JUL 8 '68

My Life with History

My Life with History

AN AUTOBIOGRAPHY

BY

John D. Hicks

UNIVERSITY OF NEBRASKA PRESS · LINCOLN

Portions of Chapter II follow closely "Then (1891) and Now (1966): Some Comparisons and Contrasts," *Nebraska History*, XLVII (June 1966), 139–155, and "The Urban Revolution," *Pacific Northwest Quarterly*, LVII (October 1966), 181–187; a few paragraphs of Chapter III originally appeared in *The American Tradition* (Boston: Houghton Mifflin Co., 1955); and parts of Chapter IV are drawn from "The Personal Factor in the Writing of History," *Pacific Northwest Quarterly*, LV (July 1964), 97–104. Chapter V first appeared in modified form as "My Years as a Graduate Student," *Wisconsin Magazine of History*, XLVII (Summer 1964), 279–290; Chapter VI as "My Six Years at Hamline," *Minnesota History*, XXXIX (Summer 1965), 213–226; Chapter VIII as "My Nine Years at the University of Nebraska," *Nebraska History*, XLVI (March 1965), 1–27; Chapter IX as "My Ten Years on the Wisconsin Faculty," *Wisconsin Magazine of History*, XLVIII (Summer 1965), 303–316; and Chapter X as Lucile C. Hicks, "Letters from Florida," *Prairie Schooner*, XI (Summer 1937), 146–165. Used by permission.

Publishers on the Plains

UNP

MANUFACTURED IN THE UNITED STATES OF AMERICA

To the Memory of My Parents

Preface

It is easy to pinpoint the beginning of this book. Early in December, 1962, five years after my retirement, William N. Davis, Jr., State Archivist and a former member of the University of California history department, had me up to his house in Sacramento for a dinner in my honor. Present also were a number of mutual friends, several of whom had worked with me as graduate students in Berkeley. After dinner Bill asked me to speak to the group, but said he would like also to play a record by Samuel Eliot Morison, "The Faith of an Historian." Which would I prefer to come first? Oddly, I had not foreseen the inevitability of a speech, so I said: "Play the record first and maybe it will give me some ideas." He did and it did. The contrast between Morison's eastern and urban background and my western and rural origin became the basis for my remarks. About a year later, when my turn came to read a paper for the Kosmos Club, an organization of Berkeley professors, I wrote down my Sacramento comments into a little essay entitled "The Personal Factor in the Writing of History." Taking myself as a case in point, I asked: What were the influences that had determined my attitudes toward historical scholarship? Why had I written as I had? With whatever candor I could command, I set down my answers.

The domino theory may have no relevance to what happens in Southeast Asia, but it worked for me. When I showed my Kosmos Club paper to Robert E. Burke of the University of Washington, he claimed it at once for publication in the *Pacific Northwest Quarterly* (July, 1964). Thus encouraged, I went on with another paper, this one on "My Years as a Graduate Student," and after its appearance in the *Wisconsin Magazine of History* (Summer, 1964), I wrote three more, each on a segment of my teaching record. When they, too, achieved publication, sheer momentum, plus the example of memoirs by two of my friends, Paul Knaplund of Wisconsin and Arthur M. Schlesinger of Harvard, did the rest.

vii

While this book started out to be primarily an academic autobiography, it emerges with much else included. It would be possible
to argue that the "personal factor," elaborated in my first essay, covers
everything I can remember. But as the manuscript grew, so also did
the realization that my nonacademic experiences might throw some
light on the changing customs of our time. Not only have our colleges
and universities changed in spectacular ways, but also, far more signifi-
cantly, the great metropolitan centers of today have swallowed up the
old town-and-country society of our pre-World War I years. The
folkways of a mainly agricultural America are disappearing, and we
must make terms, all of us, with an urbanized industrial America.

"The United States was born in the country and has moved to the
city." So wrote Richard Hofstadter in *The Age of Reform*. This wise
aphorism not only summarizes the history of our nation; it is also the
story of my life. For I, like so many others who came out of the
nineteenth century, was a white, Anglo-Saxon, Protestant, small-town,
middle-class, midwestern American, one of those who left the country
for the city. Of me and of many others like me it could truthfully be
said: "You can take the boy out of the country, but you can't take
the country out of the boy." That, at least in part, is what this "docu-
mentary," as the TV producers might call it, is all about. And, if I am
any judge, we can still detect in our dominantly urban society some of
the old agricultural influences that were so potent when I was very
young. To understand our urban present, we still need to know something about our rural past.

The writers of autobiographies are usually men of importance, or at
least men who deem themselves to be important. This book, on the
contrary, is written by an ordinary individual who suffers from no such
illusion. If the constant use of the first person, singular, seems to belie
this fact, it is only because of the awkwardness and transparency of all
efforts at circumlocution. The fact is that this book *is* about my life and
my observations. But there are no doubt thousands of my generation
whose background and activities have approximated to some degree
my own. My hope is that the record of what has happened to me will
reflect to some extent what has happened to many others.

JOHN D. HICKS
Morrison Professor of History, Emeritus
University of California, Berkeley

Contents

A section of illustrations follows page 180.

My Life with History

I. My WASPish Background

GENEALOGY HAS NEVER interested me much, but some information about my ancestors has inevitably come my way. Of my four grandparents I know least about my grandfather, Eli Hicks, and nothing at all for a certainty about his forebears. He was born near Greeneville, Tennessee, probably in 1808. Family tradition has it that two Hicks brothers came from England in the seventeenth century, and that one of them settled to the north and the other to the south of what became Mason and Dixon's Line. Assuming that there is some truth in this story, my grandfather probably belonged to the southern branch of the Hicks family, although undoubtedly many of the people who in his time lived in eastern Tennessee had drifted down the mountains from Pennsylvania. In any event, I am unable to establish direct connections with such northern notables as Elias Hicks, the famous Quaker preacher, or John Hicks, the Wisconsin newspaperman, or Thomas Hicks, the artist. While the name I bear is definitely an English import, its early origin is a matter of conjecture. Mrs. William Hicks Beach, who has written about the Hicks family in England, believes that the name derives from that of an early Saxon tribe, the Hwiccas, who took root in Gloucestershire during the sixth century.[1]

My grandfather, when he was sixteen years old, ran away from home and went to Hillsboro, Ohio, where he was befriended by a Quaker, whose name I do not know. Eli Hicks was married twice, and had two children by his first wife; but all I know about this first family is that a son, my father's half brother, joined the Union Army at the beginning of the Civil War, only to die in camp, presumably from pneumonia. Months after his death his body was returned to his family, and my father, then a ten-year-old boy, was permitted to "view the remains." The horror of that sight never left my father; this was the

[1] Mrs. William Hicks Beach, *A Cotswold Family: Hicks and Hicks Beach* (1909), p. 11.

reason why, as long as he lived, he always kept a light burning every night after he had officiated at a funeral.

I gather that my grandfather was a hard man to live with, severe as a disciplinarian, and with little of the milk of human kindness in his soul. One of my father's brothers, who like his father before him ran away from home, described his father as "the meanest man that ever lived." Grandfather Hicks's photograph, taken in his old age, shows a big man, probably six feet tall, with rugged features behind a bushy beard. Once, as a boy, I ran across the old man's will, signed with an X, his mark. "Couldn't my grandfather sign his name?" I asked my father, in dismay.

"Of course he could," was the reply. "He was just too ornery to."

While Grandfather Hicks's education must have been scanty, he was a great reader of the Bible, and took an intense interest in politics. Anti-slavery but not an abolitionist, he was a Know-Nothing before he became a Republican. He was greatly impressed by the Hungarian patriot Louis Kossuth, who visited the United States in 1851, and named the current baby, my father, John Kossuth Hicks. Eli Hicks was, in short, a typical product of the American frontier, in his background not unlike his contemporary, Abraham Lincoln. Indeed the stories about him that have come down to us, including that of his unglamorous participation in the Black Hawk War, are so like those told about Lincoln as to make me doubt their credibility.[2]

Grandfather Hicks did not remain long in Ohio, but drifted westward through Indiana, where I think he lived for a time, into southern Illinois. There, as a widower of thirty-three, he met and married my grandmother, a mere slip of a girl, only fifteen years old, but with a big name, Jalah Hutchinson Stallard. Jalah was the daughter of Samuel Duncan Stallard, who about 1817 had moved from Dungannon, Virginia, to Pocahontas, Illinois, where he married and where his children were born. Dungannon is in the extreme western tip of Virginia, not far from Big Stone Gap; hence my grandmother's people, like my grandfather's, were mountaineers. Stallard family records start with Walter Stallard, who came to Virginia from England in 1640 and settled in that part of Rappahannock County which later became Essex County. The Stallard family used to hold annual reunions at Dungannon, and I was asked to speak at their 1934 meeting on "any subject of a religious nature," but the depression was on, and I couldn't go.

The Duncan name also figures conspicuously among my grand-

[2] Roy P. Basler, The Lincoln Legend (1935), p. 134.

mother's ancestors, and traces back to William Duncan the Elder, who emigrated from Scotland to Culpeper County, Virginia, in 1722. According to the genealogists, my grandmother's given name came from the Duncan lineage, and was properly spelled Jaela. While her family was primarily of English and Scottish descent, her husband, so my father told me, often twitted her about being "part French and part Portugee," and there seems also to have been a Welsh strain in her family tree. She was the only one of my grandparents I ever knew. I remember her as a tiny, withered figure, hardly more than five feet tall, about one hundred pounds in weight, with sparse grey hair drawn tight back from her forehead to form a knot on the back of her head. I never knew her to smile. When I greeted her politely with the inquiry "How are you, Grandma?" she invariably replied, "Jes' tol'able." I was not an unattractive child, but she never petted or kissed me—it didn't occur to me that she had never been particularly fond of anybody. I showed her the respect due her age, but the grim facts of life had left her emotionally drained. Until the time of her death at over eighty years of age, Grandma Hicks lived with her youngest daughter, my Aunt Anna, and carried a generous share of the household duties. According to my father, she had wept at seventeen because she would never have any children. But when I asked her, as for some reason I often did, "How many children did you have, Grandma?" she always replied, "Nine that lived." From other sources I learned that there were eleven or twelve in all.[3]

Sometime during the 1840's Grandfather Hicks and his family joined the migration to the New Northwest and settled on a farm near Red Wing, Minnesota. But well before the Civil War they were on the move again, this time to Nodaway County, Missouri. Since both of my Hicks grandparents are buried at Clearmont, Missouri, close to the Iowa border, I assume that they must have located in that vicinity. Once in a conversation with Joseph Schafer, superintendent of the State Historical Society of Wisconsin and a great authority on frontier history, I think I stumbled onto the reason for this last move. Commenting on the Hicks variant from the normal frontier habit of following isothermal lines into the West, I asked Schafer why my grandfather should have departed from custom to go south from Minnesota instead of west. "Where did he come from?" Schafer inquired.

"From Tennessee by way of Indiana and Illinois," I replied.

[3] Nancy Reba Roy, *Descendants of William Duncan, the Elder* (1959), pp. 5, 11, 16, 22.

"That's easy," said Schafer, "the old man's feet got cold, and he wanted to go where he knew the weather would be warmer." There was something of the rover in the old man, however, for even Missouri wasn't all he had hoped it to be. In his later years, my father told me, he longed to move to California.

During the Civil War irregular skirmishes between Union and Confederate sympathizers—bushwhacking—was not uncommon in northwestern Missouri. Grandfather Hicks, as a staunch Union man and a member of the Union League, was an occasional night rider, although my father's recollections tended to cast some doubts on the objectives of these nocturnal excursions. Father had two older sisters who came of age during the Civil War period and, to the great disgust of my grandfather, were wooed and won by stay-at-home Democrats. "The Lord had a grudge against me," he used to say, "and paid me off in Democratic sons-in-law." Another favorite remark, often quoted but less original, characterized the opponents of the GOP even more forthrightly. "All Democrats may not be horse thieves, but all horse thieves are Democrats." The "haves" and "have nots" of yesteryear.

My mother's people were of New England origin and they seem to have kept painstaking records of all births and deaths. My mother's name, according to the entry made by her father in the family Bible, was Harriet Gertrude Wing, but she always claimed that the proper spelling of her first name was Harriett. Her father, Charles Cuthbert Wing, was born in Schoharie County, New York, on April 1, 1818, the eldest son of William Russell Wing and his first wife, Phoebe Cuthbert. The Wing farm was some twenty-seven miles west of Albany, about a mile from what was then called Esperance, on the Buffalo and Albany turnpike. In his old age William R. Wing moved to Nodaway County, Missouri, where by that time three of his sons, including Charles Cuthbert, were long-time residents.[4]

The Wing family beginnings in America are a typical chapter out of the history of early New England. The English progenitors of the Wing line to which I belong were John and Deborah (Bachiler) Wing. John Wing, born in Banbury in 1584, became a Church of England clergyman of some distinction. He was an Oxford graduate (Queen's College), his published sermons ran to many volumes, and he had a good living—£500 a year—from the various congregations of English

[4] Information furnished by Mr. and Mrs. Alexander W. Miller of Glens Falls, New York.

merchant adventurers he served in Germany and Holland. His wife's father, Stephen Bachiler, was also a Church of England minister, but of such strong nonconformist leanings that his vicarage at Wherwell, Hampshire, was taken away from him. Probably he infected John Wing with his views, for the two were apparently planning a joint move to New England while John was visiting in London in 1630, but John died unexpectedly and Bachiler had to carry out the project on his own. Despite his seventy-one years, he took his daughter, Deborah Wing, and her four sons with him to America on the ship *William and Francis*, one of the ten that had brought Winthrop and his company over in 1629. The ship landed at Boston on June 5, 1632. Bachiler promptly established a church at Saugus, only to be forced out by the ruling clique in Boston. He went next to Lynn, then to Ipswich, and finally back to England; but the Wing family, now headed by the oldest son, John, stayed in Saugus until 1637, when they moved to Sandwich, some seventeen or eighteen miles southeast of Plymouth and within the Plymouth colony. The second son, Daniel, from whom my grandfather was descended, eventually embraced the "peaceful Quaker doctrines" and became a substantial citizen of Bristol County. Some of Daniel Wing's descendants, whether "harried out of the land" or not, eventually migrated to New York.[5]

Grandfather Wing came west several years before the Civil War and settled first in Gentry County, Missouri, where my mother was born, then later near Maryville in Nodaway County. I know nothing of his education, but I have a few letters that he wrote to my grandmother, when she was his fiancée, which prove that for a pioneer farmer he had a pretty good command of the English language. In these letters and in the records he made in the family Bible, he obviously took great pains with his penmanship, a somewhat ornate Spencerian. According to my mother, he read a great deal and welcomed joyfully the invention of the kerosene lamp, which enabled him to read at night. She remembered the first such lamp the family acquired. Like many migrants from the East, he had no faith in land that would not grow trees and, when he came to Nodaway County, chose a remote timbered tract instead of open prairie land close to Maryville that might have made him rich. One of my mother's childhood memories concerned his three yoke of oxen, named Buck and Berry, Jack and Jerry, and a third

[5] George W. Wing, "The Wing Family in America," *The Owl*, XV (March, 1914), 1310–1314; (June, 1914), 1330–1331.

jingle that I have forgotten. The oxen were belled so that they could be found each morning when needed, but they often escaped discovery by lying quietly in the woods and never shaking a head. Grandfather Wing also kept a few sheep, for another of mother's stories concerned a butting bellwether who regularly lifted her over the fence on her way to school. Grandfather suffered much from malaria, but probably even more from the drugs he took to cure it. He lived to a ripe old age, although toward the end his mind was not very clear. The pictures I have seen of him as an old man reveal little except his frailty, but an early daguerreotype shows him as a handsome young blade, wearing a very impressive topper. He was short of stature and carried no excess weight—a little man, in comparison with my Grandfather Hicks.

While Grandfather Wing was of unimpeachable Quaker descent and an avowed abolitionist, he had nevertheless, for some reason unknown to me, lost his official status as a Quaker. My grandmother, who was also of Quaker lineage, was no longer regarded as "within the pale" after she married him. Perhaps his beliefs had changed, or perhaps his first wife was not a Quaker, or perhaps there was some undisclosed skeleton in the closet. His abolitionist views did him no good in Gentry County, where proslavery sympathizers were numerous, and may have accounted for his move to Nodaway County. He was an integrationist on principle. When he employed a Negro on his farm, as he sometimes did, he insisted that his colored hand eat at the family table. "Anyone good enough to work with me," he maintained, "is good enough to eat with me." At the outbreak of the Civil War his oldest son, Stephen, who was only eighteen, was determined to enlist in the Union Army. Because of his youth, his father tried to dissuade him, but yielded at last to his entreaties and drove with him all the way to St. Joseph, the nearest enlistment center. When confronted by the stark reality, however, young Stephen broke down and cried and wanted to go back home. But Grandfather Wing would stand for no such nonsense, and Uncle Steve went to war. His regiment, he told me, was beset by illness and saw little or no fighting, although it was in reserve during several large battles, including Murfreesboro. The war wrecked Uncle Steve's health, but he lived out the century. I knew him as a small, bearded shadow out of the past; judging from the photographs I have seen, he closely resembled his father.

My grandmother, Elizabeth Otis Button, like the man she married, stemmed from a long line of New England Quakers. She was born

February 10, 1825, in or near Danby, Vermont, the daughter of Thomas Button, whose father, Joseph Button, had come to Vermont in 1785 from Rhode Island. For a time Joseph Button kept a store in Danby "which was about the first store in town," and he also manufactured potash. He "was considered one of the wealthiest men of his day," and was a very prominent member of the Society of Friends. When the rift came in 1828 between the Hicksites and the Orthodox Quakers, Joseph Button took the side of the Hicksites and broke openly with Dr. Harris Otis, leader of the Orthodox faction, who happened to be the father of Lydia Otis, the wife of Thomas Button. To compound the bad relations between the two families, Thomas Button was so addicted to drink that Lydia, in a moment of despair, left him and went home to her parents. To her dismay, her father-in-law prevented her from retrieving her three small daughters, the youngest of whom was Elizabeth, and undertook to bring them up in his own family. My grandmother remembered a pretty lady who came to see the three little girls secretly when they were at play and cried over them. As matters turned out, however, Thomas Button soon drank himself to death, and his widow—the pretty lady—married one Solomon Haviland, a Quaker, whether Hicksite or Orthodox I do not know. Joseph Button seems then to have relented, and Lydia got her children back. Eventually Solomon died and Lydia married again, once more to a Quaker, Henry Green. This elderly couple, as Grandpa and Grandma Green, visited the Wing family in Missouri when my mother was a little girl, and greatly impressed the Wing children with their fine Quaker garb, their good manners, and their precise Quaker speech.[6]

Lydia Otis's father, Dr. Harris Otis, was born in Scituate, Massachusetts, in 1775, and came to Danby in 1793. He was sixth in descent from John Otis, an emigrant from Barnstaple, Devonshire, who had followed his strongly nonconformist pastor to Hingham, Massachusetts, in 1635. Dr. Otis, my great great-grandfather, was less than twenty years of age when he came to Danby, but, according to an industrious Danby chronicler, had already "passed through a thorough course" of preparatory medical training, obtaining some of it, no doubt, from his father, who had been a surgeon in the French and Indian War. The lot of these frontier doctors, whatever their training or their lack

[6] J. C. Williams, *The History and Map of Danby, Vermont* (1869), pp. 120, 211–212.

of it, was incredibly hard. According to the same chronicler, they "were often obliged, in visiting their patients, to travel over half-made roads, and by marked trees, through storms, by night and day, sometimes encountering wild beasts, and fording streams at the hazard of their lives." Dr. Otis no doubt had all these experiences, and perhaps because of them turned his attention more and more to farming, for, our chronicler continues, "he became a distinguished farmer, and left at his death, one of the largest fortunes ever accumulated in the town."[7]

Through Dr. Otis I am able to trace my ancestry back to a passenger on the *Mayflower*, Richard Warren, whose great-granddaughter married an Otis. For a long time I knew of the *Mayflower* connection only as a family tradition and was inclined to discount it. But Mrs. Clara S. Paine, long the valued Secretary-Treasurer of the Mississippi Valley Historical Association, put me straight on the matter. During the 1920's she and I were both residents of Lincoln, Nebraska, and regularly each year we took a train trip together to the annual meeting of the Association, wherever it happened to be held. She was a great genealogist, and on one occasion drew me into a conversation about my ancestors. When I told her about the *Mayflower* tradition, she at once insisted that it was almost certainly correct, and offered to find out for sure if I would only send her what data I had. When finally I got around to this task, she sent back, by return mail, the missing links. I still have the notes I sent her, written in ink on a piece of yellow paper, and duly embellished with her penciled-in amendments. As compensation for her efforts, she demanded that I join the Nebraska Society of Mayflower Descendants, which I did. So far as I know, I am still a member in good standing. My fondest recollection of the Nebraska Mayflowers is an interchange of remarks that occurred at one of their annual dinners. One lady genealogist, after an animated recital of her "line" to a bored male guest, inquired brightly: "And what is your line?" To which he replied with greater accuracy than relevance: "The Union Pacific."

I know comparatively little about my mother's mother, Elizabeth Otis Wing—her silverware retained the Otis rather than the Button initial. When she was twenty-three years old, on October 18, 1848, she was married to my grandfather, a widower thirty years of age. During the next thirteen years she gave birth to seven children, three of whom died in infancy and one of whom, Charles Cuthbert, Jr., died at nine-

[7] *Ibid.*, p. 211.

teen of what almost any layman would now be able to diagnose as acute appendicitis. My grandmother was a heavy woman, not very tall, and so completely bald on the top of her head, like a man, that she always wore a wig. Family pictures reveal large, firm, resolute features, despite the flesh, but her weight, coupled no doubt with the rigors of frontier life, brought her to an untimely end. She died in 1872, of undetermined causes, when my mother was only fourteen. There were three girls left, one older and one younger than my mother, but the older daughter was soon married, and even before that my mother accepted the responsibility of keeping house for the family.

In any sense of the word, my mother was one of the most unforgettable characters I have ever met. She might have been a half inch over five feet tall, certainly not more than that, but she was a presence in any room. Of obviously excellent lineage, but born in a log cabin (on March 6, 1858) and educated in the most primitive of country schools, she achieved without benefit of high school training a degree of excellence in some subjects—algebra, for example—that I was never able to equal. At nineteen she herself began to teach in country school, an occupation that she followed for the next eleven years. Her father, prematurely old and ill, went to live with her older sister, and her younger sister soon married, so she was on her own. She saw much of her sisters, however, and helped them with their problems; for as long as they lived they remained a closely knit group. In the schoolroom she was a strict disciplinarian, one who was in demand to tame schools that under weaker leadership had got out of hand. When a big boy whom she had asked to apologize for some misconduct replied that it would be "a damned pretty apology he'd make," she expelled him on the spot, and made it stick. There were fifty to seventy-five children of all ages crowded together in one room; the "three r's"—readin', 'ritin', and 'rithmetic—predominated. Wages for the teacher were twenty to thirty dollars a month; on one occasion, when the free silverites were locally in the ascendancy, it was paid entirely in silver dollars. As the teacher, Mother boarded around, and she declared that once, as she took up quarters with a new family, the farmwife inquired: "How old air ye, Miss Hattie, or d'ye know?" Some of her stories matched those told in Edward Eggleston's *The Hoosier Schoolmaster*, for example, of girls in long dresses and many petticoats, reaching to the floor while reciting, to pull up an undergarment on which to blow their noses, of six-year-old twin boys who had chewed tobacco since they were four and couldn't wait until recess for a refill. My mother solved the expectoration problem by seating the twins near a knothole in the floor, a target that they never once missed. Summers she improved her professional competence by attending teachers' institutes, long the best facility for teacher training that the Middle Border afforded. But it was probably from experience rather than from precept that she learned to delegate to big children the task of teaching little children in every corner of the schoolroom.

One bitter winter Mother tasted defeat as a disciplinarian. A member of the school board visited her just as school let out one afternoon to report damage to the school "property." She didn't need to be told what property was involved, and when her caller left she waded through the deep snow to the boys' outhouse. Opening the door, she looked out directly on the winter landscape; not a splinter of lumber remained, except for the front and side walls that were visible from the schoolhouse. She then had to admit reluctantly that there were some things a man teacher could do that a woman teacher couldn't. She chose not to apply for that school again.

The big event of Mother's younger years was a visit she undertook during the spring and summer of 1881 to Glens Falls, New York, a Wing family center, founded, indeed, by one Abraham Wing and a Quaker group in 1783, and originally known as Queensbury. The relatives that Mother visited, however, were members of the Otis clan, mostly named either Otis or Haviland, but nevertheless durably Quaker. I have a number of letters she wrote back to her sister, my Aunt Sarah, about the trip. The first night out her train was delayed in Creston, Iowa, for eight hours, after which the engine broke down and there was another delay. She arrived in Chicago the second night at twelve o'clock, and stayed until morning at the Grand Pacific for $4.75, to her an outrageous overcharge. She then boarded a "fast express," but it took her still another twenty-four hours to get to Buffalo, where she changed trains again, then went on to Albany and another change before arriving in Glens Falls. The things she saw on the trip amazed her; for example, seven kinds of fences in New York: "stone, stump, willow, rail, board, wire, evergreen hedge." Glens Falls struck her as a beautiful village, with fully half of the houses of brick or stone, and streets that were not parallel but that "run in every direction," with "hardly a house that stands straight. They stand with the street." To her unaccustomed eyes Aunt Hannah Haviland's well-appointed home was very impressive. "Her bedroom," she wrote her sister in Missouri, "is as large as your sitting-room," and her whole house "is furnished from top to cellar just as nice as can be, not one foot of rag carpet in it." Cousin Julia had "eighteen rooms in her house besides the halls and clothes rooms, all nicely carpeted and furnished." When Mother attended a Friends meeting, she was duly impressed with their "splendid minister." Years later, however, she told me her mother's stories of more primitive Quaker meetings, where people always waited for the Spirit to move them. One of these stories, only a little changed, I suspect, through the years, concerned a dear simple sister who rose to say: "As I was drivin' to meetin' this morning, I watched the horse switch his tail and switch his tail to keep the flies away. And this teaches us," she continued, "that we should switch our tails and switch our tails to keep the sins away."

Mother got around. She visited a Presbyterian church, which she described as "the most beautiful edifice I ever saw. An elegant pipe organ occupies nearly one end and extends most to the ceiling and the pews are all elegantly cushioned. They pay $20 a year for a seat." In a somewhat less religious mood she "went with Nettie to see a minstrel troop parade. It was quite a show, all dressed up in fine uniform[s] and such a nice band of music." Naturally, she and Grandma Green (once Lydia Otis) visited Uncle William Otis in Danby, Vermont, the place their branch of the Otis family came from. "I could never imagine such high mountains and such wild scenerie [*sic*]," she rhapsodized, her usually correct spelling deserting her. "But most of the farms," she wrote her father, "are old tumbled down looking places. I tell you, Pa, old Nodaway with its broad fields rich with grain will look good to me when I get back." Fortunately, however, Uncle William's place was "in perfect order" and she could report that her relatives "all keep up their farms very nicely." When I was a boy she told me about this visit, and took some pride in a *faux pas* she had committed when commenting on a bin of Uncle William's corn. "Why do you raise all that pop-corn?" she asked incredulously.

"Young lady," Uncle William replied sternly, "I'll have you understand that that's the finest corn raised in New England!" But it didn't look like much compared with what Nodaway County could do. She also told me of her uncle's prowess in making maple sugar, much of which he traded in, pound for pound, at the store for ordinary sugar.

Apparently Mother's Glens Falls relatives liked her, for they urged her to stay on for a full year. When she said she couldn't afford it, they intimated that they would take care of her; and when she objected to that—as she certainly would—they urged her to get a job at the local academy. They seem also to have done something about her wardrobe. When her sister, Sarah, wrote asking her if the clothes she had brought with her were all right, she replied that they were, "what there are of them." Aunt Hannah took her downtown and got her a new dress. "It is called satin cambric," she wrote, "and has a rainbow bow on it and a lace tie." She was not quite sure whether Aunt Hannah or Grandma Green had paid for the gift, but she was as pleased with it as any young woman would be. When she decided that a four-month visit was long enough and planned to go home, Aunt Hannah offered to pay her way back to Missouri, but this Mother wouldn't permit. "I told her if I couldn't have raised enough to get home on, I should not have come." She yielded to her relatives' importuning, however, that she go with them to Boston; but to meet that additional expense she asked her sister to lend her fifteen or twenty dollars, promising to pay it back when she got to teaching school again. Aunt Sarah must have come through handsomely, for I have a letter she later received from Mother in which Mother not only enclosed twenty dollars of her debt out of her October, 1882, "order for $42.85," but promised more later.

Her trip to Boston, "with Julia and Ezra to visit Amelia," was an experience to remember. She wrote: "[We] spent one whole day in Boston looking at the wonders I shall tell you about when I get home. And then we spent one day at the seaside, took two splendid steamboat rides 30 miles each. Took a nice sea-bath, put on a bathing suit and then walked right into the ocean. Men and women went in together. . . . the water so cold it most chilled us through. It was a very hot day and we were cool the rest of it." Cousin Amelia took her Missouri guest "all around," and "paid all [her] car fare and boat fare and wouldn't allow [her] to spend one cent and Ezra made [her] a present of [her] ticket to Boston from Glens Falls."

From Boston she went back home to Missouri; the ticket to St. Joseph, "by the way of Maryville," cost her $37.85. She took a sleeper from Boston to Buffalo, where she got off to spend a few days with relatives who lived near Angola. But from Buffalo west she made no mention of sleeping cars. No doubt she just sat it out.

My father's youth was quite a different story. Born in Illinois,

October 30, 1851, he moved with his parents as a small boy to their new home near Red Wing, Minnesota, where he grew to manhood. Years later, while I was teaching at Hamline University in St. Paul, I went with him by train to visit the scenes he once had known. He recognized the Red Wing setting—the river and the bluff—but the town was not the same. We hired a driver who showed us around, and Father spotted the site of the old academy he had wished to attend, but did not, because, as he put it, his father wouldn't let him. We drove out into the country to the Featherstone Church, which had not changed materially since he had attended it as a boy, then on to what had once been the Hicks farm. The buildings were different, but Father saw something about the farmhouse that looked familiar and asked permission to go inside. There he found the old log house he had known as a boy; the outside had been weatherboarded, but inside, despite improvements and enlargement, he could recognize the original walls. Neither in the town nor in the country could he find anyone he knew, or who knew anyone he had known. Finally he directed the driver to an old, almost abandoned cemetery, and there he found them all. Tombstone by tombstone he visited with them as I listened. It was a moving experience.

My father was married first when he was about twenty-five years old, and farmed for himself near Skidmore, in Nodaway County, Missouri. He was deeply religious, a heritage, no doubt, from his mountaineer ancestry, and early "felt the call" to preach. But his first wife, Maria Barber, opposed his ambition to enter the ministry because, in her opinion, he was inadequtely educated for such a profession. After her death, or perhaps before, he became a "local preacher," a status in the Methodist Church not unlike that of a lay reader in the Episcopal Church. I still have his last "Renewal of Local Preacher's License," dated February 14, 1889; but these licenses were issued annually, and no doubt many others preceded it. Maria Barber was of a short-lived family and died in her middle thirties, whether from cancer or from preventable disease, I do not know. I have heard both stories. She left Father with three small children, Grace Bertha, who must have been about nine, Mabel Maria, perhaps seven, and William Newton, only three. For more than two years after their mother's death the children lived with some of their Barber relatives; but on March 6, 1889, my mother's thirty-first birthday, she and Father were married and promptly took the children to their new home. My mother, both before and after her marriage to my father, encouraged him in his desire to become a regularly ordained preacher. Lack of formal education had no terrors for her; there were ways of overcoming such obstacles. Father received his first appointment as a "supply" because he was not yet ordained, about the same time he and Mother were married, and they took up residence with their ready-made family in the Methodist parsonage at Pickering, Missouri.

The Methodist Church, or the Methodist Episcopal Church, as it then was named, laid out a stiff four-year course of study for beginning preachers, which Father undertook and completed successfully. After two years he was ordained a deacon, and after four years, an elder, the highest order in the Methodist Church. Wrinkled "sheepskins" attesting to these attainments always decorated the walls of his study, although his rapidly growing library made it increasingly difficult to find a place for them. Father never got over feeling handicapped by the fact that he was not a college graduate; I've heard him say many times, a little ruefully, that if only he had had a college education he would have become a bishop. A bishop in the Methodist Church, I hasten to add, is primarily a general superintendent; the Methodist episcopacy is an office, albeit a high one, not an order.

The organization of the Methodist Episcopal Church was a very significant factor in my father's life, and indirectly in my own. The Methodist system of government, derived as it was from the Church of England (which in turn owed much to the Roman Catholic Church) had its authoritarian aspects, although the accepted church term was "connectional," not authoritarian. Every ordained preacher was a member of some Annual Conference, a unit which geographically would include perhaps a whole state, or more likely some major fraction of it. In Missouri, for example, there were two Annual Conferences, one for the counties to the north of the Missouri River, and one for the counties to the south of it. Each conference had the right to examine and admit new members, but in making such decisions it was conscious of the fact that for each new member it admitted there must be an available church. "No church without a preacher and no preacher without a church" was a cardinal feature of Methodist policy. An Annual Conference was divided in turn into districts, each of which would include perhaps twenty-five preachers in contiguous territory. Over each district a presiding elder, or as he was later called, a district superintendent, had limited authority. Once each quarter he was expected to visit each charge in his district, to occupy the pulpit, and to hold a quarterly conference. It was his business to know what was going on in all the churches of his district.

But the final and definitive authority in Methodist circles lay with the particular bishop who presided over a given session of an Annual Conference, and who at its close read a list of the appointments to which he was assigning the various members of the conference for the coming year. At his discretion a preacher might be assigned to the church he had served the preceding year (subject to the time limit) or he might be assigned to a different charge. In my youth the five-year rule (originally one, then two years) was in vogue—a preacher might not receive the same appointment more than five years in succession. Once my father was moved by this rule when neither he nor his congregation would have preferred it that way. In practice the bishop generally took the advice of his presiding elders, whom he also appointed, in assigning the preachers to their posts, but legally he could use his own judgment if he chose, and he sometimes did. He could also transfer preachers, with the consent of the other bishop concerned, from one conference to another, a prerogative he exercised with considerable discretion. Large congregations were increasingly able to make their influence felt in the choice of their ministers, but the ordinary town or village church simply had to take the man it got, "asking no question for conscience sake." Any local church, however, could make things sufficiently uncomfortable for any preacher it did not like to ensure that he would be moved at the next conference, but this was a hazardous undertaking, for cantankerous churches often wound up with cantankerous preachers. I once heard Bishop Henry W. Warren defend convincingly the Methodist system of leaving to experts, i.e., to bishops and presiding elders, the proper pairing of preachers and congregations.

The Methodists duly acknowledged popular sovereignty, however, through an elective General Conference, held every fourth year—the same year in which American presidential elections are held. By my time half the delegates to the General Conference were clergymen, elected by the various Annual Conferences, roughly in proportion to their membership. The other half were laymen, who owed their seats to Lay Conferences, which paralleled the ministerial Annual Conferences. The General Conference was the supreme lawmaking body of the Methodist Church and laid down the rules of discipline its members were supposed to observe; but its most exciting function was the election and retirement of bishops. While the rule "once a bishop always a bishop" was scrupulously observed, bishops who were deemed overage were retired from active duty rather ruthlessly, and an occasional arbitrary or incompetent bishop might be retired ahead of schedule. Since it took a two-thirds majority of the General Conference to elect a bishop, the weeding-out process was very thorough—the men who made the grade were usually of first-rate ability.

The Board of Bishops acted as a kind of supreme executive for the whole church. Each year it elected a presiding officer who might technically be described as the head of the church, but in fact this assumption would be quite inaccurate, for he had no more power than any other bishop. In my youth the Board of Bishops had the duty of assigning the various bishops to the Annual Conferences over which they were to preside in any given year. They made it a policy to ensure that each bishop made the rounds of as many different conferences as possible; as a result, my father received his appointment from a different bishop practically every year. There were missionary bishops, however, who were assigned more permanently to some designated foreign field, such as Africa or India. Later on, the General Conference decided that all bishops should be associated with specific areas; after that, the same bishop would normally preside over all the Annual Conferences in his area year after year. In general, the territory assigned to a Methodist bishop was much larger than a typical Protestant Episcopal or Roman Catholic diocese, while Methodist presiding elders, or district superintendents, performed most of the duties that fell to bishops in other episcopal churches.

The Methodist hierarchy, with its rather considerable powers, lent itself inevitably to politics. My father used to say that there were three political parties in the United States: the Republican, the Democratic, and the M. E. Church. Among Methodist preachers there was naturally much concern over the annual appointments, and undoubtedly those who stood in well with the presiding elders and the bishop got the choicer plums. But the good opinion of the higher-ups had to be earned. The preacher who regularly confronted large and growing congregations, who could point each year to a reasonable number of converts and new members, and who could collect in full the various benevolences solicited by the church rated better than those with less satisfactory records. Church benevolences, incidentally, were administered, not by the bishops, but by powerful general boards, such as Home Missions, Foreign Missions, and Temperance. The Methodist Church thus followed the example of the American political system in setting up a number of administrative agencies quite completely divorced from both the executive and the legislative branches of its government.

Since Father stood well in the various tests of excellence that the church authorities esteemed, he was never moved except at his own request or by the time limit. As a matter of fact, he regularly was permitted to choose his next appointment from among the charges open at the time. While there was little, if any, moving of one preacher to make way for another, it was generally well known by Conference time where, for any reason, there "had to be a change." Sometimes, I am sure, Father could have had a better appointment than the one he chose, but he was always deeply conscious of his educational limitations, and asked only for pulpits that he knew he could fill acceptably. He was universally popular with the other preachers, and was often mentioned for presiding elder, but he promptly shot down all such trial balloons.

Local government was spelled out in detail by the church *Discipline*, which the General Conference might revise from time to time, subject to well-established precedents and to a constitution adopted early in the nineteenth century. There was a Board of Trustees in which ownership of the local church's property was vested, and a Board of Stewards whose business it was to see that the expenses of the church, including the pastor's salary, were met. Naturally these posts went mainly to diligent and faithful church members, but Father occasionally induced an outsider of financial affluence and integrity to accept a place on the Board of Trustees. Whatever the technical arrangements, these officers were in fact chosen by the pastor himself. Father was a good money-raiser and indoctrinated his stewards in suitable business methods. He insisted that his salary be paid monthly, whether the money had been collected or not; if necessary, it was up to the church officers to borrow the amount of their shortages from a bank. He made it clear that donations in kind were totally unacceptable; he might give and receive gifts, and did, but only as any other person might do the same thing. His salary was to be paid in cash, "for the labourer is worthy of his hire." He saw to it that church bills were paid promptly, and he always paid his own bills the same way. I was early made to understand that, if one is out of money one borrows at a bank—never from an individual—and pays one's bills on time. Because Father always managed to live within his income, his credit was always good. My mother shared his views on finance completely; indeed, I do not know to what extent his ideas may have originated with her. If there was no other way to balance the family budget, she rented a room to some schoolteacher, or took in boarders. I've even known her to bake bread for the local hotel and make money by selling it at ten cents a loaf. Father's salary while we lived in Missouri was never more than eight hundred dollars a year, plus the parsonage we lived in, but we never thought of ourselves as poor; indeed, we were in fact as well off as most of our neighbors.

Father always saw to it that the church property under his care, including the parsonage, was well maintained. He was a better than average amateur carpenter, owned a fine chest of tools, and loved to build. If a woodshed or a chickenhouse, or even an additional room on the parsonage, seemed desirable, it soon appeared, mostly the work of his own hands. In one town he found the church building too small for the congregations he drew and short on Sunday school space. So he raised the funds and worked out the plans for its enlargement. It still stands—I visited it recently—not beautiful, but adequate. For such matters as these the Methodist system of itinerant preachers was not without its advantages. Somehow the charges to which my father was appointed always seemed to need the physical face lifting he was so well fitted to supply, while he was often followed by a carefree intellectual or a faith-blinded pietist who—in my father's expression— "wasn't worth his salt" in common-sense practicality. More than once I've heard my father express his annoyance with the way in which so many preachers let the church property run down.

This is not to say that Father was not deeply religious; on the contrary, he was as dedicated a Christian as I have ever known. When he prayed, he talked with God on easy and familiar terms. One got the impression that the two understood each other perfectly. He believed sincerely in the doctrines and practices of the church, and stressed in season and out the Arminian principle of "whosoever will." He saw no virtue whatever in the Calvinist notion of predestination nor in the assumption that anyone once in grace was always in grace. He was convinced by observation that almost anybody could backslide; indeed, he knew full well that it took quite a bit of personal effort not to do so. He was more than a little skeptical of what he called "the holiness crowd," people who had received a "second blessing"—one up and beyond mere conversion—which had made them wholly free from sin. "Whenever anyone claims that he can no longer sin," I've heard him say, "it's about time to lock the chickenhouse." Father's religion called for more than faith; one must be a doer as well as a believer; "by works a man is justified, and not by faith only."

Father was a great revivalist, an earnest seeker after souls. He was a magnetic and inspiring preacher who drew people to him, and was never happier than when he could move great numbers to come forward and kneel at the altar in search of salvation. Once each year, according to the custom of the times, he held a "protracted meeting," with revival services every night for weeks. Sometimes he brought in a professional evangelist to help him with these prolonged sessions, but he could himself inspire sinners to repent. He possessed a native eloquence and a gift of words that rarely failed him. He was not a deep thinker, and sometimes seemed to be more the exhorter than the preacher. But his sincerity was not to be doubted, and his congregations knew that his deeds backed up his words. His grammar was not always impeccable, but his lapses into the language of his youth were rarely noted by his auditors, who regularly were pretty short on grammar themselves. My mother, however, never failed to point out the flaws she noted, and as time went on they grew less frequent. His pronunciations of Bible names and of unusual words that he had culled out of books were now and then quite idiosyncratic; to this day I have to watch myself to keep from perpetuating some of his mistakes. These faults, of which he was quite conscious, no doubt had much to do with restraining him from seeking a higher position in the church.

My father's active ministry lasted twenty-seven years. During this time he served eight different churches—five in northwestern Missouri and three in Wyoming. His first charge, Pickering, Missouri, was a circuit, meaning that he preached intermittently at several different points—five, I believe—each at some distance from the other. The original Methodist circuit rider was a product of the American frontier, a preacher who rode horseback over long distances and preached to whatever congregations he could find in the area assigned to him. Since these early circuit riders had to be on the road most of the time, they were preferably unmarried. But by the end of the nineteenth century the frontier was gone and conditions had changed. Circuits consisted merely of churches that were too poor to pay a full-time preacher, but that, by joining forces, could raise the five hundred to six hundred dollars it took to maintain a preacher and his family. For all Methodist preachers were now expected to be married, and even those assigned to circuits felt obliged to drive a horse or a team rather than to ride horseback from the place they resided to the various country churches and schoolhouses at which they preached. Sometimes these latter-day circuit riders preached at three different places each Sunday, once in the morning, once in the afternoon, and once at night. Even so, preaching services at any given country church or schoolhouse might occur only every second or third week, although Sunday schools, duly supplied with low-cost "literature" by a thriving Methodist Book Concern, met with greater regularity, with or without benefit of clergy.

The Pickering appointment, which lasted two years, was the only circuit Father ever held. His next charge, Westboro, was a station, that is, he served only one congregation. This was not because the town was larger, for it was not, but rather because the numerous country members preferred to come together in one central church. After four years at Westboro, we were five years at Grant City, and three years each at Mound City and Hopkins, all within a radius of thirty or forty miles, and all within the Maryville district. This meant something. If a preacher made good, his presiding elder would do all in his power to keep him within the district; if, on the other hand, he had serious faults, a "horse trade" was in order, with each presiding elder trying to get the better of the bargain. I've heard my father say many times that you could never trust a presiding elder when it came to trading preachers. Problem characters, and there were always a few, might even be transferred out of the conference altogether. I recall one, for example, who was surprised in too great intimacy with a lady friend and was quietly transferred to California, where, it was hoped, he would lead a better life. For the Hicks family the business of moving, even these short distances, was always an interesting experience. The first one I remember, from Westboro to Grant City, was accomplished with the help of farmer relatives, who loaded all our possessions into lumber wagons, canvas-covered for the purpose, and drove the distance between the two towns. On later moves we sent our household goods by rail, but usually the family went by horse and buggy. We made no use of hotels; if the destination was greater than one day's journey, there were always friends or relatives who would take us in.

The part then played by churches in the social life of rural and small-town America can hardly be overestimated. There were from three to five Protestant denominations represented in each community. Catholic churches were rare, for most country people were Protestants and most Catholics lived in cities. The variety of Protestant denominations, however, gave the incentive of competition to church activities, which began the week with something for the faithful to do practically all day Sunday. For Methodists there was Sunday school at ten o'clock, morning worship at eleven o'clock, Junior League for the children at three o'clock, Epworth League for the young people at seven o'clock, and evening worship (with liberal congregational singing) at eight o'clock. During the weekdays there was prayer meeting, attended mainly by the older and more pious members, on Wednesday evening; choir practice for the musical contingent on Thursday evening (because of the rows that regularly broke out among the choir members, Father always spoke of them as his War Department); church dinners and socials to raise money for a new organ or some other worthy project at irregular but frequent intervals; and, usually in the fall, those long-drawn-out revival meetings, the purpose of which was to save the souls of the sinful and to gather into the fold the current crop of lambs.

Where we lived in Missouri, the churches were practically all evangelical, and differed little in doctrine, except for immersion, a much discussed subject on which the lines were quite clearly drawn. The Presbyterians would not immerse; the Christians—or Campbellites, as Father always called them—and the Baptists would stand for nothing less; while the Methodists, who rejected totally the doctrine of baptismal remission, sprinkled babies whose parents wanted them christened and allowed unbaptized adults to decide for themselves the way in which they wanted the rite performed. By a curious oversight, my mother, whose upbringing was Quaker, was admitted to membership in the Methodist Church without ever having been baptized at all. My father could have remedied this situation with a few drops of water any day he chose, but he thought of it as merely a good joke on the Methodist Church and left the matter as he found it. Whatever doctrinal differences might divide the churches, they agreed completely on a strict code of moral conduct, based on the Ten Commandments and the Sermon on the Mount. And they proclaimed these views in season and out. The boys and girls who grew up on this kind of moral diet rarely had to think twice to know the difference between what was right and what was wrong.

II. Boyhood in Missouri

I WAS BORN in the Methodist parsonage at Pickering, Missouri, January 25, 1890, but my first memories are of Westboro, my father's second pastorate. Everything in a preacher's family centers around the church, so it is not surprising that among my earliest recollections is the practice of going to church with my parents each Sunday morning. Methodism at that time still retained some of its primitive aspects, such as shouting, for example. I recall vividly the behavior of one little old Westboro lady who regularly got this urge when the preacher waxed emotional. On such occasions she bounced up and down the aisles like a rubber ball, praising God, shaking hands with all the brethren, and kissing all the sisters. Congregational responses, such as are still common in many Negro churches, were also the rule; and a preacher could easily measure the headway he was making by the chorus of "Amens" and "Hallelujahs" that punctuated both his prayers and his sermons. With a child's gift for imitation, I quickly picked up this technique, and one morning almost put a visiting presiding elder out of business, as he led us in family prayers, by coming out at appropriate intervals with a loud "Amen" or "Dod Drant it!" "Young man," he said, as he rose from his knees, "you just about ruined me!"

I remember—or I think I remember—Father's first effort to immerse a woman in running water. For some extremists it was not enough to be immersed in a pool or a baptistry; they demanded water in motion, like the river Jordan. So when Father—not without some privately expressed annoyance—had to baptize a sister so disposed, he hunted up a spot in a nearby river, really not much more than a creek, where the water seemed deep enough, and led her in. She was a long, lanky female, and he had got her only halfway down to the water when he found himself in a serious predicament. Inexperienced in such matters, he had kept his feet too close together, and they had sunk so far into the muddy bottom of the stream as to completely destroy his

22

freedom of movement. Either he had to let go of his charge or go down with her. He chose the latter alternative as the more gallant, and the two disappeared together. As I saw my father go under, I lifted up my voice in a mighty wail, but he came up in due time and pulled the bedraggled sister out, shouting and happy. Once to please a convert who insisted on river baptism in midwinter, Father performed the ceremony through a hole cut in the ice. The woman later died of pneumonia, and Father never did that again. The immersionist sects, he often noted, thrived better in the South where the water was warm than in the North where it was cold.

During my youth I saw my father baptize probably hundreds of people. Most of them he sprinkled with water at the railing (or altar, as the Methodists called it) that surrounded the pulpit rostrum, but many he immersed. Once after a big revival he borrowed the baptistry of the neighboring Christian church in order to make about thirty immersions. The pastor of this church, as an experienced performer of the rite, advised Father not to overtire himself by baptizing more than fifteen persons at a session. Father saw the point and acquiesced, but could not forbear wondering out loud how John the Baptist could ever have managed when "Jerusalem, and all Judaea, and all the region round about Jordan" came to him for baptism. Once I saw Father immerse a number of penitents in a farmer's round watering tank next to a windmill. (Grant Wood has a picture of just such a scene.) The tank was only about three feet deep, so the farmer had taken pains to fill it to the brim. When Father and the first of his subjects stepped in, the water overflowed mightily, much to the pleased and very vocal surprise of a circle of small children who had edged up close to see the show.

Near Grant City, Missouri, Father's third charge, was a little town named Allendale. This town, by some chance, was a favorite spot in our time for trying out new preachers, among them two English Wesleyans who came to the United States with no knowledge of immersionist practices. Ponds were common in that part of Missouri, and each of the former Wesleyans commandeered one of them for baptismal purposes. The first of the Wesleyans operated from a post out in the middle of the pond. With his left arm around the post, he used his right hand to grasp each victim by the back of his collar and then plunge him under, face first. The other Wesleyan lined up his group in a row, all kneeling with the water up to their necks, then waded along in front of them, ducking each person's head under as his turn came. Not canonical maybe, but certainly total. These ceremonies, I hasten to add, I did not witness, but they were a part of the Methodist folklore with which I grew up. They reflect the very spirited interest that the people I knew as a boy took in the mode of baptism, one of the very few items of church doctrine that divided them.

I had the advantage of older children in the home for only my first ten years. My half brother, Will, who was seven years my senior, quit school by the time he was sixteen or seventeen and went to work on a farm. As an excellent farm hand, he commanded wages of twenty dollars a month, the maximum for our vicinity. He could have married a farmer's daughter and grown rich on unearned increment, but like most farm boys he wanted above all else to get away to the city. So he soon found a job as a railway brakeman, working out of Creston, Iowa. Occasionally, when he happened to be on a train that came through our town, he would take me with him into the engine, an experience to remember. I knew him last as a switchman in Minneapolis, where he worked nights because he could make more money that way. He died of lung cancer or pneumonia in his early fifties, leaving a wife and four grown children. My next older half sister, Mabel, made me her special care until I was about eight or nine years old, when she began to teach country school and was never again regularly at home. After seven years of teaching, she married and became the mother of two daughters. She was a rare soul, hospitable to a fault, with a hearty welcome for visitors and a great yen to help the sick and afflicted. Whenever illness or death befell any of her friends, she showed up unannounced to take over the management of the distressed household along with her own. She wore herself out with good works and died at sixty. My oldest half sister, Grace, figured very little in my childhood, and was married at twenty. She waited eight years for her first baby, then had two boys in quick succession, only to lose them both from pneumonia when they were four and one respectively. Later two daughters brought her much happiness, but she died before they were grown. After my parents moved to Mound City, when I was about ten years old, my younger sister, Hattie, born in 1896, and I were the only children at home.

I am sure that family relationships meant more to children when I was young than they mean to children today. No doubt the greater mobility of the present age has served to scatter kinfolks over much wider areas now than then; also, rural Americans may have known their relatives better than urban Americans. Certainly the existence and frequent appearance of aunts and uncles and cousins was something I took for granted as a child. When we lived in Grant City, my mother's youngest sister and her husband, Aunt Annie and Uncle Will Barber to me, lived about a mile south of town, while my father's youngest sister, Aunt Anna, whose husband was a Swiss immigrant named Balthazer Knobel, lived at the extreme eastern edge of town. Uncle Will was doubly related, for he was a brother of Father's first wife; naturally we accepted all the Barber tribe, most of whom lived not more than a day's drive away, as blood relation. Uncle Will and Aunt Annie had an only daughter, Hazel, two years older and much smarter than I but no larger, who was my constant playmate. She teased me horribly, but we were devoted friends. There were three little Knobels, one of whom, Edmund, was about my age. Uncle Baltz died young; indeed, before the birth of his last child. Soon after the baby was born, Aunt Anna, Grandma Hicks, and all the Knobel children came down with the measles. (My father had this children's disease at thirty-eight and I have not had it yet.) So my mother took the new baby to nurse along with my sister, Hattie, who was about the same age. Unfortunately, Hattie had none of the family immunity and the case of measles she caught nearly ended her life. But Mother always maintained that she could never have lived with herself had she not taken over Aunt Anna's sick baby. Edmund and I saw much of each other as long as our family lived in Grant City. Later he graduated from the University of Missouri with a distinguished record as a football star— "Dobie" Knobel to the sports fans. He became a soils expert, and the number of Library of Congress cards headed by his name in any Union catalog makes my similar offering seem puny indeed.

A favorite visitor in our household, at least as far as I was concerned, was my mother's Aunt Hannah Haviland. For most of her life Aunt Hannah lived in Glens Falls, New York, where she entertained lavishly and drove a fine span of horses, but later she joined her son, a physician, in Butte, Montana. She was a salty old character right out of the eighteenth century, without the slightest embarrassment about using a four-letter verb in its proper context. This idiosyncracy combined oddly with the Quaker manner of speech to which she adhered with great tenacity. "Sairy," she once said to my Aunt Sarah, who was suffering from indigestion, "if thee could fart a little, thee'd feel better."

Tall and imperious in demeanor, with large, firm features and head held high, she impressed me mightily. Her hair was white when I knew her, but in her youth, she said, it had been "red as a fox's tail." As a young girl she had married a rich cousin much older than herself—her name was Haviland both before and after her marriage—so she was for many years a widow. In due time her wealth wore away, but her patrician spirit never dimmed. My father tired of her easily, but I thought she was great fun and easily picked up from her the Quaker jargon, which I can still handle creditably, if permitted.

My Aunt Sarah, Mother's older sister, was also quite a person. Aunt Sarah's husband, Elmus Lovett, died when she was only twenty-six years old, leaving her with three small boys. She was a handsome young woman with a rare sense of humor and had many suitors. But she never remarried. Her youngest son, Donald, after whom I was named, contracted from a fall what was then called "hip-joint disease" and died before I was born. The two older Lovett boys, Charley and Roy, were grown by the time I knew them, and lived with their mother on a farm near Maryville, Missouri. Charley soon got married, farmed for himself for a while, then moved to Oklahoma, where he became first a traveling salesman for a drug company, then a minor politician.

Both the Lovett boys were strong Republicans, for the following reason, according to my mother. During the campaign of 1880 they came to her with a serious question: "Aunt Hattie, who should we yell for? Garfield and Arthur? Or Hancock and English? Are we Republicans or Democrats?"

"Well," replied their Aunt Hattie, with dubious nonpartisanship, "your father was a Democrat, but your grandfather is a Republican. Why don't you ask your grandfather?" So off they went to find him.

"Grandpa," they demanded, "What are we? Republicans or Democrats?" Whereupon the old man set their minds for life.

"Of course you're Republicans, you little fools, you. Get out of here." From that time forward their partisanship never wavered. Eventually Roy went to Oklahoma, too, and became a Republican postmaster.

Roy's first effort to get away from the farm, however, was to join the gold rush to Nome, Alaska. Borrowing more of his mother's money than he was ever able to repay, he suffered the usual disappointments and came home broke. After that he and his mother rented a succession of Nodaway County farms near Maryville, each of which I visited for weeks at a time—what better thing was there to do with a small boy, when school let out, than to send him off to his relatives on a farm? An added attraction was my cousin Hazel, who went to live with Aunt Sarah after her own mother, my Aunt Annie, died. Cousin Roy took me with him on all his farm activities, at least as long as I could keep up the pace. Once, when he was pumping water for the hogs, his elbow, unbeknownst to him, knocked me off the pump platform into a deep hog wallow. When he turned around I had disappeared beneath the slime, but he spotted me and pulled me out, bawling lustily. I followed the plow behind him, rode on the hay wagon, watched with interest while the bull performed his duties, bounced bareback on a dependable old horse named Bollie, who stopped and waited for me when I fell off, tagged along on fence-mending expeditions. I was not, properly speaking, a farm boy, but I grew up knowing pretty well what farm life was like.

As a small-town preacher's son I had many other contacts with the country. Rural church members invariably accounted for a goodly number of Father's flock, as the number of teams tied each Sunday to the hitch-rack beside the church building abundantly attested. Several of the more prosperous farmers always served on the Official Board, and Father paid pastoral calls on them and other farmers. His comments as we drove through the farm land were those of an expert; by the time he got to a given farmer's house, he could tell how this particular owner (or renter) was doing, and what his chances were for the coming harvest. Renters, incidentally, rarely fared very well; I gathered from my father's comments that that was the reason they were renters. We scanned the horizon for weather signs, and my father knew them all. He talked to the farm families about farm problems, farm prices, and the incredibly bad weather. Either it was too hot and everything was burning up, or too cold and everything was in danger of being frosted, or too wet, or too dry. Occasionally we watched the exciting process of mowing and threshing the grain, and inevitably we saw a lot of what we called corn-picking, a job that in those days had to be done strictly by hand. I never knew anything about scientific agriculture, although it was a required subject in one school I attended, but I knew something of the ritual of farming as practiced in the Middle West at the turn of the century.

As a matter of fact, my father as an ex-farmer brought the farm right into town with him. This meant plenty of chores for the boys of the family, and after my brother left I was the only boy available. We always had a big garden and grew our own vegetables, so I learned about spades and hoes and rakes and how to use them. Father was particular about his garden tools and demanded that they be kept clean at all times to prevent rust. To this day, when I put away a dirty spade (as I usually do), my conscience tweaks me a little. If Father were around, I know I wouldn't dare not to clean it properly. I also got the care of the family horse, and the colt, when there happened to be a colt. It took endless hours to fuel up and service those old hay-burners. Storing hay in the hayloft, pushing it down into the manger, currying and brushing the animals, cleaning the stable, harnessing up and hitching the horse to the buggy or road wagon, or whatever vehicle we happened to own. (Once we had a surrey with a fringe on the top.) The buggy, or substitute, had to be washed and kept polished. Washing a car may be work, but at least a car has flat surfaces and disclike wheels. How many boys would know today what every town and country boy then knew, that there are exactly sixteen spokes in a buggy wheel? And none of our current crop of juveniles could ever have experienced the feeling of relief that came when the sixteenth spoke of the fourth wheel—sixty-four spokes in all—was finished.

The family cow also took a lot of doing. Once when I was eleven years old and my father was away at Conference, I went with Mother as she grumpily left the house to do the milking. "Let me do it! Let me do it!" I insisted.

"You don't know how," she objected, "and I've no time to teach you."

"Just let me try," I continued. That was my big mistake. By some mischance, I *did* know how, without ever being taught. On his return Father promptly resigned the milking job in my favor, and from that time on it was one of my never ceasing morning and evening chores. I even learned how to shoot a stream of milk into the mouth of the pussycat who sat expectantly at my elbow. It was my duty, also, to drive the cow to pasture each morning after she was milked, and to drive her home from the pasture each evening before she was milked. And that wasn't quite all, for I had to deliver to cowless neighbors the extra milk that my mother thriftily sold them at five cents a quart. Occasionally I was even drafted to operate the churn, for Mother usually made her own butter.

Other obligations that I accepted, willingly or unwillingly, included sawing and splitting the wood used for fuel; bringing a goodly supply into the house each evening; getting up early each morning to start a fire in the kitchen stove; carrying in hard coal for use in the base-burner; feeding the chickens and (horror of horrors) cleaning out the chicken house; mowing the lawn—always a big lawn—the hard way, maybe not with a scythe and sickle, but at least with a lawn mower that had to be pushed; filling the lamps with kerosene (coal oil, we called it); trimming the wicks; and, when there was no girl to do it, washing the chimneys. And so on indefinitely. When I read of gangs of boys breaking into houses, cluttering up the road with "hot rods," and robbing pedestrians, I give thanks for the chores that in my youth kept so many boys out of mischief.

The houses I lived in as a boy were reasonably large and, by the standards of the time, comfortable. They were usually two-storied structures, built of lumber, heated by stoves, not furnaces. They had no such irrelevancies as fireplaces, and they were totally innocent of running water and indoor plumbing, although some of them were handsomely decorated with lightning rods. Water came from a well in the back yard, or from a cistern filled with rain water from the roof. Summers, one took the weather as it came, hot or hotter, for there was no such thing as air conditioning. For the housewife, wash day came on Monday, ironing day on Tuesday, and so on, with some other desig-nated duty such as baking or cleaning for each day of the week. The rising hour was five o'clock (for farm people, four o'clock), and in winter one often milked the cow and tended the horses, both morning and evening, by lantern light.

Some of my earliest recollections concern wash day. In an age of few laundries and no laundromats the labor involved in getting out the family wash was almost incredible, especially in the early years when our family was still large. First, someone had to pump the water and carry it into the house, pailful after pailful, until the big boiler on the kitchen stove and all other available containers were filled. Next, the dirty clothes had to be sorted into batches of appropriate size, color, and character. After that (or while it was going on) some female mem-ber of the family soaped and scrubbed, usually by hand on a zinc wash-board, the worst-soiled garments, or parts of garments—the collars and cuffs of shirts, for example. This process was particularly back-break-ing, for the tub of warm-to-hot water in which it was done invariably sat on a low stool or box, over which the unhappy operator had to bend half double. After the initial scrubbing, most of the clothes—especially if they were white and wouldn't fade—went into the boiler on the stove to be boiled for a while in soap-saturated water. (Sometimes the soap we used on wash day Mother had made herself in a big black kettle over a fire in the back yard.)

After the boiling process had continued long enough, the steaming hot clothes were fished out with a wooden rod about a yard long (usually the sawed-off handle of a worn-out broom) for transfer to a hand-operated washing machine. In the earliest such machine we owned somebody had to pull a lever back and forth and back and forth until the proper degree of purity had been achieved; later we got a machine with a crank wheel that the operator turned round and round and round and round to achieve the same results. If, after all this, any items failed to pass inspection, they went back to the washboard again. As far back as I can remember, we also owned a rubber wringer, so that the wringing-out process did not have to be done by hand. In fact, I was often detailed to turn the wringer. But one wringing-out was never enough—the clothes had to be rinsed (Mother scorned the way most country women said "rensed") in clear water or bluing water, then wrung out again, then carried outdoors to be hung on the clothesline or clothes-reel to dry. This process went on, assembly-line fashion, until the last batch of clothes (overalls, socks, and such) was done.

On a good drying day, by the time the last batch went out the first batch could be brought in, but if there was room enough Mother preferred to let the whole wash flap in the breeze for a half day or so. Big washings and getting one's wash on the line early were status symbols; sometimes we managed to have the work all done and the clothes a-flapping before nine o'clock, which, incidentally, was the time we children had to go to school. Mother, bless her heart, as the harried commander-in-chief of wash-day complications, never failed to lose her temper early in the proceedings. I marveled then, and I marvel now, at her ability to chew us all out in language that contained not a single naughty word, but that in tone and tempo would have made any top sergeant green with envy. The last time I saw my older brother alive he said: "Don, will you ever forget wash day?" I had no need to reply. Quite reasonably, as I think of it now, Father always made himself scarce on Monday mornings.

As a matter of fact, my mother was a bit of a terror. To her dying day I was always a little afraid of her, and the two or three times during my teens that I stood up to her rank easily among the bravest acts of my life. She had great executive ability and should have been the manager of a string of banks or department stores; the absence of an adequate outlet for her talents was perhaps what made her so short-tempered and difficult. She made a mistake, no doubt, in dedicating me to the ministry before I was born, but it was she, rather than my easy-going father, who schooled me bluntly and forcefully in what was right and what was wrong, in what built character and what did not. I doubt if she had ever read Emerson's essay on self-reliance, but she drilled the principles it enunciated into my consciousness in a thousand different ways. "Never," she used to say over and over again, "never ask anyone to do anything for you that you can do for yourself." The debt I owe her is quite beyond my ability to estimate. If I have managed through the years "to stand on my own two feet," as she recommended, her teaching accounts for it. Let me give you a few examples.

When we left Grant City for Mound City in 1900, I was in the fifth grade, but because my class in the old school was well ahead of the equivalent group in my new school, I was put in the sixth grade. But the sixth grade was much farther along than I was, and at the end of the year I flunked. This was really not so bad, for we had moved only in April. But it was a humiliation to my mother, who simply wasn't going to have it said that a child of hers had not been promoted. My chief trouble had been with arithmetic, so my mother, who in country school had cut her teeth on Ray's *Higher Arithmetic* and knew all the answers, sat me down at the dining room table *for the summer* to do all those incredible problems, over 150 of them, as I recall, that came in my book right after fractions. Problems like: "John can do a piece of work in eight hours. (The problems all stressed hard work.) If James works half as fast as John and Richard works half as fast as James, how long will it take the three of them to do the job, working together?" Now the answer, as any sensible person would know, was that it would take three boys at least twice as long to do a given job as it would take one boy to do it working alone. But that isn't what it said in the back of the book. Nevertheless, the problem stated was a simple one; most of them were far worse. When Churchill talked about "blood, toil, tears and sweat," I thought of that summer. But with my mother's imperious voice driving me on, I solved all those problems, every last one of them, before school opened in the fall. Then I went into the seventh grade and had no further trouble with arithmetic. Probably a thousand times during my ordeal Mother quoted that abominable axiom: "If at first you don't succeed, try, try again."

My mother hadn't much time for puppy love, as she called it, but from the time I was six years old I was full of it. No doubt she knew from observation, if not from experience, the trouble it could make. When I was about ten or eleven years old I fell madly in love with a cute little girl with the figure of a match who was perhaps a year or two my junior. I would have died rather than tell her of my devotion, but of course there was really no need of that; girls always know anyway. For emotional relief I spent days, maybe weeks, composing a letter to her in which I told all. I had no notion of sending that letter; I had written it for me, and not for her, a kind of exercise in English composition. Finally I put it in the kitchen stove, where it belonged. But unfortunately the fire went out too soon that day, and my mother found my masterpiece, only slightly charred around the edges. Did she burn it? Yes, eventually. But before the cremation took place she read it to me, word by silly word, with appropriate comments and emphasis. The lesson she drew I have disregarded occasionally, but always to my sorrow. "Never," she warned me (and she was so right), "never put anything in writing that you would not have the whole world read."

Mother also made it clear that if ever I was to "amount to anything in the world," an oft-repeated phrase, I must begin to earn money and make my own way, not at some later date, but right now. To achieve this worthy end she was as full of plans as a tick is of blood. When I was about twelve years old, she sent me out to solicit subscriptions for books. She was a natural-born salesman and could have made a success of such an undertaking, but as a book peddler I didn't do very well. The first book I tried to sell was *The Beautiful Life of Frances E. Willard*, founder of the W.C.T.U. Somehow I didn't have much luck with Frances E., although I can remember selling a copy to a neighbor lady whose husband was known to fall heavily off the wagon from time to time. After my failure with Miss Willard, I tried *Up from Slavery*, by Booker T. Washington, a much better book, but with not much better luck. Finally, my mother got me into the soap business, seven bars of assorted sizes and colors all in one box, just long enough to reach from my elbow to my fingers. Price, thirty-five cents, half for me and half for the manufacturer. I did pretty well selling soap, much as I hated house-to-house canvassing, and the profits helped meet current expenses. Well, that was my mother. She might have been a hard task-master, but the lessons she taught me in personal responsibility and financial integrity would take more than one lifetime to forget.

Whatever the educationists may now think of them, I have few complaints to record about the public schools I attended as a boy. For some unremembered reason I refused to go to school until the day I was six years old, instead of starting with my class, as I should have done, at the beginning of the school year. So I was only four months in the first grade, which seems to have been long enough. I was promoted regularly, except from the sixth grade as noted, and I recall the names, faces, and personalities of all my teachers. As far as I know I was never at the head of my class, a deficiency that greatly plagued my mother, but me not at all. "I'm doing all right," I used to reply to her admonitions.

"But you are not the best in your grade," she objected.

"Well, I can't help it," I came back lamely, and to some extent correctly.

Probably the chief trouble, however, was that I was not strongly competitive, a quality that my mother tried in vain to instill in me. The only inexcusably bad showing I ever made was in my first high school year at Mound City, Missouri. Of the three teachers I had that year, one was a notably poor disciplinarian, and unfortunately, he was in charge of the assembly room during most of my study hours. The hundred or so pupils he tried in vain to control behaved shamefully, I along with the rest. In consequence my grades suffered terribly, particularly in Latin, which demanded a degree of concentration. Part of my trouble, perhaps, was my age—I was only twelve when the year began—but mostly I just didn't study.

The fates were kind to me, for that year we moved from Mound City to Hopkins, where the high school was so thoroughly regimented and so totally disciplined that everyone in the four grades got 100 in deportment, and deserved it. We had only two teachers for a total of thirty or forty pupils, but our teachers were mature men who tolerated no nonsense. My grades picked up immediately. I remember with particular fondness the singing lessons in which all grades joined, with the teacher getting the pitch from a tuning fork and do-re-mi-ing us through lesson after lesson in an old-fashioned singing book. Another interesting feature of the school was the "rhetoricals" that we were required to put on at stated intervals, with each person, in his turn, speaking a piece or participating in some group performance. I occasionally got myself involved in a debate; one question I recall arguing was: "Resolved, that the men of ancient times were greater than those of modern times." I stood firmly by the moderns, but a smart senior girl—I was then only a sophomore—made both me and the whole modern world sound foolish.

For my junior high school year, my parents sent me to the Maryville Seminary, a Methodist secondary school fourteen miles south of Hopkins. The primary reason for this decision, perhaps, was to support a church institution, but my parents also thought that I would get a better education at the seminary, which was one of the last of the old academies so common in an earlier age. Fortunately, the trains ran at suitable times. I could leave Hopkins on a Monday morning in time to make my classes, and return on a Friday afternoon after my last class for the week. I took far too many subjects to do well in any of them, but I did get superior instruction and on the whole I profited from the experience. The four nights and five days I was away from home each week I boarded with a family my parents knew, and among other things learned to eat a far more varied diet than I had adhered to at home, where my childish whims were still too much respected. The intention was for me to graduate from the seminary, but it closed down the next year, after its property was taken over by the Northwest Missouri State Teachers College, so I had to return for my senior year to the Hopkins high school, the same that I had abandoned so incontinently the year before.

Being a preacher's son in a small town undoubtedly had both its advantages and its disadvantages, but the former, in my judgment, far outweighed the latter. Most important, I think, was the fact that my father was at home most of the time, not away at an office or a store, and played quite as large a part in my bringing-up as my mother. From the time I was a toddler, Father took me with him whenever he went downtown, or for a drive into the country, or for an occasional expedition to another town. He talked to me freely, of his own problems as well as mine, and treated me as an equal. His theological views broadened with the years, and without quite realizing it he became a strong proponent of what in more sophisticated circles was called the "social gospel." As his thinking changed, mine followed along, so that I was prepared by his teaching, in a sense, to abandon the orthodoxy that he had only modified. Generous exposure to the Bible and its precepts was a part of our daily life. Every morning, immediately after breakfast, Father read a chapter from the Bible, and we all knelt while he, or some visitor, or my mother, or I myself, after I was old enough, led in prayer. Sometimes, if Mother's temper had become frayed during the breakfast hour, Father disciplined her by asking her to lead in prayer, a recipe that generally worked, but occasionally backfired: "You can just do your own praying," she sometimes said, by way of refusal. So Father prayed for her, and all the rest of us, good and hard. If Father called on me to pray (I always hoped he wouldn't), I came through the best I could, but somehow the Lord and I never got together on very familiar terms.

For anyone brought up as I was, there was no escaping a certain close acquaintance with the scriptures. I heard the Bible read at every church service, and studied short passages, line by line, in Sunday school, memorizing for each such session a "golden text." I dutifully learned by heart the Ten Commandments, the First and Twenty-third Psalms, the Beatitudes, and other favored sections. I even learned the Methodist catechism, although I doubt if most Methodists even know that there is such a thing. On my own, I got interested in biblical history. I can recall as a child making tables of the kings of Israel and Judah, with accompanying notations to indicate which did well and which did evil "in the sight of the Lord." I learned some geography from following the missionary voyages of St. Paul, but I gagged at Pauline theology, despite my father's efforts to explain that "the elect" and "whosoever will" meant exactly the same thing. As far as I was concerned, St. Paul was an unregenerate Calvinist. Years later, when I began to teach and write history, my early familiarity with the Bible showed through in scriptural allusions that my classes often failed to follow; possibly also my literary style—if I ever attained one—owed something to the King James Version. The men who made that translation may not have known their Hebrew and Greek as well as later scholars, although sometimes I wonder if they didn't know it better, but I would like to think that a little of the clear and rugged Shakespearean prose they wrote rubbed off on me.

Another advantage I enjoyed was my father's library. It emphasized theology, with books on such weird subjects as *Eschatology* that I never cracked, but with others that I deemed readable. There was a handsomely bound set of Cooper's *Leather-Stocking Tales* that I devoured, also such dependables as Hawthorne's *Twice-Told Tales,*

The Complete Works of Henry Wadsworth Longfellow, Lamb's *Tales from Shakespeare*, and the like. When the going got tough in Father's library, I raided the school library, and brought home such treasures as Henty's *Under Drake's Flag*, which I read again and again. For a long time, indeed, Henty was my favorite author. Father also subscribed to many magazines, one of which, *The Youth's Companion*, he took particularly for me. I read every word of it every week, finding it much more to my liking than the *Sunday School Advocate* and *The Classmate*, Methodist publications handed out each Sunday. But I read them, too. When I could collect the necessary ten or fifteen cents for the purpose, I supplemented the family offerings by such newsprint classics as *The Liberty Boys of Seventy-Six*, a real thriller. My tastes were quite undeveloped, and my parents made little effort to cultivate them. I can remember mooning over such items as Mrs. E. D. E. N. Southworth's *Ishmael Worth*, and Gene Stratton Porter's *The Harvester*. But I can remember also wading through Drummond's *Natural Law in the Spiritual World*, a real eye-opener that I discovered in my father's library. My favorite reading position as a boy was flat on my stomach on the floor, elbows down to prop up my chin on my hands, and the book lying open before me.

There were other educational influences that came my way, partly, at least, because my father encouraged them. One such was the Chautauqua. We had a good one in Mound City every year we lived there, with such distinguished speakers as Mark Guy Pierce, William Jennings Bryan, and Jonathan P. Dolliver. Once I can recall going from Hopkins to the Maryville Chautauqua to hear Lieutenant Richmond P. Hobson whoop it up for the temperance cause. Music and drama, far better than local talent could provide, also appeared on the Chautauqua circuits, and it was at one of them that I saw my first "motion picture." In addition to the summer Chautauqua, the small towns in which we lived also supported lecture courses to which we always had season tickets. Some of the lectures might be worth only sleeping through, but others were quite impressive. I'm sure that my father often had something to do with the choice of speakers. My parents frowned on plays that came to the local opera house as not uplifting, but I saw some anyway, and, with parental consent, *Uncle Tom's Cabin*, which was never half as good as the book.

My father early taught me to follow the course of political events. He was a strong Republican, as were most preachers of the Methodist

Episcopal Church, the northern, antislavery wing of the denomination after the secession in 1844 of the Methodist Episcopal Church, South. One of my earliest recollections is of marching at the tail end of a McKinley-Hobart torchlight procession during the campaign of 1896, with just as big a torchlight on my shoulder as anybody's. I was aware of the Spanish-American War, the events of which Father followed through the columns of the Chicago *Inter-Ocean*. I recall the tolling of the town fire bell to announce the death of President McKinley, the mobilization of a local unit for service in the Philippines, and a certain degree of amazement, bordering on hostility, among my playmates because during the Boer-British war I reflected my father's sympathy for the British. It helped, though, in the war games that small boys play, to have someone willing to lead the British forces to certain defeat.

I can remember my father's showing me, when I was perhaps ten or eleven years old, the editorial page of the St. Joseph *Daily News*, the paper on which he depended after the war was over. He advised me to read the editorials as well as the news, something I rarely neglected to do from that time on. Father was fascinated with Theodore Roosevelt, and so, of course, was I. Both of us absorbed the Progressive point of view for which he stood. In one respect Father was rather ahead of his time. He was a strong protagonist of the Negro, and I still have the notes from which he preached a sermon on behalf of the Freedman's Aid Society, a Methodist organization that collected funds for the benefit of former slaves and their descendants. The Reverend Martin Luther King, Jr., would have regarded the sentiments expressed in these notes as strictly up-to-date. Once, after I had just read Thomas Dixon's *The Clansman*, I said something at table more or less derogatory of the Negro race. My father was ordinarily slow to wrath, but not then, for he turned on me in anger. No son of his, I was made to understand, was ever to make any such statements again in his house. Sometimes when Father found the Republican candidates too obnoxious to warrant his support, he would say: "This is a good year to vote the Prohibitionist ticket." In general I got the impression that the Progressives were the "good guys" and their conservative opponents the "bad guys." And as Alexander Pope put it, "Just as the twig is bent, the tree's inclined."

Life as a preacher's son was not without its debit side. The worst disadvantage, I think, came from our frequent moves. In Grant City, where I lived from the age of five years to ten, I was one of a large group, including my cousins, the Gibson boys, and numerous other young fry among whom I had a recognized place. (Phil Gibson, incidentally, my best friend and fifth-grade seatmate, eventually became Chief Justice of the California Supreme Court. After World War II, I met him again in San Francisco.) We played together constantly, patronized the same swimming hole, learned to skate on the same pond, staged circuses in the roomiest haymow available (the Gibsons'), ganged together to watch the annual balloon ascension at the Old Soldiers' Reunion, and so on. But at ten years of age I was uprooted, and had to make my way in the new Mound City environment. "I was a stranger and ye took me in" was not written of small boys. As a new boy in town and a preacher's son at that, I was suspect. Furthermore, my mother did me no good with my peers when she saw to it that I was advanced to the seventh grade, in spite of having flunked out in the sixth. Some of the other kids in my room, most of whom were two years older than I, ganged up to give me a bad time. Once, I recall, several of them pretended during recess that they were going to burn me at the stake, and tied me up, hand and foot, for the purpose. Fortunately, I had a friend, Earl Mitchell, whose mind was already made up to become a lawyer, and he argued me loose. At some point in his argument, he referred to the fibers in the rope with which I was being tied, and he was thereafter always known as "Fiber." On another occasion, I had just won a declamatory contest, after flailing my arms through a piece called "Bresca," only to be knocked down as I left the schoolhouse by some unknown assailant. Another time, two bigger boys caught me alone at the edge of a park and beat me up. But I always had a few good friends such as Earl, and I don't recall feeling persecuted. At Hopkins, where we moved when I was thirteen, I was a good deal of a loner, a situation by no means helped when I went to the Maryville Seminary for a year, then had to return to the local high school to graduate. Had I shown any athletic prowess, it would have helped, but I couldn't even throw a ball decently far, and was of little use in outdoor games. My father was totally unaware of such problems, but I doubt if he could have helped me any had he tried.

The religious atmosphere in which I had to live was also a bit suffocating. I was probably less than five years old when I was first made to realize that I had a soul that needed to be saved. This turned out to be a hard nut for me to crack. The "blue flower of Methodism," as some called it, was the ability to know that one had "passed from death unto life," a conscious certainty of salvation that was supposed to hit a person all of a sudden, preferably during one of the annual revivals, with a lot of the already saved clustering around to pray the penitent through. This was what the evangelical sects meant by "conversion." Somehow I was never able to make the grade, although God knows I tried hard enough. Once while I was at school in Maryville I "went forward" under the influence of some magnetic sermonizer, and after a period of painfully public prayer and penitence proclaimed to all and sundry that at last I knew I was saved. It was pure fraud, for I knew nothing of the kind. I only hoped that if I said so with sufficient conviction it might turn out to be true. My father consoled me with the thought that I hadn't sinned very hard, and therefore couldn't expect too much of a rebound, so I took what comfort I could in that. I was also brought up to believe that I had been called to preach, and in due time would hear the call; but the Lord must have had other plans for me, for the message never got through. That it would come eventually, however, I long took for granted.

I have often wondered how much of Methodist revivalism was mere emotional release. Certainly the preachers got a big kick out of the services they held. After a successful evening session they used often to come to the parsonage, where they would shed their piety, crack jokes, and tell tall tales until far into the night. A bowl of apples somehow speeded up the reaction, and that was where I came in. Father liked apples and usually preserved a quantity of them for winter use in what he called an "apple hole." This hole was dug deep below the frost line somewhere in the garden, then filled with apples, then boxed over and covered with dirt. Many's the time, after church at night, that I have burrowed into that hole for apples to lighten the hearts of the reverend clergy. Father also liked apple cider, and strove earnestly to keep it from turning to hard cider or vinegar. Once a kind friend told him that ten cents worth of mustard seed would keep a keg of cider sweet all winter. The recipe seemed to work; at least something that year arrested the customary all-too-rapid progress toward vinegar. That season, instead of bringing in apples after church, I was sent to the cellar for a pitcher of that good sweet cider. It foamed like everything, but we knew it couldn't be hard because of those mighty grains of mustard seed (see Luke 17:6). But that was the only such keg of cider I remember. Either my father's faith in the mustard seed wavered, or his prohibitionist views got the better of him, or both. In his frequent temperance sermons he always bore down hard on "Demon Rum."

In state and local politics the "wet" versus "dry" issue was predominant all the time we lived in Missouri. The Anti-Saloon League was at the zenith of its power, and its representative was as constant a visitor in our household as the presiding elder himself. Collections taken in church provided the League with the sinews of war, and nothing was left undone to make sure that the voters chose officials whose stand was right on the liquor question. Signing a saloon petition was a sure means of getting one's name taken off the church roll; there was no trial about it, the name was just scratched off. Party membership hardly counted; indeed, one might almost say that to all intents and purposes the words "wet" and "dry" had supplanted for local elections the words "Democrat" and "Republican," and in about that order. In only one of the Missouri towns in which we lived was there a licensed saloon, and in due time it was voted out. Lacking saloons, there were always bootleggers, but this misfortune would end, we were told, with the attainment of statewide and nationwide prohibition.

I doubt if my being a preacher's son made any difference in the boy-girl relationships that are an inevitable part of adolescence. More important was the fact that I was a couple of grades ahead of my age in school, and correspondingly younger than the girls in my class; until I was about fourteen, also somewhat smaller. At Hopkins my most dearly beloved was even younger than I, however, but so completely protected by her parents that I almost never saw her alone. By careful timing I was able to walk to school with her nearly every day, but she always had an annoying younger brother in tow. I think she returned my affection, but for the whole three years we knew each other we loved and longed at a distance. If my recollection is to be trusted, "going steady" was much less common during my high school years than it is today. There were plenty of group parties and "socials," after which one might walk a girl home; some coasting (I had a big bobsled my father had made for me) and skating activities in winter; and an occasional picnic. But that was about all. Once in a while, just to show that I was growing up, I took a girl to Sunday evening church, but the young ladies whose parents allowed them such privileges were always older than I, and a bit condescending. One girl in my class, whom I liked a lot even if she was a bit too old for me, was very small

—just my height when we were sophomores, but hardly up to my shoulders when we were seniors. I thought I rated pretty well with her, but one Sunday after church she told me I couldn't walk home with her as I usually did, for someone else was meeting her. I watched with dismay while a grown man, probably all of twenty-one years old, led her away. They were married in a matter of months, and when I saw her next, a few years later, she had one baby in her arms and another at her knees. Girls, I thus early began to discover, have a way of thinking of the future when boys still have only the present in mind.

My father's health was always precarious, and in April, 1906, just before my graduation from high school, he decided to take a "supernumerary" relationship with the Conference, which meant that for a year he would be left without an appointment. My mother, long mindful of the fact that she might at any time be left a widow, had induced him to invest most of their very meager savings in a house at Mound City, which meant that they had somewhere to go. As for their living, the Conference voted Father the sum of three hundred dollars. So off the family moved to Mound City, leaving me behind in the home of a Hopkins neighbor to finish out the school year. I thus graduated from high school without either of my parents, or for that matter any relative, being present, the only boy in a class of five, and not the valedictorian. That honor went to a bright twenty-year-old girl, who for good measure also roundly trounced me in a public debate that was a part of the graduation exercises. Times have changed; the Hopkins graduating class sixty years later was thirty-three, although meantime the town had actually lost in population. Farm families at the turn of the century rarely felt the necessity of sending their children to high school, while consolidated schools and school buses were yet to come. Dropouts, too, were far more common, in both town and country, with the shrinkage in the size of classes beginning at about the third grade. Well, at least I had made it through high school at sixteen, even if only prematurely rather than precociously. What next? With that thought in mind, I took the train for Mound City.

Not for many years did it occur to me that the town-and-country economy in which I grew up had any particular significance. The fact that it did mean something, however, became clear in my mind recently when I visited all the little Missouri towns I had once known so well. During the last sixty years they have declined in population from 20 to

30 per cent, but they have nevertheless lost many of their rural characteristics and have taken on city ways. Nearly all of the streets are now paved and at night are fully lighted, a status rarely achieved in my youth except in or near the business district. The fences that once surrounded every residence are gone; no need now to protect lawns and gardens from predatory cows on the way to or from pasture. The barns and outbuildings that once covered a large part of every back yard have mostly disappeared or have been turned into garages. Outdoor plumbing has moved inside; only now and then does an example of "Chick Sales" architecture survive. Along Main Street the old general stores may look the same on the outside, but within they have become supermarkets, or at least that seems to have been their intention. Everything that the people buy comes now from the city; everything that the farmers sell goes now to the city. The church buildings, while all identifiable, have been dressed up inside and out to look like city churches. The schools are city-type schools. The homes are equipped with televisions and radios that proclaim city standards. The town that once looked to the country and reflected country ways now looks to the city and reflects city ways.

Even in the country things are different. One seldom sees a horse, except where some individual makes a speciality of raising riding horses to meet the demands of city girls. Milk cows are concentrated on dairy farms. Livestock raising has become increasingly specialized; a given farm may deal mainly in feeders, taken in at one size and turned out at another. General farming as we used to know it is almost dead. Farmers' wives no longer bring butter and eggs to town to trade in at the store or to sell to dependable town customers. Milk cans no longer stand at every crossroads awaiting the creamery collection. Great tracts, whether owned by one person or rented from a number of owners, are often farmed as a unit. One enormous tractor will pull the machinery that in a single operation plows the ground, plants the corn, fertilizes the soil, and deposits the weed killer that makes cultivation unnecessary. After that nature does the work until a mechanical corn picker takes over in the fall; a mere factory on the farm.

Our new urban America, for all its vast material achievements, has not yet found itself; its problems of employment, transportation, water supply, clean air to breathe, decent standards of conduct are all unsolved, perhaps unsolvable. In contrast, the town-and-country

economy of the late nineteenth century—the horse and buggy days—
had attained a viable way of life, one that on the fundamentals met the
basic needs of the people it served. There was no problem of identity.
Each person was identified with a home, a family, a church, a school,
a community. Everybody knew who he was and he knew that everybody knew who he was. Most important in the molding of his ideals
were the church, the school, and the home. On the debit side one might
list the saloon, the pool hall, and the livery stable. The tug of war went
on between good and bad, but whatever the outcome for a given individual, the system worked for the group as a whole. Of course, for the
discontented and ambitious, there was always the safety valve of the
city—someplace else to go. But at least the small town was a good place
to be *from*, and I wonder if the city did not greatly benefit, as long as
the influx lasted, from the country-bred invaders who brought with
them the principles and practices of their youth.

III. Schoolteacher in Wyoming

No sooner had I arrived in Mound City than I found out that the family would be on the move again before the summer was over. Father's three brothers had all gone west, so I suppose that it was almost inevitable that he should follow them. One brother, my Uncle George, whom I never knew, went to Colorado as a young man and for a time lived at Rico. Another, Uncle Ben, left both Missouri and the Methodist Church to become the pastor of a Christian church somewhere in Oregon. The third brother, Uncle Joe, was the youngest of the four (Father was the oldest) and the only one with whom we kept in touch. Uncle Joe—also a preacher—had only recently accepted a Methodist pulpit at Evanston, Wyoming, and was full of enthusiasm for the West. "John," he wrote my father, "if you can barely live in Missouri, you'll be a well man in Wyoming." Father didn't need much persuading. Life on three hundred dollars a year presented problems; besides, he, too, no less than his brothers, had the blood of pioneers in his veins. So when the offer came of an appointment at Buffalo, he accepted it without hesitation. We sold nearly all our household goods, sent Father's library and a few other indispensables by freight, and took the train for Wyoming.

The Burlington Route, a way through to the West that was itself less than a quarter century old, had missed Buffalo by about thirty miles, so we landed at Clearmont, the tiny railroad town nearest our destination. Since it was too late at night for us to go farther, we put up at the only hotel the town afforded. It was a pretty primitive place, even by our standards, with rooms barely large enough to accommodate a bed and chair, and only pine boards to separate us from the other guests. My father and I occupied one tiny room, my mother and sister another. But whatever the shortcomings of our accommodations, we took them in stride; after all, we were away out west.

Next morning we set out for the Peter Watt ranch, midway between

44

Clearmont and Buffalo, where my father was to make his first pastoral call. I cannot recall whether we made that trip by stage or were met by someone from the ranch—probably the latter. But we got a good look at a stage all right, for this type of conveyance still provided the only available means of public passenger transportation from the railroad into the interior. The stages we saw were heavy two- or three-seated vehicles, about as comfortable to ride in as a lumber wagon, but considerably improved over those described in Mark Twain's *Roughing It.* We also saw and passed several of the long wagon trains that were used to bring freight from the railroad to the town in which we were to live. These trains consisted usually of about three wagons lashed together, one after another, and were drawn by as many teams as the load required—eight or ten teams to a train were not uncommon. Sometimes one of the lead horses had a rider, but sometimes a driver mysteriously guided all the teams with a single line that ran from bit to bit from the wheel horses to the leaders. Passing one of these wagon trains on the road was no light matter, especially since the right-of-way, as it then existed, could best be described as "unimproved." But the stage drivers and ranch hands who used the roads managed each passing with considerable skill. Certainly road accidents were far less common, even relative to the amount of traffic, than they are today.

The Peter Watt family were important members of the Buffalo Methodist church, so we rated a cordial reception. The ranch house was large enough to accommodate all of us overnight, and by invitation I stayed on a few days longer. I remember vaguely a large two-table dining room, where family, guests, and ranch hands all took their meals together. Most of the men slept in a nearby bunkhouse, a term that my mother, to the great merriment of all concerned, understood to be "buckhouse." Here at the Watt ranch I saw for the first time the soon-to-be familiar sights of the typical Wyoming ranch—horses and cowhands, high-pommeled saddles and vicious-bitted bridles, corrals and branding irons, and all the rest. By this time the range cattle industry had suffered many mutations. No longer did the prudent rancher expect his livestock to live off the range exclusively. Now he raised huge crops of hay, and even grain, for winter feed. This process, of course, involved irrigation and water rights, a whole new set of concepts for a Missouri boy to digest. Where we had come from, it was taken for granted that enough rain would fall, "alike on the just and the unjust," to make the crops grow. In Wyoming, provided you had the water and the water rights, you could make your own rain, although anyone could see that this job was plenty tough.

At some point on the way from Clearmont to Buffalo I got my first glimpse of the Big Horn Mountains, the first time I had seen anything higher than a Missouri River bluff. Far in the distance above the seared brown hills rose this massive band of blue, surmounted by a series of snow-white peaks, and over all the curving dome of the cloudless western sky. This bit of grandeur, for which nothing in my experience had prepared me, burned itself so deeply into my memory that to this day I measure all mountains by the Big Horns. Of the many others I have seen since, some like the Swiss Alps are higher, others like the Tetons are more elaborately sculptured, and a few like Popocatepetl and Fujiyama betray their volcanic origin, but none of them in my mind eclipse the Big Horns. I was soon to learn that they would also bear close inspection, deeper and more varied than I had imagined, with endless valleys and streams and lakes and tree-covered ridges. While we lived in Buffalo, the nearest I ever got to the top of them was within about four miles; only later, when highways brought automobile traffic across them, a kind of insult, it seemed to me, to one of nature's noblest works, did I see beyond the crest.

The town of Buffalo was smaller than it is now, comparable in some ways to the towns we had lived in in Missouri, but quite different in others. The absence of a railroad running through the town and of the customary railroad station to which all foot-loose citizens could repair to watch each train come and go, seemed particularly noticeable to us. Probably Buffalo was the largest town without these facilities in the United States. The town had four churches—Methodist, Congregational, Episcopal, and Catholic—about the same number we were accustomed to, but the church buildings were smaller, even if plenty large enough for the congregations they drew. Somehow the life of the town did not center in the churches the way it did in Missouri. Where then did it center? Down on Main Street, I think.

This thoroughfare, running vaguely north to south, bisected the town. A fairly pretentious courthouse, facing to the east, introduced the business district. South of the court house was Clear Creek, a rapidly flowing, rock-strewn mountain stream that in those days did credit to its name. The creek was adequately bridged for vehicles and pedestrians, but the roar of its waters made much more noise than the traffic that crossed it. We had not long been in town when my mother and my sister furnished us with a tale long told. As they walked across the bridge with a stiff breeze blowing, my sister warned: "Watch out, Mamma, your hat will blow off!"

"Just mind your own business," Mother replied testily, at which point her hat did blow off and floated merrily away. Never long bereft of her sense of humor, Mother promptly telephoned Mrs. Peter Watt, who lived about fifteen miles downstream, asking her to keep an eye out for the errant hat as it came by.

Most of the buildings on Main Street were without distinction, not much different from those one sees on any movie set for westerns. Between the courthouse and the creek was a hotel, the very same, according to legend, in which the Virginian got his man. A little to the south of the creek and off on a side street was a house of ill fame, although that was not exactly what most people called it. Interspersed among the usual complement of stores were at least six or seven saloons, all of which seemed to be doing an excellent business, with stage drivers, teamsters, and ranch hands generously supplementing the local trade. It was often asserted that saloon visitors from a distance who passed out during a spree were mercifully relieved of their excess cash to assure them against a too prolonged debauch. If there were any shooting scrapes, as the movie scenarios would now lead us to believe, we never heard of them; but as my preacher father viewed the scene, the Devil had the town in his clutches, and working against His Satanic Majesty was uphill business. When a Methodist bishop, presiding over the church's Annual Conference at Sheridan, rebuked the Wyoming preachers for saving so few souls, Father's retort was that it was easier to make a dozen converts in Missouri than to get a single Wyoming sinner to repent.

My first concern was to get a job. I had always taken it for granted that I should teach a few years before going to college, so began to look around for a school. By good luck, the Johnson County Teachers' Institute met shortly after our arrival. I enrolled in it, listened to the rather unimportant lectures and discussions it offered, and took the required examinations for a teacher's certificate. In those days the examinations were given personally by the county superintendent of schools, a political officer, but fortunately for me a competent and attractive young woman whom I much admired. I passed in a great variety of subjects, including such learned fields as reading, writing, arithmetic, spelling, geography, and the like, and received in return a first-grade certificate, good for four years. Also, I found a school, or more accurately, the county superintendent found it for me.

Since my school would not begin for nearly a month, I looked around for something to do in the meantime. The editor of the local paper, Hayden M. White, tried me out as a reporter, but I was no good at that; the only people I knew were church people, and nothing very exciting seemed to be happening to them. Furthermore, as a preacher's son I couldn't very well visit the saloons on Main Street where all the action seemed to be. I learned, however, of a job on a ranch just at the edge of town that might be within my capabilities. This rancher had recently purchased five hundred head of sheep, and since none of his fences could remotely be considered as "sheep-tight," he needed a herder. That sounded easy to me, so I asked for and obtained the job.

Try as I might, I could never forget my experience as a sheepherder. What I had to do was known technically as close-herding, that is, I had to keep the sheep within a given pasture area and to prevent them from getting into the road or into any of the surrounding fields. To aid me in this endeavor, the rancher provided me with a dog, who fortunately understood the game perfectly and when he was of a mind to do so could handle it virtually without my help. The trouble was that my dog was old and tired and deaf and not always on the scene. Sometimes when I needed him most he was taking a nap in some secluded spot and managed not to hear my frantic cries for help. Without a dog I might as well not have been there. When sheep decide to go in a given direction, I discovered, you can kill them as fast as they come, but you can't keep them from coming. That is unless you are a dog, in which case you hardly need even to bark, but just let your presence be known. Thereupon the wayward-minded stragglers promptly turn tail and beat it back to the rest of the herd as fast as they can go.

I acquired a very low opinion of sheep. Not only did they and the dog give me a bad time by day, they also took to dying by night. That's another thing about sheep. When one of them makes up its mind to die, there's just nothing you can do about it. Sheep seemingly have some kind of suicidal mania that makes them rather die than live. If anything knocks a hog down, he will squeal around and manage somehow to get on his feet again. But if a sheep gets knocked down, it's different. The sheep just rolls over and happily accepts the fate of being trampled to death. From my angle, the trouble with a dead sheep was that I had to skin it. My employer showed me exactly how, and I learned to do it well enough, but I took little satisfaction in being a mutton mortician. For a while we lost a sheep or two each day and my life became correspondingly miserable. By the time we discovered the cause, a small patch of alkali in an out-of-the-way place that the sheep mistook for salt, my days as a sheepherder were about over. Another thing that gave me trouble was that we had a bum lamb or two in the herd. A bum lamb is a lamb that has lost its mother and has been brought up on a bottle by some misguided philanthropist. After that experience, the lamb is fit only to associate with humans; it has no sheep sense. Instead of running to the herd when the dog appears, it runs away from the herd. It deserves extermination and with a more experienced sheepherder generally gets it. But as for me, I would rather chase it than skin it.

I hasten to add that my duties were not at an end when we drove the sheep into a corral each night, as we did. My employer had fourteen milk cows, and I was one of the four hands detailed to milk them. So each night after the sheep were corralled and each morning before we let them out there were all those cows to milk. We all knew the easy milkers from the hard ones and did our best to outsmart each other, but try as we might there were always three cows for each of us and two left over. Somehow I always got one of the leftovers. By day the sheep demanded my attention, except for that all-too-brief period in the middle of the day when they bunched together for a siesta; but nights, after the milking was done, I took my turn at the cream separator, which in those primitive days was still hand-powered. Although home was only a mile or so away, I ate and bedded down at the ranch. Getting-up time was four o'clock, going-to-bed time, as soon as we could get there, and all this early-to-bed-and-early-to-rise business netted me was exactly one dollar a day. Sundays, however, I had off and spent at home or in church, longing for the time when I wouldn't have to herd sheep any more.

At last the time came. The Streeter school, so named for the family that lived nearest it, wasn't much of a school, but of course I wasn't much of a teacher. It was located near Kaycee, about sixty miles south of Buffalo, on Powder River below the confluence of its three forks. The school term was only six months long and the pay was only forty dollars a month; furthermore, since the school district was just fresh out of funds, I had to take my pay in warrants that I could either hold until the tax money came in, or discount at a Buffalo bank. Naturally

I chose the latter alternative so that my take-home pay turned out to be $38.50 a month instead of $40.00.

I gathered all my possessions together in a trunk and took the stage for Kaycee. I was the only passenger on the long drive south and the stage driver regaled me with tales of the Johnson County War. I had already picked up veiled references to this affair and had learned that it was a subject into which an outsider didn't inquire too closely, for altogether too many of the participants were still alive and didn't care to have their war records examined too closely. On one side of the conflict were the so-called Rustlers, although many of them, I was assured, were merely small farmers or ranchers who had never branded a maverick. On the other side were the White Caps, a name given locally to the big cattlemen and their supporters. Unofficially, at least, the Wyoming Stock Growers' Association, an organization dominated by the large outfits, many of them company-owned, was responsible for the invasion. Johnson County was a well-known center for small rancher activity, a large portion of which, the big cattlemen believed, consisted of augmenting small herds by theft, usually by branding unbranded calves. Sometimes, also brands were "worked," so that previously branded cattle could be stolen. The brand TP (T P), for example, could be changed into the shape of a coffee pot (⊤P). Furthermore, from the big operators' point of view, there was no room on the range for both large and small ranchers, and since the big operators had been there first, they felt that they had a kind of priority right to the range.

In the spring of 1892, therefore, the Association, or at least certain individuals who acted in its name, organized a detachment of invaders, some of whom were gun-toting Texan hands recruited in Denver for the purpose, and some of whom were bona fide members of the Association. Riding northward from Casper, these vigilantes trapped and killed two Rustlers near Kaycee, then continued their northward march, with Buffalo as their objective. When the news of the killings reached Buffalo, almost everyone who could obtain a horse and a gun, perhaps two hundred persons in all, rode southward to repel the "invasion." The White Caps were now within seven miles of Buffalo, but on discovering themselves to be hopelessly outnumbered, they retreated to the TA ranch, located about thirteen miles south of Buffalo and owned by one of their sympathizers. There they prepared for a siege, but were probably saved from being themselves massacred when a contingent of federal cavalry from Fort McKinney arrived on the scene to end the war. During my trip to Kaycee the stage driver pointed out the route taken by the invaders and the ranch house where the invasion had collapsed. He made a good story of it, and what he told me tracked pretty well with what I read later about the episode.

I don't remember what it cost me to get to Kaycee, which was then a mere dot on the map, but the man who let me ride with him from Kaycee to the Streeter ranch charged me three dollars, three whole days of sheepherding. The Streeters received me with the cordial welcome given strangers everywhere in the early West. David Streeter was a man in late middle age, married to a woman much younger than himself, and blessed with children that, as far as age went, might better have been his grandchildren. I remember five boys, two of whom were old enough to have quit school, and three of whom were my pupils. There was also a little girl under school age, and the family was not yet complete, for eventually, I learned later, the Streeters were blessed with twins. Mrs. Streeter boasted of the fact that she had never been attended by a doctor during childbirth, and that she had frequently acted as midwife for other frontier women. She was very scornful of prospective mothers who thought that they must drive all the way to Buffalo to have a baby, and felt that one neighbor who made it only halfway before her baby arrived got her just deserts. Mr. Streeter was a homesteader who had come to Wyoming from Nebraska, the kind of nuisance farmer that the big cattlemen despised. But he was a devout Seventh Day Adventist, so transparently honest that it never occurred to anyone to accuse him of being a rustler. He had cleared of sagebrush and greasewood some land along Powder River and had fenced it to protect a large meadow and garden, but a considerable part of his holding was higher in the hills and unimproved. He owned a few horses, a few cattle, a few sheep, and a large flock of chickens, and mowed hay from his meadow and grew his own vegetables. Somehow he eked out a living; no one ever went hungry and everyone had something to wear, often purchased, when it had to be purchased, from a mail-order house. The Streeters agreed to provide me with board and room for thirteen dollars a month. They had a six-room story-and-a-half log house, and accepted me as just another member of their large family. Nights I shared an unheated upstairs bedroom with the oldest son, Clarence, who was perhaps two years my senior.

This lad more or less took charge of the "schoolmarm," as he always called me. He taught me how to sit a saddle western fashion, and occasionally even let me ride his little bronco stallion. Weekends he and I roamed far out over the hills, sometimes in search of the Streeter horses and cattle, sometimes just for the sake of the ride, but always with the smell of sagebrush in our nostrils. If we came upon a sheep wagon and felt hungry, we went inside, whether the sheepherder was present or not, helped ourselves to whatever food we found, and took off without so much as leaving a thank-you note. When I equated such conduct with theft, Clarence was vastly amused. It was the law of the range, he said. Everyone had the right to help himself to food, provided only that he washed whatever dishes he used. Occasionally we saw a sheepherder at work. His band would number about two thousand (to my five hundred), and he sometimes had two dogs (to my only one). When his dogs needed direction, he gave his orders by gestures rather than by word of mouth. And the dogs did their work with uncanny skill. Ordinarily each sheepherder was stranded alone out on the range, but from time to time a camp-tender would bring him supplies and, when necessary, move him to a new location. Cattlemen despised sheepmen and clung to the legend that cattle would not feed where the scent of sheep had spoiled the range. The real trouble, of course, was that the sheep could eat the buffalo grass right down to the roots, leaving nothing that the cattle could get hold of.

We saw many sights that were completely new to me. Once we came upon two men who were riding fence in search of breaks in the barbed wire. One of them, spying a rattlesnake going into a hole, promptly pulled it out by the tail with a pair of pliers. Standard procedure, he insisted. What has happened, I wonder, to all the prairie dog villages we used to see? And to the owls who occasionally took over a whole dog town and perched solemnly on the mounds that the former tenants had made? And to the legend that prairie dogs, owls, and rattlesnakes all lived happily together in the same holes? (That one I never fell for.) Once we rode out along Salt Creek, and my companion pointed out oil slicks, the significance of which was entirely lost on both of us. Once in bitter winter weather we rode halfway to Sussex, a mere post office like Kaycee, to spend the night with a gang of workmen engaged in building a flume. The men took us in cheerfully, shared their grub with us, and made space for our bedrolls in one of their tents. It was the first and last time I ever slept on frozen ground. I don't recommend it. Next day we rode on to Sussex uninvited and collected a good meal before we turned back home. More than once we presumed on this kind of western hospitality. I arrived at an easy generalization. If there were women around, the food was materially better than when men did the cooking.

Sometimes I rode out with the younger boys. On one such occasion, I can recall coming upon a heard of antelope, seven or eight of them. My twelve-year-old companion promptly unfastened his rifle and opened fire, but the beautiful beasts bounded nonchalantly away. Fire-arms were a commonplace to these youngsters, but I had no interest in guns and let them do the shooting. They made a steady, but rather un-rewarding, war on coyotes, rabbits, ducks, and other wildlife. We never got lost, however far we might wander from home. On clear days— and most of them were clear—there were the mountains to the west of us, Pumpkin Buttes to the east of us, and Powder River somewhere alongside; besides, these children knew the terrain as well as I knew the streets of any of my several home towns.

Board with the Streeters presented certain problems, for as Advent-ists they made some effort to restrict themselves to a vegetarian diet. After a long period of living up to their principles, however, they got hungry for meat, fell from grace, and killed a calf. If you have ever eaten freshly killed meat after a long spell of vegetable diet, you know exactly what happened to us, all of us, big and little, the saved and the unsaved. Perhaps the Streeters could accept the punishment that befell them as their just due, but I had no such consolation. Regardless of its effect on us, however, we all kept right on eating the meat as long as it lasted, and by the time it was all gone the competition for our limited outside plumbing facilities had died down. Then we became vege-tarians again, although, whatever the church teachings, the Streeters did not consider milk, chickens, and eggs forbidden, which helped a lot. We drank a kind of ersätz coffee, made from a baked mixture of bran and molasses, whether because of the teachings of the church or because coffee was too expensive, I do not know. Probably the latter. So we really did all right. The presence of a large number of hungry children at table tended to break down whatever inhibitions I had acquired, and I learned to reach and help myself. I put on weight.

The "little red schoolhouse" of New England fame had suffered quite a change on the Wyoming frontier. The one-room cabin in which I taught was built of symmetrical pine logs, with plaster chinking in between. Some of the chinking had disappeared, thus ensuring the occupants of the building against the danger of inadequate ventilation. The inside and outside walls were identical. The roof rose slightly on each side of a low gable to meet the long, slender ridgepole that held it up, but it was flat enough to be dirt-covered. On this elevated soil a feeble growth of grass had taken root, thus making my headquarters the kind of house that had elicited from Mark Twain on his first visit to the West the remark that never before had he seen a house with its front yard up on top. On rainy days the roof leaked, not just a little, but a lot. After our county superintendent in making her required rounds had visited us one day, she reported back to my mother that she had to move her chair three different times to get away from as many different drips. She also predicted that I would never stick it out to the end of my term, but that thought never entered my mind. I recall only two other visitors to the Streeter school, both cowboys, judging from their costumes, but both total strangers to all of us. They dropped in one day unannounced, sat silently for an hour, then went on their way, leaving the "schoolmarm" slightly shaken, but unharmed. I never found out who they were or where they came from.

Our school equipment left a good deal to be desired. The schoolhouse had four windows, each supposed to contain four large panes of glass. Since there were no fences on two sides of the schoolyard, however, range animals seeking shelter had unfortunately knocked out several of the panes, and one of my first chores was to board them up. I tried to get some new glass, but failed. The schoolroom was thus a bit gloomy, but in good weather I could allow the door to stand open to let in more light. The floor was made of wide boards with wide cracks between them, into which, I fear, went most of each day's sweepings. We had two small squares of dilapidated blackboard, a few ancient schoolbooks, homemade desks conscientiously hand-carved to suit the taste of each new user. We carried our drinking water from the nearby Powder River, and let the "powder" sink to the bottom of the pail before we took a drink. There was the customary potbellied wood stove, which on cold days it was my duty to keep going. To get the necessary fuel, the Streeter boys and I took a team and wagon to a nearby pine ridge and scrounged great quantities of pitch pine, so dry and full of pitch that I could light a stick of it as big as my arm with a match.

Nine pupils appeared the first day of school, one of whom, a five-year-old, greeted me with the disconcerting query: "Say, Mister, is you a man or a kid?" I really didn't know. I had never had a course in education (not that it necessarily would have helped me much), and nothing in my experience gave me a clue as to how I should work out a daily program. Somehow I managed. I can remember writing to my sister, Mabel, who was still teaching country school in Missouri, asking what I should do with the little children while I was involved with the older ones. She sent me back sewing cards and other helpful busywork, but I found that the best solution, the weather permitting, was to send the small fry outdoors. In throwing distance from the schoolyard there was a prairie dog town, but I never heard of a prairie dog getting hurt. My pedagogy, I suspect, was as primitive as my surroundings, but I saw progress as a result of my teaching then, progress such as I have seldom seen since. I taught children to read who had never known how to read before, and I *knew* I had taught them something. I taught them long division and fractions and I knew by the light in their eyes when they had caught on. I taught them about the stars and the movements of the heavenly bodies, and I got from one undersized lad of nine who had listened with rapt attention this priceless comment: "Gee, I just thought the blamed things was pasted up there!"

The Streeter children and I had only a half mile to walk to school, but the others came from much farther away. One of the homes that contributed to my charges was actually even more primitive than the schoolhouse in which I taught, for the logs used in building it were of crooked cottonwood, and it had both a dirt roof and a dirt floor. The floor, however, showed signs of being constantly swept, for under each bed post was a cone of undisturbed earth, rising volcano-like from the level that was now to the level that once was. Such houses were still a commonplace in this area.

Oddly I do not remember being homesick. I listened recently to a job corps worker explain that among the youths he had to deal with those from the most deprived homes suffered the worst cases of homesickness. Perhaps it was because I was not from a deprived home that I could make the necessary adjustments. It never seemed to me that I was doing anything unusual; my mother had had similar experiences when she had taught school in her teens, and I took it all for granted. To ward off loneliness I wrote letters to all of my friends and relatives and received in turn an inordinate amount of mail. Three times a week the mail carrier delivered the mail to a box a mile away, and it was barely out of his hands when I retrieved my share. At the Teachers'

Institute in Buffalo I had joined a magazine club, and as a result received many more magazines than I could have subscribed for on my own. So, much of the time, I read and wrote, just as I have been doing ever since. On the rare occasions when the Streeters paid a visit to one of their distant neighbors, they took me with them. On one such Sunday excursion, I recall, they stayed too long and decided to spend the night. Since I had to be on hand for Monday morning school, Clarence and I walked back after midnight, a seven-mile hike. We vowed we'd never again be caught on such a junket without saddle horses.

Christmastime my father borrowed an extra horse and, with my younger sister for company, drove down from Buffalo to bring me home for the holidays. When we arrived, my mother noticed with a mixture of shock and amusement that I had outgrown all my clothes without noticing it, and that I had not had a haircut for three months. I didn't grow long hair because I liked it that way, but simply because there was no barber available. Mrs. Streeter occasionally operated on the children with the help of a gravy bowl and a pair of scissors, but the results were not such as to inspire confidence. My father had taught me how to use an old-fashioned straight-blade razor, so I remained clean-shaven, but I just kept on brushing my hair back. As soon as Mother was able to suppress her mirth, she herded me into the kitchen for a homemade haircut before she would let me be seen outside the house, then at the earliest possible moment sent me downtown to buy some new clothes.

After three months more at the Streeter school, I learned of an opening out on French Creek, five miles up over the mesa and into the mountains from Buffalo. There the school year was divided into a fall term of six months and a spring term of three months. The spring term session lacked a teacher, so I applied for the job, got it, and was soon teaching again.

The French Creek school was quite an advance over the Streeter school. It paid fifty dollars a month instead of forty dollars, my warrants didn't have to be discounted, and I could save board and room costs by living at home. I bought myself a horse named Fritz for fifty dollars, an apology of a saddle for about half that sum, and prepared to ride back and forth to my school each morning and evening. Someone did me wrong on that horse—one of father's parishoners, no doubt. He was an oversized two-year-old, amiable, well-broken, and mountain wise. I've seen him stand with three feet on solid ground and hunt around patiently to find footing for the next step forward. But when he galloped, or as we said, 'loped, he had a way of leading with the wrong foot—or something—that simply shivered his rider's spine. Nevertheless I rode him for more than a year, then sold him for what I had paid for him. By that time it was evident that he would not much longer remain riding-horse size; eventually, I was told, he grew into a big awkward plow horse. I should have tried him out better and inquired a little into his ancestry before I bought him, but after my Powder River experience I had assumed that all western horses were easy-riding broncs.

My French Creek schoolhouse was built of logs, but with a high-gabled shingled roof, and with the inside walls and ceiling plastered. I had about twenty pupils and they attended far more regularly than some of my Powder River youngsters. There was no shortage of schoolbooks or other needed supplies, and I knew considerably more about what to do. I had pupils for every grade from the first to the eighth, but by doing some drastic consolidation I managed to cut down the number of recitations to the equivalent of four or five grades. One advantage of the ungraded school that became at once apparent was the way in which the lower grades learned from what was going on up front. I soon made no effort to discourage this kind of eavesdropping. As for discipline, I had no real trouble, except from one oversized thirteen-year-old girl, who loved to annoy me, and knew just how to do it. But the other children had her number even better than I did, and were as much embarrassed by her conduct as I was. She was bright enough, and I suffered through the problems she made me, but I resolved then and there never to make teaching my life work. Recently I had the pleasure of meeting the daughter and grand-daughter of a little ten-year-old girl I had taught on French Creek. I told the granddaughter—now herself a ten-year-old—quite truthfully that her grandmother was the prettiest little girl in my school. And did that get a good response!

On French Creek as on Powder River my education proceeded along with that of the children I taught. I saw things we didn't see back in Missouri where I was born: three eagles—two old ones and a young one—perched on as many fence posts, as I rode into my school-yard one morning; a twelve-year-old girl riding up with her horse in a lather because (or so she said) she had been chased by a gray wolf;

a nearby beaver dam in process of construction; trout-fishing a few steps outside the school fence—if the fish were biting well, the noon hour sometimes lasted more than sixty minutes. These, and a thousand other things out of the Rocky Mountain West, I saw and experienced.

After the first spring term I taught nine months longer at French Creek, so that my career as a country school teacher lasted two full years. Vacations served still more to acquaint me with my surroundings. My father had acquired a horse and buggy (a one-seated road wagon, to be more precise), and I went with him and my mother on a number of distant pastoral calls. Father's horse was a difficult Roman-nosed character name Mike, lent to the preacher by a rancher friend because, as the lender admitted freely, no one could do anything with him on the ranch. Mike was a big horse and full of spirit—the first time he saw an automobile he jumped right over a six-foot fence. He was also a balker. The rancher must have sensed that Father knew about horses; otherwise he could hardly have played his pastor so dirty a trick. When Mike balked, Father patiently got out and led him a while; eventually, since he was never able to create a scene, he gave up balking as not worth his time. When we left Buffalo and Father turned him back to his owner, Mike's deportment had become correct and dependable, even though he was still a lot of horse. With Father and Mother driving Mike, and with me riding alongside on the spine-jolting Fritz, we took many interesting trips. Once we called on a family who lived on the shores of Lake De Smct, a journey that inspired me to find out what I could about the kindly Jesuit missionary after whom the lake had been named. On another occasion, in order to visit a Methodist family who lived on a ranch south of town in the Big Horn foothills, we retraced half the route I had taken to Kaycee. I marvel now at the way in which I could then ride twenty-five or thirty miles without experiencing any of the agonizing aches and pains that later on would have been inevitable. My only mishap with a horse came, not with Fritz, but with a borrowed horse who knew how to blow himself up as big as a balloon when his saddle was being cinched. Unaware of this pleasantry, I was galloping along on him at a good clip when my saddle turned and the horse ran away. Fortunately, as I fell I was able to get my feet out of the stirrups, or my career would have ended right there.

We made several trips out to visit church families who lived near the place where Rock Creek leaves the Big Horns. I knew nothing then about the writings of Frederick Jackson Turner, but later I took due note of his claim that out in the West the "cake of custom" was easily broken. His observation, I think, reflected well the freedom from conventional restraints that teenagers enjoyed in my time, with horses (not automobiles) as our means of conveyance. Once out on Rock Creek I joined a group of boys and girls my own age bound for a trip far up in the mountains. We took along on pack horses enough grub to last several days, a few cooking utensils, a tent for the girls, and bedrolls for the boys. Seemingly no one ever thought of such a thing as taking along an older person as a chaperon. There was, in fact, no need of a chaperon. At night the girls slept in their tent and the boys unrolled their beds out in the open. I still remember gazing up in wonder at the stars—for about two minutes—before going to sleep; also, the annoyance that the boys sometimes felt, especially when the fish were biting well, at having to look after the girls. Had we broken the cake of custom? Or, for the skeptics, was the cake of custom simply too strong for us? Either way, conventions that were still binding in Missouri had lost their force in Wyoming.

On another occasion the Hicks family and a number of other Methodists went together far up Clear Creek and camped near a mountain lake. Once arrived, we explored the nearby trails on horseback. As his mount for this purpose, Father borrowed a race horse, so called, from some misanthropic parishioner. This little mare, whatever her breeding and training, proved to be totally useless in the mountains, for she assumed that every trail was a fairway. So we had to leave her in camp. On one of our side trips, my mother rode the dependable Fritz, while Father and I rode whatever horses were handy. This trip turned out to be for me a very sad occasion, for the stays of Mother's corset wrecked my saddle. When Father discovered what was happening, he made Mother take off the offending garment, and tied it, garters dangling, on the back of his saddle. Then, with a whoop and a holler, he rode into camp for all to see. The Reverend had his moments.

My spring vacations came when the Buffalo High School was in session, and one year, being still of school age, I joined the senior class for several weeks, read a little Virgil, studied a little German, and listened in on a few other courses. I was received cordially by the teachers, one of whom, Winifred Hughes of Cozad, Nebraska, took especial pains with me. I corresponded with her for years afterward. My time with the students, however, was too short for me to be fully accepted by them. They treated me well enough, but they regarded me with some suspicion as a preacher's son, an outsider, and a Missourian. For some reason Missourians in Wyoming were then held in low esteem; Missouri was the last place a person should be from. My small sister cried about it, but I don't recall that it bothered me much. I had one other contact with the school, or more accurately, with the school building. One summer vacation the janitor (not yet known as a custodian) left town for a month, and paid me good wages to discharge his duties.

Twice during my teaching years I took the trip from Buffalo to Sheridan, the only other large town in our part of the state. Once I went with my parents to the meeting of the Methodist Annual Conference, and once with the Buffalo superintendent of schools to a teachers' convention. The road between the two towns was approximately the route of the old Bozeman Trail, and I can recall taking time out to inspect the monument built in honor of the men who lost their lives in the Fetterman Massacre (December 21, 1866), near old Fort Kearny. My father's comment revealed the affection he had begun to feel for his new environment. "I don't blame the Indians," he said, "for fighting to keep this country." They had certainly lost it, except for some small reservations, none of which was close to where we lived. The only Indians we saw while I was in Wyoming were imported to enliven the local rodeo, which we always attended. On one return trip from Sheridan I took the bus—or stage, as we still called it—probably the first automotive vehicle in use between the two towns. It was a four-seated, open-air, topless contrivance, with an underpowered engine (probably a two-lunger) that could hardly make it up the grades. We did just fine going downhill, however, except once when our driver speeded up to cross a muddy creek bed at the bottom of a hill and stopped abruptly instead. We all had bruised knees except a drunk in the back seat who opened his eyes only long enough to ask "What happened?"

As a preacher's son and a potential preacher, I could not escape any of the activities associated with the church. This meant teaching a Sunday school class, attending all other Sunday services, and in addition showing up for Wednesday evening prayer meeting and Thursday evening choir practice—I sang a noisy bass. Father's mind must have broadened considerably in the new environment, for I recall that one of our leading sopranos was a saloonkeeper's wife—in Missouri such a thing could never have happened. Perhaps it was the choir practice that stimulated my interest in music, for when I was a small boy my mother, after spending a total of thirty-five dollars on my musical education, had given me up as a lost cause. Probably she was right, but I took piano lessons for about a year while we were in Buffalo, and learned to play badly a few hymns and "The Flower Song." Somehow my fingers would never do what I told them to do. Most of my youthful associates in Buffalo were Methodists, but I shocked them and my parents by dating with some regularity a charming little Congregationalist. Rank heresy.

Several years later, after my exposure to Turner's ideas on the significance of the frontier in American history, I began to see my Wyoming experience in a new light. Turner in his youth had observed at Portage, Wisconsin, the retreat of the fur traders and the Indians before the advance of civilization. His father was a newspaper editor who recorded in his weekly issues the arrival of newcomers, their mingling with the old-timers, and the resulting changes in the region's way of life. What made America so different from Europe? Turner asked. Why did American democracy develop certain characteristics little noted in the democracies of the Old World? Was not the fact that every portion of the United States had at one time or another gone through the frontier process—a process that he himself had fleetingly glimpsed as a boy—was this not an overlooked factor in the making of the American nation? It was easy for me to go along with Turner, to believe with him that the frontier West was the most American part of America, and that its repetitive influence had played a unique role in shaping the nation's course. I knew something about the frontier legacy of equalitarianism—there were no social gradations on Powder River. I thought I understood what was meant by frontier individualism—one brooked few restraints and did what he pleased within wide limits in the West I had known. There was an abundance of optimism out there— pioneers like David Streeter had bet their lives on the future of Wyoming. There was "coarseness and strength"—one met it every day up and down Main Street, Buffalo. There was much "breaking the bonds of custom, offering new experiences, calling out new institutions and activities." If in my time I overemphasized the significance of the frontier in American history and underemphasized the influence of eastern and European contributions, I came by my opinions naturally, as naturally, let us say, as our urban historians come by theirs. The truth, perhaps, is that Turner was right for his time. It was nineteenth-not twentieth-century America that he was trying to explain.

Not long ago my wife and I spent a few days in Scottsdale, Arizona, where overprivileged residents of the upper Middle West go to escape the rugged winters that afflict their natural environment. Inevitably we gravitated toward the street where local merchants offer tourists unique articles of uncertain value at a great price. Long ago I learned that I suffer less on such occasions if I keep away from the scene of slaughter, so I was standing around near the entrance of the store, when a well-dressed middle-aged man—the owner, perhaps—drew me into conversation. We worked over all aspects of the weather, including the fact that Buffalo, Wyoming, had set the low temperature for the preceding day.

"I used to live there," I mused.

"Why, that's my home town," he replied. "What's your name?"

"Hicks," I admitted, "but I was there only a short time. You wouldn't have known me. My father was the Methodist preacher."

"Was your father's name John K. Hicks?" he continued.

"It certainly was," I replied.

"Well," my interrogator announced triumphantly, "he baptized me. My name is Cullen Watt and yours is Donald Hicks."

Of course I had known Cullen Watt. In fact, he was one of the children who went along on that Methodist picnic far up in the Big Horns, and his uncle was the Peter Watt on whose ranch we had spent our second night in Wyoming. Cullen Watt knew Wyoming as only a native son could, and he went back there each year, he told me, to hunt big game.

"And do you know," he complained, "they not only make me pay a high out-of-state fee for a hunting license, but they even make me hire a local guide."

IV. Undergraduate at Northwestern

INEVITABLY I grew impatient with life as a Wyoming country-school teacher; not only was I conscious of my youth and inadequacy, but I also thought of my job as primarily a means to an end, and the end was a college education. The family assumption had always been that it would take me four years of teaching to save enough money to put me through four years of college. But by the time I was eighteen years old —the normal age for an entering freshman—I couldn't wait any longer. If necessary, I told my parents, I could drop out for a while at the end of my sophomore year and earn the money I would need to complete my college course. Also, I objected to attending Baker University in Baldwin, Kansas, the place my parents had picked out for me, and chose Northwestern University instead. Northwestern, I argued, was the best the Methodists had to offer; besides, my Uncle Joe, whom I much admired, had gone there.

I still accepted without protest the idea that I was to become a Methodist preacher, and my parents, as I can see very well now, were on guard against anything that might turn my thoughts in a different direction. Only years later did I learn that a local banker had told my father that there was a place for me in his bank if I would take it. Father turned the offer down without telling me about it; he would take no such chances. Our presiding elder, Rev. J. C. Bickel, a scholarly gentleman whom I much admired, aided and abetted my parents. In his capacity as district superintendent, he visited us four times a year, and never failed to talk over my future with me. He accepted the Northwestern decision cheerfully, but came up with a suggestion that would have tied me quite firmly to a ministerial career. Why not, he advised, enter Garrett Biblical Institute first, as was still within the rules, and work in my college course later? That way I could get a job as a student preacher, and preach my way through both the university and the Institute. But somehow this program seemed to me a little like putting the cart before the horse; wisely, I think, I decided to go to Northwestern as a freshman, and to the Institute only after graduation from liberal arts.

In the fall of 1908, knowing full well that my funds would not last for more than two years, I took the train to Chicago. Two of Father's parishioners, my music teacher and a spinster friend of hers, both about twice my age, happened to be making the trip at the time I had to leave, and they took me in tow. They introduced me for the first time to a railway pullman, and I was duly impressed, both with the service we received and with the expense it involved. My escorts left me in Chicago, and an hour later I arrived in Evanston, suitcase in hand, to face the world alone, for I had not a single acquaintance on the Northwestern campus.

I had read the catalogue with great care, however, and registration presented no serious problems. My greatest disappointment was that a conflict of hours prevented me from taking the beginning course in Greek, as I had planned. In those days the classical language requirements were still strong. Admission to the program I meant to pursue assumed four years of Latin in high school, and to obtain the B.A. degree a student must choose between a fifth year of Latin and three years of Greek. I decided to meet this requirement the hard way, by taking Greek, inasmuch as Greek was recommended for all ministerial candidates. Since I had only three years of Latin to present and had forgotten all the Greek I had learned in a first year Greek course at the Maryville Seminary, I wound up taking a Virgil class in Fiske Academy, the Northwestern preparatory school, and postponed beginning Greek until my sophomore year. Instead of Greek I reluctantly registered for introductory German. My other courses—English, math, and gym—were wished on me by requirements. I was awful in gym. If grades had been given in that subject—I think they were not —mine would have been the lowest in the class. But I passed in my other subjects with B's, except German, in which I drew only a C. I saw not a single A until my junior year.

On the whole the easiest phase of adjustment to college for me, and no doubt for many other students, was inside the classroom. Classes were not overly large and the teachers were the best I had ever had. Methods of instruction in the courses I took were not vastly different from high school—harder and more exacting, perhaps, but that was all. Probably the most distinguished scholar among my teachers was

Georg Edward, a native of Germany with quite a reputation as a poet. Unfortunately, Professor Edward, whether consciously or unconsciously, was a promoter of disorder in his classroom. Bedlam broke loose the minute he opened the door. It was the only such college class I ever knew, but the trouble was 100 per cent the teacher's fault. Once, when he was called out of the room, a member of the class took charge and restored order immediately. I learned a little German that year and had an incredible amount of fun. Years later I came to know Professor Edward outside class, and came to value his friendship greatly. A bachelor when I first knew him, he presently married a Virginia girl to whom hospitality was a birthright. My friend, Freeman Galpin, and I were often in the Edwards' home. It grieved us deeply to learn that during World War I Edward suffered much unwarranted persecution as an enemy alien and eventually lost his job. Why should it be good for a native American to be loyal to his country but evil for a native of Germany to be loyal to his?

My second year in college was not unlike my first, with the Greek course I had coveted instead of Latin, with more German, more English, and my first college course in history. Again I was lucky in my teachers, for they were men of character whose imprint upon their students went far deeper than the subject matter they taught. If I had to single out the one greatest teacher I ever had, I suppose it would be John A. Scott, who, like all great teachers, taught us himself as well as his subject and his students. Scott's subject happened to be Greek, but as I have often pointed out to my educationist friends, both the Greek and the Latin words meaning teach, διδάσκω and doceo, take two accusatives. One does not teach either students or subjects, but both. The grammarians may not bear me out, but I think there is a possible third accusative—the teacher himself. I got a lot more than first-year Greek and second-year Homer from John A. Scott. I even attended a Sunday school class he taught in order to get still more of that important third accusative. I also met up with other dedicated teachers who taught their subjects, their students, and in varying degrees themselves. Northwestern in my time was a great place to be a student.

It is hard to remember just how and when one learned anything, but I credit my college courses with greatly improving my facility in the use of the English language. My second-year German teacher was George O. Curme, then regarded as the world's greatest authority on German grammar. There was no fooling in his classes. Foreign languages came hard for me, and I never learned to read or speak any of them very well. But Curme, by insisting on idiomatic translations, did make it clear to me how much English I could learn from studying German. From Latin and Greek I got a pretty good idea of the anatomy of language, something that proved to be an enduring asset even after the declensions and conjugations I had learned had evaporated. I learned much, too, from the courses I took in English language. At Northwestern, during these years, English literature and English language were two different departments, not because the division made any particular sense, but more likely because of clashing personalities. In both my freshman and my sophomore years I was exposed to the English language group, which bore down hard on the mechanics of language, the rules of grammar, the meaning of words (we spent the second half of my freshman year on Smith's *Synonyms Discriminated*), and correct writing practices. We wrote, and wrote, and wrote, and our themes were handed back to us promptly with the most precise and specific criticisms.

The leader of the pack, J. Scott Clark (not to be confused with John A. Scott), had written a book in which he had laid down a rule for and against practically everything that could be done in English composition. The numbers that these rules bore in the book greatly simplified, as was intended, the correction of themes. If one carelessly split an infinitive, the number of the violated rule, penciled in red, bore eloquent testimony to that fact. Or, if one started a clause with the words "not only" and failed to follow it up with the balancing "but also" (not just "but"), another red number hit the culprit in the eye. Wooden, maybe, but well calculated to keep the writer's feet on the ground; if, nevertheless, he cut loose and flew too high, there was also a rule on that, with a number. Mark Twain is said once to have told Rudyard Kipling: "Young man, first get your facts straight, then depart from them as you will." The way we learned to write was somewhat analogous; if we did something unorthodox, we at least knew what we were doing. During my second year I had a course with Clark himself in which we tore apart the literary styles of a dozen or so great writers of English prose and discovered in the process just how our instructor had come by the rules and practices he held so dear.

It was not until my second year that I encountered my first lecture course. The subject was English history and the lecturer was Arthur Guy Terry, whose skill on the rostrum kept his students in a hypnotic spell throughout each hour and left them in a state of eager anticipation for the next. No one ever taught me how to take notes, but Terry's logical organization and effective presentation made note-taking easy. He himself used no notes and drew on the blackboard, as needed, without even the use of an eraser, maps of the country, the region, or the battle he happened to be talking about. His ability to make historical characters live was almost Shakespearean. Later I took his course in Western Europe from the French Revolution to the twentieth century. World War I was yet to come, but unwittingly, perhaps, he set the scene for it. As another of his students wrote me in the fall of 1914: "Whatever would we have done without History G?"

I had a valuable course, too, with James L. Lardner in what was still called oratory, and had once been called elocution. Happily, both words soon lost their meaning, and "speech" took their place. Lardner, indeed, encouraged even then the direct, unadorned type of public speaking that the twentieth century has come to demand, even of preachers and politicians. For "a dollar a crack" Lardner coached me privately for a competition I had entered, and I took second prize—a much needed twenty-five dollars. My speech on this occasion was not original—the contest did not call for that—but only a reproduction from memory of Bryan's 1908 Democratic convention speech supporting the nomination of Kern for Vice-President. It was a good speech, as political speeches go, and Bryan, with his customary eloquence, had commanded his auditors' attention.

The hardest problems of my freshman year were extracurricular; I suspect that most college students find that to be true. Northwestern then had no dormitories, but I found a satisfactory room on Church Street—not far from the First Methodist Episcopal Church, as a matter of fact, which seemed like a good idea to me. My roommate was an older student with whom I had little in common; we never became close friends and I do not now even remember his name. Together we paid thirteen dollars a month for the downstairs front room of an undistinguished old residence. A block away I found a boarding-house that gave its patrons plain food for four dollars each per week. These expenditures were minimal, but I could see at once that my savings would be exhausted long before two years were up unless I made some money on the side. So I put myself on the YMCA calling list for odd jobs and was soon busy afternoons and Saturdays with such energetic activities as rug-beating and leaf-raking. The second semester

I found a place where I could earn my room rent by cleaning and waxing the floors, sweeping the sidewalks in front of the house, and the like. Also, I shifted from the boardinghouse to a cafeteria, where I could get adequately nourishing meals for less. Many times I paid only eight cents for my breakfast.

That first year I went to church regularly as had always been my custom and became a steady patron of the Evanston Public Library. Just how I found the time to read, considering my course requirements and my outside work, I don't now quite see, but I can recall reading, among other things, all the works of George Eliot that I had not read before. As a schoolboy I had conceived a great admiration for her writing, and here was the chance to catch up on what I had missed. My greatest lack was companionship. I made a few acquaintances in class, but none that ripened into friendship. It was my loneliness that led to my joining a fraternity. Early in my freshman year two fraternities had given me a good "rush" and bids, but I had declined, partly on the ground of cost and partly because I had a notion that fraternities weren't particularly worth while. But the members of the local Delta Upsilon chapter, some of whom I met regularly in my classes, kept an eye on me, and when they sensed that I was weakening, they reopened their bid. So sometime in the spring of 1909 I became a Delta U.

Whatever may be said for and against fraternities—and I think I know most of the arguments on both sides—fraternity life was a great thing for me. Toward the end of the second semester I moved into the chapter house and acquired a roommate my own age with whom I could become friends. I then had a campus home—a place where I felt I belonged. For the first time in my adolescent life I felt that complete acceptance into a group that means so much to a teen-age boy. Everyone knew I was hard up financially, but that made no difference. Indeed, it was quickly decided that in my sophomore year I should have the job of waiting tables for my board—a job regularly reserved for the chapter member who seemed to need it most.

Not only that; as a sophomore i was elected chapter treasurer and had the fraternity accounts to keep. When I got a good look at the books, I was horrified. My predecessor had made only the most casual and inaccurate entries, and an avalanche of unpaid bills soon descended on me. Casting up accounts, I found the chapter so deeply in debt that I could think of no other way out than an appeal to the alumni for contributions. So I wrote as persuasive a letter as I could, had it printed, and sent it out to every chapter alumnus. The response was terrific—we were able to pay off all our debts and start even again. Dues collection from some of the active brothers was not easy, but I hounded them and few escaped. I also nagged the rushing committee into extraordinary activity, and encouraged the pledging of as many new men as possible. Among those on whom I personally pinned a pledge button were two lifelong friends, William Freeman Galpin, later the official historian of Delta Upsilon, and George Seymour McCullough, now a retired colonel in the United States Army.

My fraternity contributions were mostly internal. I won no letters in athletics—once I went out for track, but I got a Charley horse the first day and never appeared again. I became an avid football fan, but was content to be a spectator rather than a participant. I took part only sparingly in campus affairs, although later, in a junior class play, where by some incredible mischance I was miscast as a football hero, I proved to the complete satisfaction of all concerned that I could not act. I belonged to the Oxford Club and the Hinman Literary Society, but those organizations existed primarily—or so it seemed to me—to have their group pictures published in the *Syllabus*, the student annual. Members of the Oxford Club were all prospective candidates for the ministry, with their eyes on the future rather than the present, while the Literary Society had become little more than an echo out of the past.

My involvement in social affairs was almost nil. Indeed, it required the greatest urging from my fraternity brothers to persuade me to take a few dancing lessons so that I could attend some of the fraternity dances. I liked girls, but I kept away from them, partly because they were too expensive for my pocketbook, and partly because I was determined not to become involved as yet with any one girl. Besides, I never learned to dance very well, and going with girls at Northwestern in my time meant going to dances. Quite literally, the only place one dared put his arm around a girl in those days was on the dance-floor. A tradition, deeply instilled in the Northwestern coeds, demanded that men must keep their distance. One of our first charges to fraternity pledges was that they must not attempt to take the kind of liberties with Northwestern coeds that they were accustomed to getting away with in their own home towns. No necking or spooning. If they tried it, they would get not only themselves into trouble, but the whole fraternity as well. Times have changed, I am told.

I remember only one major college prank. Late in my freshman year the word spread quietly from one Sherman Avenue fraternity house to another that all hands should gather about midnight near the Beta Theta Pi house to launch a motor boat the Betas kept in their back yard. The boat was notably unseaworthy, but the Betas were credited with capitalizing on its presence for rushing purposes. I have never noticed that any fraternity was ever particularly modest about proclaiming its virtues, but the Betas quite outdid all the rest of us in asserting their preeminence. Maybe this fact accounted for the generous response to the call for mobilization. Here was a chance to take the self-confessed leader down a peg or two. So a crowd of about a hundred or more non-Beta fraternity men swooped down on the boat with the intention of launching it in Lake Atwell, so called, a small puddle on the campus where Harris Hall now stands. Lake Atwell, commonly believed to exist as a source of supply for biological specimens, was not much larger than the Beta boat, and not half as deep. But we all agreed that the correct place for the Beta boat was down among all those amoebae.

Our army had too many generals and too few privates. Inevitably our commanding officers talked too loud and awakened the Betas, who quite unsportingly called the police. But we—the privates—finally got the boat on our shoulders and started up Orrington Avenue toward the main entrance to the campus. The numerous company of student officers who circulated about us warned us not to drop the boat, if the police should come, but to let it down easily so as not to injure it. They told us that they had their scouts out to spot the police, and would warn us in plenty of time to get away before the enemy arrived. Unfortunately, however, no one had anticipated a flanking tactic, and the police came upon us from a side street unannounced. At first sight of them we who were serving as boat-bearers let the boat down so easily that we knocked her bottom completely out, or perhaps, more properly, in. Then we all scrambled for the bushes to hide. I lay for a solid hour behind a lilac bush and watched with thumping heart while the police dug less fortunate students out from under nearby porches and shrubbery. By a miracle, they missed me and two or three others nearby. Eventually we got together and crept back along alleyways to our respective houses.

Actually only a few arrests were made, and the only penalty assessed against these victims, as far as I recall, was that they must pay for the damage done to the boat. This was considerable, but a collection was taken up to which all participants in the Beta Boat Burglary contributed, and the obligation was discharged. Since none of this disorder occurred on the university campus, the university authorities took no official notice of it, leaving the students to redeem their hostages the best they could from the toils of the law.

As an eager seeker after knowledge, I made it a point to see a little of Chicago. From time to time, usually with some more experienced fraternity brother as a companion, I elbowed my way through the Loop, discovered the Field Museum and the Chicago Art Gallery, attended a few plays, saw Babe Ruth as a pitcher win his own game with a home run and Ty Cobb hit a three-bagger. Northwestern was too far from Wyoming for me to go home for any of the short vacations, but I somehow found enough money to spend Christmas with one or the other of my two married sisters, both of whom lived in northwestern Missouri. Chicago always seemed an alien place to me, a place to escape from with all possible speed. I felt more at home in Evanston, with its broad elm-lined streets and its long lake shore; indeed, I came to love the "shining big sea-water" almost as I loved the Wyoming mountains. To this day I feel most comfortable when I have either high mountains or a wide expanse of water in sight; preferably both, as in the San Francisco Bay area. But I never got over being a country boy at heart. I still cringe at the sight and smell of industry, and I recall with especial distaste the days when the wind blew from the southwest and reminded even North Shore residents of the existence of the Chicago stockyards.

Predictably I ran out of money by the end of my sophomore year and felt obliged to take time out, as I had anticipated, to restore my solvency. My father, after completing his third year at Buffalo, had moved to Wheatland, a much newer and less distinctively western town located in southeastern Wyoming about one hundred miles north of Cheyenne. I had already spent the summer of 1909 in Wheatland and felt certain that I could obtain a teaching job in that vicinity; if not, there would be other openings. In fact, I had worked during my first vacation in the local railroad station, helping check in and check out both freight and express, and taking a hand with loading and unloading. That experience was not unimportant, for I learned a good deal about the transportation business that I could hardly have found out in any other way. Most of Wheatland's residents had moved into the state after an irrigation project under the Carey Act of 1894 had brought water to the Wheatland flats, and since most of them were from the Middle West, the community had a distinctly middle western flavor. Except for the necessity of irrigation and some sugar-beet culture, agriculture in the Wheatland area was about what I had known in Missouri. Individual farmers rarely owned more than 160 acres of land, and for the most part they engaged in general farming. The words "farm" and "ranch" had in this area quite different connotations.

To my surprise I failed to get a school. There were many country schools not far from Wheatland, but none that craved my services. Luckily, however, I was taken on as a clerk in a general store, operated, theoretically, by D. Miller and Son, but in fact by D. Miller in person. D. Miller was a character. He was of average height, but big-framed and impressive in size, with a prominent grizzled mustache, a loud, seldom-stilled voice, and a gruffly friendly but commanding way. No one ever doubted who was boss when he was around. He was perhaps sixty years old, always wore a round-brimmed, flat-topped black hat and a loose, ill-fitting suit. The minute he entered the store—a big, rectangular two-story affair with a full basement—he began to shout orders at the top of his voice. Despite his brusk exterior, he was a kind and considerate person. I suspect he gave me a job because his wife, a good Methodist, suggested it. He was not a church member, a fact he often noted, but he prided himself on his honesty. "Honesty is the best policy," I've heard him say a hundred times. "I know," he always added. "I've tried 'em both."

There were eight employees in the Miller store, some of whom had specialized duties. Only two of them were women, one in charge of the dry goods department, and the other a bookkeeper, installed regally on a high platform, overlooking the main floor, where she also made change. There was a buyer, who knew more about the stock than D. Miller himself, a shoe and clothing salesman who rarely left his special domain, and four general clerks who operated mainly in the grocery department, but were on call to sell furniture and other household items stored on the second floor. There was a warehouse back of the store for goods too bulky to be kept in the basement. One of the general clerks doubled as deliveryman, driving a one-horse wagon around town as needed. Another, imported for the purpose, spoke the kind of German required to communicate with the Russian-born Germans who worked the sugar beets. I was the youngest of the group

—I came of age that year—but I think I did my full share of the work. I could on occasion pinch-hit for the German clerk, not that I knew much conversational German, but I could at least remember the German names of most of the items the "Russians," as we called them, wanted to buy, and could say a few sentences with an accent that amused them vastly.

We sold incredible quantities of everything. Most of our trade was in groceries and other necessities, and the farmers who bought from us usually laid in a good quantity of supplies each time they came to town. Sometimes there was a little barter involved, for many farm wives brought in eggs and butter, for which we gave them credit at the going price. The eggs we sold out again over the counter or packed in crates for a more distant market; the butter, more often than not, was pretty strong and went into a box or barrel to be sent to a creamery for renovation. Once in a while we got an order from a distant ranch —the Swan Land and Cattle Company was one of our customers— and would pile up on the floor as much as a thousand dollars worth of goods for the purchaser to haul away. Prices were fantastically low, compared with the prices we now know—two pounds of Arbuckle's coffee for thirty-five cents, for example, and sugar at five cents a pound. Most of the country trade was on credit, and collections were often a full year in coming in—if crops were bad, longer. D. Miller was generous with credit; if he ever turned anyone away, I don't remember it. Partly on this account, I think, he rarely lost anything more than the interest on his money; the people who bought from him appreciated his trust in them and paid up when they could.

One of Miller's fetishes was to discount all his bills. He never wanted to owe anybody anything any longer than it took for him to pay the bill. Also, he bought in quantities—by the carload whenever that was possible. I've sweated through unloading whole railway cars of flour, sugar, potatoes, and the like, no small undertaking at the time, for while I was five feet, nine and one-half inches, in height, I was as thin as a rail and not very long on muscle. A sack of sugar weighed 100 pounds and a sack of potatoes 125 pounds. Another unique principle on which Miller operated was that clerks were worth either fifty dollars a month or sixty dollars a month, but never more or less. (I was in the fifty dollar class.) Hours were long, but nobody quibbled at that. The day began at 7 A.M., when all the men took part in sweeping out the store. It ended at 6 P.M., with an hour off for lunch—a ten-hour day. By staggering meal hours we kept the store open all day long every day except Sunday, when it was closed all day; the era of Sunday openings had not yet arrived. Saturdays we worked until 10 o'clock at night, with an extra hour off for dinner, thus making the work week 63 hours. Dull days, which were inevitable, greatly exasperated the boss. We learned to keep out of sight when there were no customers to serve, assembling furniture upstairs, cleaning out the warehouse, re-ordering the basement, or, more daringly, filling up vacancies on the shelves. There was little loafing on the job; Miller always thought he had hired too many clerks anyway, and we knew a loafer would get the ax.

I deserved a day of rest on Sunday, but this was not to be. There were two outside points near Wheatland where the Methodist preacher was supposed to appear one Sunday afternoon each month. My father's health was unequal to this extra burden, so he and the presiding elder —a new one, E. B. Rawls—hatched up a scheme whereby I was to take this extra burden off my father's shoulders. It would be good practice for a neophyte, and they figured that I was young enough to take the punishment. After two years in college my feelings about my future career were somewhat mixed; I had always assumed that I was to be a preacher, but I was beginning to have unconfessed doubts about it. I was eager to help my father, however, so I accepted $150, I think it was, from the Methodist Home Missionary Society to serve those outside points. Father had a driving horse and a road wagon; with this means of transportation I carried the gospel to the little town of Uva, north of Wheatland, and to a schoolhouse somewhere out southwest. My sister often went with me to play the organ while I led the singing; if she couldn't go along, by careful selection of the hymns I sometimes played the organ myself.

Getting up a sermon each month was one of my hardest tasks. Father had a good library of its kind, filled with such works as the *Expositor's Bible*, a multivolume commentary on the scriptures, but I had in-adequate time for reading and thinking. I preached my first two sermons to Father's Wheatland congregation and felt immensely dis-couraged with the results, although the people were kind enough to say that I had done well. Then Father took me in hand and showed me how to create a sermon. One had to take a text that could be pried apart into several headings, and that could somehow be applied to the lives of the people who composed the congregation. I got so that I could work up something passable, even with inadequate time, but I felt miserably inadequate and somewhat hypocritical. I taught a Sunday school class in Wheatland each Sunday morning, whether I preached that afternoon or not, and frequently I led the congregational singing at the evening service. Whoever told me I could sing made a great mistake, but I could carry a tune and beat time.

This year of hard labor pretty nearly laid me out. By the time I left for Northwestern in the fall of 1911, I was down to 120 pounds, and little more than skin and bones. My parents had apparently worried a little for fear I might have tuberculosis, for Father constructed a floored tent in the parsonage yard so that I could sleep outside whenever the weather made it possible. But no one ever mentioned the matter of overwork, and I don't recall ever having seen a doctor the entire year. On the whole my job experience was worth the effort. The family principle that "hard work never killed anybody" proved to be correct, and I had learned a lot I never could have learned in college. One unanticipated result, however, and one that neither my parents nor I had foreseen, was that I had got my fill of preaching. I now held a local preacher's license from the Wheatland Quarterly Conference, which to please my father I permitted to be renewed for the next few years. But I had begun to doubt seriously that I could ever become a preacher.

On my return trip to Northwestern, Father accompanied me as far as Denver, and together we saw the sights available to tourists. Except for man-made creations, such as the Moffit Railroad, they did not seem to me to offer much that Wyoming could not equal. Financially speaking, I would have been far better off to have attended a university closer to home—the University of Wyoming, for example, or Denver University, which like Northwestern had a Methodist background. But I even spent a part of my hard-earned cash on the Denver spree, confident that I could make it somehow through the next two years. One windfall that I could count on was an invitation I had received from the parents of Seymour McCullough to live with their family during my junior year. They had moved to Evanston from the Chicago north side and had taken a house diagonally across the street from the Delta Upsilon fraternity headquarters. Their son, Cy, as everyone called him, had shown a greater interest in extracurricular activities than in his studies, and they thought that if I roomed with him I could steady him down a bit. Their idea was to give me board and room free, but this I refused to accept. So we agreed on a compromise; I would pay them fifteen dollars a month, the estimated extra cost to them of my keep, and would earn the rest by setting Cy a good example. On the strength of this bargain, I decided that I would forego all efforts to earn money during the college year, and devote my attention primarily to my studies.

The McCulloughs were a wonderful family. Both Cy's parents accepted me as if I were their son and did everything possible to make me feel at home. Cy had a much younger brother named Jim, of whom I remember little, except that he was always bringing home a case of poison ivy which bothered him hardly at all, but made his mother frantically ill. Cy also had a teen-age sister, Carol, whom I adored— had she been a few years older I would have fallen hopelessly in love with her. Fortunately, she regarded me as merely the same kind of general nuisance that any brother was bound to be. My influence on Cy proved to be minimal, although he and I were the best of friends and still are. It took World War I to straighten him out. He found a career to his liking in the army, rose eventually to a colonelcy, and became an expert on military history. Cy's father, a practicing civil engineer, was one of those rare all-around scholars who knew quite a bit about almost everything. His influence on me was infinitely greater than mine on his son. Indeed, I think I owe more to him than to any other man except my father. Much as I learned from my teachers, I learned more, I'm sure, from the long after-dinner conversations I had with Ernest McCullough, day after day, month after month. He talked to me on equal terms, and drew me out on a great variety of subjects. He was in no direct way responsible for my decision not to enter the ministry, but he did help me to think for myself. By the end of my senior year I knew for a certainty that the ministry was not for me, and in a strained and difficult interview I communicated that fact to my parents. Ernest McCullough, like his son, entered the army during World War I, and he, too, found the military life to his liking. Mrs. McCullough, whose health had never been good, died, as I recall, while her husband was still in service. As long as she lived I always felt that I had a second home in Evanston.

Somewhat to my consternation I discovered that during my absence in Wyoming I had been elected president of the Northwestern chapter of Delta Upsilon, an office to which I was re-elected the succeeding year. I took my duties seriously and they were a considerable distraction. The fraternity in my days was a relatively cohesive group, but there was a certain, more or less shadowy, division between what we called the roughnecks on one side, and the purity squad on the other. I was clearly identified with the purity squad, but the roughnecks were much more fun and I saw a good deal of them. My closest friend was Freeman Galpin, who became treasurer of the chapter and worked conscientiously with me to keep it financially solvent. Between us, we more or less ran the works, although not without some protests from the side lines. It was not easy then, and it is not easy now, to develop in young men a sense of either individual or group responsibility. But there were always a few substantial members on whom we could depend, chief among them, as I now recall, Percy Walsh and Fred Bollman.

While fraternity matters consumed quite a bit of my time, the fact that I was living outside the house and was free from odd-job employment made a vast difference in my grades. I had never won an A in any course during my first two years, but in the first semester of my junior year I received an A in every course but one. My lowest grade was in Greek, the subject to which I devoted more time than to any other. I can recall many mornings when I rose at five o'clock to sweat out my seventy lines of Homer before breakfast. I did best, perhaps, in zoology, the course I chose (just why, I do not now recall) to fulfill the science requirement for the B.A. degree. The lecturer in this course was William A. Locy, and his book, *Biology and Its Makers*, was our text. Locy's method, both in his lectures and in his book, was to unfold biological knowledge in the order of its discovery rather than after some systematic scheme. We got the idea that scholarship in the field had just begun, that far greater discoveries than any yet made lay in the future. In the laboratory we saw with our own eyes the overwhelming evidence that supported the evolutionary hypothesis; hard on my theology, maybe, but too obvious to be disputed. Unlike many of my classmates I had little trouble in learning to use a microscope, and I took real pleasure in observing and recording what I saw through it. I could not draw, but I could diagram, and it soon became apparent that I could see the things I was supposed to see.

Locy rarely, if ever, appeared in laboratory sections, but one day he called me out of the laboratory into his office to tell me that he had examined my lab books and was pleased with what he saw. He suggested that I consider going on in zoology. It was too late; after all, I was a junior taking a freshman course, but if I had taken that course as a freshman rather than as a junior, I might never have become a history teacher. Certainly no member of the history staff ever called me into his office and told me that I should go on in history. When the time came for that decision, the solicitations all ran the other way.

It would be quite too much to say that Locy's influence guided me into a genetic approach to history. That conception dominated historical thought during all my undergraduate years. John Fiske, for example, whose somewhat oversimplified interpretation of American history had not yet become the favorite target of revisionists, worked this idea to the limit in his various books on early American history, and he was only one of many. Applied to America, the biological analogy was particularly convincing. The planting of colonies, the development of new institutions, the growth of a distinctive American culture with periodic flowerings were all there to see if one chose to see them that way. History was like a tree, the roots, trunk, branches, and leaves of which were all growing at the same time.

In these later troubled years I am not so sure of this analogy as I used to be. Sometimes I wonder if history is not more like a series of unrelated explosions, differing widely in intensity, and with mankind forever engaged between blasts in the hopeless task of picking up the pieces. But I can never write it that way. Whatever I undertake to do always manages to start off with seedtime, continues through a period of growth, then may possibly decline and die, but, if so, not before new seed is sown. Nor, try as I may, can I ever eliminate the idea of progress, "ever onward and upward." I doubt very much if the civilization of our time copes any better with the problems that confront it than earlier civilizations coped with theirs. But when I pour it in sour, like that, it always comes out sweet.

Toward the end of my junior year my perennial problem, finances, began to catch up with me again. What I had saved the previous year, it transpired, would see me through the current academic year, and that was about all. A fraternity brother, Ellwood Griscom, who worked as part-time night clerk at the Greenwood Inn, a south Evanston residential hotel, told me of an impending vacancy there; I applied for it, got it, and left the pleasant McCullough environs, where I had more or less failed in my efforts with Cy, for the totally impersonal accommodations of the Inn. I had a good room and free board in return for four hours of night duty—from 11 P.M. to 3 A.M. The Inn was an old frame building, a real firetrap, and my main task was to make the rounds every half hour with a time clock, which I punched at numerous points on every floor to prove that I had been there. I got no chance to sleep while on duty, and found to my dismay that during my free time I couldn't get to sleep readily, either before 11 o'clock at night or after 3 o'clock in the morning. When vacation time came, although I had been expected to stay on, I resigned and went home. But by that time another break had come my way. Another fraternity brother, Trescott ("Tessie") Merrill, had a job in the Northwestern library that, as a graduating senior, he was giving up. He recommended me for the place and I got it, to begin the following September.

My new job was a honey. It would pay me fifty dollars a month, twelve months a year, a total of six hundred dollars—a living, as costs then were, with a month or more of summer vacation. The hitch was that I had to put in full library time, forty-one and one-half hours per week. That meant that I could not take a full college program. By my senior year, however, I was a few credits ahead, and I found that by taking an examination in solid geometry, which I had not had in high school, I would have only twenty-two credits to earn for my degree— eleven each semester. That summer in Wyoming I worked up solid geometry on my own, with occasional assistance from the current Wheatland high school principal, passed the examination with ease, and won the three extra credits. Also, I learned in advance the books to be assigned in third-year German—a tough Schiller course with Curme that included *The Thirty Years War* and *Wallenstein*—and read them all during the summer under the tutelage of a Wheatland Lutheran preacher.

My senior year was probably the hardest of the four. Most of my time at the library I put in at the circulation desk, where the calls for books kept me busy practically every minute I was on duty. I did learn a lot about the titles and outsides of books, especially in history, the subject that had become my major. But I had far too little time to look into them. I put in twenty-four of my library requirement of forty-one and one-half hours per week by working all six nights from six o'clock to 10 o'clock; the other hours were interspersed during the day as my classes would permit. (The library was closed on Sunday.) Besides the third-year German, I was taking third-year Greek and two history courses. Most of my study time went to my Greek course; but for- tunately two of my fraternity brothers were taking the same course, and we frequently worked out our assignment together. That may have helped some, but often the first chance I had to hit the books came after ten o'clock at night, when the library closed. I roomed at the fraternity house that year with Galpin, who also had a library job. He and I had one of our history courses together, and that helped some. I had to trust far too much to my summer preparation in German; as a result I often made a dunce of myself in class, trying to translate passages that I had not seen for months. Given time, as on a written examination, I could usually puzzle out anything in a foreign language that I had ever translated before, so I pulled through in the end.

My grades were not as good as in my junior year, but they were good enough that in June, 1913, I received my B.A. degree, without Phi Beta Kappa, I hardly need to add. According to student gossip, Phi Beta Kappa at Northwestern was in my day in grave danger of becoming a sorority (not that this would have made any difference in my case). Selections for membership were made strictly on a grade-point basis, and the girls regularly got better grades than the men, partly, men gripers maintained, because men teachers were doing the grading. Moreover, girls at Northwestern in these years regularly out-numbered men, an additional threat. And further, Northwestern drew many of its coeds from well-to-do North Shore families, while a larger proportion of the men came from distant towns and villages, and often had to make their own way financially. A Northwestern man might thus console himself with the thought that, even if he operated at a disadvantage in making Phi Beta Kappa, he had a better than even chance of landing a rich wife. Of course, I didn't even do that.

My roommate, Galpin, who always claimed credit for having in-duced me to major in history, received his degree at the same com-mencement. He was also a preacher's son who had had to work his way through. He was a year younger than I was, as were most of the class of 1913, but I had a pretty good alibi for being a bit overage. Three of the years between my graduation from high school and my graduation from college I had had to stay out and work.

What, in addition to a parchment, did I have to show for my four years at Northwestern? Quite a bit, I think. I had gained enough mental maturity, for example, to discard my original plan for entering the ministry. My belief in the fundamentalist theology on which I had grown up had evaporated. This was not due to any doubts deliberately planted by my teachers or to any specific books that I had read. It was just a part of coming of age intellectually. The old-time religion no longer made sense. I suppose I could have retreated to Unitarianism or to broad-church Episcopalianism, but somehow this solution had no appeal for me whatever. I thought of myself as a Christian, for I believed in the ethical teachings of Jesus and the Judaeo-Christian concepts of right and wrong. But as far as I was personally concerned, this was something to live rather than to preach.

In regard to politics, too, I had begun to think for myself. Brought up on the G.A.R. type of Republicanism, I found that it no longer satisfied. I came to the university the same year that Taft ran for President on the Roosevelt record, and I suppose I would have voted for Taft if I had then been old enough to vote. But I was a little shaken by a speech I heard Bryan make on campus that year. To an uproarious student audience, few of whom supported him, he read an excerpt from a Republican editorial which first quoted what it assumed to be a Bryan speech, then tore the quotation literally to bits. But by some mysterious error the quote was not from a Bryan speech at all, but from the current Republican platform! Possibly I only reflected the progressive spirit of the times when I went along later with the insurgents in their war on Taft, and supported Roosevelt for the 1912 Republican nomination. But I could forgive neither Roosevelt nor Taft for their failure to seek an accommodation, one that might have led to a progressive candidate acceptable to both factions. So, while I voted for Roosevelt in the Republican primary, I voted for Wilson in the election. After all, Wilson's program seemed to me quite as forward-looking as Roosevelt's, and a united Democratic party might accomplish more than a divided Republican party. I even sold this line of thought to my father, who for the first time in his life voted for a Democratic candidate for President. My mother, also a lifelong Republican, cast her first vote—the voting privilege was already accorded to women in Wyoming—for Wilson. Later both of my parents had their regrets when they discovered that Wilson was not dependably "dry."

Among the other items worth mentioning that derived in part from my university years was an increased ability to get along with and understand young men my own age, even though many of them were of a far less serious cast of mind than I was. This growing tolerance extended also to other people's points of view. I had learned, too, how little I knew. Certainly the erudition of such men as Curme and Scott and Locy was enough to inspire humility in their students and to discourage arrogance. Try as I might I could never match their scholarship. But, per contra, I had gained considerably in self-confidence. My fraternity experience demonstrated that I had at least a little capacity for leadership. Significant for my later career was the discovery that history was interesting and exciting. I got this not only from my contacts with Terry, who was a brilliant lecturer, but also from William V. Pooley, who was not. Pooley introduced me to medieval history, a subject of enduring fascination—the background and explanation of the modern Western world. From such offerings as Walter Dill Scott's social psychology and Norman D. Harris's Asia and Africa I learned how basic history was to all the social sciences. If I were to continue with graduate work, there was no longer any doubt about the subject I would choose.

V. In Quest of a Ph.D.

THE PROBLEMS that face graduate students in our "multiversities," as former President Clark Kerr of California once so aptly termed the overgrown campuses of today, serve inevitably to remind oldsters like myself of how different conditions were when we did our graduate work. The intimate relationship that then existed between candidates for higher degrees and their teachers seems to be breaking down. In those less frantic years, when university professors were not so harried by numbers, a kind of academic apprentice system prevailed; each graduate student learned his trade by close association with a few more experienced practitioners, and in particular, a major professor, with whose name and fame he was branded for life. Nowadays everything is becoming so diffused and impersonal. Unable, as I have admitted, to give up the idea of progress, I should be willing to concede that the new system is better than the old, or at least better for our time. But I have my doubts.

By chance my encounter with the old system of graduate training coincided with the three years that immediately preceded American entrance into World War I, a period that in so many ways marked the end of an epoch. When finally I decided, late in my senior year, that I could never become a Methodist preacher, I had to choose some alternative goal. My two years as a country-school teacher had left me with a low opinion of the teaching profession, but at length I made up my mind to get a master's degree, then teach for a while in high school, and thus buy time to think out my next step. Since I had made history my undergraduate major—a rather weak major of only twenty-four units —history would have to be the subject for my master's degree. I screwed up my courage to interview James A. James, head of the Northwestern history department, on the matter, and obtained his somewhat reluctant consent to my proposal. His reluctance, which happily he later forgot, was well justified, for I had made only a mediocre record in his favorite course, the history of the West, which stemmed from his early contacts with Frederick Jackson Turner of Wisconsin.

I was restricted to Northwestern for my first year of graduate work by the fact that I could keep for another year the job in the university library that I had held as a senior. It was a good job, paying enough for a student to live on, but it was also a full-time job. My poor showing in Professor James's course was not unrelated to this situation, but probably owed more to the inexorable demands on my limited time made by third-year Greek. Seemingly it never occurred to anyone, hardly even to me, that my library hours plus my classroom hours added up to well over eight and one-half hours a day, including Saturdays. And only rarely could I sneak in an hour of study while on duty at the library; my best study time came after ten o'clock at night.

Since I had got by as a senior with this tight schedule, there seemed no reason to suppose that I couldn't do the same as a graduate student. How I managed, I don't quite remember. No doubt the requirements were not as stiff then as they are now, and at least I didn't have all that Greek to do. Professor James presided that year over a seminar of which he was later very proud, for five of its members eventually obtained their Ph.D.'s and became well known in the history profession—Reginald Aragon, Raymond Chambers, Ernest Lauer, Freeman Galpin, and I. I learned a little of research methods from Albert K. Heckel, a Cheyney-Pennsylvania Ph.D., who taught us to distinguish between original and secondary accounts, and put us to work on Hakluyt's *Voyages*. I wrote a thesis about Illinois on the eve of the Civil War, mainly using newspaper sources that I found in the library of the Chicago Historical Society, and from which I quoted far too extensively. For this latter sin I was severely criticized, but the thesis was approved, I passed the oral examination, and in June, 1914, I received my M.A. degree. My knowledge of history at that time was even more fragmentary than I have since come to expect as normal for newly created M.A.'s.

For better or for worse I was never to teach in high school. My Northwestern sponsors, most especially William V. Pooley, a Wisconsin Ph.D., saw enough promise in me to warrant them in recommending me to the University of Wisconsin for a teaching assistantship, which in due time I was offered and accepted. The stipend amounted to only three hundred dollars a year, barely half a living, but my parents agreed to lend me an equal sum, so in September, 1914, with the world ablaze in war, I arrived on the Wisconsin campus. There was then little thought that the United States would ever be involved in the war, but if anything more was needed to whet my appetite for history, the war provided it.

Many of my courses at Wisconsin reflected the war interest. Carl Russell Fish offered a seminar, which I took, on the American Civil War. My first report was on the organization of the volunteer army in 1861, and I did it well enough to receive Fish's high commendation. This was long before Fred Shannon did his work on the subject. After my graduate days were over, I adapted the theme to Minnesota, and, thus amended, it became my first published paper.[1] My next report for Fish was on the Department of the West, with headquarters at St. Louis, during the early months of the war. After what I found from that investigation, no one has ever been able to convince me that John C. Frémont, as a military man, was anything less than a delusion. The following year, I think it was, Fish gave a lecture course on the history of American neutrality, to which I listened with eager interest, for it did much to bring Wilsonian diplomacy into focus.

All the time I was at Wisconsin I served as one of Fish's three assistants in his large introductory course. This is where I learned the fundamentals of American history. Fish put on a marvelous performance, although his bubbling wit, his incorrigible ham-acting, and his exaggerated New England accent caused many duller academicians to doubt his scholarship. But as a matter of fact he was a Channing-Harvard product who knew his subject thoroughly, and gave one of the solidest courses, despite the fun it was, I ever took. He loved the hilarious "skyrockets" that regularly preceded, punctuated, and followed each lecture, and knew how to provoke them in maximum profusion. The class also enjoyed the horseplay, and thought up pretexts to promote it. Once when Professor Sellery came in just before class to confer with Fish, the two won an immediate and resounding "skyrocket": "Fish and Sellery."[2]

---

[1] "The Organization of the Volunteer Army in 1861, with Special Reference to Minnesota," *Minnesota History Bulletin*, II (February, 1918), 324–368.

[2] A "skyrocket" was a student cheer consisting of a prolonged hiss, followed by the simulated "boom" of a rocket bursting, then a long-drawn-out "a-a-ah," and ending in a shrill whistle and the chanting of the honoree's name. It was a commonplace in my time, but later was rarely given in class except after the final

My work as Fish's assistant, aside from the pleasure of attending classes and the grind of reading mid-terms, consisted mainly in conferences with students in groups of three or four on their outside reading. We assistants divided up among ourselves the extensive reading lists that Fish made available, took notes on each selection we read, and then exchanged our notes. We thus fancied that we could tell whether the students in their oral reports had read what they claimed to have read or were just bluffing. Obviously, however, if we could exchange notes, so could they, but at least we concentrated in these conferences on the readings rather than on a rehash of the lectures, a practice that in later years I found my own assistants prone to follow. Many times I argued with Fish that the groups were too small to get up a good discussion, so one summer, when I was his only assistant and the numbers quite overwhelming, he let me do it my way. With ten or a dozen students to a section, I found that we could get up a pretty good head of steam. It was in leading these discussions that I first discovered whatever knack I had for arousing student interest and participation. Furthermore, it was fun. Maybe it would be all right for me to become a teacher, after all.

My second year at Wisconsin (I was a fellow then, with a stipend of four hundred dollars, but the same teaching duties), I entered Frederick Logan Paxson's seminar, and chose him, as graduate students were then permitted to do, for my major professor. This meant, among other things, that I would be guided by him principally in the writing of a thesis (we rarely used the word "dissertation"). To satisfy this requirement Fish wanted me to do a history of the National Guard, an excellent subject that I suppose I should have jumped at, but I was determined to work on something pertaining to the West. Probably this interest was due less to Frederick Jackson Turner's hypothesis than to the fact that my Wyoming experience had made me feel terribly western. When Turner left Wisconsin for Harvard in 1910, Paxson had been brought in to fill the vacancy in the field that Turner had

---

lecture of the semester as a mark of appreciation for the professor and the course. In the mid-1950's the custom was abandoned, to be replaced by mere hand-clapping. Distinguished visitors to the campus, on being honored with a student "skyrocket," were, unless forewarned, frequently baffled and offended by the initial hissing. I once saw William Howard Taft's expression turn from a deep scowl to a broad smile as he comprehended the meaning of this salute.

made famous. Paxson was not a Turner student, and not even a westerner, although he had taught at the University of Colorado from 1904 to 1907 and had written a colorful book on *The Last American Frontier*, published in 1910.

Paxson, when I first knew him, was a young man well under forty years of age, full of mental and physical vigor, an admirable exponent of "the promise of American life." As a McMaster-Pennsylvania Ph.D., he had inevitably acquired an enormous respect for newspapers as sources, and he made constant use of them in building up his knowledge of both western and recent American history, the two fields in which he gave lecture courses. Less glamorous on the platform than Fish, but with a rapid-fire, Gatling-gun style of delivery that always commanded attention, he took pains to make each of his lectures a carefully wrought unit. All of us who had any real interest in history found them deeply exciting. Paxson had by this time given up his earlier decision to specialize in diplomatic history and a later flirtation with the Civil War. He showed the enthusiasm of the convert for the West, which long commanded his main attention. In recent American history, however, a subject to which he was increasingly drawn, he was essentially an originator. If not the first, he was certainly among the first to bridge in scholarly fashion the gap between the Reconstruction period and current events. Regularly his lectures in this course ended with the day before yesterday.

At the time I became his student Paxson was much impressed with the writings of Francis Newton Thorpe, and wanted to make me an authority on the constitutional history of the western states. He brushed aside my suggestion that I should like to write on some aspect of Populism, and plunged me instead into the morass of state-making, during the last half of the nineteenth century, across the wide Missouri. I foundered around in the subject for many months, writing one dismal report after another, until I realized that I could never hope to finish the job in the immediately forseeable future. Since I had only limited time and means at my disposal, Paxson finally agreed that what I had planned as one chapter out of a projected six or eight could be expanded into a thesis, and the remainder held over, perhaps for my future life work. So my thesis, when it was finally accepted, concerned only the constitutions of the six northwestern states admitted in 1889 and 1890. I learned a great deal of value from my explorations into state constitutional history, but I was never very proud of my thesis, and later came to regret that it achieved publication.[3] After obtaining my degree I did not pursue the subject further.

The third man in American history at Wisconsin during my graduate-student days was Winfred T. Root, whose interest lay in the colonial period. Root was hardly comparable to Fish or Paxson as a lecturer, but he was a meticulous scholar, and in the classroom put his ideas across with clarity and forcefulness. Revisionism in colonial history was already well advanced, and Root, another Pennsylvania Ph.D., had the facts to show that there was a British as well as an American side to the disputes between the colonies and the mother country. Since neither Fish nor Paxson touched seriously on colonial history, whatever I started with in that subject derived mainly from Root. Root also gave me invaluable advice on my research, and helped me convince Paxson that I should hold my thesis down to garden size instead of trying to cultivate the oversized farm—or ranch—that Paxson had laid out for me.

The history department at Wisconsin had not yet granted a great many doctor's degrees, and the procedure was less formalized in those years than it became later. Students in American history, however, were expected to present minors in European and English history, and in particular to show competence in some field earlier than the discovery of America. Pooley's course in medieval history at Northwestern had aroused my interest in that subject, although Pooley was an Americanist—a Turner Ph.D.—and had taught medieval history with some reluctance. At Wisconsin I fell under the spell of Dana C. Munro and George Clarke Sellery, two of the ablest scholars I have ever known. The term "intellectual history" was not then in general use, but it describes perfectly the course on medieval civilization I took from Munro, and the two courses, one on the Renaissance and another on the Reformation, that I took from Sellery. Both Munro and Sellery were superb lecturers, and later I tried consciously to pattern my style after theirs. Like Paxson, they believed in making each lecture a self-contained unit that could stand on its own feet, and before class they put a brief outline of the topic for the day on the blackboard, a kind of promissory note on which they regularly delivered. For the forty-one years I taught I also followed that procedure. To my great regret, then

[3] *The Constitutions of the Northwest States*, University of Nebraska Studies, XXIII (January–April, 1923).

and later, I was never able to work into my schedule a course given by W. L. Westermann, whose distinction in ancient history was already acknowledged. But I saw him often, and he took a kindly interest in my welfare.

From another great scholar, A. L. P. Dennis, I had a dazzlingly brilliant course on nineteenth-century England. Dennis knew that he could never get through a hundred years of English history in a single course if he tried to cover every aspect of it, so he sketched in briefly the outlines of one limited period at a time, then went into greater detail on some single theme, a different one each year. When I was in his class the subject he stressed was diplomacy. He lectured without notes, in topic sentences and paragraphs, and never seemed at a loss for exactly the right word. In all the other history courses I took at Wisconsin, students were required to present a long term paper, which counted for about one-third of the final grade. Dennis allowed us, if we chose, to compile instead a syllabus of the period covered by the course, and I elected this option. I was flattered when he told me that my syllabus was so good that he would like to keep it. Naturally, I consented, but I often wished for it later. I had typed it myself on the old Smith-Premier double-decker I had bought for fifteen dollars, and had made only a single copy. I also pounded out all my term papers and my thesis on that already obsolete instrument. I never learned the touch system, but I learned to touch all the keys.

Professional indoctrination, I suspect, was on a somewhat less formidable scale then than now. First-year graduate students were held for a course in historical method, but my Northwestern work was accepted in lieu of that. There was also a course in bibliography, or historiography, but aside from a few brilliant lectures from Victor Coffin I remember little about it. Munro gave a course on great historians, but disdained all Americans except Henry Charles Lea. Both Paxson and Fish took notes on three-by-five slips or cards, so most of us became three-by-fivers. The importance of research and writing to our future careers was not overlooked, but neither was it overemphasized. I, for one, got the impression that our first duty was to teach, but if we were any good we were expected also to find time for writing and research. Good teaching was stressed both by precept and example. "Learn to lecture! Learn to lecture!" Paxson said to me repeatedly. He also on one occasion stood me up in front of his class in the history of the West to see how well I could present the subject of my thesis. I acquitted myself well enough to elicit expressions of approval from members of the class, but Paxson, who sat in the back of the room with a few invited guests, was not one to spoil a neophyte with flattery.

In those days the Ph.D. in history demanded an outside minor, that is, a minor in some related field. I chose political science, and made no mistake in so doing. As lecturers the political scientists with whom I worked were not the equals of the historians, but they were men of eminence in their specialities, and had much to offer. From Frederick Austin Ogg I took a course in the governments of Europe; from A. B. Hall, a course in constitutional law; from Chester Lloyd Jones, a course in political theory (begun, but not finished by Ambassador Paul Reinsch); and from Stanley K. Hornbeck, a course in international law. The three courses first mentioned were more or less traditional, with a good textbook, plenty of additional reading, lectures, and class discussions. But the Hornbeck course was unlike anything I have ever known before or since, and deserves special mention.

To the best of my recollection, there were only seven students in this course the semester I took it—three of them graduates, and four undergraduates. The class met in the auditorium of the law school, a large semicircular room with a capacity of two or three hundred, and a high judge's throne up in front. At the beginning of each session Hornbeck entered the room with judicial formality, mounted the rostrum, solemnly occupied the throne, and confronted the nonexistent multitude. For some unknown reason the seven members of the class seated themselves at great distances from each other, a matter of which our presiding officer took no notice whatever. The regular assignment for each day was sixty pages in Scott's *Cases on International Law*. In due time there came a question from the chair, addressed to no one person in particular, and sometimes not closely related to the cases we had read. Whether Hornbeck's method was a shrewd device to stimulate discussion, as I now think probable, or the product of total unpreparedness, as we all then thought, the result was strikingly effective. From then on the three graduate students, with whatever tact they could muster, took over (the undergraduates quickly descended to the status of ciphers), and with some difficulty refreshed the instructor's memory, first as to the facts involved in the cases under discussion, and then as to the law. As a pupil, Hornbeck was often stubborn, difficult, and uncooperative, but usually, by the end of the period, he came around to our point of view. Whether this was all a pretense or what it seemed, it was enormously successful. We learned a lot. I recall, also, that I got special commendation for a paper I turned in on the doctrine of continuous voyages, or something like that. It *was* a good paper, even if I had had to whip it up in record time.

Language requirements for a Wisconsin Ph.D. were then unalterably French and German. For the latter I felt reasonably well prepared, for my minor as an undergraduate at Northwestern had been in German, and I brought with me to Wisconsin a certificate, signed by George O. Curme, one of the greatest names in German philology, to the effect that I could read German passably well. Ph.D. language examinations at Wisconsin were then oral affairs, given by a designated member of the language department concerned. Fortunately, the German instructor who had the duty the year I came up was a Curme student; he was much impressed with the document I showed him, but explained that under the rules he had to examine me anyway. I had found in the library a German textbook in American history, and had it in hand, hoping that I might be asked to read from it. While I had not had time to read much of it in advance, I had found out that it was easy German; I knew also that with the familiar subject matter I would be able to make pretty good guesses at any words I failed to recognize. All went as planned. Then my examiner pulled down a book from his shelves and pointed to a passage in it that told about Kaiser Wilhelm II "dropping the pilot," Bismarck. Well, I knew that story, too, so the German examination was easily off my mind.

The French ordeal was not to be so simple, for my knowledge of French was strictly limited. At Northwestern my roommate, Freeman Galpin, and I had hired a pretty coed to tutor us in that subject for a few weeks, but I hadn't learned very much French, so decided to register at Wisconsin for a first-year class in the subject. I soon got discouraged, however, with the slow progress in reading of the mostly freshman students, and dropped out in order to have more time to read on my own. To my consternation I learned at the end of the semester that the only way I could escape an F in the course was to take the final exam. So I took it, and rated a C. What I didn't know about French irregular verbs was a lot.

When finally I had read enough French to justify the try, I went to the appropriate member of the French department, carrying along a

big, fat, dull book on the reign of Louis Philippe that I was sure I could
read forward and backward. Historical French, I had discovered, was
easy; my worry was for fear I might be asked to read some esoteric
literary or philosophical French, which I knew very well I could never
do. Imagine my consternation when my examiner asked me to read a
long paragraph from the Louis Philippe book in *French*. I could have
translated every word of it easily, but as my friend Bill Hesseltine put
the matter later, I was never one to encourage the French to mis-
pronounce their language. "You hav'n't had much French, have you?"
my tormentor noted. Then he began pointing to two or three words in
the middle of a sentence in the middle of a paragraph, all idiomatic
expressions, and asking me what they meant. Sometimes I could come
up with the answer, sometimes I could not. At last he pointed to a
sentence far down in a paragraph, and said: "You won't know the
first two words in that sentence, but translate the rest of it." I knew the
first two words. So he slapped the book shut, signed my paper, and
told me good-by. Whew!

Before my time, to the best of my knowledge, the examination for
the Ph.D. in history at Wisconsin had been merely an oral affair, and
I was among the first, if not the first, to be saddled with written preliminaries. When the time came that I thought I could struggle with
this problem, Professor Paxson, at my request, provided me with a list
of a dozen comprehensive questions on the whole of American history,
from Christopher Columbus to Woodrow Wilson. As yet, the department had not worked out rules on when, where, and how long the
candidate should write, or how, if at all, the examination should be
monitored. I was told that I might take the questions with me, write
out the answers at my convenience, and bring back my contribution
when it was finished. I understood that the examination was to be an
affair of honor, with the answers to be drawn only from what I carried
around under my hat, although I don't remember that anyone ever
said as much to me. I wrote all my spare time on those questions for the
next three weeks, and brought back a stack of bluebooks that resulted
in an immediate departmental decision to limit thereafter the writing
time for all such examinations. The only comment on my intemperate
behavior from Paxson that I can recall was an inquiry: "Where in the
world did you pick up your amazing knowledge of bibliography?"
My reply came easily: "Working in the Northwestern University
library." I might have added—but did not—that I knew many of the

books I had mentioned from the outside only; no doubt if it had been necessary I could have given their Dewey decimal call numbers also.

One of my two minor examinations was in European history, mainly medieval and early modern, and the other in English history. In each case the procedure was the same as in the major examination, but I must have been warned not to overextend myself, for the number of bluebooks I turned in was much more modest. It was undoubtedly true, also, that I knew less about these subjects than about American history. In English history Dennis asked me to write on four out of seven questions, a terrific break, for three of the questions he listed had me floored at sight. In European history Sellery was not so liberal with choices, and on a few items he stumped me completely. I recall his stopping me in the hall one day, after he had read my production. "Who wrote *The Imitation of Christ?*" he inquired severely.

"Thomas Aquinas," I replied, repeating a misstatement on my paper.

"Who?" he demanded, glaring fiercely down on me through the bottoms of his bifocals.

"Thomas à Kempis," I corrected myself, weakly.

"That's better," he said, and stalked on. But even my second answer, I gather, needed qualification.

My final oral examination turned out not to be the unpleasant experience I had anticipated. According to the Wisconsin custom, Paxson as my major adviser was chairman of the examining committee, with Fish, Sellery, Chester Lloyd Jones, and an outsider whom I had never met before completing the panel. Paxson yielded to Fish, with whom I visited pleasantly for half an hour. Sellery took me on next, and wooled me around enough to let me know that the occasion wasn't any pink tea. We were debating the relationship between the Renaissance and the Reformation, with me championing earnestly the views I knew he held, when he suddenly turned me over to Lloyd Jones. Without indulging in any preliminaries, Jones brought me up short with the question: "What are the chief elements of due process of law?" There was a long pause while I made the transition, but at length I came up with the words, "Notice and hearing." I should have added "jurisdiction," but I didn't think of that until later. After my initial stumble, Jones and I got along all right. The outside member worried me with questions about western mining law, suggested by my thesis. I soon gathered that he, too, was in the dark about some such matters, and was mainly seeking information that I certainly didn't have. When he found that out, he called it quits.

I expected that Paxson would now put me through my paces, but he adjourned the examination without asking me a single question. Later I asked why he had let me off so easily. His explanation was that he had waited until the rest had finished so that he could come to the rescue, if necessary, but that I didn't need his help. I have followed the same course with my own candidates many times since, but not always successfully, even when I have exerted myself to the limit. What slaughters many students, I am sure, is fright. I wasn't frightened of these men; at least four out of the five were my friends, and they remained so as long as they lived.

Obtaining a doctor's degree in history three years after one's bachelor's degree is rarer now than it was then. Perhaps we were picked greener in our time than our successors are today, but there were some other considerations. None of the graduate students in history that I knew at Wisconsin were married, and none of them, I'm sure, even considered marriage as a possibility until after the coveted degree could be achieved and a job found. We consciously and determinedly kept away from girls, somewhat to the irritation of the charming young women about us who were also working for degrees—or for husbands, as the case might be. We were frightened to death of becoming involved. Most of us were hard up, and there were then no fat fellowships available, such as now exist, to enable us to put in any more than the minimum time. We were expected to finish in three years, and we did so if it was humanly possible.

The library was our headquarters. We arrived there promptly at eight o'clock in the morning, and rarely left the building, except for classes, until closing time at night, ten o'clock. We had stack privileges, of course, but no private desks or cubicles where we could gather and hold the books we were using. I remember once trying to sequester in a remote corner a dozen or so volumes that I very much needed to keep together, only to be found out and told off in no uncertain terms by the lady martinet who headed the circulation department. If ever I did such a thing again, I learned, my stack privileges would be revoked forthwith. Another time I incurred her wrath by bringing a bottle of ink into the stacks. I meant no harm; fountain pens were permitted, and mine had an unpleasant way of running dry. But there was a rule against ink. I might have got by all right, except that I couldn't get the cork out of the bottle and went to the desk for help. My ink was confiscated, and I was almost ordered out. Men were given to understand, also, that they were supposed to keep their coats on, however hot the weather, particularly if they wore suspenders. The atmosphere was somewhat more relaxed in the document, newspaper, and manuscripts rooms, although in the latter, understandably enough, we were forbidden to use pens, or even indelible pencils.

In those days the graduate students in history had access to two seminar rooms on the first floor, one dedicated to American history and another to European history. Here we met frequently to read, argue, and gossip. I doubt if there were more than twelve or fifteen of us, all told, who were seriously working for doctor's degrees, so we came to know each other well. Our discussions neglected few subjects of consequence, and they helped us mightily in forming our opinions. War news, and the prospect of American involvement, came to occupy a disproportionate amount of our talking time. My closest friends were Merton Coulter and Theodore Gronert—one year the three of us had rooms together—but I remember with particular admiration Katharine Gallagher, who was probably the best scholar among us, and John Oliver, who went out of his way to lend a helping hand to those of us who were his juniors.

Hard as we kept our noses to the grindstone, we took time off for a few diversions. Once a week, regularly, we attended the current vaudeville show at the Orpheum. On Sundays several of us would often take long walks—I remember one in which Coulter, Gronert, and I made it all around Lake Mendota. When we could afford it we sometimes had a big dinner, usually out at Middleton, or if we felt really rich, down at Ben Stitjens, back of the Park Hotel. While we tended to go about in groups, we each had certain separate interests. For example, I was still loyal to the Delta Upsilon fraternity, often ate my dinner at the house, and joined in the customary postprandial hoopla. On rare occasions I went along with some of the erring brothers for a Saturday night binge, the object of which was to have a drink at every bar around the square, a rather major undertaking in those days. With limited cash and even more limited capacity, I never got more than halfway around, but neither did I ever fail to reach home under my own steam. I lived most of one year and two full summers at the Delta Upsilon house on North Francis Street, close by the lake, and learned of necessity to paddle a canoe and to swim.

The summers were wonderful, mainly because the chapter rented out the third floor of the house to guests for the season, among whom, for the two summers I spent there, were a family from St. Louis by the name of Hahn. The parents, Ike and Hannah, were the salt of the earth, and their six children, a son several years my junior and five beautiful daughters ranging in age from seven to seventeen, were certainly the savor. I fell for them all so completely that they promptly adopted me into the family and treated me as one of the group. The parents and the son are now gone, but the girls are all alive, and we still keep in touch. Emily later made her mark on campus by defying a ruling of Dean Sellery's and transferring from Arts and Science to Mining Engineering, in which course she graduated, only to win distinction as a writer rather than as an engineer.

It would not be fair to omit mention of the contributions that our professors and their families made to our social life. The Paxsons then lived in the old Turner house across the street from the Delta Upsilon headquarters, and I saw them frequently. I first met Jane and Emma, the two older Paxson children, aged six and four respectively, down at the North Francis Street beach, and with some difficulty won their confidence. They had been taught not to take up with strange men. The Paxsons were Quakers, and used the familiar form of address within the family, but not with outsiders. I can recall Jane saying, "John, this is for you; and Emma, this is for thee." I could talk this way, too, but one such lapse in Mrs. Paxson's presence taught me that I had overstepped my prerogatives. I was not within the pale. The Paxsons however, had me in for meals; included me in card games ("Fred," said Mrs. Paxson on one such occasion, "thee'd better have played thy ace"); and even took me with them on family picnics. I can also remember inducing Mrs. Paxson, whose patrician grace and beauty I much admired, to go out on Lake Mendota with me for a canoe ride. What a nerve! Fish was then unmarried, and handicapped by an invalid mother, but we American history neophytes were occasionally in his house, as well as in Root's.

There were also organizational activities. Some kind of history club existed, consisting of both faculty and graduate students, which met occasionally for an evening of talk at the house of some faculty member. To this group, for example, graduate students who had attended the 1914 meeting of the American Historical Association in Chicago reported their impressions. I can recall trying to describe some of the eminent historians I had seen in action; also a comment by Paxson then or later that nearly all of the men who had achieved distinction in American history were still alive. Another faculty–graduate student group, recruited from many departments, met occasionally in some public place for drinks and a meal. Stanley K. Hornbeck laid aside his classroom dignity and played a leading role in this group. It was here, I think, that I first met my lifelong friend Harold S. Quigley, a graduate student in political science. I also recall one evening when Frederick Austin Ogg invited several of us to his house for an after-dinner meeting with some celebrity. When we arrived, we found, to our quite unnecessary embarrassment, that the dinner group was in evening clothes. We, of course, hadn't any.

When, late in 1916, President Samuel F. Kerfoot of Hamline University in St. Paul, visited the Wisconsin campus in search of a new history teacher, Professor Paxson arranged for me to meet him. Paxson knew that Kerfoot was a Methodist preacher and that I was the son of one. Naturally the two of us hit if off together very well—we always did. Kerfoot mentioned as a possible salary sixteen hundred dollars, to me a fantastically large sum; but when his formal offer came it was for only fourteen hundred, a real comedown. I was inclined to argue the matter, but fortunately showed Paxson the letter of protest I had written. He advised me to file it in the category of "letters not sent," which I did— in a wastebasket. I then accepted the offer with becoming enthusiasm. I was really lucky to get any kind of offer that year; not many jobs were available.

Since I had missed the spring deadline with my thesis, my diploma arrived just barely in time to justify the Ph.D. after my name when I began my teaching duties at Hamline. My parchment—whether real or imitation, I do not know—bore the signature of Charles R. Van Hise, the close friend of both Turner and LaFollette who had done so much to establish the reputation of Wisconsin as a great liberal university. I should have had the document framed and hung it up somewhere, but I never did, and the last time I saw it the mice had taken off quite a corner of it. But neither mice nor men could diminish my respect for the university that had granted me the degree, nor for the able group of scholars with whom I had studied. If I had my life to live over again, I would not wish to change very much the events of those fruitful years.

VI. Hamline University

HAMLINE UNIVERSITY, when I first set foot on its campus, was still
definitely in the small college class, with a student body of well under
five hundred. It was located where it is now, in the Midway district of
St. Paul, along Snelling Avenue. Efforts to move to a new location
less threatened by industrial penetration were long insistent, but the
governing authorities finally decided, while I was at Hamline, against
a new campus. Talk of altering the name of the institution by sub-
stituting "College" for "University" was likewise rife but failed to
achieve results, primarily because of the risk—real or fancied—involved in seeking a charter amendment. Incorporated in territorial
times, Hamline had obtained valuable special privileges, including tax
exemption, that it could not afford to lose. Until after World War I
there were only five buildings on the campus proper, two of which,
University Hall and Science Hall, took care of all the classes; the other
three were a library, a gymnasium, and Goheen Hall, a dormitory for
women. Nearby, however, were a president's house; a converted residence known as the Annex, which took care of the overflow from
Goheen Hall; and the inevitable football field, with bleachers.

Hamline was affiliated with the Methodist Church, and abundant
evidence existed to demonstrate that this connection was not merely a
technicality. The president of the University, Dr. Samuel F. Kerfoot,
was a Methodist clergyman, and so also were two or three other members of the faculty. Chapel was a daily exercise, with definitely religious
overtones. While faculty members were expected to take their turns in
leading chapel, the President was usually on hand, and more often than
not delivered what amounted to a short sermon. Invited guests, of whom
a disproportionate number were clergymen, also spoke at chapel. While
the Middle West was growing up the Methodist Church had a definite
policy of establishing an institution of higher learning in each state, and
Hamline University served that end for Minnesota. The purpose of

such an establishment was not only to spare the children of the faithful such dangers as were involved in attending the "godless" state university, but also to save for the church as many potential preachers and lay leaders as possible. Across the street from the campus was the Hamline Methodist church, which a large proportion of the faculty and the student body attended regularly. On campus the YMCA and the YWCA enjoyed much official encouragement.

The president of the university then held and exercised wide prerogatives. He might act occasionally in the name of the board of trustees, to which the Minnesota Annual Conference of the Methodist Church had entrusted the university, but in practice the authority was his. He could hire and fire all members of his faculty at will. Ordinarily he respected tenure rights acquired by long service, but neophytes had to take their chances—if he thought they hadn't made good, they had to go. He made it a definite policy, I'm sure, to hunt out bright young men for such openings as occurred, and then to keep them as long as he could. The financial resources at his disposal were limited, and the turnover in the faculty was high, but he did recruit many able young men. I suspect that the principal reason why he chose me for the vacancy he had in history, however, had little to do with scholarship. He was impressed with the fact that my father was a Methodist preacher, and that I had myself once held a local preacher's license. But he also had respect for the Ph.D. I had just achieved from the University of Wisconsin; the more Ph.D.'s an institution like Hamline could point to on its faculty, the better its standing with the various accrediting organizations that were beginning to throw their weight around. Kerfoot was president of Hamline all the time I was there. He was a tall, spare, fatherly type, slow to anger, and benevolently tolerant of youthful shortcomings. His earnestness and honesty of purpose could hardly be questioned. He consulted the faculty freely, both as individuals and as a group, and left to them most decisions on academic matters—the curriculum, for example. He believed in high standards and did what he could to promote them, but he believed also that the students under his care had precious souls that at all costs must be saved.

Kerfoot brought me to Hamline to modernize the teaching of history in the college. Before my time Dr. George S. Innis had been in charge of the department. He was a dedicated Christian whom everyone loved, but his attainments as a scholar were moderate. Students rarely failed to get high grades in his courses; gossip had it that he only counted the pages of examination bluebooks instead of reading them. Some perverse characters even claimed that they had won their A's by writing and rewriting the Lord's Prayer, page after page. Whatever the truth of such charges, President Kerfoot decided to place Dr. Innis in charge of education courses, and to give the new man a completely free hand in history.

Since I was the entire history department, decisions were easy to reach—I could have a department meeting standing on a street corner waiting for a streetcar, and often did. In working out the new history program I took account of what the catalogue set forth as previous practice and what I could at least pretend to be qualified to teach. I found Greek and Roman history in the lead positions, and I let them stand, although in each case followed by a helpful rubric that the course would not be given during the current year. That device also let me out of English history, which I might have undertaken except for the conviction that European history, beginning with the fall of Rome (whenever that was), would serve better as a freshman course. For the sophomores I decided in favor of American history, after the pattern laid down at Wisconsin by Carl Russell Fish. There would also have to be an advanced course for juniors and seniors, and on that I floundered for a while. I can recall giving American colonial history one semester, and problems in American history probably more than once. But the pattern soon worked itself out nicely; experience proved that in the freshman course on European history I could get no further than the Peace of Westphalia (1648). So the junior-senior course became European history, 1648 to the present. I also explained to the President that it was impossible for any one person to teach all history, and that we would definitely have to get someone better qualified than I was for the projected courses in ancient and English history. As for Asia, Africa, Latin America, and the islands of the sea, we left all that over for unforeseeable expansion.

My propaganda in favor of a larger staff soon showed results. The President had long had his eye on Harold Scott Quigley, who was a Hamline graduate, a former Rhodes Scholar from Minnesota, and a Ph.D. in political science from Wisconsin. Quigley had taken his degree the same year I had taken mine, but had got his first job at Princeton. I had known Quigley at Wisconsin, and strongly supported the idea of adding him to our faculty, although I wasn't very optimistic about Hamline's being able to take a man away from Princeton. I also planted the thought that Quigley could teach English history, as well as political science—a dirty deed, I'll admit, but I needed help. The net result was that Quigley left his instructorship at Princeton for higher rank and pay at Hamline to teach both political science and English history. As might have been expected, Quig took the double beating for only one year, and I joined him in his demand for emancipation from English history, pointing out, however, that we simply had to have someone else to teach that subject. By good luck, I had just the man to nominate for the place in my old friend and classmate at Northwestern, W. Freeman Galpin, who had acquired a Ph.D. from Pennsylvania and was available. Galpin got the job, but I saw to it that he also took over those courses in Greek and Roman history that I had marked "Not Given" for two successive years. Galpin stood it for a year, then took off for Michigan, where he had been offered an instructorship strictly in English history. I then turned to the University of Minnesota for help, and plucked a great prize in Theodore C. Blegen, another Americanist like myself, but willing to teach temporarily outside his field. Blegen outlasted me at Hamline, but my friendship with him, and with Galpin and with Quigley, grew mightily with the years, surviving all our various moves.

My experience in teaching at the college level was one of the best things that ever happened to me. In any large university I would have had little, if any, opportunity to teach outside my speciality. At Hamline I was obliged to draw upon everything I had ever known about both European and American history, and to find out a great deal more about both. I doubt if I have ever worked as hard, either before or since, as I did during my first two teaching years. Despite the illusion that a small college means small classes, my classes were relatively large. I had to take care of about 150 freshmen, and since the classroom assigned to me would accommodate only half that number, I met them in two sections of about 75 each. Two days a week I lectured; the third day I quizzed the class orally on the work of the week. By seating the students and keeping before me a seating chart, I soon learned the name of every member of the class, and developed a technique for asking each person at least one question each quiz period. I followed much the same practice with my courses in American history and in modern European history, both of which normally came close to filling the room. My teaching load was twelve hours a week, not bad, considering that one of my three-hour courses was a repeat. Also, by my own choice, my class schedule was concentrated on eight o'clocks and ten o'clocks six days each week. That program continued until after I was married, when my bride drew the line against eight o'clocks. I read all my own bluebooks. With a total of about 250 students in my classes, this was no mean chore.

During the early years, however, it was the lectures that threatened to get me down. I had been too well brought up at Wisconsin ever to go to class unprepared; hence every lecture I gave for the first time cost me two, three, or more hours by way of preparation. The library resources on campus were not especially good, and as yet I owned few books, but there were materials enough available to keep my nose to the grindstone. I tried to make each lecture a self-contained unit, as most of my Wisconsin teachers had done. Like some of them, each day I put an outline on the blackboard to give my students advance notice of what I intended to say. At first I used full notes, sometimes even writing out whole introductory sentences, but I took pains not to read my lectures—or at least not to seem to read them—and as time went on the notes became less and less necessary. I also adopted early the practice of writing memos to myself after each lecture about what was wrong with it; on the basis of these criticisms, together with whatever new information I had gleaned, I reworked my lectures year after year. My lecture notes, like my research notes, I kept on three-by-five-inch paper slips, so that it was easy to make modifications by taking some slips out and putting others in. During my early years—I think this would be valid for all of my time at Hamline—I brought in far too many details and tried to say too much, with the result that I talked too fast. Later I slowed down, said far less, but probably got over more to the class. Eventually I discarded full notes in favor of brief outlines designed primarily to keep my attention fixed on a few main points. Without such guidance I found the temptation to chase rabbits all over the field well-nigh irresistible. I always stood to lecture, made the most of what I had learned by precept and example about public speaking, and used every device I thought legitimate to command the attention of the class.

Most Hamline students came from Minnesota, probably in greater proportion from the small towns than from the cities. They reflected fairly accurately the national origins of the Minnesota population, a fact that the names on my class rolls demonstrated clearly. I soon learned to pronounce Scandinavian and other non-English names correctly. With respect to church affiliations, Methodists were understandably numerous among the students, but nearly every other Protestant denomination was also represented. There were even a few Catholics, one of whom, Daniel C. Gainey, was a universal favorite, and later became a prominent Minnesota businessman and a member of the board of regents of the University of Minnesota. Dan was one of the many boys who worked their way through Hamline, and he claims to have made some money by pressing the professors' pants. We had a few foreign students—Chinese, Japanese, and European—but not enough to give the campus the kind of international flavor so characteristic of American colleges and universities of today. I remember only one Negro student, a friendly dark-skinned boy who was accepted with no slightest evidence of discrimination—unless, indeed, in his favor. He enjoyed a kind of special status that a representative of his race might resent today.

In quality of scholarship the Hamline students showed every gradation, but the best of them were as capable as any I have taught anywhere. Sometimes students who couldn't get by at the state university tried to transfer to Hamline, and a few may have succeeded. But the stock retort of the official who ruled on their transcripts was: "Sorry, but our hospital facilities here are overcrowded already." We had the customary dropouts, usually due to poor grades or inadequate finances, and we lost a good many students who transferred at the end of their sophomore year to other institutions. However, some others who had expected to leave developed a warm loyalty to Hamline and stayed on for graduation. As a group the Hamline students were earnest, eager young people, determined to make their way in the world.

To my great delight my students seemed to like my courses about as well as I liked giving them. Discipline was no problem despite the easy familiarity that engulfed the campus and my youthful looks (I was only twenty-six when I came to Hamline and was often mistaken for a freshman). I made it a point in class to address all students by their last names, Mr. or Miss as the case might be, but on campus I called them by their first names and they generally called me John D. I had come by that handle accidentally. As a child everyone had called me Don for Donald, my middle name. But at about twelve years of age I struck at this—Don was too undignified; even dogs were called Don. So I demanded to be called Donald, and thanks to an opportune move to another town I got away with it pretty well. Until I went to Northwestern I parted my name on the side; in all my high school textbooks it appears as J. Donald Hicks. The J. was for John, my father's name also, and one member of the family by that name had seemed enough. When I entered Northwestern, however, by an understandable error my name got into the student directory as Hicks, John D. That did it. My financial status was so unlike that of another John D. who was then current in the news that his name—and mine, really—became my nickname, on the same principle, no doubt, that a six-foot, six-inch, giant is sometimes called Shorty. Finally, almost of necessity, I accepted the rearrangement of my name as official.

Once while I was at Wisconsin my mentor, Professor Paxson, had told me abruptly, "You can't get married until after you've taught for five years." He needn't have worried, for I came to Hamline with a ready-made family. Shortly before I had gone to Wisconsin, my father had left Wheatland for Douglas, another Wyoming appointment, but two years later, because of high blood pressure and a serious heart condition, he decided to retire from the ministry—or, to use the cruel church term, was "superannuated." By common consent, he and my mother and my younger sister, Hattie, who by this time had completed two years of college work at Baker University, the Kansas equivalent of Hamline, came to St. Paul to make a home for me. By pooling our financial resources, we knew we could make ends meet. Father's annuity from the church after twenty-seven years of service was three hundred dollars, so that his income and mine together were seventeen hundred dollars, a lot more than Father had ever received in any of his active years.

My mother soon had things all figured out. I had borrowed a total of seven hundred dollars from my parents to see me through graduate school, and with interest at 7 per cent, compounded annually, I owed them substantially more than that. As an undergraduate at Northwestern I had borrowed about half that much from a Methodist Church fund, but the Church, fortunately, could wait. By way of repayment on the family loan, I would take care of the twenty-five dollars a month rental for which we got a comfortable little six-room house. In addition, I would pay my parents thirty-five dollars a month board and room for myself, and a like sum for my sister. That brought the old pay check down to pretty slim proportions, but I had lived on less, and felt no grievance. We continued this arrangement for two years, until my sister had graduated from Hamline and was prepared to teach in high school. Then my father, critically ill, decided to move back to the scene of his last pastorate in Missouri. I continued to send home about half my salary each month until my father's death in 1919, and substantial sums to my mother after that. I gave up bookkeeping on my obligation, but my mother never did. Thanks in no small part to her interest in my finances, I was seven hundred dollars ahead of the game when I got married, exactly five years after I began to teach. Meantime my sister had helped me pay off my Methodist Church debt. Maybe we had to pool our resources during those years, but if anyone thinks we were poor he has another think coming. We were rich in everything that counted.

Before the end of my first year at Hamline the United States entered World War I. War fever ran high on the campus and led almost immediately to the organization of an ambulance unit for which about forty of our best students volunteered. The unit saw active serive in France and sustained serious losses. On June 5, 1917, along with nine and a half million other young Americans, including many of my students, I registered for the draft, but for better or for worse my family commitments saved me from military service. The Selective Service Act of 1917 provided for five classes of enrollees, the first of which consisted of all able-bodied young men who were unmarried, had no dependents, and were not needed at home in agriculture or industry. Class three, which included unmarried men with dependents, was exactly tailored to my condition, so that without hesitation or argument I was deferred. Undoubtedly if the war had lasted longer I would have been transferred to class one, but in those days before social security it was deemed expedient not to complicate conditions on the home front by calling up men with dependents, unless absolutely necessary. Later in the war Professor Paxson, who had joined the committee on public information in Washington, offered me a first lieutenancy to come to the national capital and help him. I declined on the ground that my family needed me and that I was at least equally useful to the war effort as a teacher. I think I was right, but for a long time—both during and after the war—I felt stigmatized because I had not worn a uniform.

I taught fledgling soldiers, however, or at least I tried to teach them, in the Students' Army Training Corps (S.A.T.C.), a device designed to keep the nation's colleges and universities alive despite the draft that fell so heavily on men of student age. The idea was to make each campus over into an army camp in which most of the male students divided their time between ordinary classroom activities and military instruction. Beginning with the fall of 1918, our Science Hall was transformed at government expense into an army barracks, practically the entire male section of the student body donned uniforms, and the campus resounded to the unmistakable sounds of military drill.

The program was of course unworkable; there is good authority for the dictum that no man can serve two masters. What can a distracted teacher do when an army sergeant appears at his classroom door, interrupts the proceedings with a loud command for Private So-and-So to report to such-and-such a place p. d. q., then departs noisily, followed by the uneasy victim? Try to pick up the pieces after a few such incidents. And who has priority when it comes to study time, or scheduled tests, or other requirements? And just where do the coeds and the nonuniformed students fit in? We all tried hard to make the proper adjustments, the President, the faculty, the students, and the somewhat unlettered military commandant, but it just couldn't be done. The college authorities knew nothing about how to run an army post, the army knew nothing about how to run a college. One well-intentioned—but deeply revealing—order posted by the commandant recited: "There will be improvised study every night from eight to ten." Supervised? But whether improvised or supervised, it was all the same.

To add to the general confusion there was an outbreak of the flu among the student-soldiers, but a sensible local doctor commandeered a large residence, kept the sick boys in it until they got well, and didn't lose a single patient. Maybe freedom from classes and drill worked the miracle. When the fighting ended, November 11, 1918, the S.A.T.C. clamored to go home. What little discipline had existed before now evaporated almost completely. There was enough red tape to hold things together until Christmas vacation, but when that time came, to the great relief of all concerned, the S.A.T.C. disappeared.

During my first two years at Hamline I had little spare time to devote to research, but I well remembered the admonitions of my Wisconsin teachers that one must write to get anywhere in the history profession. Besides, I liked to write. So I got out the old seminar report I had done at Wisconsin for Carl Russell Fish on the "Organization of the Volunteer Army in 1861" and reworked it with special reference to Minnesota. This task introduced me at once to the library of the

Minnesota Historical Society, then housed in the basement of the state capitol. Newspapers provided most of the material I needed, and the contrasts between raising the army in 1861 and in 1917–1918 kept my interest alive.

At the suggestion of Professor James A. James of Northwestern University, whom I managed to see from time to time, I also began work on the papers of Ignatius Donnelly, a choice collection which the society had fortunately acquired. By the time I got to this task the society was housed in its new building on the capitol plaza, and its manuscript division, under the able direction of Grace Lee Nute, had the Donnelly Papers in excellent order. Out of them and other pertinent material I was able to write an article on "The Political Career of Ignatius Donnelly" that the *Mississippi Valley Historical Review* published in its June–September issue of 1921. Thus began my long sustained interest in Populism.

Naturally I made the acquaintance of Solon J. Buck, then the superintendent of the Minnesota Historical Society, and author of *The Granger Movement* (1913), from its publication a classic in the field of agrarian history. Buck gave me much encouragement in my work, and once even tempted me with an offer—at a salary well above my Hamline earnings—to become a member of his staff. I declined, for by that time I was so devoted to teaching as a career that I viewed anything that might lead me into something else as sheer treason. Buck understood. We often attended historical meetings together, and it was perhaps he who got me the opportunity to read a part of my Donnelly paper, before it was published, to one of the section meetings of the American Historical Association at a Washington convention.

I recall that incident clearly. My paper was well received, and as I left the rostrum a distinguished-looking gentleman who sat far down in front congratulated me warmly. As I walked out into the hall to greet Dean Loren H. Batchelder, a member of the Hamline faculty who had asked me to meet him there, I was followed by another distinguished-looking gentleman who said to me: "Do you know who that was who spoke to you?" I did not. "That," he said, "was Albert J. Beveridge." It was then my turn to inquire of someone else who my thoughtful informant was. "That," I was told, "was Claude H. Van Tyne." It took me some time to get back to normal.

My determination to write, aided no doubt by my personal friendship with Professors James and Paxson and my persistent appearance at national historical meetings, paid good dividends. Twice during my years at Hamline I was invited to teach in summer session at Northwestern University, and once at Wisconsin. The small stipends I received for such service—about two hundred dollars per session as I recall—helped balance the family budget, while the opportunity to work in other libraries and with other students was not amiss. Also, I made new friendships with other young teachers of history, among them Reginald McGrane of the University of Cincinnati, who taught with me at Northwestern, and Paul Knaplund of the University of Wisconsin, who was just beginning his long and distinguished career. After any given summer excursion I returned to Hamline with new, even revolutionary, ideas that never seemed to pan out. Once after expressing myself volubly in faculty meeting Dean Batchelder cut me down to size with the remark: "Young man, that won't work. We tried it twenty years ago."

A problem of the small college that had never occurred to me before I came to Hamline may be described bluntly as competition for students. Minnesota, like many other western states, had just about all the small denominational colleges that it could support. Naturally, each college left few stones unturned to induce all the students who might possibly be interested in it to come its way. The state university, which for lower fees offered more kudos and a greater variety of courses, was hardest to deal with, and the various state teachers' colleges came next.

One summer our energetic young business manager, Ivan T. Jones, known inevitably as "I. T." or "Ivan the Terrible," asked me to accompany him on an extensive tour of the state in quest of students. I accepted—probably for a small fee—and had the time of my life. We set out in a Model T Ford and visited nearly every town that had a high school in a triangle that stretched from the Twin Cities to Minot, North Dakota, to Duluth and back. Our technique in each town was simple. First, we would go to the local newspaper office and acquire a copy of the town paper published right after the recent graduation exercises. It always contained a complete list of the graduating seniors. Then we would inquire our way to some available member of the class and ask him (or her) what each of his fellow graduates was planning for the following year. Those who were definitely committed to places other than Hamline we crossed off our list. To the Hamline prospects we offered congratulations and encouragement, and found out from them who among their classmates might be amenable to a little arm-twisting. All who might conceivably be interested in Hamline, and sometimes others too, we called on and sang in no uncertain terms the praises of the college we represented. Maybe we influenced a few to go to Hamline who might otherwise have gone elsewhere, and probably we kept some waverers in line—but I wondered then, and I wonder now, if our expedition really paid off.

We developed a good sales talk. First and foremost was the personal attention that a student could get in the small college. He would soon know everybody and everybody would know him. He would meet his teachers, not only in the classroom, but everywhere he went. This was almost painfully true. In a small college it took everyone available to make a right good crowd for anything. Both faculty and students were urged to turn out for all the games, debates, and other events on the calendar. If you weren't there, your absence was noted and your stock went down correspondingly. So we bore down hard and feelingly on togetherness. At a large university a student would be lost in the shuffle; in a small college he couldn't get lost if he wanted to. These arguments meant a lot to many small-town boys and girls and to their parents. We also stressed the point that the small-college freshman would have classes with the oldest and wisest men on our faculty, and would not be turned over to mere graduate student assistants or inexperienced instructors, as so often happened in large universities.

We denied vigorously that standards were lower in our college than in the state university, but we pointed out that if a student was down in his work at Hamline, somebody would care and would try to help him. And Hamline, we noted, in comparison with some other Minnesota colleges, enjoyed the great cultural advantages of a city environment—libraries, museums, theaters, and all that. This line of talk may have won a convert now and then, but probably it also lost an occasional student, for there were many parents who were not eager to see their darlings subjected to the temptations of a wicked city environment. We talked about the great guys we had on our faculty, the exciting leaders in our student body, and the brilliant prospects our football team had for the coming year—whatever its previous record. We didn't do any recruiting of athletes, however; that was a specialty which rested completely in other hands. In fact, if any such thing was being done, I, at least, didn't know about it.

During the regular academic year the business of promotion took a different form. Pamphlets singing the praises of Hamline appeared at intervals, although I had nothing to do with their preparation. One such, designed by a well-intentioned, if inept, colleague, was entitled "Making Squirrel Tracks for Hamline," and had cute drawings of such tracks on its cover. It was never sent out. "They'll think we're all nuts," said the registrar, as he chucked the entire printing into a wastebasket.

On several occasions I—and I'm sure other faculty members also—represented Hamline at high schools throughout the state, probably at times when high school and college vacations failed to coincide. These trips I made by train, occasionally riding the caboose of a local freight to make connections. Salesmanship took the form of a call on the local high school principal, usually just before a morning or an afternoon session. Explaining the purpose of my visit, I asked an opportunity to address the senior class, and usually had no trouble in getting it. My little speech—I learned to keep it short—stressed the advantages of higher education and invited students who would like to talk over their future plans with me to meet me for a few minutes later in the day. For such interviews the principal usually made his office, or some other suitable room, available. Only once, in some large town in southern Minnesota—perhaps Winona or Rochester—did I meet a rebuff. On this occasion the superintendent of schools not only denied my request to speak, but practically threw me out of his office. He was himself promoting a fifth high school year to serve as the equivalent of the freshman year in college—an incipient junior college program, I suppose—and he would tolerate no poaching on his preserves.

I view with considerable regret the drowning in numbers that is now changing the character of the American small college. At Hamline the student body must this year number well over a thousand, too many to permit the kind of intimate college life we knew while I was there. But what has happened to the universities is even more appalling. Often I am asked by parents about where they should send their children. Should it be to a large university, or what we now call a small college? My reply invariably begins with the words "That depends." Good students with well-adjusted personalities will do all right anywhere, but only those who answer such a description should go to one of our great, oversized universities. Average students will do better in a good small college, and below-average students will hang on longer and probably learn more in such surroundings than anywhere else. I have always been impressed, however, with the disproportionate number of graduate students who come to the universities from small colleges. The reason for this, I think, is that members of the faculty in small colleges can more easily spot real excellence in their students, and urge the right ones to go on. Furthermore, as a training ground for university teachers, the small college, in which teaching of necessity must be highly esteemed, can hardly be surpassed. For these and many other reasons, the small colleges, in these days of rapid population growth, well justify their existence.

Social life at Hamline these days was pretty inbred; the faculty saw each other and the students, and the students saw each other and the faculty. Picnics by classes or other units at some not too distant spot were frequent in appropriate seasons, and my sister and I were deemed to be adequate chaperons. We usually took such trips by public transportation; the automobile had not yet got in its deadly work. Each spring there was also a big steamboat excursion down the Mississippi and up the St. Croix, then back again, a trip that took all day and that everybody attended. The great problem on these occasions was what to do about dancing, upon which the Methodist discipline still frowned. What amounted, in effect, to a happy compromise was the inevitable result; dancing was officially forbidden, but somebody could always play the piano, so everyone danced who wanted to. Everyone knew that the President and most of the faculty had no serious scruples about dancing, but also that some of the rural Methodist clientele did. Thus everyone was satisfied. To the opponents of dancing one could cite the rule; to those who favored it, the fact. There was no mandate against liquor, simply because in those preprohibition days such a rule wasn't needed; certainly if anyone ever took any liquor along on those occasions, I never knew it. But, of course, I was faculty.

During my first two years at Hamline, while my parents and my sister were still with me, the problem of my father's health was an ever present concern. Rest and the absence of responsibility helped him considerably, and for a time he was able to accept a "supply" appointment in a St. Paul working-class neighborhood. In all his previous ministry he had never known city workers; the experience was thus an eye-opener to him, and to the rest of us. He liked his flock, however, and they were immensely proud of him. Ordinarily they had rated only a fumbling beginner, but Father looked, acted, and dressed the part of an honest-to-goodness parson—the kind some of them had known only in the old country.

Father's time was running out, and eventually he had to give up his little church. Well or ill, however, he always managed to put in a vegetable garden. One spring during the war he and I even obtained a garden plot on the edge of town where we "fought the Kaiser" by planting rows and rows of potatoes. Unfortunately, the potato bugs were not patriotic, and did our crop in. Father recommended the correct proportions of an appropriate insecticide, but I doused it on so liberally as to kill not only the potato bugs but also most of the potato plants. I think we harvested about as many potatoes as we put in.

One reason Father decided to leave Minnesota, I am sure, was the weather. The two winters we were there together were probably the coldest I have ever experienced. During one of them the total snowfall measured about eleven feet, and some of the first snow was still on the ground when the last snowfall came. The thermometer dropped to twenty degrees below zero frequently, and once to as low as forty below. Sidewalks became trenches, and it took a hard lift to get a shovelful of snow over the top. In the campus buildings we were usually comfortable, although our heating plant had its erratic moments. I recall one warmish day when I found the library overheated and opened a window. Miss Anna Davis, the lady librarian, known to all the students as Anna Maud, promptly closed it. "You know," she explained, "there are lots of times when we can't get enough heat in here, so we have to take it when we can get it." At home we had a good furnace and kept warm, but Father longed for a gentler climate and an earlier spring. So in the summer of 1918 he made the move back to Mound City, Missouri, where he bought a tiny house next door to my sister Mabel's, and practically in her yard. The change was made the more palatable for both my parents by the fact that my sister Hattie had landed a teaching position in the Mound City high school, and could continue to live with them.

After my family left for Missouri, I moved in with Harold Quigley, who was still a bachelor and agreed to share with me the two rooms he rented in a large residence close to the campus. For the next two years we lived together and shared experiences. Both of us had begun to cast interested eyes on the numerous young women about and to give each other much unheeded advice on the subject. We boarded at another residence two or three blocks from where we roomed, and paid eight dollars a week for meals that couldn't be had now for less than four or five times that amount. I don't remember what we paid for our rooms, but it wasn't much.

Despite the good food and pleasant companionship, I missed the advantages of a home of my own; besides, I was in love. Before the end of my fourth year I became engaged to one of my senior students, Lucile Harriet Curtis. Such crossing of caste lines was frowned upon by all the lady professors and some professors' wives, but I told the President about it and, humane character that he was, he said it was all right. Lucile was nearly ten years my junior, so to let her grow up a little and to make sure that we had made no mistake we agreed that she should teach for a year in high school before we were married. Since Quigley had accepted an offer to join the political science department of the University of Minnesota and I had no interest in living alone, I invited my now widowed mother to come back from Missouri and keep house for me for a year. Quite unwittingly, I had taken on a double hazard; I had turned my girl loose among the wolves, and I had installed in my household her natural competitor. But when the year was up Lucile and I were married at her home in St. James, Minnesota. Naturally, Harold Quigley was my best man, and President Kerfoot tied the knot. Six weeks later I helped Quigley get married and saw him and his bride off for a two-year tour of duty at Tsing Hua College in China. After my marriage my mother returned to her own home in Mound City.

Our marriage, from the first, was a complete success. "There's a divinity that shapes our ends." This good fortune was due in part to our common backgrounds. If my father was a Methodist preacher, hers was a Methodist Sunday school superintendent; we had protested against many of the same things. We were both products of a small-town environment. We had similar ancestry and similar family traditions; indeed, on our mothers' side our family lines crossed a couple of hundred years back, somewhere in New England. Lucile's parents were both college graduates—unlike mine, who only wished they were—her father from Michigan State and her mother from Knox. Her father was owner and editor of the *Watonwan County Plaindealer*, and as newspaper people, her parents read books, esteemed learning, and understood instinctively the importance of writing and publication. Lucile was the oldest daughter among five children, had learned as a matter of course about keeping house, could make an applie pie, and all that. But my young wife's qualifications, as I was eventually to learn, went well beyond the domestic virtues. Once Paxson had remarked for my benefit that a university professor without a competent wife was in the same predicament as an opera star without a good manager. Only when I was old enough and wise enough to be pleased about it did I realize that there was a stronger hand at the helm than mine. There couldn't have been a better marriage; after forty-seven years, three daughters, and ten grandchildren, I ought to know.

One day while Quigley was still at Hamline and we were leaving the campus together, we were stopped at a street corner by Rev. Herbert G. Leonard, pastor of the Hamline Methodist church, a man of great intellectual distinction whom we both admired. He laid down a challenge to us—he even called it that. "You two men," he said, "can go elsewhere, if you wish, and rise in your profession. But why don't you resolve, here and now, not to accept the offers that will come your way, and build your lives into this college?" Well, we felt a little as the rich young ruler must have felt when he asked the Good Master, "What must I do to inherit eternal life?" and was told "Go sell that thou hast, and come follow me." The young man went away sorrowful, and so did we, for we knew in our hearts that we could never follow our pastor's advice. Our dedication, we concluded, was not to any particular college, but to teaching and to the fields we taught. Quigley soon after accepted his call from the University of Minnesota, while at the end of my sixth year, because I couldn't do any better, I took an offer that came my way from the North Carolina College for Women. I didn't much want to go south, and I felt a little hurt that the University of Minnesota had overlooked my splendid possibilities. Dean Guy Stanton Ford, Professor August C. Krey, and other Minnesota historians were very kind and helpful to me, both then and later, but the offer never came. I knew that I had to leave Hamline soon, or I would have to take Dr. Leonard's advice, whether I liked it or not.

My rank at Hamline the first year I was there was assistant professor. The next year I drew a promotion, the only one I ever asked for, to full professor at sixteen hundred dollars. I went to the North Carolina College for Women (now the University of North Carolina at Greensboro) as a full professor, and a year after that I went to the University of Nebraska at the same rank. My teaching career thus assays one year as an assistant professor and forty years as a full professor, with a couple of deanships and no less than four chairmanships thrown in. I can remember complaining to Professor Paxson, shortly before his death, about the frantic way in which younger members of the history department at California were gunning for higher ranks. "Tut! Tut!," he said reprovingly, "You don't know anything about it." As usual, he was right.

VII. To North Carolina and Back Again

IT WAS NOT without deep foreboding that in 1922 I took off for Greensboro, North Carolina. Not only was I dismayed at the thought of spending the rest of my life in the Southeast, a section of the United States of which I knew comparatively little, but I also had certain professional misgivings. I was concerned about the necessity of teaching women only, I deplored the fact that I would not have a single class in American history, and I regretted the lack of any opportunity to work with graduate students. I was not unduly driven by ambition, but I had the normal desire to rise in my profession; besides, there were now three of us to think about—Jane Harriet, our oldest, had arrived the preceding March. Whatever my doubts, I accepted my new position in good faith, knowing that I might never have another chance to move but hoping secretly that my stay in the South would not be too prolonged.

We made our journey to North Carolina in two laps. On the way south we stopped off at Evanston, Illinois, where, thanks again to my former teacher, now Dean James A. James, I was to teach in summer session for a third time. We had already rented, sight unseen, a furnished apartment on Davis Street, near the Northwestern railroad station, and I shall never forget the startled look on the face of the housewife we supplanted when we appeared on her doorstep. I had assumed, quite naturally I thought, that the place was ours from the day my rent on it began; what she thought, I'll never know, for she certainly wasn't expecting us. We waited her out, for we had no place else to go, and at length she grumpily departed. Our temporary abode was an inconvenient second-story flat, with five rooms strung together in a row and no rear exit. Lucile had a time getting the baby's daily wash on the line. Furthermore, Jane Harriet was a colicky infant and I doubt if our neighbors ever adjusted to her presence. Afternoons, when my classes were over, we took her in a baby buggy to the lake shore, but I insisted on choosing a different route each day because she cried so much. We had feeding problems in those days that pediatricians have now pretty well solved.

Our summer in Evanston was made delightful by the presence nearby of the Hahn family, whom, as already noted, I had known as summer visitors in Madison, Wisconsin. The Hahns had moved recently from St. Louis to Chicago and now lived in easy reach of us on the north side. They accepted Lucile and the baby into the family as they had earlier accepted me, and we saw a lot of them. Lucile was a little unprepared for the open evidence of affection between the beautiful Hahn daughters and her young husband, but she put up with it without undue protest. Rose, the oldest of the Hahn girls, was now married to a young Chicago lawyer, Mitchell Dawson. The Dawsons lived north of the Loop in what had once been a sumptuous Gold Coast stable, which they had leased and rebuilt to suit their taste. The younger girls, Dorothy, Emily, Helen, and Josephine, were still at home. Mannel, the only son, was married to Nancy Koonsman, a promising young sculptress, and was not in evidence that summer, but he and his wife ultimately became our lifelong friends. She even did a plaque of me. Eventually most of the Hahn family became residents of Winnetka, Illinois, and we made it a point to see them every time we came through Chicago. Years later, when Emily had gained fame as a writer, we were to meet her and her husband, Charles Boxer, in both England and America.

After Evanston we found our way by rail to Greensboro, a long, hard trip at best, but made infinitely worse by the railway shopmen's strike of 1922. At length we found ourselves stranded in Salisbury, North Carolina, still a considerable distance from our destination. We went to a hotel, registered, were shown to our room, got the baby quieted down, and fell into bed. Almost immediately there was a loud rapping on our door, to which I replied with some irritation. "You forgot to register for your wife," I was told.

"Well, please do it for me," I replied.

"No, that won't do," came the answer. "You'll have to come down to the desk and do it yourself." So I got up angrily, dressed, went down to the lobby and corrected my registration. True enough, I had signed only my own name, reverting, I suppose to my practice as a bachelor. So I added after my name in the register—one of those big bound books that most hotels were already discarding—the words "and wife and baby," inquiring of the clerk at the same time if he didn't think the presence of the baby was a sufficient guarantee that we were a married couple. He said nothing. I went back to bed, muttering to myself that if this was a sample of North Carolina, why had I ever left Minnesota.

In Greensboro the chairman of the department, Professor W. C. Jackson, took charge of us and did everything humanly possible to help us adjust to our new environment. The college owned several unfurnished houses, one of which we rented, but we had to buy our own furniture, no easy feat with a baby and without a car. Fortunately, I had only a short distance to walk to my office—the first one I had ever rated—and to my classes.

Teaching southern girls proved to be no great challenge. Most of them were a year younger than their northern counterparts, for most southern public schools then provided for only eleven grades instead of twelve before graduation from high school. The girls were docile, studied hard, got good grades, and longed for matrimony, the only career to which, with a few exceptions, they aspired. Socially speaking, the campus was badly located; with about twelve hundred girls at NCCW and half that number in another Greensboro women's college, there were simply not enough eligible young men available to meet even minimum demands. Campus rules were unduly restrictive and the girls were correspondingly restive, although not half as rebellious as northern girls would have been under similar circumstances.

Southern prejudices ran deep, but they hardly affected me at all. The year before my arrival Professor Paxson, according to a story I heard, had fared less well. After a series of lectures he had given on the campus, one of the girls who had heard him was found weeping in her room because, she said, she was afraid Dr. Paxson was "neither a Christian nor a Democrat." On the latter score she might have been right. The fact that I was not teaching American history probably saved me from even stronger criticism. No one could ever have persuaded me, for example, either then or later, to refer to the Civil War as the War Between the States. On the other hand, had I been permitted to give a course in the history of the American frontier, as I did later elsewhere, I could hardly have overlooked such significant local items as the Battle of Alamance, the scene of which I visited, or the organization of the State of Franklin. Maybe in this way I could have identified myself more closely with my historic surroundings. I found, indeed, that I was completely at home with the occasional country people I met. They talked the same language that I had talked in Missouri as a boy, full of hauntingly familiar tones and elisions. Lucile, on the other hand, was astonished to hear country people speak without a Scandinavian accent. That was all she had ever heard from those she had met in Minnesota.

Entirely new to us was the presence in the community of large numbers of Negroes. There was an all-Negro section in Greensboro, and in addition several enclaves of Negroes tucked in here and there among the whites. As yet there was no pretense of equality between the races; the Negroes all "knew their place" and kept in it. The tremendous dependence of the southern whites on the Negroes was no doubt more obvious to us than to those who had lived with this situation all their lives. In practically every southern middle-class household there was at least one Negro servant, while such labor-demanding activities as the maintenance of the college buildings, dining halls, and campus grounds were exclusively in Negro hands. The college, indeed, and no doubt many other southern institutions, depended for its functioning on a kind of Negro underground, about as numerous and in its way about as important as the whites who were more in evidence. The ruler of the campus underground, known affectionately as "Uncle William" Peebles, was said to be quite a tyrant, not only in his dealings with his own people, but also with the numerous lady professors. When referring to the latter, he was wont to shake his head sadly and say: "These here wimmin; you can pacify 'em, but you cain't satisfy 'em."

While seemingly there was little strain between the two races, there was a more somber side. The sight of a gang of Negroes—convicts, I suppose—working the road in front of my house under the supervision of white men armed with guns, curdled my blood and strengthened my determination to leave the South when opportunity offered. This wasn't the kind of environment in which I wanted to bring up my children.

The caste system of the South, we discovered, was by no means confined to the racial barrier. The white millworkers were also a class apart. They lived in a separate community adjacent to where they worked, and they had nothing to do with either the Negroes or the middle-class whites. One could almost identify still another class, the mill owners, who lived in a district of bigger and better houses and kept pretty much to themselves. By tacit agreement, the Negroes had the run of the downtown area one evening each week and the mill-workers another. All this was hard on my middle western, small-town equalitarian sensibilities.

We were not long enough in Greensboro to make a place for ourselves there. The college community was friendly enough, but we did not really become a part of it, although we attended teas, receptions, and public meetings, and received and duly returned invitations. On occasion we had dinner with the girls at one of the two large dining halls for students; being the only man present among six hundred girls was quite an experience. We saw little or nothing of the Greensboro townspeople, and I had the feeling that however cordial they might seem superficially, they would always regard us as outsiders—mere educational carpetbaggers. We attended church on Sunday, as everyone did, but when it came to transferring our membership from the Methodist Episcopal Church to the Methodist Episcopal Church, South, my northern prejudices got the better of me. I just couldn't do it. My motives, however, were somewhat more complicated than that. I could not bring myself publicly to reaffirm doctrinal beliefs that I no longer held. From this time forward I ceased to be a church member.

Despite these personal reactions, I am sure that southern identification with the nation at large was complete after World War I, more complete, probably, than it is today, when the civil rights issue has risen to the surface. One thing I noted with interest. The Greensboro students could sing every stanza and every verse of "The Star-Spangled Banner" without missing a word, something northern students could rarely do, and something I have never been able to do. They could do the same by "Dixie," but that I could have foreseen.

Our happiest memories of our Greensboro days came from two close friendships we formed while we were there. One of them was with Charles B. Shaw, the college librarian, and his wife, Dorothy, our next-door neighbors. Charles, or maybe one of his predecessors, had succeeded in getting a new library building, but its bookshelves were startlingly empty. We conspired together on how to fill them and found, to our considerable dismay, that getting the money was the least part of the problem. I learned then that you don't just go out and buy a library, a fact that is painfully apparent nowadays in California as we struggle to establish new campuses, new colleges, and new universities. Libraries have to be built from the ground up, and the process takes a long time, partly because other libraries have already cornered so many of the books you need. The Shaws stayed in Greensboro longer than we did, then went to Swarthmore, where Charles was librarian until the time of his death. Somehow over the years we managed to see each other repeatedly.

The other choice friend from Greensboro days was Harriet Elliot, who headed the political science department. Harriet really opened my eyes to the world of politics; I had long had liberal tendencies, but Harriet was militant in her liberalism, and knew why. Later, when she was prominent in the Franklin D. Roosevelt administration, I had the pleasure of introducing her to Governor Philip LaFollette in his office at the state capitol in Wisconsin. The two hit it off perfectly, and the conversational sparks flew in every direction. Phil was then advocating New Deal expenditures in billions rather than hundreds of millions to defeat the depression, and no doubt Harriet carried the word back to Washington.

Lady Luck plays a prominent part in anyone's career. We had hardly got settled in Greensboro when I received an invitation to read a paper at the December meeting of the American Historical Association. This was the break I needed, and I accepted with alacrity, but how was I to write such a paper? My findings on "The Origin and Early History of the Farmers' Alliance in Minnesota," which exploited about all I had found out about that subject, were already on the way to publication.[1] Had I been in Minnesota, I could easily have gone on with that theme, but what did I know about the Farmers' Alliance in North Carolina? The subject suggested itself, but I had to find out what I could do with it. The college library yielded exactly nothing, so I tried the Greensboro Public Library, which by good fortune had a file of the Greensboro *Daily Record* during exactly the years for which I needed it. I learned also of another newspaper prominent during the period, the Greensboro *Patriot*, discovered its back files in a local newspaper office, and dug into them. The trail pointed next to the *Progressive Farmer*, a paper that had been closely identified with the southern Farmers' Alliance movement and Populism. So I went to Raleigh, where the paper was still published, and pored over its old volumes in the editor's office. I also visited the headquarters of the North Carolina Literary and Historical Association and picked up such additional data as its collection yielded. By the time the convention met in late

[1] *Mississippi Valley Historical Review*, IX (December 1922), 203–226.

December, 1922, at New Haven, I had put together a paper that I was not ashamed to read.[2]

By chance Lucile still corresponded with a former Hamline student, Jeanette Joachim, who now lived with her husband and children at Newport News, Virginia, so we cheerfully accepted her invitation for Lucile to stay there while I went on to New England. The trip from the North Carolina interior to the Virginia coast, which we took entirely by rail, was in those days a long and painful experience, involving many delays and much changing of cars. North–south transportation in these parts was easy enough, but facilities for travel east or west left much to be desired. The train trip ended at Norfolk, and we had to get to Newport News by ferry. Our hosts received us cordially, despite the fact that unbeknownst to us they had recently become the parents of a new baby. They hadn't told us for fear the news might have changed our plans. Lieutenant Joachim was a naval air officer who was stationed at Langley Field. He showed me over the installations there, including an air tunnel being used to test experiments in airplane design. A ferry across Chesapeake Bay landed me on the Cape Charles side, where I boarded a northbound train. Attending national conventions also paid dividends, I was learning, in making me more familiar with the geography of the United States.

At the AHA meeting Lady Luck continued to show me favor. In the large audience to which I read my paper was Frederick Jackson Turner, and I learned later that he thought well of my effort. Far more important, however, was the presence of Guernsey Jones, chairman of the department of history at Nebraska, who apparently had already got favorable reports on me, probably from Fred Paxson and Guy Stanton Ford. Jones looked me up, and after my return to Greensboro invited me to visit Lincoln at the university's expense, obviously to be looked over by Chancellor Samuel Avery and other interested individuals.

Lincoln was only about a hundred miles from my birthplace in northern Missouri and not much farther from Mound City, where my mother made her home. Only Mother wasn't there, for by this time she had come to visit us in Greensboro. Thereby hangs a tale. The year Mother kept house for me in St. Paul my sister, Hattie, had left the Mound City high school for a better position in Tracy, Minnesota.

---

[2] "The Farmers' Alliance in North Carolina," *North Carolina Historical Review*, II (April 1925), 162–187.

This meant that Mother, at least during the winters, had to live alone. She didn't like it. So the fall Lucile and I went to Greensboro she decided to pay an extended visit to her sister, my Aunt Sarah Lovett, in Bristow, Oklahoma. After a few months it became apparent that the two sisters, much as they loved each other, simply couldn't get along together. So early in 1923 Mother showed up on our doorstep in Greensboro. Lucile was kind and deferential, but two queen bees in one hive are too many. So when I took the train to Lincoln that spring, I saw to it that Mother went with me as far as Mound City.

I suppose there is no ordeal harder for the young teacher to endure than being looked over officially for a new job. Guernsey Jones was the soul of kindness and extended me every courtesy, but there was one thing he did that I could never explain. Without consulting me in advance, he scheduled me for a public lecture on "The Role of the Farmer in American History." Later I might have extemporized rather painlessly on such a theme, and with adequate notice I could have had something to say even then. As it was, I simply changed the subject to "My Impressions of North Carolina," and reported on what I had seen and done down south. Nobody seemed to care what I talked about; apparently it was sufficient to demonstrate that I could talk. Chancellor Avery was among the hundred or so persons in my audience, and he offered no comments on my speech, pro or con. Whether because of it, or in spite of it, I received in due time an offer of a professorship at four thousand dollars a year, five hundred more than I was making in North Carolina, although I had augmented my NCCW salary a little by teaching an extension course—"moonlighting"—once each week in Charlotte, North Carolina. Even so, the Nebraska offer was more than adequate; I could have been had for less.

I felt a twinge of regret and some embarrassment at leaving NCCW so soon, but the Nebraska opportunity was one that I could not possibly pass up. It meant teaching exclusively in my own field, something I had never before had a chance to do; it meant teaching both men and women instead of women only; it meant working with graduate students. So I made what apologies I could to my Greensboro sponsors, and at the end of the year gathered up my wife and baby and our few belongings preparatory to the move back to more familiar surroundings.

Our return to the Middle West did not proceed exactly according to schedule. I had accepted an offer from Finla Crawford, whom I had known as a graduate student at Wisconsin, to teach in the 1923 summer session at Syracuse University. An additional attraction was the presence there of Freeman Galpin, my roommate at Northwestern and my colleague for a year at Hamline. Lucile and I had it all figured out. We would go together to Washington, D.C., where I would put her and the baby on the train to Minnesota, via Chicago. While she visited her parents in St. James, I would stay in Washington for two weeks, working in the Library of Congress, a *sine qua non* for all aspiring writers of American history. Then we would meet in Syracuse. But when we got to Washington the baby got sick and we panicked. More experienced parents would have known that she stood as good a chance of getting well, from whatever she had, without the presence of her father as with it. But we ditched the Library of Congress project and took off as a family unit for Minnesota. The child, of course, was practically well by the time a doctor saw her. After two weeks, with our financial resources somewhat impaired, we entrained for Syracuse. Neither then nor later did it occur to either of us that I could spend as much as six or eight weeks away from the family; wherever I went, we all went.

Sight unseen again—we should have known better—we had rented another upstairs apartment, this one on the third—or, as it turned out, the attic—floor of an old house not far from the campus. Lucile took one look at the place and said she wouldn't live there. I didn't like it either, but it was cheap and I had the "sanctity of contracts" on my side. This time she had to carry the baby's wash down three flights of stairs, the local mosquitoes were small enough to go right through our screens (we covered the baby's crib with mosquito netting), and the weather was incredibly hot. The regular tenant whose place we took was a bachelor teacher with many books, mostly on low shelves in easy reach of our sixteen-month-old infant. She examined and rearranged all the books she could bring down, but not according to any approved pattern. We didn't much mind.

Both the Crawfords and the Galpins put themselves out to show us a good time. Galpin was already married when he came to Hamline, so Gladys, his wife, and Lucile were old friends. In fact, we had done a good bit of our courting baby-sitting with the Galpin's first infant, who was correspondingly older than ours. We drove around central New York a little and saw what sights Syracuse afforded, among them the still visible channel of the old Erie Canal and New York Central trains running right down the middle of the city's principal thoroughfare.

I had pleasant quarters at the university and taught classes that included some graduate students. Among the latter I remember best Philip Auchampaugh, who was already a great Buchanan fan. Later he won his Ph.D. and wrote voluminously, if not convincingly, on his favorite theme. I met him repeatedly thereafter, particularly after he joined the faculty of the University of Nevada and I went to California.

We were still in Syracuse at the time of Harding's death and followed in the newspapers the course of his funeral train as it went from San Francisco to Washington and then back to Marion. From the respectful crowds that appeared along the route, and from the unrestrained post-mortem encomiums, some historians have drawn the conclusion that Harding had became very popular with the American people. I don't think this was true. Even at the time, I thought the mourning for Harding seemed a little forced, and as far as I was concerned it was totally nonexistent. I had voted for Harding on the assurance of such respected Republicans as Hughes, Root, and Hoover that a Harding victory was the best way to get the United States into the League of Nations, a desirable end that the Democrats had been unable to accomplish. After Harding took an exactly opposite course, I felt betrayed. The return to isolation, which he so firmly promoted, together with the other mistakes of his administration, turned me permanently against both him and the party that had nominated him. I never again voted for a Republican for President.

We had missed Niagara Falls on our honeymoon; in fact, we had settled for a lakeside cabin thirty miles from Minneapolis. So, Syracuse being where it was, we planned to include a glimpse of the Falls on our journey west. Lucile, who is a master strategist when it comes to figuring out how to see new places, had it all worked out. We would go to Buffalo, make the side trip to the Falls, return to Buffalo and from there take a ship across Lake Erie to Detroit, then board the train for Chicago, change stations in a Parmelee bus, as one always had to do, and from Chicago take the train to Mound City, on our way to Lincoln. It was a good plan and seemingly feasible.

We would have followed it all right had not a restaurant in Buffalo served me some tainted food. On the way back from the Falls I became deathly sick, and only with the greatest difficulty managed to get by taxi from the railroad station to a hotel. There we found a long line at the registration desk, and after Lucile lost her place in it several times because of having to chase the baby, I elbowed my way to the counter and demanded a room at once. The clerk took one look at me and obliged. We tried to get a doctor, but it was midnight before he showed up. Meantime, I had concluded that my days were numbered and had briefed Lucile, not once but many times, on her course of action after my demise. Her instinct told her that I would live, but she agreed that we would have to give up the ship passage across Lake Erie and make new arrangements for the rest of our trip. Next morning I was sufficiently alive that I could care for the baby while she went down to the water front—a scary experience—to cancel our ship reservations, and to the railroad station to work out a new schedule.

As soon as I was able we took the train for Chicago, with barely enough money to get us there. We always slept the three of us together in a berth, for Lucile was afraid to be left alone, and I was afraid to trust her with the baby, for in those days she slept so soundly. But even one berth cost a lot, and after paying for it we were down almost to pocket change. (Once, on an earlier trip, we could get only an upper. I didn't sleep a wink for fear of falling out, but Lucile and the baby slept just fine.) Fortunately, we had friends in Chicago, Tom and Frances Carter, to whom we could appeal for help. With complete confidence we wired them to meet our train and to bring along enough money to see us through to our destination.

How did we know the Carters so well? That takes us back to our Hamline days, when Frances had been Lucile's best friend and Tom the college YMCA secretary. Their courtship and ours had coincided in point of time. Indeed, we frequently went out as a foursome, and sometimes when we attended movies Frances and I had made it a point to sit together, as far as possible from Tom and Lucile, because they so often embarrassed us by laughing hilariously at the slightest provocation. Only after the movie was over would we change partners. At our wedding in 1921 Frances had been Lucile's maid of honor and Tom, to whom she was then engaged, had assisted Quigley in keeping me breathing.

As a matter of fact, Tom and Frances had gone with us on our honeymoon. After the wedding reception, Lucile and I had taken the afternoon train from St. James to St. Paul, where we spent the night, while Tom and Frances stayed on with friends in St. James. Next morning, whom should we meet a block from the hotel but Tom and Frances, who had come to the city on an early train, and were wandering about disconsolately until Frances could get a train to her home town. Tom would gladly have gone with her, but she hadn't as yet sold her parents on her engagement, so she ruled that out. Without quite realizing what we were doing, we spoke up generously: "Why don't you come with us? We are eligible chaperons now!" In their frustrated state, that seemed to them like a good idea, and they took us up on it. We phoned to the resort where we had reservations, asking for two single rooms for our guests, and got a favorable reply. Imagine our consternation when we found on our arrival late at night that we had been given one two-room cabin and that there was nothing else available. So Lucile and Frances occupied one room, while Tom and I occupied the other. Fortunately, however, Tom and Frances took long walks each evening. They were married soon after, and by the time we wired them from Buffalo they were living in Chicago.

Tom was an ordained Methodist preacher who had served as a chaplain in World War I. He decided while at Hamline to work for his Ph.D. in social psychology with C. H. Judd at the University of Chicago. That hurdle surmounted, he accepted an offer from Albion College in Michigan, where he spent his entire teaching career. The Carters met our train as we had requested and lent us the money we needed to be on our way, both couples with another tall tale to tell. We have seen them now and then since they rescued us in Chicago, and have corresponded with them irregularly.

At long length we arrived at my mother's home in Mound City, with the Nebraska venture just around the corner.

VIII. Nebraska

BEFORE automobiles and buses made local travel easy, people who lived in small towns knew their railroad connections well. Mound City was on a Burlington branch line that ran from Villisca, Iowa, to St. Joseph, Missouri. Coming from Chicago, a passenger had to change cars at Villisca and maybe wait over at Clarinda for the arrival of another train, but he at least got all the way to Mound City by rail. If he came in from Omaha, he got off at Bigelow, three miles short of his destination, and unless some kind friend or relative met him, took the hack to Mound City over a bottom road that ran through deep mud or frozen ruts or swirling dust, depending on the weather. To get from Mound City to Lincoln, he drove about ten miles to Napier, then boarded a train from St. Joseph that would cross the Missouri River at Falls City on its way to the Nebraska capital. As for Napier, the following conversation, overheard on a railway coach, will suffice:

"Where y' goin', boy?" asked a little old lady.

"To Napier," he replied.

"Lan's sake, chile," she protested. "Napier ain't nowhere."

As soon as I was fully recovered from my Niagara Falls illness, my brother-in-law, Robert E. Terhune (Mabel's husband), took me to Napier and put me on a train for Lincoln, where I was to rent us a house. We had had all we could take of apartment life in Evanston and Syracuse, so a house it had to be. On my arrival in Lincoln, one of my future colleagues, Roy Cochran, took me in tow and helped me with my search. We found nothing of the right size available, so I settled for one of those utterly characterless, boxlike frame structures so common in the Middle West—three rooms downstairs, three rooms up, a wide front porch, all painted an uncompromising battleship gray. The rent was too high and the house was too large, but after consulting Lucile by telephone, I took it, then returned to Mound City to collect the family. By the time we all got to Lincoln, our furniture had arrived from Greensboro, but there wasn't enough of it. So we had no choice but to go broke again buying some more.

Nevertheless, we took great delight in our new surroundings. Almost immediately Lincoln became home to us. It was then a city of about fifty thousand people, not too large and not too small. Stately elms flanked its wide streets and glossed over the plainness of even such houses as ours. As far as we were concerned, this would be a good place for us to spend the rest of our lives. Most important of all, we found new friends, young people our own ages, with their children on the way and their futures to make. Two couples we came to know well were new arrivals like ourselves. I first met Cliff Hamilton, a young chemist, and his wife, Frances, while they were house-hunting at the same time I was similarly engaged. Joyce Hertzler, a sociologist, and his wife, Flo, were also as new to Lincoln as we were. Other young couples who had come to the university earlier put themselves out to make us feel welcome. Except for Guernsey Jones, our best friends were not connected with the history department, but were drawn from widely different interests. We saw much of John and Nell Rice, Townsend and Elizabeth Smith, Paul and Marjorie Sears, and Fred and Georgia Upson. John was a classicist, Townsend a physicist, Paul a botanist, and Fred a chemist.

There were many others. Guernsey Jones was unmarried, but he took quite shine to Lucile and was a constant caller at our house. He was a connoisseur of fine china and brought with him each time he came a gift for her to treasure. He found bargains for us that we bought for a fraction of their value and that still decorate our table. We knew other bachelors, too, among them three members of the English department, Sherlock Gass, Kenneth Forward, and Orin Stepanek, all of whom later married. Delightful older people took us in, such as the Paul Grummanns and the Max Westermanns. We joined a Faculty Dancing Club and Lucile grimly undertook to make my dancing less intolerable. But with my one Methodist foot and my one Quaker foot, what chance did she have? However that might be, we soon had a sense of belonging in Lincoln that we could never have acquired in a southern city.

We even bought a lot and built ourselves a house far out on "N" Street, about two miles from the campus. We started the project during our second year in Lincoln with fifteen hundred dollars pressed on us by my mother, who thought her money would be safer with me than with the bank. She was so right; the bank failed disastrously a few weeks after she took her money out. As students of economic history will recall, that happening was altogether too common among western small-town banks of the period. Our new home was of wood construction, but veneered with brick and stucco to give it a more impressive exterior. It was further distinguished by a steep roof and a high central gable over the front entrance. Downstairs, it had three rooms and an enclosed porch; upstairs, three bedrooms, a small study, and a sleeping porch; besides this, a full basement, an attic, and an outside garage. The contract price was $7,200 for house and lot, but it probably cost me $7,600 before it was habitable. I recall that the carpenters were not unhappy with wages at seventy-five cents an hour. The purchasing power of the dollar has certainly changed, but we thought prices were ridiculously high even then. For about the same price, the same contractor was also building at about the same time a brick-veneered colonial house for the Hamiltons a few doors from ours. We were neighbors for many years.

Even before we moved to our new home on "N" Street, we had acquired our first automobile, a broken-down Model T Ford sedan that Bob Terhune had sold me for two hundred dollars. In Greensboro we had weighed the alternative of buying a car or a piano—we could not afford both—and the piano had won. Perhaps I should explain, parenthetically, that my young wife had already decided to continue with her music, despite the distractions of matrimony. Her mother, who was a music teacher, had seen to it that her daughter had had a start in piano, violin, and voice, but eventually the singing interest had won out. Although Lucile took piano lessons in Greensboro, it was primarily with the idea of learning to play her own accompaniments. Not without a certain amount of feminine guile, she chose the piano over the automobile, knowing full well that in the long run she could be perfectly sure of both. In Lincoln distances proved to be too great for us to get around conveniently without a car, although I made it a point to walk either to or from the campus practically every day. Like most American couples who buy their first automobile, we were never again without one. Vacations we could make it in two days to Lucile's home town in Minnesota, and in less than one to Mound City.

In our day Lincoln was a very clubby sort of place, and some of the organizations that then existed probably still endure. One such group, consisting of our most intimate friends, made it a practice to get together frequently at one another's houses for potluck dinners, each couple bringing a dish. Strange as it may seem now, those of us who had children could then afford domestic help, usually a college girl who lived in, and for a few dollars a week plus board and room was available for daytime chores and for baby-sitting when we went out of an evening. In this particular "dinner club," John Rice more or less led the works, with Menckenesque diatribes against every sort of sham and pretense. A Rhodes scholar, Rice had taken a first in classics at Oxford, although I always believed less because of his knowledge of Greek and Latin than because of his native brilliance. He and others among us made constant use of the word "humanism," the definition of which seemed to vary with each user, but we wrestled earnestly with whatever ideas anyone thought he had. The one common denominator that ran through our talk was that there was a hell of a lot wrong with the world, whether in education, in religion, in literature, or in business, and that something ought to be done about it. Rice left Nebraska before I did, and the place was the poorer for his going. He could stir up more argument in a few minutes than any other man I ever knew. He later wrote a book, *I Came Out of the Eighteenth Century*, a delightful book in some ways, but unbecomingly unkind to Nebraska and some Nebraskans, including Chancellor Avery and other members of the university community. The University of Nebraska certainly was not Oxford, and it had many faults, but it carried the brightest torch for learning to be found anywhere between the Missouri River and the Pacific Coast.

There were several somewhat more formal men's dinner clubs in Lincoln, and I belonged to three of them. Most pretentious was The Club, or, as some called it derisively, the *The* Club, which consisted of a dozen or fifteen of Lincoln's well-established business, professional, and university leaders. After a sumptuous home dinner, provided in turn by the various wives, one member read a paper, on which afterward every other member commented in turn. As I recall, the papers were quite uniformly good, and the comments worth listening to, if only one could keep awake after eating so much. Another club, The Twelve, with somewhat similar membership, followed the same practice, but permitted the wives—known as The Taggers—to be present at dinner, although afterward the women made themselves scarce. The third such organization to which I belonged, The Crucible Club, had a somewhat larger membership, drawn in the main from young business and professional men. They met at a hotel or the University Club, and went through the customary after-dinner ritual. Once in a while we struck pay dirt, as for example in a heated argument between a physician and a scientist over whether the future of medicine lay with the bacteriologists or the chemists. Subsequent events have proved that they both won. In general, members of this club regarded me and my ideas with some disdain. I stood up for the farmers, voted for such impossible characters as Norris, LaFollette, and Al Smith, and showed too little respect for what I would probably have called then the Rotarian way of life. But I found a few choice friends in this group, among them Paul F. Good, later an Omaha lawyer, and Walter Locke, a journalist of real distinction, now deceased.

In addition to these clubs, membership in the university faculty meant involvement in a very active, almost mandatory social life. Arthur M. Schlesinger, who had encountered much the same thing at Iowa City, once asked me: "How in the world did you manage to get any work done?" I don't know; but he did, and I did.

Adjustments to the University of Nebraska came easily. The main campus was unfortunately located near the business district of the city, campus buildings showed the remarkable unconcern for architectural consistency then—and still—so characteristic of American universities, and all serious thought of landscaping lay well in the future. But my new university home looked good to me. I can remember thinking to myself as I settled into my Social Science Building office, "The lines are fallen unto me in pleasant places; yea, I have a goodly heritage." The Department of History was then filled with dissension; despite its small size (six members, as I recall), it had only recently ceased to be three departments—English history, European history, and American history—each headed by an unyielding chief. But now it was united in name, if not in fact, under one head. I got along well with the chairman, and departmental problems did not at first trouble me. I had been warned about Fred Morrow Fling, well known for his work on the French Revolution and for his personal inflexibility. "So you're going out to Nebraska to have your Fling!" quipped one of my friends, in commenting on my new appointment. But when the learned professor and his wife called on us, our baby daughter occupied the entire time untying his shoestrings, a circumstance that kept the conversation on a pleasantly low level. When we returned the call, however, it was different. The master took me into his library, showed me his books (a truly remarkable collection), then sat me down at a table opposite him, and began to quiz me. He was past master at the art—my oral Ph.D. examination at Wisconsin was as nothing in comparison. After an hour or more he seemed satisfied, and we rejoined the ladies in the living room. My relations with him from that time on were never unfriendly, if often difficult.

I early conceived a very genuine admiration for Chancellor Samuel Avery. He was a diamond in the rough who looked more like a farmer, uncomfortable in store clothes, than like the head of a great university. He was deeply intent on building up his faculty, and admitted over-paying some recent acquisitions—including me—in order to beat out prospective competitors. He was a shrewd judge of men, who could strike a keen balance between the virtues and defects of any given individual and use him for what he was worth. In analyzing character he sometimes thought out loud, and maybe said too much. "You can't make a parlor cat out of an alley cat," I've heard him observe, in ex-planation of a certain professor's deficiencies. He could squeeze a penny hard, especially on minor items—always expected and delivered a tight budget. In his regime salary increases were difficult to come by; if an increase in rank in lieu of salary would satisfy, he would keep the cash and let the credit go. One dean who made overgenerous promises to his faculty, Avery likened to a small boy who in advance of their appearance promised out more kittens to his friends than his expectant mother cat delivered. I can recall being invited to his office and greeted with the comment: "I don't like it for members of the faculty to con-spire *against* the Chancellor, but I've no objection to their conspiring *with* him. Let's do a little conspiring." Out of that particular conspiracy came the selection of Herman G. James to be dean of the College of Arts and Sciences and dean of the Graduate School, both at the same time, a sound as well as frugal idea, I thought. The fewer deans, the better.

Off as well as on the campus Avery was an astute politician. He got along well with his board of regents most of the time, but was content with only a bare majority on his side when he couldn't do better. The board he had to deal with was elected, one from each congressional district, a situation that sometimes brought out the cynic in him. Commenting on the relative merits of appointive and elective boards, I've heard him say: "Whichever you've got, you'll wish it was the other." His frugality and conservatism appealed to the state legislature, which during the years I was in Nebraska showed similar traits. In dealing with politicians, he asserted feelingly that conservative Republicans were the easiest to handle, conservative Democrats next, liberal Democrats considerably more difficult, and liberal Republicans quite the worst of all. I think probably he had something there, even if in those years I did class myself with the last-named group. I had good company. George W. Norris was a United States Senator from Nebraska all the time I lived in the state, and C. A. Sorensen was his able campaign manager. On several occasions I met Norris at Sorensen's house. Sorensen's two sons, later much in the news, were about the ages of my first and second daughters.

Most of my classes at Nebraska were large, particularly in the survey course which filled the Social Science auditorium, but they were all in American history, the students were responsive, and the library facilities were adequate. There was then no pampering of teachers as to the work load. In addition to the survey course, which was designed primarily for sophomores, I taught two lecture courses for upperclassmen, one on the history of the West, and the other on recent American history; also a seminar for graduates. The survey course I had given before at Hamline, but I now included in it for the first time the colonial period, and revised every lecture again and again. The other courses I had never given before, and for several years they absorbed a large part of my time. The day of dependence on graduate students for use as section leaders, or teaching assistants, had not yet dawned in Nebraska, although in large courses we did have paid readers. For this assignment we sometimes chose able undergraduates, a last resort which I deeply deplored and rarely used.

In the history of the West I followed the pattern that Paxson had laid out at Wisconsin, beginning with the colonial frontier of 1763, and following the frontier across the continent, step by step, until 1893, the date Turner delivered his famous paper on "The Significance of the Frontier in American History." An easy, but not always accurate (Nebraska, for example) definition of when a given frontier grew up and could be abandoned to make way for a discussion of its successor was when the territories concerned became states. Sometimes I threw in a few extra lectures at the end in order to bring in the four states admitted later—Utah, Oklahoma, New Mexico, and Arizona. I can recall also lectures comparing the Canadian frontier with the frontier of the United States, and raising questions about a world frontier. I had to put this course together without benefit of Paxson's *A History of the American Frontier* (1924), but as soon as this book appeared it became our text, and sent me scrounging for new lecture material. From the first year, however, we had Turner's collected essays, and made much use of them in the discussion periods I held at regular intervals. For this purpose I divided the class into several small groups, over each of which I presided in person. In my advanced courses I read all the bluebooks myself, and also the term papers I required of each student. This seemed normal to me; my teachers both at Northwestern and at Wisconsin had assumed the same responsibility. Mari Sandoz, whom I had known as an undergraduate, told me later that I had commented favorably on a term paper she wrote for me, noting her admirable understanding of frontier conditions. I'm sure she merited whatever compliments I paid her; her *Old Jules* is one of the most moving narratives of the frontier that I have ever read.

My course in recent American history was not technically so named, for one of my colleagues had preempted that title for a course he gave in current events. So I called the first semester "The Cleveland Era," and the second, "The Roosevelt Era." There was then no occasion to ask which Roosevelt. Partly because of the competition from the current events course, and partly because of rigorous prerequisites laid down to satisfy Dean James, my classes in these courses were very small and very select. Under these conditions I could make use of an informal lecture system that worked very well. I prepared a careful outline from which I could have lectured, if necessary, but instead of trying to do all the talking myself I encouraged the students to contribute whenever their information was adequate. What they didn't say that needed to be said, I tried to provide. Student participation was enthusiastic, and about one hundred per cent for each period. When I succeeded Dean James in 1929 I gave up this course, however, out of deference to my administrative duties. Furthermore, as long as I remained in Nebraska my principal interest lay in the history of the West. It was only after I joined the faculty of the University of Wisconsin that I began to turn definitely toward the twentieth century.

My first efforts to direct graduate work occurred at Nebraska, and it was my great good fortune to welcome a steady stream of really superior graduate students into my seminar. I quickly discovered that an abundance of excellent sources existed for the pioneer period of Nebraska history, and, dedicated Turnerian that I was, I steered my flock in that direction. In Nebraska, and in every other western state in which I have lived, some of the old-timers invariably did a tremendous service to the cause of history by collecting and preserving the records. Impressed as they were with the process of transforming a wilderness into a civilized society, and incidentally with the importance of their own contributions to that end, they made every effort to promote the "remembrance of things past." In general their contribution was strictly antiquarian; they were not in search of hidden meanings or new interpretations. But they kept the sources, and in due time nearly always founded a state historical society to help take care of them. The old-timers got minor assistance from the genealogists, although in the new western areas ancestors beyond a generation or two back always lived somewhere else.

The Nebraska State Historical Society, when I arrived on the scene, still had its principal collection in the ground floor of the old university library. Plans for a new building adjacent to the state capitol had gone awry after the foundation was laid, but the pressure for space was so great that the Society roofed over the basement walls, and installed therein well-filled bookshelves. On occasion I braved an inch or two of water on the floor of this cellar to explore such reserves as were stored there, but for the most part my students and I found what we needed in the Society's campus headquarters. Old newspaper files, territorial and early state documents, pamphlets of every sort and kind, and some manuscript collections provided the all-essential material for historical investigation. As yet, not nearly enough had been done by way of organizing and classifying the Society's treasures, but we had the advantage of two knowledgeable individuals to help us find the items we sought. One was the "superintendent," as he was then called, Dr. Addison E. Sheldon, an old-timer himself, who had been around long enough to know a great many of the Nebraska pioneers and to remember more about them than they had ever known about themselves. The other was the librarian, Mrs. Clara S. Paine, widow of a former superintendent, who patiently directed the search part of our research.

Of great importance to us, also, was a three-volume work by Albert Watkins, the *Illustrated History of Nebraska* (1906–1913), a production of extraordinary merit. Watkins was a native of England who had come to Nebraska by way of Wisconsin and Iowa. As a former school-teacher and newspaper editor, with one foot in politics—he was postmaster of Lincoln from 1885 to 1890, and a leading opponent of free silver—he knew whereof he wrote, and he wrote it well. Part of his *History* was "mug-book," but that part, too, was of great value to us. While Watkins' volumes were by no means complete enough to obviate the need for further research, they did provide us with a springboard to almost every conceivable subject. I made good use of them, and of Sheldon's extraordinary memory, when I was writing more than a score of sketches of early Nebraskans for the *Dictionary of American Biography*.

Most of my graduate students were candidates for the M.A. degree who were either planning to teach, or had already taught, in high school. In those days, fortunately, the requirements for an M.A. included a thesis, and student reports on their progress toward this goal provided the *pièce de résistance* of our seminar. I encouraged each member of the group to find a subject that would have some special meaning for him (or her, as the case might be, for there were always a number of women in the group). The origins of a student's home town, an early Indian outbreak, the opening up of new trails (Nebraska was a highway to the farther West), the building of branch railroads, the careers of prominent citizens, the family trail to Nebraska—all these and many other local subjects furnished grist for our mill. One of the most perspicacious of these theses was Jesse E. Boell's "Bryan Before 1896," which demonstrated among other things the author's genius for digging out original sources. Sometimes the subject led beyond the state borders, but if so, we followed where it led; two such theses that were particularly good were Fern McBride's "Steamboating on the Upper Missouri," and Everett Dick's "The Long Drive."[1] I should have kept a card file indicating by author and title all the master's theses written under my direction, but this was one of my many sins of omission. A few of them that were related in some way to Populism I noted in the bibliography of *The Populist Revolt*.

Only two of my students completed their work for the Ph.D. with me at Nebraska. One of them, Annadora Gregory, wrote about Crete, Nebraska, and Doane College, its particular pride and joy. The other, Charles Lindsay, was from Wyoming, and with my encouragement wrote a thesis, later published, on *The Big Horn Basin* (1932). We lacked most of the material he needed, but he traveled the region over

[1] Dick's thesis was published in the Kansas State Historical Society *Collections*, XVII (1926–1928), 27–97.

and hunted it out from army posts, Indian reservations, town libraries, and the like, a laudable example of both search and research. Lindsay died shortly after receiving his degree, while swimming across the Shoshone River, probably from a heart attack, for he was a powerful swimmer. As a matter of policy I encouraged most of my M.A. students who wished to take a Ph.D. degree to finish their work elsewhere. Among such were Everett Dick, now a professor of history at Union College; J. Martin Klotsche, now chancellor of the University of Wisconsin, Milwaukee; and William F. Zimmerman, now academic vice-president of Midland College, Fremont, Nebraska. Dick and Klotsche took their doctor's degrees at Wisconsin, Zimmerman at Cornell. A. Bower Sageser, now of Kansas State University, at Manhattan, started his Ph.D. work with me, but finished it after I had left for Wisconsin. George T. Hunt also began with me at Nebraska, but followed me to Wisconsin and took his degree there. I like to think, too, that I contributed something to the career of Emma Beekman (Mrs. Aristotle Gavras), whom I knew first as one of Fling's disciples, but who turned to American history and took her Ph.D. in that subject at the University of Southern California. Mrs. Gavras is now a member of the faculty of the Los Angeles Trade-Technical College.

In a very literal sense I worked with my graduate students. The old University of Nebraska library was cramped for space, and we trod on each other's toes as we ransacked its historical resources. In the Historical Society quarters the crowding was even worse. One result of my close proximity to my students was that I was forever at their mercy; when they had a question to ask, it never occurred to them not to interrupt me. Possibly I could have stopped this informality by a slight show of impatience, but I don't recall that the thought ever entered my mind. As a matter of fact I got as much as I gave. My students all knew what my interests were, and the interruptions were often to tell me about some item they had dug up that they thought I would like to have.

Despite its relative youth, the University of Nebraska had even then a good library, partly, no doubt, because of pressure exerted by E. Benjamin Andrews, chancellor from 1900 to 1908. Andrews was a well-rounded scholar, a distinguished historian, and a former president of Brown University. During the 1890's, while still at Brown, he had openly espoused the free silver cause, and when asked by his board of regents to discontinue the airing of his monetary views, had promptly resigned. His action precipitated a terrific row over freedom of speech, and the regents backed down. Andrews withdrew his resignation, but remained at Brown for only one more year before accepting, first the superintendency of the Chicago public schools, then after two years the chancellorship of the University of Nebraska, where his views on free silver were less a liability than an asset. Andrews' activities at Nebraska provide a shining example of the leavening influence of the East on the West. It is true that before his coming the University was already showing signs of an increasing intellectual maturity; Charles E. Bessey, for example, the acting chancellor who preceded Andrews, was one of the nation's leading botanists, while Roscoe Pound, whose pre-eminence in the legal field was soon to be unchallenged, and his sister, Louise Pound, later a great authority on American literature and folk-lore, were already members of the Nebraska faculty. Nevertheless, it is fair to say that under Andrews' guidance the University of Nebraska shook off the last remnants of frontier provincialism and took its place among the important universities of the nation. Will Owen Jones, the brother of Guernsey Jones and the highly intelligent editor of Lincoln's leading daily, no doubt had this thought in mind when he answered the query of a supercilious eastern visitor, "How far east do you have to go to find a really good library?" "To the British Museum," came Jones's instant, if somewhat cryptic, reply.

Whether because of its location in the heart of the Populist country, or because of Andrews' influence, or both, the university library possessed the finest collection of free silver pamphlets I have ever seen, while the Historical Society was rich in Populist lore. My first instinct was naturally to write on Populism in Nebraska, but I discovered that John D. Barnhart, then teaching at Nebraska Wesleyan, had a Harvard Ph.D. dissertation on that subject in the making, while Raymond C. Miller, at the University of Chicago, was engaged in a similar task on Kansas. Since A. M. Arnett's *The Populist Movement in Georgia* (1922) had already appeared, soon to be followed by several other state studies on southern Populism, it seemed evident that the thing for me to do was to aim at an all-over treatment of the subject. Meantime, however, to satisfy the insistent urge for publication, I began to turn out a series of articles on various aspects of the agrarian revolt. During this period I was characterized, not inaptly, by one critic as an "indefatigable monographer," who could write an article but not a book. *The Populist Revolt* (1931) was a long time in coming, I'll have to admit, but in due time it arrived. I dedicated it, appropriately I thought, to my graduate students, many of whom had worked on subjects related to the general theme.

It is only fair to point out, however, that I had benefited greatly from research in libraries other than those of my own university. My previous library contacts had served me well, but I needed to examine much more material that was available only at a distance. In the 1920's grants-in-aid were not as easy to come by as they are now, but I solved this problem in part by accepting summer appointments at other institutions. My first such opportunity was at the University of Minnesota in 1925, but this did little more than to take me back to already familiar sources. The most rewarding of my summer excursions was to George Washington University in 1927. This position I owed to the kindness of Samuel Flagg Bemis, the great authority on American diplomatic history. A fact that came to my attention much later made Bemis's invitation to me seem especially good-tempered. When I was invited to the University of Nebraska, he was the only other person seriously considered for the place, and he could hardly have been less eager to get away from Whitman College in Walla Walla, Washington, than I was to leave Greensboro. As it turned out, however, Bemis went to Washington, D.C., as a research associate of the Carnegie Institution, at about the same time that I went to Nebraska, while the next year he became a professor of history at George Washington. So for his purposes he was much better off than if he had gone to Nebraska. In any event, I owe a great deal to him for having made it possible for me to spend a summer at the national capital.

My classes at George Washington were scheduled for the early morning and the late afternoon in order to suit the convenience of the federal employees, who constituted so large a proportion of the students. This arrangement not only left them free for their regular daily duties, but also enabled me to spend about six hours each day at the Library of Congress. There I dug out much data on the Populists that I had not seen before, most especially from the *National Economist*, the official organ of the southern Alliance, and the *People's Party Paper*, edited and published by Tom Watson. The Library of Congress authorities gave me a study high up in the building, with a view window opening toward the Capitol and the Washington Monument. It was an inspiring setting. By rare good fortune, the summer I was in Washington was one of the coolest the city had known in years—we had a fire in our fireplace on the Fourth of July—so my activities were in no way hampered by the weather.

Two years later I taught my fourth summer term at Northwestern. By this time I was engaged principally in writing rather than research. My location on a campus other than my own, however, was a great boon, for I thus avoided much of the routine work that would have come my way had I stayed in Lincoln. That summer I made good progress with my manuscript.

The fourth and most exciting of the outside appointments I held while a member of the Nebraska faculty was at Harvard, where as visiting lecturer I took over the work of Frederick Merk for the first half year, 1931–1932. Merk remained in Cambridge, however, on leave in residence, so that he was on hand to show me every courtesy. Arthur Schlesinger was also present and equally helpful. I had known Merk while we were both graduate students at the University of Wisconsin, while Schlesinger and I had met frequently at historical association meetings. No doubt I was selected as Merk's stand-in primarily because of my interest in the history of the West, but besides his course for upperclassmen in that subject, I was permitted, also, to give the first half of the large survey course in American history.

I was impressed with the general excellence of the Harvard undergraduates and appreciated the cordiality of their response to my efforts. They had a way then in large lecture courses of applauding lectures that they liked, a type of approval that I had previously associated only with public audiences. My first few lectures in the survey course drew only the customary respectful silence, so I was quite unprepared for the good hand I got on what had seemed to me a particularly difficult and complicated lecture on the American states during the Revolution. Thereafter I always rated some applause, although I could measure very well the degree of my success in the minds of my students by the volume and earnestness of their response. Far more important was the way in which I was obliged, practically every day I lectured, to hold an after-meeting on the platform. Students came up with interesting questions and with polite disagreements. They loved to bait me into whooping it up for the West and discounting the East. The latter stance, with their superb self-conceit, they thought very funny. They were also amused by my confident prediction that in 1932 the United States would elect a Democratic President.

I had three readers as my helpers at Harvard, all candidates for the

Ph.D. degree: Ralph W. Hidy, Raymond P. Stearns, and George W. Adams. We came to know each other very well, and I have followed their subsequent careers with great interest. They have lived up splendidly to the promise they then showed.

One of the amazing things about these trips we took to other campuses was the insouciant way in which we would pack our children and a few necessities in our car and take off confidently for our destination, however distant it might be. The summer I taught in Minnesota, Lucile was very pregnant with our second child, but that fact deterred us not at all. Our one concession to her condition was to rent rooms in a rooming house rather than to take a place by ourselves, as we might have done. We had feared that any extra space might tempt some of our relatives to visit us. As it turned out, both my sister, Hattie, and my mother showed up anyway. By this time Hattie had taken a master's degree in history at Wisconsin, and had a good teaching position in Oshkosh. But she chose this particular summer to get married, and she and her husband, Frank Ducker, spent part of their honeymoon with us. While the newlyweds took a room in another house, they ate with us regularly. When Mother also appeared unexpectedly, we got her a room next to ours. Since the summer proved to be intolerably hot, we would all have been more comfortable in a house where we could have spread out. We never made that mistake again. After summer school, to rest up a little, we drove three hundred miles farther north to spend a few days with the Quigleys at their cabin on an island in Turtle Lake, not far from Bemidji. Our Jane Harriet and their Margaret were then too nearly the same age to live together in peace, so we were soon on our way back to Lincoln again.

All this driving was the more remarkable because of the condition of the roads at that time. Some states, Minnesota among them, had begun systems of good roads, but others, including Iowa and Nebraska, lagged considerably behind. The Nebraska policy was strictly "pay as you build," and dirt roads were still the rule. On one of our return trips from St. James, we decided to take a cutoff from Sioux City to Lincoln, only to involve ourselves in an all-day downpour. Usually Lucile did the driving in emergencies, but that time she lay down on the back seat and cried, while I slithered through the hub-deep mud. On these earlier trips, with Model T Fords and unpredictable roads, we were content to average 150 miles a day. Later, with better cars and better roads, we could do 300 miles or more.

When we went to George Washington, Jane Harriet was five years old and Carolyn was one and one-half. We drove the entire distance, spending the nights at tourist homes, for motels were not yet available, and getting in and out of hotels with small children presented problems. In Mound City, which of course we visited on the way, Lucile ran our car over one of those much-too-high buttons with which in those days small towns often marked the centers of intersections. The impact quite literally knocked the bottom out of our crankcase. A local mechanic picked up the pieces of metal from the road, welded them together again, and by working night and day got us on our way after a long week end. Meanwhile, our five-year-old had broken out with what looked to us like chicken pox, but a kind local doctor diagnosed it as hives and assured us that travel would make it no worse. When we got to Washington, the second daughter broke out with what was unmistakably chicken pox, so that was that. But by this time we were comfortably settled in a Takoma Park house.

The trip to Cambridge outdid all the rest. We started from Lincoln with a new Nash—before this we had had mostly used cars—and with three children, for our Marjorie had arrived only about six months before. To help with the care of the offspring, we took along our maid, Hattie, a girl of perhaps twenty who for a year or more had been practically a member of our family. In those days cars lacked the roomy rear-end trunks that are now standard, and travelers had to strap their baggage on the running boards or on a carrier that folded down over the rear bumper. Lucile conceived the idea of having a deep box built on the rear carrier, a box big enough to hold all our gear, and so equipped we started out. Naturally we had to visit all the relatives who lived along our route, so we stopped first to see Lucile's people in St. James, then the Duckers in Oshkosh. On these occasions, and many others, I had to retrieve much absolutely essential feminine equipment from that big black box. Invariably these necessities had found their way to the very bottom layer. This operation in itself was well calculated to promote family dissension, but the worst was yet to come.

By the time we left Oshkosh we knew that there was something wrong with our engine, but we had about worn out our welcome in that town and felt that we had to be on our way. Our plan was to drive to Manitowoc, take a ferry across Lake Michigan to Ludington or Muskegan—I forget which—drive on through Port Huron to Ontario, visit Niagara Falls again, call on our friends, the Galpins, in Syracuse, and feel our way along through New York and Massachusetts to

Cambridge. We had good maps to guide us, and for the times good roads. But things soon began to happen. When we got to Manitowoc, there was our ship awaiting us, so we drove right on it, congratulating ourselves on having got there just in time. To our consternation, the craft had no sooner got well out on the lake than it began to bear unmistakably north, instead of to the southeast. Only then did we discover that we had taken the wrong ferry and were on our way to Frankfort, fifty miles or more too far north. That in itself would not have been so bad, but within ten miles after we were on the road again our engine began to gasp its last. We made it to a little town called Beulah, found a garage, and discovered that we had a cracked engine block. The new Nash model we had bought turned out to have too small a radiator, and somewhere along the road, when our engine was badly overheated, someone had put in cold water. The Beulah mechanic assured us that, if we could wait around several days, he could extract the damaged engine block and send it to Traverse City to be welded together again.

What to do in the meantime? We found a tourist home for the first night, but it was so terrible that Lucile borrowed a car from the local station agent and went on a hunt for better quarters. Finally she found a summer cottage on nearby Crystal Lake that we could rent, but we would have to provide all our sheets, pillowslips, and towels. Thinking of all those hundreds of freshly laundered diapers in the trunk of the car, she took the house and we lived there for a week while the repairs proceeded according to plan. The weather was warm, the children spent most of the time in the water, and the diapers served numerous purposes for which they had not been intended. Finally our engine was taken apart and put together again. I had grave doubts as to its durability, but there was nothing to do but try it out.

The repair job lasted us across Canada and as far as Syracuse, no farther. So I traded our car in on a used Nash with a whole engine block, and we were soon on our way again. Since there was no place for the big black box on the car we had acquired, we gave the contraption to the Galpins in exchange for an old steamer trunk they found in their attic, then sent the trunk by express to Cambridge. Fortunately, we had allowed ourselves plenty of time for the trip, so that before my teaching duties began we were comfortably located in an Arlington Heights house and our two older children were in school, learning from their Irish classmates how to speak New England English.

Our trip home in late January, 1932, was less eventful, but we were plenty crowded on the first lap. One of our favorite friends from Lucile's college days was a former school nurse at Hamline, Mamie Doebler Mack. "Doebie," as everyone called her, was a tall, red-haired, freckled-faced marvel of efficiency and good humor. Whenever we had serious illness in the family, or a new baby to be cared for, Doebie always responded to our plea for help. Our Marjorie, almost from birth, had had serious ear infections, and developed one that Christmas. Maybe there were other reasons why Doebie was in Cambridge, but at any rate when we started for home she was with us. We decided to go back by way of New York, where Doebie would leave us for another adventure, and see something of the city. New England winters can be at their worst in January, but our luck was good and we set out in perfect weather. We had expected to find a tourist home on the outskirts of the city, but we arrived on a Sunday with traffic at a minimum, and almost before we knew it we were all the way downtown. I remembered a little hotel on Forty-second Street where Galpin and I had stayed years before, and parked our car in front of it while I investigated rates. When I asked the clerk what he could do for a lone man with six women—Lucile, Doebie, Hattie, and the three daughters —on his hands, he showed becoming sympathy and, believe it or not, put us all up comfortably for nine dollars a night. The depression was still on. After a short stay in New York we drove uneventfully across New Jersey, Pennsylvania, Ohio, Indiana, Illinois, and Iowa before we met our first snow. Only from Omaha to Lincoln was there any serious evidence of winter.

The Populist Revolt made its initial appearance in print while I was in Cambridge. Among my colleagues, Arthur Schlesinger and Paul Buck read it approvingly, while from Henry Steele Commager, whom I hardly knew, I received a heartening letter. Contemporary reviews were for the most part flattering, but a generation later the book became a frequent target of revisionists. Except for a few minor points, my critics did not challenge my findings factually, but they did object to some of my interpretations. By this time I could, in certain instances, agree with them, although seemingly it never occurred to anyone that events of the intervening years might have changed my mind on anything. For example, when I wrote *The Populist Revolt* I was still uncritical, as were most American historians, of Turner's theories, and found greater significance in the passing of the frontier than I would now think reasonable. As I saw matters then, the lack of a new frontier to which to go was an important consideration, alike for the distressed farmers of the West, where the frontier had only lately disappeared, and for those of the South, where the Civil War and Reconstruction had virtually revived post-frontier conditions. While this line of thought was not altogether without merit, I would now give greater emphasis to the effects of the agricultural revolution, and particularly to the increasingly international aspects of American farm marketing. As a matter of fact, early in 1954, well before the publication of Richard Hofstadter's criticisms in *The Age of Reform* (1955), I wrote a little piece in this vein for Broadcast Music, Inc., which no doubt reached a few listeners over the air, and two years later was published in *The American Story* (1956), edited by Earl Schenk Miers.

My statement that the Populists had begun "the last phase of a long and perhaps a losing struggle . . . to save agricultural America from the devouring jaws of industrial America" has also received criticism. While the farmers are now in a small minority, it can be argued that they are doing all right, and they certainly haven't been devoured. They began to prosper, indeed, even before World War I, and they certainly prospered during it. Such emotion as my statement reveals, however, can be traced readily to the time in which it was written. During World War I the American farmers had responded cordially to the slogan "Food will win the war," and had achieved a capacity to produce in greater quantities than they could market profitably after normal production began again in Europe. While the war was on, the federal government had fixed agricultural prices at a lower figure than the law of supply and demand would have warranted, but after the war it took off its price supports, and allowed the farmers' income to drop abysmally. Throughout the decade of the 1920's the holders of power in Washington branded nearly every farmer effort to get government help as "economically unsound," while at the same time defending the necessity of a high protective tariff and other benefits for manufacturers. It is possible that my sympathy for the earlier movement of protest was compounded by the conditions I saw about me. A quarter of a century later, when the farmers had learned after World War II how to obtain substantial governmental aid, the situation had a quite different look, although hardly anyone would now deny the overwhelming superiority of industry over agriculture.

Perhaps a few other items stressed by the revisionists are worthy of note. Some of them have taken my observation that many Populist demands won later acceptance to mean that I regarded nineteenth-century Populism as the primary cause of twentieth-century Progressivism. I would not so interpret my comments; certainly the Progressive urbanites had many quite separate reasons of their own for embracing so much of the Populist program. I will concede cheerfully that I did not evaluate adequately the importance of middle-class participation in the twentieth-century reform movement until after the publication of George E. Mowry's *The California Progressives* (1951), but I was writing about the Populists, not the Progressives. My failure to brand the Populists as anti-Semites and nativists also worried some critics, but I think that the critics were much farther off base than I was. Indeed, later investigations seem to show that the Populists were, if anything, more charitable toward the Jews and the foreigners than were the general run of Americans. As for the argument of some so-called new conservatives that the Populists introduced into American politics a spirit of demagogic intolerance and authoritarianism that culminated in the activities of such persons as Senator Joseph R. McCarthy of Wisconsin, there could hardly have been a more glaring misrepresentation. The Populists favored the use of governmental power to restrain misconduct on the part of the great corporations only because there was no other power strong enough to protect the agricultural interest. Undoubtedly they put too much faith in the efficacy of legislation, but this was—and is—an all-American, not strictly a Populist, trait.

Sometime during the middle 1920's Guernsey Jones became incapacitated because of illness, and I took over from him the chairmanship of the Department of History. This task involved much less paper work than is almost universal in departmental offices today, and I held down the job without so much as a part-time secretary or typist. I had only one department meeting during my four years as chairman, for the clashing personalities within our group made it completely impossible to transact any business that way. So I gathered support for what I thought should be done by consulting individually with each member. Quite obviously we needed new blood, and we achieved some results along this line. As a first step, to take over Professor Jones's work in English history, we brought in Glenn Gray, a Notestein Ph.D. from Cornell, whose course in English constitutional history, a pre-law requirement, greatly pleased the Law School faculty.

It was a matter of deep concern to me that we had no one in the department primarily interested in either ancient or medieval history, and as a long step in the right direction we succeeded in adding to our staff Charles Henry Oldfather, a Wisconsin Ph.D. who had studied under Westermann and Rostovtzeff and had taught for ten years at Wabash College. While classics departments, in these days when students of the "dead" languages are not very numerous, readily volunteer to take over courses in ancient history, it has always seemed important to many of us in the historical profession that the history of the ancient world should be taught by historians. Too often the classicists are primarily interested in philology, and as history teachers approach their subject more from the language than from the historical point of view. Oldfather was a great tower of strength to the department and the university; eventually he succeeded me, first as chairman, then as dean. In medieval history we first brought in John L. La Monte, a Harvard Ph.D. who left us for Minnesota after two years, then Robert L. Reynolds, who after a similar interval returned to Wisconsin. We then got Edgar N. Johnson, a Chicago Ph.D. who stayed at Nebraska for a long time. The Department of History also collaborated with the State Historical Society to invite James L. Sellers, a Wisconsin Ph.D. then teaching at Wisconsin, to join us, giving part of his time to the Society and part to courses in American history. Sellers soon came over full-time to the department, which he served with great distinction for the rest of his teaching career.

I had no faintest desire to become an administrator, beyond such limited duties as I exercised as chairman, and I can honestly say that the deanship I held at Nebraska sought me out, not the reverse. When Dean James left Nebraska in 1929 to become president of the University of South Dakota, his double deanship was divided between my friend Fred Upson as dean of the Graduate School, and me as dean of the College of Arts and Sciences. Since John Senning at the same time took over as chairman of the political science department, a post James had also held, James took great delight in pointing out that it took three men to replace him. Perhaps I should have declined a job in which I felt so little interest, but I accepted it in part to keep it out of more ambitious hands. I had come to believe—and this is still my opinion—that our universities suffer much from over-administration. I knew that I had no desire for power and would interfere as little as possible with the prerogatives of the teaching staff. Despite my fancy title, I still considered myself primarily a teacher, and proved it both by giving up my chairmanship and by retaining three out of the four courses I taught.

I suppose I was really not a very good dean; certainly my heart wasn't much in the job. I inherited from Dean James an efficient secretary, Florence Beers, who knew the routine of the office and discharged her responsibilities well. It never occurred to me to seek additional clerical help; we had enough. Indeed, my first two decisions as dean nearly put our office out of commission. I directed, first, that we would keep no records available elsewhere in the University, and second, that there would be no revision of the Arts and Sciences requirements for degrees while I was dean. Like most such faculties, ours had tended to change the requirements so often that the ink was hardly dry on one new plan before another new plan was adopted; it was a rarity for a senior to graduate under the requirements that existed when he was a freshman. I had lived through enough revisions of the curriculum to realize how like such an ordeal was to a general revision of the tariff by Congress. Every department, like every economic interest, was out to get all it could for its own aggrandizement. This was natural enough, for every instructor who was worth his salt thought of his subject as fundamental to learning. But the log-rolling necessary to get any agreement among the various contenders for spoils would almost put Congress to shame. University professors are terrible infighters; they operate with no holds or weapons barred. So while I was dean we avoided this kind of bloodshed.

It was my policy also to interfere as little as possible with the various departments. I had the duty of selecting departmental chairmen, and during my two and one-half years as dean I exercised this prerogative once, when after much consultation I brought in Thomas M. Raysor, a Harvard Ph.D., to head the English department. I remember Raysor best for a great personal service he did me. Once he called at my office to ask if I had any manuscripts that I would like him to read critically; he was fresh out of such punishment, and missed it. I handed him a typed copy of *The Populist Revolt*, which I had not yet submitted to a publisher. He brought it back a day or two later with some excellent suggestions, and the flattering comment: "This is a good book. It will make your reputation."

As dean I also had annual budget recommendations to make, the most serious and time-consuming of my duties. The budget sheets we used displayed three columns, one for the chairmen, one for the appropriate dean, and one for the chancellor—the final answer. I always conferred with the chairmen before they made their recommendations and tried to hold them down to figures that would be acceptable on high. As a result, the chairmen's figures and the dean's figures were usually identical, and were usually accepted, for I knew in advance about how much the Chancellor would assign to Arts and Sciences. I had no separate dean's budget, except barely enough to carry my office, and happily no largesse of any kind to distribute. Nor did I have any responsibility for student discipline; I would never have taken the job had it called for such duties. We had a separate dean of students on whom that responsibility fell, poor chap.

Despite the limited interpretation I placed on my duties, I did, however, attempt to assert some leadership. Unfortunately, I had not yet learned the first rule of effective university administration. Under no circumstances should a president, or a chancellor, or a provost, or a dean appear to have any ideas. If he wants something done, he should carefully and unobtrusively plant the thought in some unexpected place, wait patiently for it to take root and grow, act as surprised and suspicious of the idea as possible when it is brought to his attention, then yield reluctantly to overwhelming pressure. One thing I thought a dean should do was to read the catalogue. This is by no means a simple undertaking, and if persisted in too long at a time is guaranteed to produce migraine. But I tried. One thing I discovered was that many courses seemed to overlap with many others, and I thought something ought to be done about it. I found, for example, that there were at least five separate courses in statistics, given in as many different departments. Why, I innocently suggested, should there not be one course in the fundamentals of the subject, then, if necessary, others building on this foundation? I soon discovered that I had stirred up a veritable hornets' nest—there were at least fifty good reasons why this could never be done. Before the statistical confusion that resulted, I retired in some disorder.

I had another idea, by no means original, but it seemed good to me. One problem of the College of Arts and Sciences was that every other undergraduate college—Teachers, Engineering, Business Administration, and the like—made use of Arts and Sciences courses to fill out its curriculum; in some of them, indeed, our courses provided from three-fourths to four-fifths of their programs. Not only that, the professional schools, Law and Medicine, designated certain courses we gave as pre-law and pre-medic requirements, and kept a sharp eye on their content. Because of outside insistence, we felt obliged to offer certain special courses, business English, for example, that of our own free will we would hardly have thought necessary. For our own freshmen we required a three-hour course in English, but some of the other colleges were unwilling to spend so much time on so unimportant a subject, so for their benefit we offered a two-hour watered-down substitute. Our beginning mathematics course, I always thought, represented less what our mathematicians thought desirable than what the Engineering faculty wanted us to teach their students. Arts and Sciences was thus to a very great extent a mere service college for other schools and colleges, and had no real soul of its own. For this situation, which still exists to some extent in nearly every American university, I think now that there is probably no remedy, but I wondered then out loud why all parties concerned shouldn't agree on a common program for the first two years and begin their divergences thereafter. I would even have given up my cherished dream of avoiding curriculum revisions if by so doing we could all have adopted the same requirements for the freshman and sophomore years. Well, this trial balloon was shot down so fast that I couldn't even find the fragments. So I gave up reform.

I also found out that I couldn't trust reporters. For what reason, I don't quite know, but in general it seems true that the newspaper world is determined to make university professors look as ridiculous as possible. Once, in talking with an affable reporter from an Omaha newspaper, I dwelt on some of the problems described above, and facetiously —I thought—quoted Hartley Burr Alexander, a distinguished professor of philosophy who had recently left Nebraska for Scripps College. Disgusted with the way in which students worked more for degrees than for an education, Alexander suggested that society could save itself much trouble by awarding degrees at birth. All babies weighing nine pounds or more should receive a Ph.D. degree; all eight-pound babies, an M.A.; all seven-pound babies, a B.A.; all six-pounders and under, a teacher's certificate. The reporter panned me roundly for making light of serious things, and his story went all over the country. I received numerous letters of protest, most of them from teachers college professors who were angry that I had placed their product so low on the totem pole. I never again tried to be funny with a reporter.

Three episodes made me regret deeply that I had ever become a dean. After Avery retired, the regents made Dean Edgar A. Burnett of the College of Agriculture acting chancellor, partly because he was the oldest of the deans and was not regarded seriously as a candidate for chancellor. As acting chancellor, Burnett leaned over backward to seek faculty advice and conciliate faculty opinion. Because of this characteristic, many of us urged that he be made chancellor, even though his term of office might be short; and this was done. But as chancellor he no longer felt the need of faculty advice, and took many actions that I, at least, could not approve. One was the very harsh treatment he meted out to two faculty members who made the mistake of drinking some yeast beer (this was during the prohibition era) at a student party in a campus building. I defended these men before the board of regents, while the dean of the Law School—a somewhat better lawyer—acted as prosecutor. The punishment assessed was out of all proportion to the crime; but it would have been even worse had not a lawyer on the board detected from the evidence (as I did not) that the whole thing was almost, if not quite, a frame-up, or at the very least a double cross. On another occasion a member of the sociology department was offered his salary for the rest of the year to resign and get out of town. His crime was that, while he and his wife were out at a party, a baby sitter at his house had misbehaved with a boy friend, whose influential father insisted that the wicked sociologist was somehow to blame. Knowing full well that I would protest, the Chancellor directed that the story be kept from me until the victim had left the state.

The third episode had to do with the depression. Nebraska salaries were then pitifully low, but at least we had salaries. Nevertheless, the Chancellor decided that, to conciliate public opinion, all salaries should be lowered by a flat 10 per cent. This action was ordered in the middle of a biennium, with the money to run the university for the coming year already appropriated. Nor was the sum thus saved returned to the state treasury; it was spent, most of us thought, for far less important things than teachers' salaries. I reminded the Chancellor that President Hoover, as a means of holding the depression in check, had urged businessmen not to reduce wages or salaries, and I remember well the reply I got. "That's one point," the Chancellor asserted firmly, "on which Hoover was wrong." When in the spring of 1932 I received an invitation to join the Department of History of the University of Wisconsin at the same salary I was receiving at Nebraska, I accepted without first referring the matter to the Chancellor. It is only fair to admit, however, that I would have accepted this offer under any circumstances. Professionally it was a long step forward, and I didn't want to be a dean anyway.

Glad as I was to escape from my administrative perplexities, it was not easy for me, or for my wife, to leave Nebraska. It was almost like leaving home again; many of our happiest memories are associated with the years we spent in Lincoln. We came with one small daughter; we left with three, only one of whom was still very small. We came with a few acquaintances; we left with many close friends, the kind one doesn't lose by separation, but for that reason misses all the more. We can never forget the generous welcome we received as we arrived, nor the continuing evidence of good will that accompanied us as we went on our way. My students, whom I had not forsaken when I became a dean, were a constant joy, perhaps the most appreciative students I have ever taught. They flocked to my office, and I received them gladly; they sent me flowers when I was ill; they gave me some carefully chosen books when I met them last; in the days of a well-known "gloomy dean," they called me the "jolly dean." The faculty I had sought to serve were equally gracious; I think that I retained the confidence of an overwhelming majority of them to the end. They had a going-away dinner for us and gave us presents, a part of the middle western way of life that we understood and liked. It was hard to leave, and maybe we should have stayed. But one can't have it both ways; we did what we thought we had to do.

IX. Wisconsin (Part 1)

My CALL to the University of Wisconsin came in 1932, shortly after our return from Cambridge, and while the Great Depression was almost at its worst. I did not go directly from Lincoln to Madison, for I had long before promised to teach in the 1932 summer session of West Virginia University and felt obliged to keep my word. Normally the family would have gone with me to Morgantown, but our oldest daughter chose that particular time to contract pneumonia and was in no condition to travel. I felt guilty about leaving all the packing and moving to Lucile, but apparently not guilty enough to do anything about it. I doubt if I could be so callous today. By a stroke of luck one of my Nebraska colleagues, a distinguished architect, was driving east with his wife and young son at exactly the same time that I needed to go to Morgantown, so I rode with him and shared expenses as far as Uniontown, Pennsylvania, a good break for both of us. This was the summer of the Bonus Army—the B.E.F.—and we saw many veterans along the road, some accompanied by their families, hitchhiking their way toward Washington. It was not a pleasant sight.

My six weeks at Morgantown, in the heart of the coal-mining area, opened my eyes still further as to the real meaning of the depression. The house I lived in overlooked the Monongahela River, and one day, as I took in the spectacular view, I was startled to see a long column of men on the opposite side of the river advancing like an army toward the bridge—a march on the city of unemployed coal miners. Word of their coming had apparently preceded them, for as I watched, a delegation of city officials crossed the bridge to meet them. After a brief conference the marchers did an about-face and departed the way they had come. The promise that restrained them, as I soon learned, was not jobs, but food. By this time the local relief funds in West Virginia—city, county, and state—were exhausted, but fortunately the national government had agreed at last to lend money to the states for relief

154

purposes. Later I visited some of the mines. Coal at the tipple brought seventy-five cents a ton, when it could be sold at all. Miners were lucky if they got one day of work a week. The mining villages, with their drab, unpainted houses, were a horror; on the streets the people walked listlessly about, when they bothered to walk at all, as in a slow-motion movie. It was time for a change.

In Chicago, as I passed through on the way to Wisconsin, I saw still more evidence of the depression. Arriving early on a hot August morning, with some time to wait before I left for Madison, I walked along Michigan Avenue and saw hundreds of men sleeping in the doorways of buildings, on park benches, or anywhere they could find enough space to lay themselves down. Some of them had covered their heads with newspapers. It was daylight, but they all seemed to be asleep; perhaps they lacked the will to wake up and face the day. I found my way to a hotel and waited in the lobby until it was time to catch my northbound train.

Meanwhile Lucile had successfully moved all our worldly goods from Lincoln to Madison, and was at the station with our three daughters, Jane Harriet (ten years old), Carolyn (six and one-half), and Marjorie (one and one-half), to meet me. She had also rented us a house on the edge of Madison's University Heights district, a house quite comparable to the one we had left unsold in Lincoln—the depression again. The rental, to be sure, was about twice the sum of the monthly payments we were making on our Lincoln house—the first, but by no means the last, of a number of financial surprises that came our way. Pending the time when we could take over our new domicile, Bob and Sarah Reynolds, whom we had known while Bob was teaching at Nebraska, absorbed us into their family; but the occupants of our new house were slow about moving out, so to relieve the Reynolds family of their self-imposed burden, we took a little cottage in Shorewood Hills near Lake Mendota and stayed there a week or so. Four years later we traded in our Lincoln house on a handsome dwelling of colonial design in Shorewood Hills, and lived in that delightful suburb the rest of our stay in Wisconsin.

We were quickly at home in Madison. I had become familiar with the place as a graduate student, and some of the old connections still endured. Paul Knaplund, chairman of the history department, I had known since 1919, when he and I had taught together in a Wisconsin summer session. Paul and his wife, Dorothy, received us cordially and helped us get acquainted. Mrs. Marvin B. Rosenberry, wife of the Chief Justice, whom I remembered as Lois Kimball Mathews, professor of history and dean of women, threw a formal dinner party for us at which we were introduced to Governor Philip F. LaFollette, and Mrs. LaFollette. The university community accepted us as if we had always been there. Walter Sharp of the political science department and his wife, Doris, lived only a half block from us, and were soon our intimate friends. Fortunately, we were still young enough to form the kind of friendships that only youth can cement. When we get older we tend to build walls around ourselves that neither we nor our new acquaintances can ever get through. As a young married couple with children we fraternized easily and understandingly with other young couples who had children. The city of Madison, like Lincoln, had only two primary interests, the university and the state government; most residents, directly or indirectly, sold their services to one or the other. For better or for worse, the university faculty kept pretty well to itself, although the relations between town and gown were not unfriendly, and there was some crossing of caste lines.

The history department had changed greatly since my graduate-student days. Munro and Dennis and Westermann had all gone east, and Sellery had become dean of Letters and Science. The "big three" in American history under whom I had studied—Fish, Paxson, and Root—had ceased to exist. Root had gone to the University of Iowa as head of its history department; Paxson had left for the University of California, Berkeley; Fish was dead. Paxson's acceptance of a California offer was what paved the way for my return to Wisconsin. When in the spring of 1932 he made his decision known to the department, Fish was still alive and, as the obvious choice to replace Paxson as chairman, began his search for a new man (or so I was told) by removing my book, *The Populist Revolt*, from the office shelf and taking it home with him. In a matter of days he wrote me what he chose to call a "love letter," inviting me to join the Wisconsin staff. Of course I accepted. The news of Paxson's going and my coming, at a time when academic transfers were relatively scarce, attracted the attention of *Time*, which noted the double move, but not without its customary flippancy.[1] Shortly afterward word reached me of Fish's death from a streptococcic throat infection. To take over his teaching duties the department's choice fell upon William B. Hesseltine, a Virginian by

[1] Vol. XIX (May 30, 1932), p. 32.

birth and an Ohio State Ph.D. Bill and I arrived in Madison at the same time, and together with Curtis Nettels, who had replaced Root in Colonial history a few years before, we began the awesome task of trying to restore the prestige of American history at Wisconsin. In this undertaking, as in all other departmental efforts, we could rely on the courage, good judgment, and tenacity of our chairman, Paul Knaplund, and the extraordinary political acumen of our dean, George Sellery.

Paxson's departure was perhaps unnecessary. Years later he told me that if, after Fish's death, anyone in authority at Wisconsin had asked him to stay, he would have done so. This would not necessarily have meant my elimination, for I could have taken over Fish's work. I have always felt that Paxson's decision to leave came mainly from the distaff side. Helen Paxson was a tall, handsome, imperious woman of Philadelphia Main Line standards who respected conventions and showed some disdain for those who did not. Fish's wife, Jeanne ("Janie"), whom he had married when they were neither very young, was of French origin, small, dark, and volcanic, a character actress who dearly loved an impish role and with a few mischievous remarks could blow any genteel conversation to bits. Fish and Paxson respected and admired each other, and in academic matters stood firmly together. But Janie's devotion to the startling and unexpected could hardly have set well with Helen. I have no footnotes to offer for this unsolicited opinion. But I knew both women well, and I'll bet a dollar. . . .

My classroom duties at Wisconsin followed closely the pattern I had cut at Nebraska. In the 1930's the notion that only research mattered and that teaching was relatively unimportant had made little headway at Wisconsin; at least in the Department of History good teaching not only was expected, it was demanded. Failure to excel along this line was as certain a road to disaster as failure to publish. Tradition demanded also that the beginning courses in each subject be taught by a senior professor; beginners, it was assumed, couldn't do much to harm upperclassmen, but freshmen and sophomores needed to be inspired, and deserved the best we had to give. Since Hesseltine was much younger than I was, and relatively untried, and since Nettels' speciality lay in the colonial period, it fell to my lot to take over Fish's large survey course in American history. I could not be Fish—I could only be myself—but I heard few complaints. When, after a few years, it became apparent that Hesseltine would be at least equally effective with beginners, he took over the survey and made an institution of it.

Bill and I became devoted friends and remained so for all the rest of his life, although we disagreed violently on nearly every important issue, whether related to historical interpretation or to current events. In his specialized courses he continued Fish's interest in slavery, the Civil War, and Reconstruction, while I kept on with recent and western history. With Nettels increasingly recognized as one of the nation's leading colonialists, we three pretty well covered the American field. Maybe Wisconsin was no longer what it had been in the olden days— we had to live with that refrain—but it was still on the map. We added others to our group as opportunity offered, among them Fred Harvey Harrington, now president of the university, and Earl Pomeroy, now professor of history at the University of Oregon. But with a depression budget to restrain us, our possibilities for expansion were limited.

The two courses for undergraduates on which I concentrated principally were the history of the West and recent American history. I had worked hard on the former at Nebraska, and did what I could at Wisconsin to maintain the reputation that the course had achieved under its originator, Frederick Jackson Turner, and his successor, Frederic Logan Paxson. I was flattered, rather than offended, when now and then comments appeared on the Turner-Paxson-Hicks over-emphasis on western history. But I found that the recent American course demanded more and more of my time and thought. The whole subject was in a constant state of flux. When I first began to teach the course the beginning date was 1873, omitting only the political aspects of Reconstruction. But gradually the beginning date had to be moved forward to make way for unfolding events at the end. By the time I left Wisconsin we were starting with Bryan and 1896. Paxson's *Recent History of the United States*, which appeared first in 1921 and was repeatedly revised, gave us a text, but historians were now giving serious attention to the post-Reconstruction decades, and new interpretations followed one another with bewildering rapidity. In the concluding lectures of the course I was forever building a new bridge to the present, then rebuilding it again and again and again. I wonder now what my earliest lectures on the New Deal and the outbreak of World War II must have been like. They were certainly drawn from the rawest kind of source material; nothing else was then available.

I came to believe very earnestly in the worthwhileness of recent history. It seemed axiomatic that the present could be understood only in the light of the past. But if historians were to skip the recent past simply because the perspective was somewhat blurred and the facts were not yet all in, the usefulness of history in evaluating the present and in planning for the future would be correspondingly diminished. It was up to the history guild, or so it seemed to me, to put the events of the just retreating years into the most meaningful pattern possible. I worked at this task with all my heart, and made it a point to include in my last lecture news gleaned from the morning papers.

During my later years at Wisconsin I offered a one-semester course in American social history. After the publication of the Schlesinger-Fox "History of American Life" series, such a course became almost mandatory in American universities; and with our cramped financial resources it was apparent that either we would drop behind the procession or I would have to give the course. It was an interesting experience. I ruled out as completely as possible all political and economic factors, then tried to piece the remaining fragments together into a sensible pattern. There was some truth in the remark of Paxson, which I suspect he borrowed from someone else, that the undertaking was not unlike trying to nail jelly to the wall. Political and economic history weave together readily and provide an almost essential background for every other kind of history. Remove them, and a reliable scheme of organization is hard to find. The device to which I resorted was the examination of cross sections of American life and thought at intervals about a generation apart; if the students already knew their political and economic history, the plan worked very well. Later, at the University of California, I lengthened this course to two semesters and offered it for a number of years. The students ate it up; I think it was the most popular course I ever gave, probably because the subject matter so readily lent itself to hilarity. I never felt comfortable with the course, however, and at the first opportunity turned it over to someone else.

Teaching history to undergraduates at a university the size of Wisconsin meant primarily lecturing to them. In the beginning courses we had assistants who once each week met the students in small groups, and in the history of the West I continued the practice I had begun at Nebraska of dividing my class into three or four sections for occasional informal discussions, which I led in person. But with classes numbering often well into the hundreds there was no alternative to lecturing. The wholesale denunciation of this system of instruction, so common now among critics of our educational procedures, is not entirely warranted. If the lecturer is as deeply devoted to his work as he ought to be, he can communicate his interest to his students. He will be at pains not to bore them by a droning recital of dead facts; rather he will show by example how exciting it can be to think one's way through a succession of historical relationships. He can, and should, present the latest thought on any given topic, together with such shadings as may derive from his own reflections. He can, and should, tell his students where they can look for further light on the subject and for alternative points of view. He can, and should, whenever opportunity offers, relate what went on at an earlier time with what goes on today. He will find that the very task of giving oral expression to his ideas tends to sharpen them, and sometimes leads to flashes of insight that he might otherwise never have had. Some of my very best thoughts, as I esteem them, have come to me in this way.

Apologists for the lecture system can argue also that the conscientious lecturer dares not face his class unprepared; indeed, the larger the class, the more insistent the need for careful preparation. The lecturer must have thought out in advance exactly what he means to say; in practice he may say more, or less, or something quite different, but he should never be driven to careless improvisation. He must know, also, how to hold the attention of his class, how to get his message across. And he'd better *have* a message; if he does not his students will be quick to recognize that fact and to turn their thoughts to better ends. It is quite true that not every good teacher can lecture effectively to large classes; our universities should take cognizance of this fact and make their teaching assignments accordingly. Certainly this was the the policy of the Wisconsin Department of History, both when I was there as a graduate student, and later when I was a member of the faculty. Sometimes the men we had to use as lecturers let us down, but in recruiting we made every effort to take on only scholars with some promise of platform ability.

Why classroom discussions are generally considered so superior to lectures as a teaching device, I fail to see. Chronically, half or more of any student group will arrive on the scene totally unprepared. Every teacher knows the anguish involved in first pumping ideas into a class, then pumping them out again. He knows, too, the irritating loss of time due to dealing with bluffers and smart alecks—a few of both are almost always on hand. Perhaps the discussions do more than the lectures to promote self-expression on the part of a few students, but it should not be forgotten that the art of listening is also one which needs cultivation, and that students can learn much about how to express themselves by hearing someone else express himself well. On the whole, lectures tend to make reasonable terms with the varying abilities of the students. The superior students get a lot from what they hear, the average students get something, and even the poorer students generally get a little. Competently led section meetings, held after the lectures and designed to promote discussion of both the lectures and the assigned readings, can be very helpful. But when I hear university graduates commenting on the great teachers under whom they have studied, the great teachers, more often than not, turn out to have been great lecturers.

Regrettably, term papers, or "topics," to use the local metonymy, once almost always required in upperclass history courses at Wisconsin, were by the 1930's no longer so universal. An extra credit for such a task was common, but the problem of overwhelming numbers had greatly weakened the usefulness of this excellent teaching device. The descent toward so-called objective tests, however, had only barely begun, and essay-type examinations, read by the instructor himself, were the rule in all advanced courses. I may be wrong, but my impression is that the proportion of students who were unable to write acceptable English was smaller then than it is today. On my desk as I write is a letter, just received from a student in a neighboring college, addressing me as "Proffesser."

My graduate students, considering the numbers involved, absorbed a disproportionately large share of my time. The depression, and no doubt also the changes in teaching personnel, cut down our seminar enrollments by perhaps half, but even so my group rarely, if ever, numbered less than a dozen. I soon learned that the earliest frontier of Wisconsin, unlike that of Nebraska when I arrived on the scene there, had already received much attention, both from such distinguished scholars as Reuben Gold Thwaites, Louise Phelps Kellogg, and Joseph Schafer, and also from a host of graduate students brought up on the frontier diet by Turner and Paxson. I observed, too, that the State Historical Society of Wisconsin, thanks to the collecting efforts of Lyman Draper and others, had acquired the sources necessary for regional as well as statewide studies. I signed a few theses that dealt with an early frontier, such, for example, as Lena Mitchell Jamison's "The Natchez Trace," [2] and George T. Hunt's *The Wars of the*

---

[2] *Journal of Mississippi History*, I (April 1939), 82–99.

Iroquois (1940), for the supervision of which Louise Kellogg provided more expert assistance than I was able to give. But in general the theses that came out of my seminar, even when they began in frontier times, extended well beyond that period into the post-frontier years, such, for example, as Robert Fries's *Empire in Pine* (1951), which traced the story of lumbering in Wisconsin from 1830 to 1900, or Clare Marquette's "The Business Activities of C. C. Washburn," whose career in Wisconsin and Minnesota spanned a period of four decades, beginning in the 1840's.

The importance of post-frontier developments gave point to Turner's corollary hypothesis on the significance of sections in American history; a number of his essays that emphasized this theme were published in a book by that title the year I came to Wisconsin. As time went on I found my interest turning away from the frontier and more and more toward the history of the whole section in which I had lived most of my life, the Middle West. Indeed, I conceived the idea of writing a history of this section from the earliest times to the present that would point up its continuing significance in the life of the nation. No longer could I regard the frontier—if ever I had—as an adequate key to American development; in particular, economic influences, both national and international, were essential to the understanding of nation and section alike. One of my graduate students, Benton H. Wilcox, in a Ph.D. thesis and a published article, "An Historical Definition of Frontier Radicalism," [3] made it quite obvious that frontier radicalism could "be explained most clearly by practical economic factors rather than by reference to frontier psychology," while numerous other critics of pure Turnerianism began to appear.

My proposed history of the Middle West failed to materialize, although Turner himself in his posthumous book, *The United States, 1830–1850* (1935), produced a hundred-page chapter that was admirable as far as it went. My own contribution was confined mainly to two essays that originated as papers read at historical meetings, "The Development of Civilization in the Middle West, 1860–1900," and "Our Own Middle West, 1900–1940." [4] In these papers I tried to argue that the culture of the Middle West was not merely derivative,

[3] *Mississippi Valley Historical Review*, XXVI (December 1939), 377–394.

[4] *Sources of Culture in the Middle West*, ed. Dixon Ryan Fox (1934), pp. 73–101; *Democracy in the Middle West, 1840–1940*, ed. Jeanette P. Nichols and James G. Randall (1941), pp. 97–117.

as some eastern historians seemed to think, but had an originality of its own based both upon its more recent frontier experience and upon its equally free access to world influences. The West, I insisted, was less the child of the East than a bright—maybe brighter—younger sister who had enjoyed much the same educational opportunities but had drawn a less affluent husband. My more mature reflections along this line I published years later in an essay somewhat curiously entitled (not by me) "A Political Whirlpool," in *The Heritage of the Middle West*, edited by John J. Murray (1958). In this article I took account of the rise of great cities in the Middle West, a subject generally ignored by Turnerians. Had I remained longer in Wisconsin, it is just possible that I might have written the book I had in mind.

My interest in the twentieth century, however, soon began to overshadow my interest in the Middle West. With the New Deal unfolding before our eyes, I found my graduate students, and I with them, eager to undertake studies that would provide background for and perhaps explain the reform impulse that was currently in the ascendancy. As for Populism, we tended to regard that subject as a bit passé, although Leon Fuller, a holdover from Paxson, made an excellent study of Populism in Colorado.[5] Our interest tended to center, rather, on the Progressive movement, both state and national. I can recall theses dealing with the course of reform in such neighboring states as Missouri, Iowa, and Minnesota, but because of the inaccessibility of the LaFollette papers, none on Wisconsin. It was in my seminar, also, that George E. Mowry began his work on *Theodore Roosevelt and the Progressive Movement* (1946), the first of his three excellent volumes on this and related subjects.[6] As for my own activities, I set myself the task of finding out what had happened to the farmers of the Middle West after the decline of Populism. This undertaking would either fit into my larger study of the Middle West, or would perhaps become a book all by itself. I wangled a research assistant, Theodore Saloutos, to help me with this work, but in the end it was he who wrote the book, while I became little more than a silent partner in the enterprise.[7]

[5] "Colorado's Revolt Against Capitalism," *Mississippi Valley Historical Review*, XXI (December 1934), 343–360.

[6] The two others are *The California Progressives* (1951) and *The Era of Theodore Roosevelt, 1900–1912* (1958).

[7] Theodore Saloutos and John D. Hicks, *Agricultural Discontent in the Middle West, 1900–1939* (1951); published as a paperback under the title *Twentieth Century Populism* (1954).

My interest in the farmers did not blind me to the equally important role that labor was playing, and had played, in the struggle for reform, but there was little in my background to encourage me in trying to exploit this theme. My seminar, which occasionally included some of Selig Perlman's students—notably Philip Taft—taught me more on this subject than I taught them, and I also had an opportunity to learn something from Perlman himself, whom I knew well and greatly admired, and from John R. Commons, whom I met frequently and found still brilliant in his old age. My colleagues in economics had so much to offer in the field of labor, and I so little, that students of labor history usually wound up in that department rather than in history. One of my Ph.D. men, Maurice Neufeld, after doing a somewhat unusual thesis on certain aspects of the World's Columbian Exposition,[8] became a successful labor historian, but I can claim little credit for that.

During this period at Wisconsin we had a very good practice with reference to our Ph.D. candidates. We expected students who were writing a thesis on some aspect of European history to spend at least a semester in Europe, and those who were writing on American history to spend a like period in Washington. We obtained permission from the graduate office for all such students to register in person, and then take off, or even, if necessary, to register *in absentia*. The semester of residence abroad or in Washington was recorded on the books as a part of the three-year residence required for the degree. Since the University of Wisconsin was then committed to the principle that the Ph.D. would be granted only on the basis of residence, thesis, and examinations, rather than courses taken, the scheme worked out very well until World War II complicated matters for the Europeanists.

The persistence of the depression, even after the New Deal began, tended to make life difficult financially for many students, both graduate and undergraduate. After the National Youth Administration (NYA) program got started, some of them qualified for payments of fifteen dollars a month for such nonteaching jobs as the university was able to provide. We found room for a considerable number of these young people in our history office; occasionally, we learned, a part of their slender earnings they sent home to their parents. Faculty members had students in for meals more frequently than the demands of courtesy

[8] "The White City," Illinois State Historical Society *Journal*, XXVII (1934–1935), 71–93.

required, and donated such essential items as overcoats to students who lacked them. The problem of Ph.D. placements was critical and absorbed much faculty attention. On this matter an Extension Division program, also geared to the depression, helped us materially. Since many high school graduates were finding it impossible to begin a college course away from home, the university attempted to take its first year's program to them. Circuit riders who drove from town to town in university automobiles taught such basic courses as history and English at several different places; four or five of them, representing as many different departments, made possible the off-campus completion of the whole freshman year. Many of our fledgling Ph.D.'s got their start in this way. The hardships faced by so many of our students tended to make me, at least, and no doubt many of my colleagues also, extremely sympathetic with the efforts of the New Deal to care for the needy and to get the national economy moving again. But this feeling was by no means universal. I can recall, for example, ex-President Birge telling me to my face that my open support of FDR's court-packing scheme "had reduced my usefulness to the university by fifty per cent." Birge was never one to pull a punch. Once when someone asked him for advice as to what party to support, he is reputed to have replied: "I generally vote the Democratic ticket when I can do it without making a fool of myself."

Undoubtedly my failure to produce the specialized studies I had dreamed of writing was in considerable part due to my deep involvement in a textbook project. This undertaking owed something to my having accepted the Nebraska deanship three years before I came to Wisconsin. I had long cherished a secret desire to write a textbook on American history, and had even blocked out two very tentative beginning chapters while I was teaching at Hamline. But some textbook peddler who visited the Hamline campus discouraged me, and I knew, too, that this kind of writing was regarded by the profession with considerable contempt; a good scholar was not supposed so to "prostitute" his talents. Also, most fortunately, I realized that I did not yet know enough to write a textbook. Nevertheless, it seemed obvious to me then, and it still does, that history, to be meaningful, must be put together; one might lay a thousand Ph.D. theses end to end and still be far short of the mark. Synthesis, I reasoned, was as necessary and important as original research, and required about as much by way of originality. In this frame of mind I was certain eventually to yield to temptation, and the temptation came from no less a personage than my former major professor and close friend, Fred Paxson, who was doing a revision of his *Recent History of the United States* and asked me to write an early history to pair with it. The two together, he hoped, might serve as a text for beginning courses. I thought the matter over a little and agreed to undertake the task. I was suffering from the customary illusion that it wouldn't be very difficult to write a textbook; all I would need to do would be to write up the lectures I had worked out; even a busy dean (or, as some put it, a "dizzy bean") could do that.

I was so wrong: I doubt if there is any more difficult and painstaking type of historical writing than is required to produce a good textbook. If one has taught long and conscientiously, the outline, to be sure, exists, at least in a rudimentary way, but filling it in is quite a different thing. In lectures one can skip lightly over subjects he doesn't know very well and few students will notice the difference. In a textbook he can take no such chances; every few sentences he must stop to check the accuracy of his data and to fill in the gaps that he had never noticed before. Often he finds that secondary accounts serve only to confuse him, and that he must of necessity consult the original sources. Furthermore, new interpretations crowd in upon him, and he must constantly stop to rethink his conclusions. Even his over-all outline comes in for constant reconsideration. All historical writing is a kind of compromise between topical and chronological treatment; how far should he go with one subject before he takes up another? And what sequence can he follow that will least confuse the students who so regularly assume that whatever comes earlier in the book happened before whatever comes later? And how can he guard against introducing a subject, following it halfway through, then dropping it for chronological reasons and forgetting to return to it? Many times I have pointed out to my students how much simpler it would be if historical synthesis could follow the example of a symphony orchestra, with the various instruments, each representing some significant development, all blending together to produce a harmonious whole. Instead, the historian has to do the best he can to convey his enormously complicated message on a single instrument that can produce only one tone at a time. These are some of the problems that make textbook writing exceedingly hard and exacting work. As a result, good textbooks are as few as poor textbooks are numerous. It took me nearly all of my spare time for the next six or seven years to produce *The Federal Union*.

Times have changed in the textbook business. Nowadays publishers compete vigorously for prospective authors, and frequently, even before a word is written, offer them not only contracts but also large advances. No one except Paxson ever asked me to write this book, and his publishers, the Houghton Mifflin Company, agreed at his request, not mine, merely to examine whatever copy I might submit to them. Just before I came to Wisconsin I sent in the first half of my manuscript. Months later I received an encouraging letter with irrefutable evidence that someone had examined my production with painstaking care. In fact, each of my sixteen chapters had received the grade A, B, or C. I was happy to get A's or B's on all but three chapters, the first two and the last. Why, I was asked, somewhat testily, did these three fail to measure up to the others? The answer was not hard to find. As for the first two, I had blanketed in without revision the half-baked chapters I had written at Hamline some ten or fifteen years before. As for the last one, I had written it hurriedly, and with every intent of rewriting it, while teaching in the summer session at West Virginia. When I had reworked these three chapters to the editors' satisfaction, I was assured of a contract, but I received no advance on this, or any other book I ever wrote. Even before *The Federal Union* was published in 1937, however, the publishers were after me to do a succeeding volume, paralleling in point of time Paxson's *Recent History*. Paxson's revision, the publishers had decided, while suitable for upperclass courses, would never meet the needs of beginners. So, with Paxson's blessing, I was no sooner done with one textbook than I began another.

When I began *The Federal Union* I had scarcely considered the matter of royalties. What I wanted primarily was to do a good book, one that neither Paxson nor I need be ashamed of. At Nebraska my salary of $6,000 a year as dean meant, until the depression was well along, $500 a month for twelve months, with additional pay for summer session. At that time Nebraska made no deductions for retirement funds or other such frivolities, and withholding taxes were well in the future. Indeed, I had no federal income tax to pay, since the rule then held that state salaries, including state university payrolls, were not taxable by the federal government. And the state of Nebraska had no income tax. My original call to Wisconsin set my salary at $6,000, but with the prospect of a small cut, perhaps 5 per cent. When I asked for moving expenses, I was told that Wisconsin had a rule against such payments, but that, as a gesture in this direction, my salary for the first year would be $6,500, but only $6,000 thereafter, subject to that small cut. Well, when the cut came it was more than three times the predicted percentage, and left me with about $5,300 a year, plus summer school pay, which was always kept at a minimum; university teachers, it is sometimes said, are the only employed persons who regularly receive half pay for overtime. During the depression, the University of Wisconsin, like the federal government, kept two sets of books, one showing what salaries it had promised to pay, the other showing what it actually paid. Fortunately, my stated—but not actual—salary remained at $6,500, but the first year I ever received that amount was the last year I taught at Wisconsin. Also, I discovered that the state of Wisconsin, unlike Nebraska, had a good stiff income tax, while under the New Deal the federal government had discovered that it no longer need exempt state university salaries from the federal income tax. So I paid two income taxes. Between the cuts and the taxes and the move I found myself hard up.

Then disaster struck. My youngest daughter, Marjorie, at four years of age ran the gamut of a mastoid operation, a lateral sinus operation, a jugular tie off, a streptococcic blood stream infection, empyema pneumonia, and a rib resection—at least those are some of the medical terms I remember. At one time we were told to expect brain surgery, but fortunately that didn't happen. She was in the hospital for months, with three nurses a day, each on an eight-hour shift. Eleven physicians, so a nurse told me, participated in one set of operations. I borrowed every cent the bank would lend me, on both my credit and my life insurance, and ended the ordeal thousands of dollars in debt. Moreover, we were under orders to take the child to Florida for the first winter after her illness. Happily, Marjorie recovered handsomely and is now the mother of six of my ten irresistible grandchildren. And eventually the debts were all paid, except for some unpayable debts of gratitude, particularly to two dedicated Madison physicians, Dr. Eugene Neff and Dr. Kent Tenney.

The Florida mandate posed problems for us, financial and otherwise. By chance the meeting of the American Historical Association in 1935 was set for Chattanooga, so we decided to postpone our trip south until after Christmas so that I could accompany the family at least through most of Tennessee. By that time they would be in a durably warm climate and could safely make their way alone. The parents of

Bob Reynolds, two of the finest people I have ever known, were looking for a temporary place to live in Madison and agreed to move into
our house while we were gone, and to stay on to look after me when I
returned alone. We also persuaded Doebie Mack, our nurse friend, to
accompany Lucile and the children all the way to Florida. Doebie had
been with us the previous summer during Marjorie's illness and had
taken one shift with the baby each day at the hospital. Once when
Marjorie was so low that the doctors excluded even Lucile from the
sickroom, they almost put Doebie off the case, too, on the ground that
she was no less emotionally involved than the child's mother. The real
trouble, we suspected, was that Doebie was never able to register that
humble and self-effacing look that doctors expect in nurses and, when
she felt like it, even talked right up to them. At our insistence she
stayed on the case.

At first all went as planned. I traded off my 1929 Nash for a 1930
Buick that was a bit roomier and had seen less punishment. Marjorie
frightened us to death a week before the time set for departure by
having to have her ear lanced again. Our doctor simply raved. "Didn't
I tell you to leave by Thanksgiving?" he protested. But for once we
got a break, and the ear healed up normally and quickly. Weighed
down by a mountain of baggage behind, and a jumble of suitcases and
humanity within, we set forth two days before Christmas. We knew
mighty well that, whatever the status of recovery, Ol' Man Winter was
just around the corner, and the sooner we could leave the vicinity of the
Great Lakes, the better.

We were none too soon. As a matter of fact, we skated along on a
glare of ice the greater part of the first day out, and made less than two
hundred miles. But we'd had a late start, and we were comforted by
repeated assurances that in another hundred miles we'd be out of snow
and ice. How little our informants knew about it! The blizzard that
we'd suspected caught up with us the next day, and we had to go to
bed again with only two hundred more miles behind us. The third
day was the worst yet. When we looked out the hotel window that
morning, the snow was so thick in the air that we couldn't see across
the street, and the head of the family positively refused to budge.
Merry Christmas indeed! But by ten o'clock the sun came out, and the
women, as usual, had their way.

As we crossed the Ohio River that day, one of the children remarked, "Oh, the river isn't frozen at all!"

"Of course not," I replied. "A river this size never freezes."

"Well, then," in a pleased high treble from the back seat, "How did Eliza get across?"

That preposterous blizzard followed us all the way through Kentucky and Tennessee, and the day after we arrived in Chattanooga another one came on. The local residents, who had thought to show us their precious battlefields, their still more precious Tennessee Valley Authority, and other glimpses of the "sunny South," were simply overcome with mortification. "We just nevah have weathah like this down heah!" they lamented a thousand times. Yes, we said, so we'd noticed. The day they'd planned the grand tour of inspection one couldn't even get a taxi across town. For all the convention saw of the outside world, it might as well have met in Minneapolis or Winnipeg. Furthermore, Tennessee still had prohibition.

It had not been our intent for the family to stay longer in Chattanooga than overnight, but the roads were so treacherous that I would not permit them to leave until the convention was over. With hotel accommodations for six people to pay for, my financial resources soon began to show signs of exhaustion. Actually, it was a full week after we left Madison when we were again able to head south, still with that old refrain ringing in our ears: "Oh, you'll have no more snow after another hundred miles!"

I stayed with the family as far as Atlanta, for I was unwilling to leave them until I'd seen with my own eyes that the roads were clear. It was just as well I went, for, beginning about fifty miles north of Atlanta, we found the scenery, including the roads, embellished by the most astounding ice pack any of us had ever seen, and we'd all lived fairly close to the Canadian border. Two inches of rain had frozen as it fell. The vegetation was covered with ice, and huge branches, unable to bear the weight, had broken away from the trees. Telephone poles were down for miles at a stretch, and in some places the wires were literally broken to bits. Atlanta was a veritable shambles. Yards and side streets were littered with broken branches and fallen trees, streetcar service had been discontinued, and once we saw the stately pillars of an old colonial porch standing stark naked out in front of the house because the roof they were meant to support had caved in. But the drive was relatively uneventful. After all, that was only our fifth day of icy roads, and one gets used to anything. We had a flat tire, due surprisingly to a horseshoe nail, that delayed us an hour, but we reached Atlanta early in the afternoon.

Meantime the sun had come out, and with the help of the traffic had cleared the main roads of ice. At last I felt safe in leaving the family to its own devices. Both women could drive, by their own admission even better than I, and besides, "in another hundred miles!" So I bought a ticket to Madison and, after giving Lucile practically every cent of money I had left, I boarded a northbound train. When Lucile protested against my penniless condition, I assured her that between the political scientists, who had just met in Atlanta, and the historians, who were leaving Chattanooga, I could surely find someone on the train to lend me enough money to buy food. I found Harold Quigley.

Back in Madison, I was soon on the usual routine, except that I had no car to take me back and forth to my classes. So I walked what would ordinarily have been an easy mile. Unfortunately, the exceptional character of that winter was not confined to the South. Every day for six weeks the thermometer dropped below zero; going to and from the campus I located three places along the way where I could warm up a little before undertaking the next lap of the voyage. It was a grim winter, brightened mainly by the almost daily letters I soon began to receive.

X. Letters from Florida

BARNESVILLE, GA., December 30, 1935.

JOHN DARLING,

My last picture of you going forlornly into the depot at Atlanta isn't a bit pleasant. I could have cried and cried, but the family seemed very quiet and sober for miles, so I didn't dare let go. Presently Marjorie remarked, very wistfully, "Gosh, he's lucky, to get to go back and see what Madison looks like!" Those weren't my feelings, for I felt that any place with you in it would be heavenly, but any place without you would be desolate.

We're in the queerest hotel yet. Three dollars for a big room heated by a natural gas burner, and containing two double beds. I get both small children. It's a big old barn of a place, with a funny little proprietor that Doebie says smells of whiskey. We're the only people on this big floor. We hav'n't a private bath, but fortunately there's a lavatory in our room.

Very soon after leaving Atlanta the roads cleared, and they were soon so dry that we went right along and got this far by five o'clock. They tell us that the ice lasts only fifteen miles farther, and that the storm did not touch Macon, thirty-eight miles to the south. Doebie is reading accounts of the storm out loud until I can scarcely write. Marietta, the next town to Atlanta, seems to have suffered worst, and is without either telephones or lights.

We stopped once and bought a sack of pecans, and in making change Doebie got them free. The man returned the whole ten dollars from her ten dollar bill, and when we discovered it we were too far along to go back. We also bought some pralines that were delicious and had them for dessert.

We're all having to go to bed so that Marjorie can sleep.

LUCILE.

JASPER, FLA., Dec. 31, 1935.

DEAR JOHN,

I wish I knew how you got home, if you got home, where you got the money to go on, and a million other things. It's simply unbelievable how much I'm used to being with you and can't get used to being without you.

We got to feeling to-day that Georgia stretched endlessly on and on, and that we'd never get into the state of Florida. We were coming along fine, congratulating ourselves on our early start and the prospect of making a hundred miles before noon, when the car acted queer, and I stopped, only to find the right rear tire almost down. We were two-and-a-half miles from a village, so we hailed a motorist, who turned out to be from Michigan, and said he'd help a sister-stater. He sent a man out from town who told us that, since it was already lunch time, he'd fix our tire while we ate. We were agreeable, so went back with him. He charged us a dollar for the whole job, and returned the good tire to the wheel. We found to our dismay, as we ate dinner, that time had changed, and we'd lost an hour, so that with an hour out for the tire and an hour for the change we'd really lost two hours. So when we got here to Jasper at 5:15 we'd gone only two hundred miles, but as I was dead tired and it would soon be dark we stopped. Besides, I saw this nice hotel, which is really a big old house turned into a hotel. Doebie persuaded the woman-proprietor to let us have one room with two double beds, and another with one big bed, all for $3.50. I slept only a tiny bit last night with the two little girls, and wasn't going to try that anymore.

To-night we are downstairs by a big grate fire—the only heat they have—writing on a card-table. Marjorie had a nice bath, and was asleep soon after seven. Carolyn is bathed, and we'll send her up soon. She's parading around in my bath-robe.

Doebie is keeping a strict account of our expenses. It takes about $10 a day, and Doebie pays her own bills.

We find that it's 209 miles to St. Petersburg, and we expect to arrive there tomorrow. The next morning we'll call on Doebie's friends, do a little sight-seeing, and then go to Palmetto, where another of Doebie's friends is expecting us. We'll look over the cabin she has found for us, but I think we'll go on to Palm Beach Friday, for I'd rather be down on the east coast where it is warmer.

The country around here is flat, but the landscape is no longer wintry. The foliage is all green, and there are huge trees that drip a long gray mossy stuff. Palm trees are getting more numerous. It rained hard all afternoon, and seems chilly and cold, but the fireplace keeps us comfortable, so you see it isn't awfully cold. Just outside the hotel is an orange tree, with a bushel or so of oranges on it, ripe and ready to eat, and nearby is a grape-fruit tree with fruit on it.

How I do long for mail, or word of you! I seem so awfully far away. When I see my baby all brown and husky, and the other two happy in school, perhaps I'll think the separation worth while, but right now life seems a hard job to live.

Happy New Year! I'm afraid we'll just sleep it in.

LUCILE.

NEAR TAMPA, Jan. 1, 1936.

DEAR JOHN,

Our lives to-day have been so full of adventure and excitement that to-night I'm all tired out, and discouraged and blue. We got a nice start this morning after a cozy breakfast in front of a roaring grate fire. It was still cold and cloudy when we started, and when the proprietor's wife told us that in a hundred miles we'd see a change we laughed right out. But she was right. In less than a hundred miles we began to shed our winter clothes, and leggings and coats piled up in the car until we could scarcely see over the luggage. And at 11:30 we had a flat tire again! When we got out to investigate, off came all our coats, and still we nearly roasted. We hailed a motorist again, who sent two men from a filling station a quarter of a mile away. We used our own jack and tools, and with everyone helping we finally got the tire changed. We're using the spare from now on, for I think it must be better than this one that has gone bad three times.

By noon we were in Ocala, and had lunch. We found that we were only five miles from the famous Silver Springs, and nothing doing but the family must all go sight-seeing. So we spent two hours viewing the most wonderful under-water loveliness you can imagine. We were in a glass-bottomed boat, and Marjorie convulsed the crowd by asking in an awed voice, "Why, Mother, is this a magic glass?" We had a time of it not to spend too much on souvenirs. I thought we might not be able to eat for a day as it was, for the trip cost $1.00 per adult, and fifty cents for children under twelve.

By 3:30 we started again, and at 5:10 the car stopped, and refused to go. We were simply nonplussed, and worked and worked to no avail. A man came along, and he worked a while, too, but finally gave it up and walked to a town (we were just on its edge), and sent out a garage man. He fussed around, and found a dirty carburator, cleaned the screen, and then the engine ran beautifully. We ate hamburger sandwiches, even Marjorie, and decided to drive on to Tampa. Marjorie was tired, and I hate night driving, but Doebie and Jane Harriet were hell-bent on it.

Finally I saw a cabin camp, and stopped. It's 70°, and seems warmer, so here we are in one cabin with two double beds, a cot, a lavatory, and a toilet that won't flush, all for $2. I'm getting so sick of traveling and getting nowhere, and living out of suit-cases, that I could settle anywhere soon. Goodness knows, if there's anyplace warmer than this, we wouldn't want to be there. Tonight I had to get out summer underwear, sox, and dresses for everyone.

LUCILE.

BRADENTON, FLA., Jan. 2, 1936.

DEAR JOHN,

We made an early start this morning, got breakfast in Tampa, and arrived in St. Petersburg about 10:30 a.m. We called on two of Doebie's friends, and the second one asked us to lunch. We all appreciated a home-cooked meal so very much.

After lunch this woman who had fed us took us all over St. Petersburg to see the sights. The city reminds me a little of our old home in Nebraska, for its streets are so very wide, and the country so very flat. The trees, however, are mostly palm trees, and there are far more of them than Lincoln has. We went out on the big pier, where they have concession stands much like those on the Chicago municipal pier. We fed pop-corn to the sea-gulls. They are so tame that they fly by and pick it out of your fingers, or catch it if you throw it up to them. The children got a big kick out of that. We snapped some pictures, too. There were a number of pelicans flying around, and I got a picture of one of them on a post behind two of the children. It was hot in the sun, but the breeze from the gulf was chilly. We wore no coats until later.

At 3:45 we took the ferry across to Bradenton. And were the children thrilled! It was a big ferry, took half an hour for the trip, and cost $1.95 for the lot of us and our car. I forgot to say that we came from Tampa to St. Petersburg over a long bridge, and got a real thrill out of going right over the bay.

We arrived at Palmetto about five o'clock, and found Doebie's friend in that town. She gave us a delicious chicken dinner, which we all gobbled down as though we were starved. I never saw Carolyn or Marjorie eat so much. We've had pretty poor food lately, and home cooking simply overcame our manners, and we gobbled.

I could get a cottage near Palmetto for $25 a month, but it is at the beach, twelve miles away, and the children would have to take a bus to town each day for school. I can't quite see that. Bradenton, where we are to-night, may be better, but its beach is six miles away, and I'm quite discouraged. No, I really knew we shouldn't spend time and money coming this way. We're terribly tired of hotels and traveling, but I guess we must go on until I like it. The children have stood the trip so very well, and their colds have disappeared in this mild climate. But how much longer can we hold out? And can I find what I want if I do go farther? A house near both beach and school is what I seek, and goodness knows where it is. Two real estate men stopped me in St. Petersburg with offers of nice bungalows for about $40, but they weren't near a beach.

Doebie's friends tell me I must have title papers for the car and my driver's license, registration cards, etc. There is no school tuition, but when you enter children in school you have to buy a Florida license and must have the proper credentials. They paid $10 for a Florida license when their children went to school. Of course that's St. Petersburg, and the regulations are said to differ from town to town.

I got your card written at Atlanta, and, as the children say, was I glad to get it! I wanted more word from you so much. I hope you're sending letters in care of Doebie's friend in Palmetto, for we'll get them sooner that way than if you waited for our address. I have spent less than $50 as yet, and I think I can hold out with what I have until the 7th or 8th. I do hope I'm settled by then. This uncertainty is so trying, but I do want to be happy where I locate. More to-morrow.

LUCILE.

LAKE WORTH, FLA., Jan. 4, 1936.

DEAR JOHN,

I've so much to tell you that I scarcely know where to begin. But I suppose the best place is where I left off in my last letter, which was at

Bradenton. I didn't even look over the cabins there, and I suppose I really should have done so, for I am now paying $50 a month, and glad to get a house at that.

Well, we went on from Bradenton Friday morning, with a late start, for they didn't fix the tire until morning because it needed a new inner tube. About ten o'clock we struck off straight across the state, heading for Ft. Pierce on the east coast. It seems one doesn't travel across state in Florida, for we got into the most deserted regions I've ever seen. With our characteristic luck we took a state highway for the first fifty miles instead of what must have been the better route. Our road led through the jungles, or everglades, or whatever one should call the lush green foliage and tropical scenery that swallowed us up. It was so very deserted. Not a farm house, not a car, not a human-being in sight. I was really frightened for fear something would go wrong with the engine, or we'd have a flat tire and be stranded there forever. But the country was really amazingly beautiful, with its high palm trees and evergreens and ferns abounding. And it was simply alive with birds. Now we know where they all come to when they fly south. There were huge lovely white birds, pink-gray flamingoes on long legs, beautiful red birds, and blue birds, and birds of every size, shape, and color. Doebie's eyes fairly popped all the time.

Our road, which started as a rather narrow black-top, soon began to get narrower and narrower, until it was wide enough only for one car. In addition, it was very full of chuck-holes. It was really fortunate that we didn't have to pass a car. At last we reached Arcadia, a nice little city in the wilderness. It was nearly noon, but not quite time to stop and eat, so we asked about the next stop, only to learn that we must go through just such barren country another sixty miles before we'd reach another town. We got sandwiches, cookies, and a bottle of milk, checked the oil and gas, then started on. This time the character of the country was entirely changed, but equally deserted and forlorn. It was perfectly flat, entirely devoid of trees, and again as empty of humanity as it could be. Soon it began to rain, and poured buckets. We stopped the car and ate lunch, feeling completely isolated from the world, then drove on through the downpour to Ft. Pierce.

When we arrived there at about three o'clock, the town band was out. We began to feel important, but discovered, of course, that they were expecting some celebrity from Virginia, and hadn't meant to play for us. We sought the chamber of commerce to see if any houses were available, and a man took us (the rain still pouring) to see the only two houses he had, which were utterly impossible. We decided to go on down the coast and stop at a few more towns. But first we stopped at an orange orchard, got some fruit juice, and bought a bushel of oranges for a dollar. The oranges we tied on the side of the car beside one of the spare tires.

Then we pushed on to West Palm Beach, where a real estate man sent us house-hunting with a nice college boy from Philadelphia as a guide. Before dinner we saw two or three houses that were offered at $300 for the season. The boy showed us an inexpensive place to eat and spend the night, and we decided to call it a day. We had two double beds in one room, so we pushed them together, giving Jane Harriet the crack. In the morning she remarked that it was the most comfortable crack she had slept on yet.

Saturday morning the boy showed us around again, and at my top price, $50 a month, we saw only two places, one a third floor apartment in a poor location, and the other a rambling cottage with only the bare necessities of life in it, the kind we might consider for a summer at a lake. The boy thought that a great bargain, and urged me to take it. He also drove us all over Palm Beach. We saw the magnificent expanse of ocean and sandy beach, with so many out sunning or swimming. The children nearly went wild to be down in it too.

We had met in Bradenton a professor from Columbia, who told us about Lake Worth, just seven miles from Palm Beach, so when we couldn't be sure of a house at West Palm Beach, we came on down here. As we parked for lunch a man came up and asked us if we were interested in houses in Lake Worth. It developed that his mother had one to rent, so after lunch we looked at it, and decided to take it at the $200 for the season she asked. That's more than I'd wanted to pay, but I'd come to the conclusion that I could do no better.

Our house is of yellow stucco, a flat-roofed, vine-covered, Spanish affair. It has two bed rooms and a sun room at the front, and a marvelous big porch at the rear. The porch opens three ways, has awnings to let down, a swing davenport, a breakfast set, and a few chairs. It's really the main living room, and at the present moment we are all out here writing. We have a big mango tree in our yard, and three or four palm trees, but white sand instead of grass.

It's been really hot out to-day; in fact, Doebie and I simply wilted, once we had the chance. I had to get out all our summer clothes, and Marjorie dug sand for hours in the front yard, clad only in her panties. The children can hardly wait to get to the beach, which is only a mile away.

The owner of the house unpacked my luggage, and has been most kind. He and his wife moved out to a tiny cottage a block away. All the natives try to rent their houses and move almost any place while the season is on.

There is no garage, but everyone says the car will be safe by the house. The gas feed got to sticking, and something ruined the case of gear-shifting, so I had to pay another $1.80 for repairs this morning.

My expenses here should not be high, but food prices seem about the same as anywhere else. By going to the dairy a mile away I can get raw milk for ten cents a quart, but I'm looking around for some that is pasteurized. Butter is forty-three cents, eggs fifty cents. Fruit is cheap, but not so cheap as we thought. Fish is plentiful and cheap.

There is a nice grade school for Carolyn about three blocks away, and a splendid high school building about ten blocks away. This town has a population of about five thousand, and is near enough to West Palm Beach that we can have the advantage of what goes on over there without the cost of living there. But to seek a home and get established without you, and without having to consider your ideas or tastes, is simply too much for my spirits, and I feel to-night like a deflated balloon.

I shall be surprised if you read all this, but it was on my chest to write.

LUCILE.

LAKE WORTH, FLA., Jan. 5, 1936.

MOST HONORED FATHER,

I take it upon myself de vous écrire une lettre.

We spent our first time on the beach this morning. There is no under-toe [sic] (or rather wasn't) to-day. Excellent time. We premons notre déjeuner dans l'auto et then we dug holes dans la plage. I dug one so deep that I could get in it and sit comfortably. While I was digging I made friends with a family from Minnesota. There was a girl my age who is going to be here just two weeks and they live near us. A guy said the schools have a ban up that new-comers can't go to school for two weeks. We're going to find out to-morrow for sure. If they do I can play with that girl.

Doebie is burned, every inch of her—no not quite every inch

because every inch wasn't exposed (I hope). Her legs are so red and burning she has to hold up her dress. Can't you imagine the effect?

I rummaged around in the lady's book-case that owns this house. J'ai trouvé deux livres, *The Shepard of the Hills*, by Harold Bell Wright, et *Isobel*, by James Oliver Curwood. Pretty good so far.

Marjorie and Mother and Carolyn are all sun-burned, all except me and my face is. But I'm just tanned on my back and legs and arms. I hadn't lost last summer's tan so much.

Salt water makes my legs smart and while digging the hole I threw sand directly upwards instead of out, and presto it came directly down dans ma tête.

Write me honored one. Love.

NAPOLEON.

LAKE WORTH, FLORIDA. Jan. 6.

DEAR JOHN,

O, how we do want mail! It seems an age since we left you in Atlanta just a week ago.

I took the children to school to-day and had no trouble entering them. In fact, everyone was most cordial, and we felt quite welcome. School begins for Carolyn at 8:30 and lasts until 12:00, then takes up at 12:45 and closes at 2:45 so that everyone can go to the beach in the afternoon. Jane Harriet's schedule is about the same, except that she eats at the high school cafeteria and doesn't get out until 3:00. I'm going to let Marjorie go to the morning kindergarten if they will take her, for there are no children nearby for her to play with, and she is quite at a loss for something to do.

A whole flock of other new youngsters registered this morning along with Jane Harriet. She can't get French or Biology, but takes Ancient History and advanced General Science. There's no music at all, and she is urging me to rent a piano. She has two study periods at school, and only four instead of five subjects, so she thinks her school-work will be a snap.

We foolishly stayed too long at the beach yesterday and are all sun-burned, Doebie worst of all. She was really ill last night from it, had chills and everything until I almost was worried. To-day she has not left the house, and has grunted and groaned and grumbled every breath. Jane Harriet got it on her nose and cheeks, and Carolyn and Marjorie are pretty red. We didn't try to go out to-day.

My parents, the Reverend John K. Hicks and
Hattie Wing Hicks, at the time of their marriage.

At five years of age.

On Fritz, the rough rider, with friends.

The Streeter School, near Kaycee, Wyoming, where I taught.

The Northwestern University Delta Upsilon class of 1913. In the back row are, at extreme left, William Freeman Galpin, and, at extreme right, Percy Walsh. I am in the front row, at the left.

Northwestern's Orrington Lunt Library, where I worked as a student.

Courtesy of the State Historical Society of Wisconsin

Carl Russell Fish

Courtesy of the University of Wisconsin Archives

Frederic Logan Paxson

The University of Wisconsin teaching assistants in history, 1915. In the back row, from the left, are Coulter, Hicks, and, second from the right, Gronert.

The Hamline University campus at about the time I taught there.

Our first daughter, Jane Harriet, with her parents and Grandmother
Hicks.

As Dean of Arts and Sciences at Nebraska.

With members of the Madison, Wisconsin, Town and Gown. From the left, E. B. Fred, Dr. Joe Evans, and, at extreme right, E. A. Birge.

Leaving for Florida, December, 1935.

Gold Trees, our home at Dutch Flat.

Southacre, at Cambridge, where we had a flat.

Teaching a class at the Salzburg Seminar.

Receiving an Army Certificate of Appreciation from General Dean,
for contributions to the Army Historical Program.

In 1968.

If I were a certain lady newspaper columnist I'd write like this:

It may not be of any significance, but we've noticed that

In Florida there are lots of Baby Austins. The owners say they take little gas, and since gas is high down here, that's a help. Also because there are no hills they do a good job of around town driving. There are coupés, trucks, delivery cars, and sedans.

That here no one has a telephone.

That few have hot water.

That the moon shines down every night (so far) in a lovely white glow from straight overhead.

That there is no twilight or dawn. Until one minute before six at night it is daylight, and at six it is night. In the morning it's dark until 6:30, and then all suddenly light and day.

That it gets really hot at noon, and stays that way until four o'clock, then cools off so that we sleep under blankets every night.

That there's a stiff wind off the ocean that's almost cold. (That's what fooled us yesterday. The wind was so cool we didn't feel the heat of the sun).

We have a night-blooming jasmine in our front yard that we think will open to-night. Its fragrance is so lovely. In the daytime it doesn't smell at all, but at night its perfume pervades the whole yard.

We bought guavas to-day from a Negro and made guava jam. We also bought fresh limes from him, and the neighbors say he has avacados for sale, too. Negroes are not allowed inside the city to live, but they have a community just outside the city limits.

No one here seems to have the slightest cold, so I don't hesitate about sending Marjorie to school. She is so pleased at the thought, for she was crushed this morning when Carolyn went to school and left her. Many of the little boys go to school bare-footed, and all the little girls are in summery dresses.

We wish so very, very much that you might be with us.

LUCILE.

Lake Worth, January 7.

Dear John,

We heard a suspicious rattling of the mail box this noon, and all rushed out (Doebie only half-clothed) to get our first mail. We got all the letters you had sent to Palmetto and gorged ourselves for an hour.

I feel so guilty being here in this summer climate while you're up there freezing among the bills. Just pay what you can, and let enough go that you can make a trip down to see us. It's heavenly hot here, and the beach simply marvelous. We may never be out of debt again enough to repeat this experience, so we might as well get all we can out of it.

We're trying to keep our expenses here at a minimum. Some things cost more, some less, than at home. I'm saving a gas bill by the damned kerosene stove, but ice costs thirty cents for fifty pounds, and we need that much every other day. I've found a place to take my washing that does it for five cents a pound, rough dry. Doebie and I think we can manage the other work ourselves, even the ironing, to save the expense of help. But I'm going to have to cash a check in another day or two.

It was a very sober baby who met her mother outside the school-house at 11:30 this morning. She clung silently to my hand all the way home. Since there were traces of tears I asked why she cried, and she said it lasted too long and she had wanted to come home. To-night she declared she wasn't going back to-morrow, and I don't know just what to do about it. If she objects too much, I won't make her go, but she really needs something to do. We can go to the beach with her mornings, but we won't want to go afternoons, too; the others wouldn't stand for that.

Jane Harriet is simply on a rampage to-night. She sits here singing ditties like

> "I wear my pink pajamas in the summer when it's hot,
> I wear my flannel nightie in the winter when it's not,
> But sometimes in the springtime, and sometimes in the fall,
> I hop right in between the sheets with nothing on at all."

Her father's influence cropping out. She said school was awfully lonely, and she'd had all the science she was having to take now and was going to be bored to death by that, and that history was another bore. Their semester closes here in two weeks, and she's worried about having to take the semester exams when she's had so little time to prepare for them. I may have to rent a piano in self-defense to give her something to do, for she devils us all the time she isn't in school.

We went swimming to-day at three, and the tide soon began coming in with huge gulps. The children surely loved riding the waves. Even Marjorie hung on to the ropes, and let the waves break clear up on her. The water is gloriously warm. We spent hours gathering shells and dipping in the ocean. We have a collection of lovely shells, and every night we gather around the table and paint them, then glue them into little novelties. On our next trip to the beach we hunt for odd sizes and shapes that will work into our patterns. Jane Harriet has made a lovely rose on a pedestal of shells, and has painted it pink and green. Next it has to be shellacked.

When you see me next I'm going to be fat as a pig. I have the most amazing appetite, and so do the children. We eat and eat. I've got to stop it or I'll be a pollywog. Doebie still groans from the sunburn. She sits and looks at it, and can think of nothing else. It's really very bad. . . .

LUCILE.

LAKE WORTH, FLA., Jan. 9, 1936.

DEAR JOHN,

At last, at last, at last a letter directly from you to me here. I doubt if it helped a bit to send it air mail, for it took from Monday to Thursday for it to reach me. It takes so long to get any word back and forth. You'll know by now that the $100 is only half my rent. If one came here in October or November or December the rent would be the same, for it's figured by the season. For me it will average $50 a month if I stay until May. We'll be plenty hot here by then, in fact, we're plenty hot already, but we're too glad to be that way to object. And then, there's always the cool breeze from the ocean, while in the shade one is many degrees cooler than in the sun. Nights are so lovely and cool to sleep that we go to bed at nine o'clock because, if we don't, it's so hard to get up mornings.

The children are thriving so very much. Marjorie is tan, and has pink cheeks and *curly hair*. This damp heat has caused her hair to kink up around her head, and she looks too cute for words. I am still having her go to school, for she was so lost all day without it. She cried again yesterday, and clung to me, and I nearly had heart failure at making her stay, but I know it's so much better for her. The first day, it seems, her nails weren't quite clean, and she hadn't brought fruit for a mid-morning lunch as the others had done, so she wasn't very happy about it. Then, when she got home the second day she sighed, and said, "Well, I'm glad that boy wasn't there to-day." This morning she had gone a whole block with Carolyn when she tore home to "ask Mother something," so I walked part way with her, and she went on the rest of the way with Carolyn's hand to bolster her courage. Carolyn, as usual, takes life as it comes, calmly and happily. She and Marjorie have played so nicely together.

I sent you a telegram New Year's eve from Jasper, Florida. Did you get it? It was a night letter, and cost me ninety-one cents when I wasn't at all sure my money would hold out, so if it didn't reach you I'm going to write in for a refund.

When you come down be sure to bring white shoes, plenty of white duck trousers, and your swimming suit. You can't wear wool clothes at all down here. As each of the children returns from school she strips immediately, puts on the thinnest sun-suit, bares her feet, and goes out to play. Marjorie has miles of sand pile, for the whole yard is sand, and vacant lots on each side and in the rear give her plenty of play sand. She can turn on the faucet outside, too, so has water to work with.

To-day a beautiful red rose is in full bloom at our front door. With plenty of water and care there seems no limit to the flowers, vines, and shrubs that can be grown here. Huge red poinsettias flourish, and big bushy azaleas with blossoms as large as a plate are quite common. Palm trees with their coconuts are everywhere, and evergreens as well. It's winter resting time for some of the trees and bushes, and they look very curious, all brown and leafless.

We spent the evening last night killing cock-roaches the size of June bugs in our living room—with a fly swatter! Other evenings we've spent on the porch, so hadn't seen them before, but last night we all gathered in the living-room, and there they were. We'd noticed shells in corners filled with insect-killer, so were suspicious. Jane Harriet and I sat with feet up, and Doebie did the dirty work.

To-day Doebie's back feels better, and her spirits have returned. She says she thinks now that she'll recover. Her sunburn made her really ill, and for a while I was almost worried about her. The rest of us are all well.

LUCILE.

LAKE WORTH, Jan. 10, 1936.

DEAR JOHN,

Your last air-mail letter reached me in two days, so I guess it pays to send them that way. And do I await them eagerly! Yes, ma-a-am, as the children are all learning to say. It's so funny to hear Marjorie say "Yes, ma'am," and "No, ma'am," to everything.

Your story of snow and ice seems unbelievable to us now. We've been here long enough to be completely translated into summer. In fact, we get an awful start when we hear the natives mention "this winter," or refer to this month as January. Both Doebie and I talk about "this summer," and make many laughable mistakes because to us it seems like June. It's really hot in the sun every day, but we still glory in it.

Doebie and I went to P.T.A. (or "P.P.A." as the kindergartners call it) to-day. It seems that even in Florida it's as hopeless an affair as everywhere else. We sang a P.T.A. song to begin with that was designed to bring out the religious worth-whileness of P.T.A. Then we all recited the Lord's Prayer. (They are great on religion down here—read the Bible and pray every day in both schools.) Then two women sang (who had no right to), and a government works woman talked about the need for adult education. She told how large a percentage of us were almost feeble-minded, and so needed to join the parents' classes. We didn't like to admit that we were feeble-minded, so refrained from joining.

We find we don't need any help. With all children gone every morning, and both of us to do the work, we manage easily. These houses are like summer cottages. We sweep out once every morning, and call it clean for the day.

Jane Harriet read all your letters yesterday, and fairly wept she was so homesick. She's been miserable at school for they are now reviewing the semester's work, and in all but mathematics she doesn't even know what they are talking about. The superintendent here told her not to try to take the semester examinations, and to try to get her credit for the first semester in Madison. Will you see her principal there about it? She's going on with her French on her own, and feels secure about that. She grieves because she's completely deprived of music, except for an old Edison here that she and the younger children play and play. Of course her chief trouble is that she hasn't yet found enough congenial friends to be very happy. She says she's going back with you when you come down.

Marjorie is running in and out in a cute pair of red trunks, and her fat little body is getting so very brown. She eats enormous meals, and is always hungry. Even Carolyn is stuffing, to say nothing of Doebie and me. We'll be too fat to look at soon, all of us.

LUCILE.

LAKE WORTH, Sunday morning.

DEAR JOHN,

Doebie and Jane Harriet have gone to church, and I have our lunch all ready to go to the beach when they return. I had to put up plenty, because yesterday we all nearly starved, although I thought I had taken more than enough. You've no idea the unbelievable amounts this family eats. Even the mamma can't seem to remember to go carefully.

I'm enclosing a picture of the Casino near which we go swimming. The Casino is out on a key, which we reach by a long causeway. It's about three minutes drive from our house. They have a fine pool in the Casino with a charge of fifteen swims for a dollar. I may buy a ticket, as one can't really swim in the ocean. The waves are too big. To-day at the Casino they have a tame seal, and to any child that can ride it goes a week's free swimming in the pool.

Marjorie walked out quite far into the ocean yesterday (I right behind her), hanging on to the rope, and a big wave broke all over her. She kept hold of the rope, and I grabbed her, but even though we all laughed she couldn't think it was funny. The ocean was calm, but every so often a big swell would slip in unexpectedly.

Jane Harriet goes all over the roped-in section, and sits and tumbles around on the ropes. Carolyn is a bit more cautious. Doebie went in for the first time yesterday since her sunburn. I hav'n't been in the water very much yet, for I don't like the waves. We picked up a whole pail full more of shells, and the children are painting them and making things with them again to-day.

I went to the library yesterday and got five books for over the week-end. They help take care of Jane Harriet's odd moments. I read Ike Hoover's *Forty-Two Years in the White House* last night, and enjoyed it immensely. The family appreciated it, too, when I read them of the antics of the Roosevelt children. Jane Harriet nearly fell off her chair when I read about them taking a pony up and down in the elevator. I have just finished *February Hill*, the book Walter and Doris gave me, and enjoyed it so much. It's the story of a prostitute and her family. Doebie is reading it now, and will die of shock, I'm afraid. . . .

The man from whom we rent says that this town is one hundred per cent for the Townsend pension plan. They have weekly meetings, are fully organized, and more than enthusiastic. I suspect the town is made up mostly of retired elderly people from the north who need the money. Everyone must be rather poor, for the houses are small, and there is little evidence of wealth.

The town looks odd to us. There are few sidewalks (none on our street), and where they are, only on one side of the street. The houses are set hit and miss, some at the rear of a lot, some half way back, some at the side, some facing one way, some another, some with no yard, some with grass and flowers, and some with only sand for lawn. Nearly all are tiny, one-storied and flat-roofed, like ours. We've seen only two two-storied houses with peaked roofs in the whole town. The place has the appearance (and West Palm Beach too) of one of our summer colonies around a lake. The houses are either very white or very yellow stucco (stăcco, Marjorie calls it), or white clapboard. I wonder how the permanent citizens live. Just camp out like the rest of us, I suppose. You can't get any of them to admit it's hot here summers, and maybe it isn't, but if this is January, I can't help wondering about July.

Last night was the first time we ever closed the doors and windows because of the coolness. It had rained a little and was damp outside. . . . This is an absolutely ideal winter climate, and I'm so comfortable and relaxed all the time that I don't ever want to live through a northern winter again. I'm rooting for you to get a job at the University of Miami. We could live on a much smaller salary down here, with no coal or winter clothes to buy.

                                                              LUCILE.

                              LAKE WORTH, FLORIDA. Jan. 13, 1936.
CELEBRATED FATHER,

I will make this letter neat and proper if you read it, the way you did the other, to everyone in Madison. To answer your questions, in the first place, no one could push our car out of the sand where it sits if they tried, so we don't lock it. In the second place, when we lock our house up we can go to the back door and push it open about an inch, take a nail and lift up the lock on the inside of the door, so you see in what security we live.

School is dry. Really I wonder sometimes why you gave me two names, because everyone makes up their own inventions out of my name. I don't have to go back to school this week because they're all taking examinations, and I don't take them except in algebra.

I miss the snow and ice and Smugs [our dog], the piano, too. I miss that most, but Mother says she doesn't know whether she can afford to rent one or not, and Doebie says she thinks they'd be expensive. So I guess I'm out of luck, but if you come down here do bring my violin at least.

Soon we are going to visit the ostrich and alligator farm where I intend to purchase an alligator all packed and ready to send, and send it to the ten o'clock Biology class (that's ours) care of Miss Weber. They can't kill me, because I'm in Florida.

Ancient history isn't as bad as I supposed, but I can think of better things.

JANE HARRIET.

LAKE WORTH, Jan. 15, 1936.

DEAR JOHN,

What a round of dinners you are having! Keep it up, it will save on the food bills.

I've let Marjorie stay at home from school this week, for she was so unhappy about going, and seemed very tired each night. But she is very lonesome all morning here alone, so next week I think I'll follow your suggestion and go over once during the morning to see her. But I'll bet she'll yell when I leave!

The children have no school after to-day for the rest of the week, so to-morrow we plan to drive down to Miami, spend the rest of Thursday there, then go on out to Key West Friday. They are advertising the ferry schedules in the papers now, so evidently the roads that the hurricane washed out are again usable. We see evidence of what the huge waves can do along the south ocean drive here, where the road is closed, and is dropping off into the beach by chunks. We'll return from Key West on Saturday, be in Miami until Sunday noon, and then come home. We've decided, since it costs so much for meals on a trip, to take along a big box of sandwiches, a cake, and some fruit. Then we can have one meal a day in our car, or by the road-side. Doebie thinks we can take our toaster and coffee-pot, too, and have breakfast at the tourist camps, where we will spend the nights. It costs only about two dollars a night in a camp, and we can dispense with baths for three nights if we have to, though it's plenty warm.

Last night Doebie and I decided we were entitled to a night out, so after supper, and when Marjorie was in bed, we walked down town. We had a great time, for we met and talked to lots of people. There is a town-hall in the middle of the town, around which is a lovely lawn, with trees and flowers, a band-shell and benches, and lighted courts for shuffle-board. We got two men to play it with us (you just *have* to have *four*), and had a fine time, although to-day I'm as stiff as can be in legs and arms. We discovered where the life of the town is, down there every evening. We walked along the streets, and everyone talked to us as if we were old friends. We met no end of people, and it was really great fun.

I also bought your birthday present, which is being sent out this morning. It's a box of fruit, ripened on the tree and delicious. Tell me if it arrives safely. I had the man put in some Temple oranges, large ones of a kind we don't get up north because they have to be ripened on the trees. We wish we might bake you a cake and help you celebrate, but we'll do that for you when you come down.

We're taking all the family to a band concert down town to-night. They put on a program with what talent they can pick up among the tourists. Last night we met a young man who is to sing. I'll write more later.

LUCILE.

KEY WEST, FLORIDA, Jan. 17, 1936.

DEAR JOHN,

Are we enjoying ourselves? Well, I should say so! We left Lake Worth Thursday morning about ten o'clock, and drove leisurely down the coast, visiting Hollywood, Delray Beach, Ft. Lauderdale, and finally Miami. At Miami Beach our visions of Florida beautiful were truly realized. Such gorgeous homes set in such gorgeous surroundings I've never seen before. It's like a fairy land, with palm trees, vines in full bloom, blossoms of every size and color, elaborately landscaped yards with fountains and pools, and even garages and servant-quarters more beautiful than anything we can ever hope to live in. Miami Beach is right on the ocean, and handsome new hotels are going up, literally by the dozens. The ones already in use are apparently well-patronized, and liveried doormen in blue, gold, and white made a profound impression on the children. The architecture of the houses is quite unusual, a combination of Spanish and modernistic designs, done in white or pink or yellow stucco, with bright awnings, red, scarlet, and blue. The general effect really baffles description. We oh-ed, and ah-ed, and oh-looked, oh-looked all the way through the town.

At Miami we hunted up the address of some people Doebie knew, only to find them gone, and then tried to find out how to get to Key West. No one seemed to know or care, even the policemen were anything but helpful or friendly. There were so many narrow one-way streets that we were constantly going the wrong direction, and getting honked off the road. About four o'clock we gave up the search for information, and headed on south towards Homestead, which we reached about 5:30. Doebie again knew some people there, and we found them. They have a grove of fruit trees on the edge of the town, and we had the fun of picking grape-fruit, oranges, limes, tangerines, and tangelows right off the trees.

That night we stayed at a curious small-town hotel with no private toilet or bath, and our rooms far apart. Doebie was quite disgusted because we had to pay $4.50 for our rooms, but we were helpless, for there were no other hotels in the place, and no tourist camps.

We learned that the one ferry a day for Key West leaves at 10 a.m. and that we have to drive fifty-five miles farther before we get to it. So we left orders to be called at 5:30 in the morning, and although Marjorie protested that it wasn't morning yet, the children were all good sports, and we got out of town by seven, still in darkness, for there was a heavy fog and mist over everything. We drove out over one causeway after another, and across one bleak island after another. We saw the awful destruction that the November hurricane had done, and the wreckage of the camp where the hundred men were killed. For mile after mile the railroad tracks were lifted clear off the road bed and set down fifty yards away, a broken twisted mass. Whole sections of the railroad were simply gone, no one knows where. The automobile roads, however, have been re-worked, and they are passable to within seven miles of where they used to go. Why anyone should wish to live out on these islands I can't possibly see. They are perfectly flat, with only small trees and low bushes. The soil is porous coral rock, and not usable, except for a truck garden now and then.

We got to the ferry an hour and a half too soon, but finally it started. It takes six and a half hours now to get across, which meant that we wouldn't arrive until four-thirty, with forty miles of driving after that before we'd reach Key West. I was afraid the children would be bored, for I hadn't brought any thing to amuse them, but they managed beautifully. Jane Harriet kidded the captain (when Doebie wasn't monopolizing him), and actually steered the boat for a long way from up in the cabin. Carolyn found a girl her own age who had a wet diaper doll, so her time was fully occupied. I spent hours holding on to Marjorie's dress as she made the rounds of the decks. The railings were so flimsy that I was in hot water for fear she might be in cold. We had dinner on the boat. Doebie and I chose turtle steak, fried in deep fat, which turned out to be delicious.

Then I made Marjorie rest, and did the same myself. For an hour and a half I sat in the car, and was completely and wholly happy. The calm, leisurely trip over the quiet waters, so blue or green or purple, brought a peace and quiet to my soul that seemed to make up for all my worries and anxieties of last winter. I think the feeling will be with me for a long time. I seemed to bargain with the Fates about life, and to tell them that now we were even for the dirty tricks of last winter. I don't know when I so thoroughly enjoyed anything as I enjoyed that ride on the sleepy old ferry.

At 4:15 we arrived at a no-name key, and drove on to Key West, through lonely keys and over countless causeways. By six we had found this hotel. We had sandwiches, cakes, and fruit with us, so we got a bottle of milk, and ate our supper in our rooms. Then I put three of the dirtiest children you ever saw in the tub, and to bed.

This is a quaint, old-world looking town, unlike any I have ever seen before. The houses are two-storied, with balconies, of Spanish architecture, or else Cape Cod cottages with green shutters. Most of the people seem to be Spanish or Negro. We plan to stay here to-morrow morning and do more sight-seeing, go to the beach all afternoon to swim, and leave on the Sunday morning ferry. We should be back in Lake Worth by Sunday night.

I feel a bit guilty about spending money for the trip. I had to cash another check before I left. But it's all really too good to be true, and I can't help being glad that we're doing it. The temperature is hot, and we've had sunshine most of the time. We wear only the thinnest clothes, and smile at Marjorie who goes about exclaiming, "Oh, I'm perspiring." Marjorie has freckles all over her little nose. She says tell Daddy "I giggle when I sleep." She should say "wiggle." I know, for I slept with her last night.

We learn that there is no mail service from here on Friday, so this letter will be a day longer than usual in reaching you. We've had no car or tire trouble so far, but my fingers are crossed. We all send love from the farthest south in the United States we can go.

LUCILE.

ABOARD FERRY FROM KEY WEST, Jan. 19, 1936.

DEAR JOHN,

We had a gay day of sight-seeing in Key West yesterday. We began the morning by a trip around the wide palm-fringed boulevard that encircles the island, after which we stopped at one curious place after another. We saw a pool of fish so tame that they would come to the surface to eat out of your hand and would let you pet them; a coral garden adorned with clusters of lacy coral in which beautiful sea-shells were imbedded; the old fort where the big coast defense guns once were, but where now there is little more by way of defense than a garrison of forty soldiers. We ate lunch where everyone was talking Spanish, and the food was Spanish—yellow rice cooked with saffron and curry powder, and delicious peppers that the children weren't so sure about. We went to the light-house, and climbed clear to the top on an open circular stair-way. From the top of the light-house (an open place with an entirely inadequate fence around it) we could see the whole island, and far out to sea. I had complete heart-failure coming down the steps, though the trouble has since centered in my right leg, and to-day I can hardly walk. The light-house keeper makes birds his hobby. Some he traps, and then bands their legs and turns them loose. Some he keeps in cages, and Doebie simply gloated over the new varieties she saw.

The flowers at Key West were the most gorgeous of any we have seen. Bougainvillaea in big bushy vines half cover some of the houses, and there are many India rubber trees, poinsettias in profusion, red, white, and yellow roses in masses, and lovely "pink-ball" trees that are simply filled with big pink flowers like our snow-balls, only pink.

We went to the docks and ware-houses, and saw men packing into barrels of ice some of the thousand pounds of kingfish they had brought in that day. We brought a dozen big conch shells for two cents each—a Negro lifted boards in the ware-house floor and brought them out. Some smelled to high heaven, and Jane Harriet got the smell all over her dress until we thought we'd have to bury her.

We visited a curio shop kept by a "Hinglishman" named Thompson who was more curious than his curios. He told us all manner of yarns. We learned that the recent hurricane didn't touch Key West proper at all, but just the nearby islands. We talked to a number of English sailors who told us more tall tales.

We all got badly bitten by mosquitoes in the hotel last night. One

of Jane Harriet's eyes was swollen shut. We hope these weren't
malaria mosquitoes. We're rather glad now for the six hours of peace
and quiet on the boat. We'll be in Lake Worth by six o'clock to-night
if all goes well.

LUCILE.

The trip to Key West ended successfully, and a few days after their
return to Lake Worth I visited the exiles. To keep up the family's
reputation for hard luck, Marjorie had contrived to acquire the scarlet
fever, or something exactly like it, the day before I arrived. We were
badly frightened, of course, but she was well within a week, and a
considerate doctor neglected to quarantine us. My visit lasted ten days,
and the vitamins I soaked up from the Florida sunshine saw me safely
through the winter. The family stayed on until April, and the letters
kept coming, but I had seen the sights and there was now less to tell.
Still, the later letters as well as the earlier ones are all carefully filed
away against the day when some interested descendant may choose to
dig them out and read them.

XI. Wisconsin (Part 2)

WHILE THE FAMILY was in Florida, I spent most of my time putting the finishing touches on *The Federal Union*, but it was not until a year later that the book was published, and a year after that before I began to receive any royalties. For our family these were the hardest years of the depression. In addition to the cost of Marjorie's illness and the trip to Florida, we were faced one year with the necessity of sending Jane Harriet to Milwaukee Downer, a girls' boarding school. She had experienced environmental problems, and our medical advisers insisted on getting her out of Madison for a while, a course that in the long run paid good dividends. But with all these extra expenses it was at least five years before we got entirely out of debt. One year, I recall, I had to let the taxes on our house go unpaid for six months. Brought up, as I was, with "a peasant's horror of debt," these were trying times.

I will not deny that in writing *The American Nation* I was interested in royalties. Whereas it took me six or seven years to complete *The Federal Union*, it took only three or four years for me to do *The American Nation*, a longer book. I had the advantage, however, of a semester's leave at full pay, made possible for me by the dean of the Graduate School, E. B. Fred, on condition that I would get clear out of town most of the time. So we took Marjorie for a second season to Florida, where I wrote, and wrote, and wrote. We left our oldest daughter, Jane Harriet, with a neighbor, and the middle one, Carolyn, with Dean and Mrs. Fred, who cared for her as if she were their own. She and Rosalie, the Freds' daughter, were about of an age, and hit it off together very well.

During our second stay in Florida we spent most of the time at Indian Rocks, near Clearwater, on the western coast. The elder Reynolds couple, who had cared for me when the family was in Florida before, had a cottage on the beach adjacent to ours, with a tiny guest room entirely separate from the rest of the house. They let me take over this room, so I had a good place to spread out my notes and books. One night a near hurricane blew the rain right through every crack in the walls, and next morning I found my belongings awash. Fortunately, most of them were retrievable and later rains were more gentle. Writing at a distance from a library presented so many difficulties that we left Florida in April and returned to Madison, where I spent most of my working time in a little-used room of the State Historical Society, aloof from both student and administrative responsibilities.

During our second Florida experience the demands of my writing cut down on the sight-seeing, but we took one memorable trip across the entrance to Tampa Bay, around southern Florida by the Tamiami Trail, and finally out to Key West. We had Marjorie and our dog, Smugs, with us, and in a separate car a Madison friend and her two small children. On our return trip we spent one night in Miami, and Smugs, who was usually entirely trustworthy, got lost. As a result we saw parts of the city that tourists rarely visit and that I could hardly recommend. We had to leave without the pooch, but the numerous inquiries we made resulted in his reappearance in Clearwater a week or two later, via express collect, gaunt and full of fleas. As a pup he had lost one eye to a passing automobile, so he was quite identifiable, although a frantic exchange of telegrams proved that there were an incredible number of lost one-eyed dogs in Miami.

Meantime one of our closest Madison friends, a physician, Dr. J. N. Sisk, had joined us at Indian Rocks, enroute to Cuba. "J. N." was just recuperating from a serious illness and needed a companion for the rest of his trip, so Lucile promptly volunteered to go with him. Since Lucile's mother, who had accompanied us this time to Florida, and Marjorie both went along, the scandal was not as great as we tried to make out afterward. I stayed on in Florida, for I was unwilling to take out more time from writing. For those who went, the Cuban adventure, by ship from Tampa, was a huge success, except that J. N. brought back too much supposedly duty-free Cuban liquor and to pay the customs charges had to retrieve some money he had left with me. Legally or illegally, I passed the required sum to him through the barred customs window. Marjorie also disregarded proprieties. When, as she got off the ship and saw Smugs with me, she ran to the customs-house fence to greet him, with a protesting guard at her heels. That Cuban liquor caused us much trouble. J. N. had expected to express it to himself in Madison, but this procedure turned out to be illegal, so we divided the booze between us, J. N. taking his half by train while I took mine by car, obtaining the extra space by shipping home a big box of clothes.

Despite many subsequent distractions, *The American Nation* was published in January, 1941. I wrote up the results of the election of 1940 before the vote was taken, leaving only the correct figures to be supplied in proof. I didn't have to unsay anything I had said, but I was soon to learn that recent elections rarely deserve the space that a textbook writer is prone to give them. When a few years have elapsed, he realizes that he can say all that is really necessary in about half as many words. In one sense this is all to the good, for when the time comes for a revision he will need all the space he can find.

Another thing I learned was that writing a textbook, particularly one on recent history, is not the last of it. Any such book has to be revised repeatedly (it's all in the fine print of the contract). Furthermore, if a two-volume work does well, the publishers demand a one-volume job, and vice versa. I completed the one-volume *Short History of American Democracy* in 1943, but for its second edition I obtained the assistance of my former graduate student George E. Mowry. For its third edition, and for the fourth edition of the two-volume text, both Mowry and another of my former graduate students, Robert E. Burke, collaborated with me.

But I am getting ahead of my story. When I finished my first text-book I had no idea that I had tied myself to a juggernaut that for the rest of my life would command so large a proportion of my time. I was more concerned then with the fact that I had got myself thoroughly caught up in university affairs, most of which were only indirectly related to my main business of teaching and research. For one thing, I became chairman of the department of history in 1938, not because I wanted the post, but because Paul Knaplund, who had long been chairman, insisted that he had had enough. Unlike some other universities, Wisconsin at that time neither paid departmental chairmen anything extra for their administrative duties, nor relieved them of any part of their teaching. It seemed only reasonable to pass this dubious honor around. But it did mean extra work, despite the unfailing support of an extraordinarily able departmental secretary, Helena B. Leute, who knew all the ropes. The task was the more time-consuming because of the devotion of the department to democratic procedures. All important decisions were made, not by the chairman, but by the members of the department acting together; there was no such thing as avoiding department meetings the way I had done in Nebraska while I was chairman there. Happily, the Wisconsin Department of History, and for that matter the University of Wisconsin as a whole, knew how to make democracy work. We in history might have serious disagreements, but once a decision was made—by majority vote—we all stood firmly behind it.

One chore that fell to my lot as chairman was making out the summer school budget. In those days of meager salaries nearly every member of the department, including the chairman, needed to teach summers in order to make a living. The university offered a premium for teaching in summer session without compensation; two such contributions over a given period of years would net one a semester's leave of absence with pay. But few of us could afford to take the bribe, and there was never quite enough summer school money to go around. When opportunity offered, both before and after I became chairman, I helped solve this problem by accepting whatever offers of summer teaching elsewhere happened to come my way. In 1937 I taught at the University of Southern California, in 1939 at Columbia University, and in 1941 at the University of California, Los Angeles.

Our trip to Los Angeles in 1937 was close enough on the heels of our Florida trip that we were still driving the same old 1930 Buick, book value at that time about seventy-five dollars. The Oakies and the Arkies didn't have much on us. We took the whole family with us, as usual, driving by way of Denver, Raton Pass, Albuquerque, Flagstaff, and the Mojave Desert. The only real trouble our car gave us was from a vapor lock that it invariably developed half way up a mountain grade. I learned always to have with me a milk bottle full of water with which to douse the gas line and carburetor whenever we got stalled. It worked. We covered a lot of territory on that trip, including on our way west a glimpse of the Grand Canyon, and on our return to the "East," Boulder Dam, Zion and Bryce Canyons, and the Great Salt Lake Basin. As we climbed eastward out of Salt Lake City we had our last vapor lock, and before our next trip I had traded our old car in.

While we were away from Madison, we were lucky in having a family from Chicago to live in our Shorewood Hills house. They paid us $250 for the privilege, a bonus we owed to Mannel Hahn, who showed me how to write the proper ad and where to run it. Acting on our own, I'm sure we would not have been so lucky. The family who moved in as we left brought with them a colored couple as servants, a fact that led some of the neighborhood children to report that their new playmates had two daddies, a white one and a black one. In any event, both the house and the yard were well cared for in our absence. That yard really took some caring for. It consisted of five city lots, three of which were still covered with oak trees.

Through some of our Shorewood Hills friends we learned of a house in Hollywood that we could rent for a paltry two hundred dollars (meaning fifty dollars profit to us), so while we were in Los Angeles we were well housed—almost over-housed, for we had six bedrooms and six baths, including an outside guest suite over the garage, available only by way of a fascinating catwalk. The original splendor of the house was somewhat decayed, but it put up a good front, thanks in part to a dominating false chimney that looked swell from the outside but had nothing whatever to back it up within. We had a fireplace all right, but it was somewhere else. My sister from Oshkosh and her small son visited us while we were there, and we did some gadding around, but mainly I battered my way mornings down Vermont Avenue (through twenty-three stoplights) to the USC campus, and afternoons drove with the family to the Santa Monica beach. It was not a good summer for writing and research. The most notable thing about Los Angeles then, as I think of it now, was the absence of smog.

Our trip to New York in 1939 involved much less driving, and by this time we had a better car. That summer we left our house in the charge of Jim and Nell Sellers. They also got our dog, Smugs, a real character about whom Jim wrote a piece, "Life with Smugs," that *Reader's Digest* should have published in its "most unforgettable" series. In New York we rented the apartment of Ralph Linton, the anthropologist, whom I had known before he left Wisconsin for Columbia. Since we lived within walking distance from my classes, we stored our car in a garage for twenty dollars a month and took the subway wherever we wanted to go, mainly to the World's Fair. This, too, was a poor season for writing and research.

That same summer my friend Bill Hesseltine was teaching at New York University, and lived with his family in Mamaroneck. We got together occasionally and plotted out a return trip to Madison that appealed to both families. Our route took us through New England, where we inspected Plymouth Rock and other historic sites, then to

Bangor, Maine, where we detoured to call on Mrs. Frederick Jackson Turner at Hancock Point, then across Maine to Quebec and down the St. Lawrence through Three Rivers and Montreal, then through Ontario and lower Michigan to Chicago and home. The war in Europe was just breaking out, so Bill and I read avidly whatever war bulletins we could get at each stop. In the province of Quebec we often were dependent on French-language newspapers, which Bill and I had to pool our language resources to puzzle out. Indeed, not only the newspapers, but everything else in our surroundings suddenly turned foreign. French Canada, I think, is in some ways more foreign than any European country I have ever visited.

Bill and I reacted quite differently to the war news. Whatever non-involvement sentiments I may have held before hostilities broke out, they soon began to evaporate, while Bill became more staunchly isolationist every day. It was just as well that we parted company in Michigan, where the Hicks family detoured to visit our old friends Tom and Frances Carter in Albion. Eventually, Bill and I learned just not to talk about certain things.

The trip to Los Angeles in 1941 was again in the company of the Hesseltines, for Bill was teaching at USC while I was at UCLA. This was the summer that Hitler attacked Russia, a bit of news that came to us when we had got only as far west as Taos, New Mexico. For once our embargo on discussion of the news broke down, and for once we agreed heartily. We both hoped fervently that the Germans and the Russians would cancel each other out. On the return trip to Madison we separated, with the Hicks family driving north to inspect San Francisco and Berkeley, and the Hesseltines heading east toward Oklahoma, where Bill wanted to look up some remote relatives. But before we separated we drove together into Baja California as far as Ensenada, which we found perfectly delightful, even if Mexico did seem fully as foreign as Quebec.

As for California, we liked it better the farther north we drove. We took Route One along the windings of the Pacific Coast almost all the way to San Francisco, and crossed the Bay Bridge, then only a few years old, to Berkeley. Here the Paxsons generously opened their house to us, although both Fred and Helen were away at the time. Perhaps they hoped thereby to impress upon us the desirability of living in the Bay Area. Our flirtation with the University of California had already begun; indeed, one reason for our taking the northern route home was to accept an invitation from President and Mrs. Sproul to attend a dinner party at the president's house on the Berkeley campus. We discovered, much too late for us to do anything about it, that the party was a black-tie affair, so I went in the best I had available, a dark green sport jacket and gray slacks. If, as I suspect, I was being looked over officially, my costume could hardly have done much for me.

Again we saw a lot of the U.S.A. We drove east through Salt Lake City, then veered northward across western Wyoming, taking a good look at the Jackson Hole country and Yellowstone National Park. We crossed the Big Horn Mountains along the northern route which took us to Sheridan, then drove on east through the Black Hills and the Bad Lands, and eventually got back home. By good fortune, Doris Sharp (our near neighbor in Madison) and her children had been visiting in San Francisco and drove back with us, our Jane Harriet riding in the Sharp car part of the time and spelling Doris with the driving. These long summer junkets paid few dividends in books written and research accomplished, but they did make us all better aware of the hugeness and the complexity of the American nation. That might even have helped me a little as a historian, for history, according to Herder, is only "geography set in motion."

While I was at Wisconsin, and probably now also, the faculty participated extensively in the making and administration of university policy. When I first came there I noted, for example, with some amazement the way in which a faculty committee, headed by Mark Ingraham (not yet a dean), worked out a graduated system of salary cuts to meet the reduced legislative appropriations that accompanied the depression. At Nebraska the chancellor, on his own initiative, had simply announced a flat 10 per cent cut in all salaries, and that was that. But at Wisconsin the faculty itself took over the problem, and assessed higher cuts percentagewise on the high salaries and lower cuts on the low salaries. Nor did the university choose to deplete faculty ranks by dismissing non-tenure members and refusing to fill vacancies, a heartless procedure that enabled some universities to boast of not cutting salaries. In a great variety of ways the principle of self-government was observed. Departmental chairmen were nominated by the members of a given department, and only in extremely rare cases did the deans fail to accept these recommendations. Deans and other high administrative officers were usually chosen as the result of faculty consensus, whether formally or informally expressed, and their tenure of office depended primarily upon their success in representing accurately faculty opinion. Or, to use an expression I heard often from the lips of Dean Sellery, "Ours is a *faculty* university."

New presidents were sometimes loath to concede this point. The system grew up with presidents chosen from the faculty, notably Charles R. Van Hise and Edward A. Birge, who knew and understood its moods. Glenn Frank, chosen by the regents in 1925, was a journalist rather than an academician and had trouble adjusting himself to the system. His Experimental College lasted only a few years, and was completely liquidated by the time I arrived on the scene. By this time, indeed, Frank had accepted the limitations that faculty opinion had imposed on him, and had become a good constitutional monarch who reigned but did not rule. In the meantime, however, he had made many campus enemies, which accounted for the fact that the faculty did nothing to prevent his ouster by the regents in 1937, despite its obviously political nature. He had many friends on campus—I counted myself among them—but we knew that if we came to his defense other and louder faculty voices would be raised against him, thus doing him no good and merely dividing the faculty. Indeed, I was one of a self-appointed committee of three, all friends of Frank, who went to him before his infamous "trial" and urged him to avoid the impending ordeal by resigning. Unfortunately, he did not choose to take our advice.

My acquaintance with Glenn Frank dated back to the time when we were both undergraduates at Northwestern. For a while we were classmates, but because I had to drop out a year for financial reasons he became a senior while I was still a junior. As students, both of us had to earn our own way, but years later at Wisconsin, when we were exchanging reminiscences, Glenn pointed out that he had had a better "racket" than mine. What he meant, but had no need to say, was that even then he was in demand as a public speaker, and could make from a single lecture more than I could make in a week, or maybe a month. We had much in common by way of background. Both of us had grown up in small Missouri towns, which are as alike as identical twins. Both of us had received a thorough indoctrination in orthodox Methodism. Both of us had outgrown our earlier beliefs and had abandoned the ministerial career toward which our parents had pointed us. But Glenn never left the Methodist Church, as I did, and at Wisconsin he made it a practice to preach the baccalaureate sermon for each graduating class.

At Northwestern Frank always managed to stand quite apart from the general student body. I remember particularly the speech he made during the commencement exercises that marked the graduation of his class. He was one of four student speakers, the rest of whom sweated their way through a memorized and uninspired performance. But Glenn ostentatiously changed his subject from the one announced on the printed program, then spoke with his usual ease and fluency, impressing everyone, as he no doubt intended to do, with his ability to speak extemporaneously on almost any subject, any time. He worked hard to achieve this excellence. I can recall going to the School of Oratory on the Evanston campus to keep an appointment with Professor James L. Lardner, and finding Glenn on the high platform of the auditorium, practicing his piece, with Lardner as coach and audience.

Abram W. Harris, president of Northwestern University, was among those who were impressed by Glenn's extraordinary ability as a speaker. This was one reason, no doubt, why Harris made Glenn assistant to the president, or, in effect, alumni secretary, immediately after Glenn's graduation in 1912. In this position, which he held for four years, Glenn quickly, and no doubt properly, separated himself still further from the student body. For example, when he attended Sunday morning services at the First Methodist Episcopal church of Evanston, where students felt welcome only in the gallery, Frank now appeared in a cutaway coat and striped pants, then the customary Sunday regalia for men who felt that they had arrived, and took his seat on the main floor in the rented-pew section. When there was no audience involved, however, he could break down and fraternize in the most friendly fashion. I recall one occasion, while I was at the circulation desk of the Northwestern library, when Glenn came in with a problem. He had to make a speech the next day on a subject about which he said he knew nothing. Together we went through the card catalogue in search of appropriate titles, and he carried off an armful of books. I've no doubt he entranced his audience.

My next direct contact with Frank came while I was teaching at the University of Nebraska. He was invited there primarily to speak to the students, but because the university had not then an auditorium large enough to accommodate the expected audience his address was scheduled for the First Methodist Episcopal church. He spoke without notes or manuscript, but with never a pause to think for the right word. I remember his theme, which was prophetic. He was arguing the case for a more effective national leadership. What the country needed, he said, was another Roosevelt, not necessarily another man by that name, but someone with T. R.'s vitality and aggressiveness (Glenn Frank?). While he was in Lincoln I attended a luncheon in his honor, and someone presented me to him with this query: "Do you know this man?"

"Like a book," he replied. But when I asked him to meet with our little group of humanists, he brushed the invitation off with what seemed to us unnecessary brusqueness. Whether he intended it that way or not, we got the impression that he regarded us as too small potatoes for him to bother with.

At Wisconsin I shared the skepticism of my colleagues about the value of the speeches from the chair with which Frank often opened faculty meetings. He never got over being a preacher, and his remarks usually dwelt on some aspect of university affairs in which he thought he could lead us to a better life. As far as content is concerned, I remember only one of those speeches. He was impressed with the imbalance between the achievements of science on the one hand and the social studies and humanities on the other. Scientific progress, he maintained, had got too far ahead. To even things up, there should be a kind of moratorium on scientific achievement in order to give the humanities time to catch up. The best face one could put on this bit of naïveté was that it was meant as a tongue-in-cheek admonition to the laggards to hurry up, but we couldn't be sure that he didn't really mean exactly what he said. He was not a deep thinker, but he had a way of clothing the obvious in fine enough words to make it sound original. His flow of words, however, while always in musical cadences, sometimes grew monotonous. The same pat phrases tended to reappear too often, and his use of such devices as alliteration drew uncomplimentary comments.

One trouble with Frank's university speeches was that they were always read, a manner of delivery that greatly reduced their effectiveness. He had no need to read a speech, for he never lacked words to express his ideas, and I could never understand why he tied himself to a manuscript. The university community never knew what a terrific spellbinder he could be when he cut loose on his own.

Frank both read and wrote books, something very unusual in university presidents, who rarely have time for either. Also, he accumulated a large library; the abundance of bookshelves he had built into the president's house was reputed to have been an embarrassment to his successor. But despite his bookishness, Frank never won faculty recognition as a scholar. There was no field in which he was a specialist; his books and articles were addressed primarily to the general public. His *Thunder and Dawn* (1932) was characterized on campus as "a lot of noise and not much light." His *America's Hour of Decision* (1934), whatever its merits, won little faculty applause. His book reviews, while lucid and well written, would rarely have rated publication in a professional journal. As editor of *Century* he was quite in his element; as president of a great university, he was miscast.

Part of the Franks' trouble at Wisconsin was the manner of life they chose to live. Instead of adapting themselves to the unpretentious ways of a small middle-western city, they tried to bring with them to Madison the high proprieties of New York society. They employed a butler and maintained a chauffeur-driven car; they entertained too lavishly, with "white tie" or "black tie" noted on invitations; they made a little too much of visiting celebrities; they gave the impression of being on their way to more important roles.

Only once do I recall the Franks' being at our house, and that was after we had been in Madison four or five years, for by then we had moved to Shorewood Hills. We used to have a big evening party each December 25, with 150 or more guests to drink eggnogs—or something stronger—listen to Janie Fish's "songbirds," a group of women who liked to sing but not all of whom could, and then sing along together after Janie's group got through. Glenn rose to the familiar tunes like an old fire horse to the sound of a fire bell and had himself a time. But when we ran out of Christmas carols he insisted on singing some Easter hymns, to the considerable dismay of some of our High Church Episcopal friends.

About two years before his dismissal, Frank for some reason quite unknown to me asked me to become chairman of the committee on honorary degrees. This group included a lot of deans, ex officio, and the president himself, if he chose to attend. Frank would have liked to use the offer of a degree as a means of bringing celebrities to the campus, and he sometimes succeeded, as for example in the case of Katharine Cornell. But the committee tried to hold him to the rule that no one should receive a degree unless his career was related in some way either to the university or to the state of Wisconsin. Unlike California, where the committee is secret and nominations come only from the president, the Wisconsin committee itself, whose personnel was well known, could initiate recommendations. From time to time the infighting got pretty tough, as members sought to pay off obligations or to win special favors. Outside pressure for degrees was also considerable, and the committee had to take the blame for candidates who were turned down. We were criticized, quite properly, I think, for refusing a degree to Frank Lloyd Wright because his matrimonial adventures gave offense to the puritans. Our most heated denunciations, however, came from the progressives, who claimed that we discriminated against their kind. We were roundly denounced for not granting a degree to Justice Louis D. Brandeis, although I had a letter from him in my files declining the proffer of a degree on the ground that its acceptance would be incompatible with his service on the Supreme Court.

The LaFollette fans tried hard, also, to get an honorary degree for "young Bob," who was then United States Senator. This recommendation would ordinarily have met with ready approval, but, by the time it reached the committee, the break between Frank and the LaFollette family had already come, and it was an open secret that the latter had marked the former for execution. It seemed indecent to me that Frank should be compelled to confer an honorary degree upon one of his probable chief executioners, so after a terrific fight I blocked the proposal in the committee. I doubt if the LaFollettes ever forgave me for that, although I actually paved the way for the Senator to receive the degree later on. I knew that William H. Kiekhofer, the Wisconsin economist, although politically a conservative, was a warm friend of the LaFollette family and personally favored granting the degree. So when I resigned the chairmanship after the appointment of a new president, as I thought I should, I recommended Kiekhofer as my successor. My recommendation was accepted, and with Frank out of the picture, young Bob got his degree.

My original stand on the LaFollette degree won from Dean Sellery, who was a member of the committee and favored the course I opposed, the nearest thing to an admission of error that I ever heard him make. I had always stood in especial awe of the Dean, an attitude dating back to the years when I was a graduate student and he was chairman of the history department, so it took courage of a high order for me to tangle with him. We had held our committee meeting at the University Club on State Street, and I had won out over his very vocal opposition. After the session was over, as I crossed Park Street to climb "the hill," whom should I meet but Sellery, standing high on the curb and glowering down at me.

"Well, you beat me," he said, and then as if by way of afterthought, "but you wouldn't have, only you were right."

Despite his often ill-concealed truculence, Dean Sellery had a charming and warm-hearted nature. I was devoted to him. The value of his service to the university during his many years on the faculty can hardly be overestimated.

It was during the Frank administration, also, that I was made chairman of a committee charged with the task of creating a University of Wisconsin Press. The recommendation of my name for this task came from my friend E. B. Fred, then dean of the Graduate School, who argued that the results of university scholarship should be presented to the readers in "beautiful books," not in the incredibly ugly "bulletins," always bound in battleship gray paper covers, that were then current. Frank saw the point and gave the project his unstinted support, but it was not easy to convert the faculty, most of whom looked askance at all suggestions of funneling funds into channels other than the restoration of salaries to their pre-depression levels. It took all the combined skill of Dean Fred and me to win the grudging consent of the faculty to a timid start, but we managed it somehow, and the press got going. It was not, of course, a printing concern, but merely a publishing agency. One of our chief troubles with the faculty was to make this difference clear, for to most of them, strange as it may seem, the word "press" connoted only a printing establishment. Once we got started, faculty manuscripts soon began to come our way, and the University of Wisconsin Press still lives.

Frank's troubles with the LaFollettes were both personal and political. I never knew the Senator personally, but the Phil LaFollettes were ultrademocratic and entertained simply, even in the Governor's Mansion, a far less imposing house than the university president occupied. People with such different tastes and values could hardly have liked each other. My guess is that Glenn's oratorical skill, perhaps unconsciously, also irritated Phil, who was no mean orator himself. I can remember remarking on one occasion: "You can't have two boy orators in the same state." Most particularly was this true in view of the fact that they both had political aspirations. On domestic policies they were not really very far apart; as far as content was concerned—but not form—each could have given most of the other's speeches without undue embarrassment. Both men were progressive Republicans to begin with; not until far into the thirties did the Wisconsin progressives divorce themselves from the Republican party. By that time the President and the Governor were completely at odds; but even if they hadn't been I doubt if Frank could ever have brought himself to leave the Republican party. Nor apparently could he bear the thought of becoming a Democrat. Regardless of his party affiliations, his transparent political aspirations were certain to irk the LaFollettes. They wanted no rivals, either in their own camp or elsewhere.

There may have been a considerable difference between the two antagonists on the role the university should play in the state. Under the elder Governor LaFollette and President Van Hise, the "Wisconsin Idea" had included the use of university experts for advice and assistance in the government of the state. As time went on, some progressives came to believe that the university should be dominated by men who adhered to progressive views and would promote progressive ideas. They regarded conservatives on the faculty with great suspicion, and ultraconservatives as fit only to be rooted out. Frank, quite correctly, held that the university must never become the tool of any one party or faction. The duty of the university was to educate, not to indoctrinate. I doubt if either of the LaFollette brothers thought the opposite, but sometimes their statements could be so construed. The demand for the elimination of "deadwood" from the faculty, for example, led some observers to conclude that the "deadwood" consisted mainly of individuals out of sympathy with the LaFollettes. Frank could be trusted to dramatize such an issue as this, whether it really existed or not. To him the rights of faculty members to freedom of speech and to security in whatever tenure they had acquired were inviolable.

While most of the university faculty were ready to concede that the regents should never have chosen Frank to be president, hiring him and firing him were two different things. Frank's presence at the head of the university no longer posed any threat to the faculty. He had long before accepted their right to a dominant role in internal university affairs. He was a kindly person who never showed the slightest desire to hurt anyone. He had his lightning rod up for a political job, and given time he just might have made it. To be sure, his personal feud with the Governor might cost the university money; but, on the other hand, a new president, chosen by a politically-minded board of regents, could become a sore trial to us; the process of bringing him to the state of grace that Frank had already attained might be long and arduous. On the whole, I found myself in Frank's corner.

The final execution came soon after Governor LaFollette had appointed enough anti-Frank regents to do the job, but the vote for dismissal was only eight to seven. At this time I was one of the six members of the University Committee, a faculty institution which existed to offer the administration whatever advice it saw fit, and to make a kind of "state of the union" report on university conditions each year. Our committee was assured by the regents—quite unofficially, of course—that if we would not come to Frank's defense we would be given a voice in the choice of his successor. Actually we couldn't do anything for Frank—he was beyond help, and we were too divided on that subject anyway. I, for one, had little hope of influencing the regents, but the president of the board and two other members met with us in the president's office. They handed us a list of seven names to consider, but it was obvious that the only name in which they had any interest was that of Clarence A. Dykstra; indeed, it was apparent that they had already decided on him. My five colleagues accepted the decision with relief, for it could certainly have been worse, but as a minority of one I protested mildly. We had just had our troubles with a president who was a journalist; what better could we hope from a city manager? Why not a faculty man, preferably someone from our own faculty who would from the beginning understand our system of operation? My personal choice would have been E. B. Fred.

Dykstra was given a warm welcome by the Wisconsin faculty, but he was in trouble with the regents after the election of 1938 brought the Republicans back into power and ended the ascendancy of the progressives. As soon as possible, the state legislature abolished the board of regents that had dismissed Frank and hired Dykstra, replacing it with a new board appointed by the Republican governor. With this group Dykstra had two strikes against him from the beginning. Dykstra's admiration for Robert Hutchins, president of the University of Chicago, also caused considerable faculty unrest, for Dyke showed a strong disposition to follow wherever Hutchins led. To please our President we set up some interdepartmental combinations that we called institutes, but we took pains to insure that the colleges and the departments would still retain their customary autonomy. The illusion that university departmentalization can separate all knowledge into mutually exclusive segments is a favorite of the nonacademic mind. Departments are essential for administrative reasons, but scholars rarely recognize any hard and fast boundaries between fields. In history, and in the other social studies, everyone poaches at will on everyone else's preserve—now we even go in strongly for the history of science. As I have often taken occasion to remark, the temple of knowledge is one, but the doors that open into it are many.

Members of a university faculty are almost always drawn into professional activities that reach well beyond the boundaries of their campus, and I was no exception to the rule. During my Wisconsin years I devoted much time to the affairs of the Mississippi Valley Historical Association (now the Organization of American Historians), and the American Historical Association. I was president of the former the first year I lived in Madison, and a member of its executive committee for six years thereafter. I served also as chairman of an *ad hoc* committee to seek a university sponsor for the *Mississippi Valley Historical Review* and to choose a new editor, tasks somewhat more difficult than they might appear on the surface. I was also a member of the executive council of the American Historical Association, and on one occasion drew the thankless assignment of heading a special committee on reorganization. Operating without a budget, our committee succeeded in modernizing the constitution of the Association and in centering its principal activities in Washington, D.C., where, according to our charter, it was supposed to have its headquarters. Shortly afterward a committee of which I was a member chose former President Guy Stanton Ford of the University of Minnesota to be both executive secretary of the Association and managing editor of the *Review*. This combination of duties was, by design, not a constitutional requirement, but it made possible a salary (the depression was still on) large enough to induce a distinguished historian to head up our Washington office. For several years I was also chairman of the committee on the Carnegie Revolving Fund which selected from manuscripts submitted to it those it deemed worthy of publication and drew on the Fund to turn the manuscripts into books. On an average we published about a volume a year. While I lived in Wisconsin I rarely, if ever, missed a meeting of either the AHA or the MVHA, although as a matter of policy—or poverty—the university refused to pay any part of the expenses of faculty members for attendance of professional meetings.

The outbreak of World War II provided another distraction from my teaching and research activities. The prewar years produced in Wisconsin a lively debate between the advocates of collective security and those of continued isolation, with the isolationists definitely in the ascendancy. For a time I wavered somewhat between the two extremes, although my sympathies were all with the Allied powers and against the Axis. After the British and French gave their cause away at Munich I wondered what use it would be for the United States to take a hand in the situation, but the events of 1939 decided my attitude, and thereafter I advocated, in season and out of season, strengthening the national defense and giving to the Allies all possible aid short of war. This stand brought me into conflict with Bundist and Communist sympathizers alike, both fanatically opposed to any American involvement in the European struggle. I can remember a certain amount of heckling in my classes—the only time in my career that this ever happened to me—but, considering the source, the interruptions didn't bother me much. After the German attack on Russia the Communists and the fellow travelers came over to my side, somewhat to my embarrassment, for I felt much more comfortable when they were against me. After Pearl Harbor even the Bundists piped down, thus restoring peace to the classroom, even if the sounds of war grew deafening everywhere else.

I loved the University of Wisconsin as I have loved no other university, and I still find it difficult to account for my decision to leave it. I turned down an offer from Harvard in 1939, partly because, in addition to a professorship in history I would for a while have had to take charge of placing the young men with high hopes and no tenure that President Conant had decided to liquidate from his faculty; also, partly because after my half year at Harvard in 1931–1932 I realized that I could never fit comfortably into an eastern environment. My children would eventually belong, but not their parents. I cold-shouldered other overtures, among them the first offer I received from California, but with many misgivings I accepted a far more attractive one that came the following year. I can remember casting up accounts —why I should stay at Wisconsin in one column, and why I should go to California in the other. On the "stay" side were my cordial relationships with the faculty, my eminently satisfactory classroom contacts, my interest in the Middle West as a field for research, and the presence of a sister, my only surviving close relative, in nearby Osh-kosh. I valued, too, some of my social connections, particularly the Town and Gown Club, a group of rare individuals, including former President Birge, Charles Slichter, John R. Commons, Justice George Nelson (until his death), Lucien M. Hanks, Dr. Joseph Evans, E. B. Fred, George Thorp, and on occasion Glenn Frank and former Governor Kohler. Except for the last two, these men dined together at regular intervals and discussed with gusto every important item in the news. I have never known their like elsewhere.

On the "go" side were my frequent policy disagreements with President Dykstra, the low salary scale at Wisconsin, the possible advantages of the move to members of my family, the temptation of a more salubrious climate, and the lure of the West for a grandson of pioneers. As I think back on it, perhaps the deciding factor was that I really didn't want to go, and was suffering from an undiagnosed attack of puritanism. Was it right for anyone to be enjoying himself so much? Perhaps a new environment would keep me from getting into a rut, and it would certainly present a new challenge. Could I, at fifty-two, start all over again, and get away with it? Whatever the reasons, in the end the verdict was: "California, here I come!"

The way in which my successor at Wisconsin was chosen provides an interesting example of the democratic procedures then in vogue on that campus. When members of the department asked me to suggest the names of such individuals as I deemed best qualified to succeed me, I made two nominations, Elmer Ellis of the University of Missouri (not yet its president) and Merle Curti of Columbia Teachers College. The first choice of the department was Ellis, mainly because of his interest in western history, a subject which had a long tradition at Wisconsin. When Ellis turned the offer down, the invitation went to Curti, who accepted. President Dykstra, who was informed rather than consulted about departmental plans, heartily approved of Ellis but was lukewarm toward Curti. The department, however, with the dean's approval, put its judgment above the President's, and went ahead. No doubt Dykstra would have agreed heartily later on that the department's judgment was in this case far better than his own.

XII. California (Part 1)

WE CAME from Wisconsin to California by train in August, 1942. We had made the trip by automobile twice before and really had no great urge to drive that long distance again; besides, the war was on, rubber rationing had begun, and our tires weren't up to it. So we loaded all our household goods and our automobile into a freight car and took the train. We were a party of five—or of six, counting Judy, Smugs' successor, who rode in the baggage car. Our oldest daughter, Jane Harriet, had just finished her junior year at the University of Wisconsin; our second daughter, Carolyn, would have been a senior in the university high school; our youngest, Marjorie, was ready for junior high. None of them wanted to leave Madison, and to appease them we resorted to shameless bribery. Jane Harriet was to have a fur coat (far more important in Wisconsin than it proved to be in California), Carolyn, a great Dane dog, and Marjorie, a horse. Eventually we delivered on all three promises, at least after a fashion. Jane Harriet got the coat in reasonable time, and Marjorie soon owned the best fifty-dollar horse in California, a black old gentleman named Harlem, who proved to be a jumper. We learned later that he had been too much for the Mills College girls to handle. But the dog business hung fire for a long time. We already had enough dogs. Judy was an "almost wirehair" who soon had pups, one of which was a remarkably perfect wirehair named Penny, whom we kept. And our Berkeley house stood on too small a lot to accommodate a great Dane. Years later, however, when Lucile and I were in England, Carolyn took matters into her own hands and bought for herself out of her own allowance the great Dane we had promised but had not delivered. When we came home a good share of our living room furniture had to be replaced or reupholstered.

The train we took to California was crowded with servicemen on their way to the Pacific, so the older girls had a ball. We hardly saw them. Everywhere the train stopped it was surrounded by buzzing groups of patriotic women with gifts for the boys who were going to war. A favorite token of esteem was a big frosted cake for whichever man in uniform had a birthday that day. By the strangest sort of coincidence there always turned out to be a birthday boy for every cake. Our train was not the swiftest on the line, for it took us about three days and four nights to make the trip. Wherever we stopped there was usually plenty of time for Marjorie to retrieve her dog from the baggage car and walk the canine back and forth the length of the train. But retrieving Marjorie before the train pulled out kept us in a perpetual state of anxiety.

We were met at the Berkeley station by Fred and Helen Paxson, who had obtained a bedding-down place for us at Cloyne Court, an apartment hotel on Hearst Street, near the campus. This hotel was inhabited mainly by elderly persons, "the home of the living dead," the girls called it. The management looked askance at both the girls and the dog, but we assured the lady at the desk that they were all well behaved, so she let us in. Our presence in the dining room, even without the dog, led to many raised eyebrows, and some comments. The older girls kept bringing in the obviously noncommissioned representatives of the armed forces that they had met on the train, and raucous sounds of mirth were rarely absent from our table. Marjorie, who was eleven, noted with interest the way the waiters carried their trays on one hand high above their heads, and imitated them in carrying out after each meal a plate loaded with scraps for her dog. If anyone smiled, it was her parents, but we rarely dared to because of the shocked expressions we saw about us. We lived in Cloyne Court for about three weeks, while we were house hunting; the wonder is that we weren't asked to go long before we checked out.

At length we found a house about two miles north of the campus on Southampton Avenue. It had long been vacant, except for rare visits from the retired lady doctor who owned it. Our real estate agent had to talk hard to the owner to persuade her to let us have it, but the patriotic motive turned the trick. Houses were too scarce in the Bay Area, our agent argued, for any to be left unoccupied. The government might even step in and take over such property. The house, fortunately, was large enough to meet our needs, with five bedrooms, an attic, a basement, and three baths. We had a view of the Golden Gate from the windows on the west side of the house, and early began to worship at that shrine. We rented the place at first, then bought it and lived in it for a total of ten years. But Lucile never really liked the house, and cast longing eyes at two vacant lots across the street. In the end we bought those lots and built on them the glass and redwood house in which we now live. By that time the daughters were all married, so we needed only a small house all on one floor, the kind sometimes described as complete with a lot of big rooms in it. For good measure the new house also had two patios, a big car port, and two outside storerooms to take care of the stuff that usually occupies an attic, not to mention back-breaking gardens all around. We quickly discovered the existence of shrubs known as "California natives," which could be counted on to survive with a minimum of human assistance, planted them in profusion, and let them grow at will. From our living room window we acquired a nearly one hundred-degree sweep of San Francisco Bay, a perpetually changing picture that we think now we could never live without.

The daughters soon accommodated themselves well to the Berkeley environment. Jane Harriet transferred to the University, was affiliated by her sorority, graduated a year later, and got a job with the army at the Presidio. I was distressed to learn that, for tuition purposes, she was still a resident of Wisconsin, and that I, although a member of the University of California faculty, must pay out-of-state tuition for her. Had I sent her back to Wisconsin to finish where she had started, I should also have had to pay out-of-state tuition for her there, since I was no longer a resident of Wisconsin. I've never quite reconciled myself to those rulings. One shouldn't become a stateless person because of moving from one state to another. Nor, for that matter, should one lose his right to vote in national elections on that account. Carolyn didn't like the idea of attending Berkeley High because of its enormous size, so we sent her to the Anna Head School for girls, from which she graduated a year later. She lacked adequate language require-ments for admission to Cal, so went to junior college in San Francisco for a year, then back to the University of Wisconsin for her second year. But her mother was unreconciled to her being so far away, so during her third year she attended Mills College. Then, because of her special interests and talents, she enrolled at the Oakland College of Arts and Crafts, from which in due time she graduated with a B.F.A. degree. Marjorie, in her turn, graduated from the Anna Head School, then from the University of California. I advised all three daughters to take the courses necessary to obtain teaching credentials, but they unanimously refused. Since their mother and I insisted that they should prepare themselves somehow to make a living, they elected one after another to take courses in shorthand and typewriting and to become stenographers. Each of them held a good job for several years, but they did not lack for masculine attention, and eventually they all married.

There was nothing in my earlier teaching experience to prepare me adequately for the impersonality of a large university in a big-city environment. Hamline University, where I had first taught, was indeed located in the Twin Cities, but the college was self-contained and quite unaffected by its urban surroundings. And while summer assignments had taken me to several great urban centers, summer visitors do not expect to identify themselves to any considerable extent with an environment in which their stay is so short. Greensboro, North Carolina, Lincoln, Nebraska, and Madison, Wisconsin, were all small cities in which the local campus loomed large. But Berkeley, although its inhabitants numbered then less than one hundred thousand, was part of a great metropolitan center, in which the university played only a very minor role. To find living quarters, both faculty and students tended to spread out over a wide area, for there were then relatively few university-owned dormitories, and no housing whatever for faculty. The Faculty Club served as a convenient luncheon center, not only for the faculty as individuals, but for the innumerable committees that university activities spawned. But, to my surprise, I soon found that acquaintances made on campus rarely ripened into friendships and off-campus connections. Departments were large. The history department, for example, consisted of about twenty-five full-time members (it is about three times that size now), as many as the entire faculty of Hamline University numbered when I taught there. Nor was the faculty of the history department very closely knit, a difference between Wisconsin and California to which I found it difficult to adjust. Indeed, while my history colleagues were uniformly courteous to me, they seemed, with a few exceptions, to regard my coming with the greatest indifference, or in some cases as an affront.

This attitude on the part of my new colleagues bothered both Lucile and me considerably, for we were used to the generous hospitality of the Middle West. Primarily, of course, what we were experiencing was only the impersonality that goes with numbers, with a "multiversity" in a metropolitan area. But there were other factors. The war was on and, with gas and tire rationing the order of the day, mobility was at a minimum; people were handicapped in whatever desires they may have had to welcome newcomers. Also, as I came to realize later, there was a certain disadvantage to my having been imported to fill a higher position at a higher salary than many of my long-resident colleagues enjoyed—over their heads, so to speak. This was not my fault; I had not sought the appointment, and had accepted it only after long hesitation and with the gravest of doubts. University of California policy was really to blame. The university had at its disposal a number of endowed chairs, each named after the individual or individuals who had furnished the endowment. In most instances these endowments did not fully pay the salaries of the named chairs, as most people assumed, but they did provide enough extra income to make possible higher salaries for the named professors than for those less fortunate. Worse still, it was generally assumed that these "super-professorships" must go to an outsider rather than to anyone who was already a member of the staff. From the point of view of the administration this made sense; why pay all that extra money for someone you've already got? On principle, however, I came to believe that the policy was wrong, and I am happy to observe that it is now being discarded. There is a kind of colonialism involved in the assumption that you must go elsewhere for your best scholars, that your university cannot be expected to grow its own. Our current and more wholesome practice, I believe, is to do most of our outside recruiting at a lower level, and whenever possible to award the named professorships to men on our own staff who have won high distinction in their respective fields. This development does not mean inbreeding, for the promotions merely reflect achievements in residence, without regard to the earlier background of a given individual. It is rather an evidence of the attainment by the university of a higher degree of self-confidence and maturity.

There is an old saying that we have often repeated to newcomers: "You have plenty of friends here; your only problem is to find them." This was our experience. If we found fewer of our friends than we had expected within the university, we found many more than we had expected outside. The families of our neighborhood, unable to travel for social events as far and as often during the war as formerly, saw more of each other, and "included us in." The Hillside Club, an organization of more than two hundred people who owned a clubhouse, put on plays, musicales, and other performances for their self entertainment, offered us membership and an opportunity for Lucile to sing and act. Out of these and similar connections came many warm friends. It is possible that university people too often herd together and too infrequently associate with people in other walks of life. That was probably true of us before we came to Berkeley, but it has not been true since.

We also contrived to see a good deal of California, despite wartime conditions. This opportunity came about through the Extension Division, which almost immediately solicited my aid in spreading the gospel of internationalism throughout the state. For a small fee and a university car in which to make the trip, I went to numerous towns and cities to speak my mind on whatever subject involving international relations I thought worth while. Having battled isolationism with all my heart before I came to California, I was not without something to say. I talked to audiences large and small, listened to their questions, and pointed out the futility of our nation's trying any longer to live to itself alone. This is one subject on which the American people changed their minds during the 1940's. The experience of Senator Arthur H. Vandenberg of Michigan was not unique; millions of ordinary Americans, swayed by the logic of the world situation, shifted from the myth of isolationism to the reality of full American participation in world affairs. "Look," said Lucile, one night on the way home after one of these lecture trips, "you don't have to make that speech anymore. The people all agree with you." But meantime we had seen enough of California to realize how rich and beautiful a state it is, and how lucky we were to have identified ourselves with it.

Nostalgia, however, is a powerful force, and I almost yielded to it. Had I received an offer to return to Wisconsin at the end of my first California year, I no doubt would have accepted it. But the offer, which for a time I awaited impatiently, came only after two years, and that proved to be too late. At that stage of my career I thought that my principal interest lay in agricultural, or to be more accurate, agrarian, history—the farmer in politics—and the plan, to which I was more or less party, was to bring me back to Wisconsin to fill some kind of liaison position involving both the Department of History and the College of Agriculture. I had no sooner made up my mind to accept the offer than doubts began to intrude. In the first place, I had heard from the history chairman at Wisconsin and the dean of Letters and Science, but had had not a word from anyone in Agriculture. Would I be expected on my return to negotiate my own position? Furthermore, how sold was I on restricting my teaching and research to a single narrow aspect of American history? Would I be content to see the courses that I had once loved and taught committed indefinitely to someone else? And what, incidentally, would my successor, chosen precisely to take my place, think of my sudden reappearance? Finally, how could the descendant of ten generations of American pioneers take the back trail? Whether I liked it or not—and I was no longer so sure that I didn't like it—I knew that I would have to stay in California.

Meantime, Professor Paxson, chairman of the California Department of History and my closest Berkeley friend, had painstakingly avoided trying to sway my decision. When I went to his office to tell him that I had made up my mind to stay, he was visibly moved. I can still see him as he rose from his chair, grasped my hand, and said only two words: "My son." It was perhaps the only time I ever knew him to express deep emotion. When he told our president, Robert Gordon Sproul, of my decision, Sproul immediately called me by telephone to affirm his delight and to ask me to listen to the campanile chimes that noon. When the clock tolled twelve, I therefore cocked an ear, and heard the bells ring out first "On Wisconsin," then "The Bear Comes over the Mountain," then "All Hail, Blue and Gold." I got the message, or at least I thought I did. But the President, when he got home that night, had to answer to his wife. "Bob," she said, "what in the world happened to the campanile this noon?"

"I don't know," he replied, "what?"

"Oh, all those wild tunes on Good Friday!" As a good Catholic, she had noticed.

Suspecting (not without reason) that Lucile had had a hand in my decision, the President sent her a beautiful orchid corsage. Well, what do you do with an orchid corsage on Good Friday, even if you are only retired Methodists? We sat home and the orchids sat in the refrigerator. The Saturday night after Good Friday we tried to get the Paxsons to join us for a night on the town, but they had a previous engagement. So the orchids rested until the third day. Then, we decided, they could at least be taken to church on Easter Sunday. Our oldest daughter, Jane Harriet, had been confirmed some years before in the Episcopal Church, so we went with her to her church, St. Mark's.

This was by no means our first such trip, but up to that time we had never rated a better seat than the third pew from the rear. But with all those orchids pinned on Lucile, the usher even on Easter Sunday unhesitatingly led us to the third pew from the front, an incident that I love to recount to my Episcopal friends, who usually manage to achieve only a faint smile.

Just as the age of normalcy had colored my Nebraska experience and the Great Depression my years at Wisconsin, so World War II was to exert a dominating influence on my first decade at the University of California. In the fall of 1942 residents of the Pacific Coast were by no means sure that their cities might not be subjected to air raids, and elaborate instructions abounded on what to do in case of such an emergency. I was for a time the air raid warden for my immediate neighborhood, and had some fire-fighting equipment (never used) stored in my basement. One night orders came through that the whole Bay Area must be blacked out. I checked all residences in my block to see that no lights were left burning, then joined Lucile to watch from our attic window while one great urban section after another, from downtown Oakland on our left, through San Francisco and Marin County in front of us, over to downtown Richmond on our right, went dark; then, when the alert was over, we watched while the lights in similar stages came on again—an eerie sight. On campus the basements of certain buildings were designated as air raid shelters (they still are), but neither faculty nor students seemed much alarmed. What was far more upsetting was the introduction of the three semester, or trimester, system, which divided the calendar year into three nearly equal periods, each about the length of an ordinary semester. The purpose of this change was to enable students to pursue their studies the year around, with a minimum of time out for vacations.

The university already had its army and navy ROTC units, but it soon had also various special programs designed to encourage students to enlist, then to continue with college courses that would presumably fit them for specialized roles in the armed services. Men so enlisted were not subject to induction under the Selective Service Act, although they might be called directly for duty at any time, if necessity required. While much more complicated and extensive than the old S.A.T.C. of World War I, the World War II programs proved to be less difficult to deal with, and the work of the university went on. Naturally, some of the men griped at the necessity of taking such courses as American history (almost a universal requirement). "What has that got to do with killing Japanese in the South Pacific?" they asked. Others, however, realized that they needed an education for peace as well as for war, and were delighted to carry forward so large a part of their normal college program. Inevitably the number of women on campus in proportion to the number of men went up, as draft boards made servicemen of many potential students and class after class in the training programs went off to war. Graduate studies, except in some of the sciences, were particularly hard hit. I had fewer students in my seminars than ever before or after, sometimes only three or four at a time.

But if my seminars were small, my other classes were large. It fell to my lot to teach one lecture section in the survey of United States history. This class met in the large semicircular auditorium of California Hall, which had seats for about four hundred. So my class numbered about four hundred. Paxson told me that a teacher might safely enroll about 10 per cent more students than he had places for, since not all of them could be expected to be present at the same time. But accustomed as I was to seating my students and having my assistants check each day for absentees, I would have nothing to do with such laxity, and took on only as many students as I could assign to seats. I had not given the survey course for many years, partly because I had no desire to lecture in competition with my own textbooks, but under war conditions I seemed to have no choice. Nor was I man enough to throw out my own books, which were in use at California long before I arrived. So I did the best I could to enrich my lectures with material not exploited in the texts. California Hall was not too large for me to make everyone in the room hear without the use of a microphone, but later, when I moved over to Wheeler Auditorium, which seated about a thousand, I needed and obtained the use of an amplifier. In that room my classes often numbered five or six hundred, and on occasion over a thousand. By that time I had given up my naïve middle western assumption that I must check on the presence of every student every day.

I had expected that my second lecture course would be the history of the West—Paxson had said as much during our negotiations. But I quickly sensed that he had no real desire to give up that course, so I filled in such neglected gaps as I noted in the history curriculum. For a long time I gave a one-semester course in American foreign policy and a one-semester course in American social history. When later we brought in Armin Rappaport to teach American diplomacy, I expanded the social history course to two semesters, and repeated it each year for several years. After Paxson retired in 1947 his recent American course fell to me, and I gave up the survey course, while another Paxson student, William N. Davis, Jr., who was also a member of our staff, took over the West. Shortly before I retired, Davis left us to become state archivist at Sacramento, and, mainly for old time's sake, I gave the West again. Since my Wisconsin days, my ideas had changed considerably, and I found myself lecturing against my notes as often as not.

Lecturing to University of California students presented some problems that I had never faced before. Whether from an excess of western individualism or from an overdose of permissiveness in progressive education, many students felt themselves under no obligation to behave in the classrooms as adult human beings. Classes began at ten minutes after the hour instead of on the hour, a practice that in itself (or so it seemed to me) gave a psychological boost to unpunctuality. There were no classroom bells to indicate when one class ended and another began, leaving everyone, including the professors, to keep his own time, whatever the clock in the campanile might register. Students thought nothing of rising in the middle of a lecture, climbing leisurely over the knees of their seatmates, and wandering out by a distant exit. Often those coming late met those leaving early. The buzz of conversation that preceded the opening of each session tended to persist for an irritatingly long time after the lecture began. In some classes, I was told, the buzz continued to the end of the hour. I was shocked. By this time I had taught, counting summer sessions, on more than a dozen American campuses, and never before had I experienced any greater disorder than a preacher might expect from a Sunday morning congregation. Although I had had no army experience, I reacted immediately and automatically like a top sergeant—probably I overreacted, for the students really didn't sense that they were being impolite and disrespectful. But I got results. While I soon left it to each student to decide for himself whether he wished to come to class or not, I made it clear that, if he did come, he was expected to come on time and to stay on to the end of the lecture, whether he liked it or not. If he had good reason for leaving early—an appointment with a doctor or dentist, for example—he should sit near the door and leave as inconspicuously as possible. And as for freedom of speech, it was to be thoroughly suppressed, except for the lecturer, throughout the hour. If a student wanted to go to sleep, that was his privilege, provided he didn't snore. In general, I found that all one had to do to get order was to ask for it. And if the students thought the lecturer had something to say worth listening to, they usually came to class.

Campus rules prohibited smoking in class as a fire hazard, so I tried to enforce that rule, not that it made any difference to me personally. I pointed out to my students, however, that there was positively no rule against chewing tobacco, which was far more nourishing than smoking it, and I recommended the cultivation of this habit by all who couldn't make it through an hour unassisted by nicotine, provided only that each person bring his own disposal plant with him. I even sang the praises of snuff, or more properly, snuss, the non-sneezing kind. Some of our pioneer ancestors, I pointed out, particularly in the South, had made it a practice to carry around under the lip or in the cheek a tidy amount of this tasty item, while others dipped the chewed end of a green twig into their snussbox, then tucked it into the corner of the mouth for further rumination. I'm afraid that I won few converts to these more effective means of using tobacco, but there was little smoking in my classes except during written examinations, during which, by common consent, the rule was quite generally relaxed.

It did not take me long to realize that my best weapon for keeping order in class was to arouse and maintain student interest. I remembered how the Chatauqua orators of my youth, such men as Bob Burdette and Richmond P. Hobson, had won the rapt attention of huge tent audiences, despite the insufferable summer heat of the Middle West, the uncomfortable backless benches on which the people had to sit, and the easy means of egress. Why shouldn't I, with much better surroundings, achieve somewhat similar results? I had always tried to lecture well; now I redoubled my efforts. I prepared painstakingly for each lecture, keeping in mind what I thought the students would want to know and how much they could be expected to absorb in a fifty-minute period. As a safeguard, I tried to keep the hour that preceded each lecture free for concentration on what I planned to say; this was the only hour of any given day in which I discouraged students from calling on me in my office. I knew that I was not an orator in the sense that my father, for example, had been; I could neither flail the air nor prance about the platform without losing my train of thought. The organization of whatever I had to say, the words I used to convey my meaning, and their significance to the young men and women before me had to carry the whole load. Students like to be amused, and occasionally I told an anecdote that might illustrate a given point. In general, however, I relied for this purpose only on such witticisms as the material I was discussing provoked. History is full of the ridiculous, and only a blind man could miss it. Nevertheless, many of my most effective lectures presented from beginning to end no opportunity for either a joke or a wisecrack.

The students responded wonderfully to my efforts. Their conduct in class, with a few inconsequential exceptions, became irreproachable. It is possible that the presence of many men in uniform, individuals who had been introduced to discipline, had an effect, while the seriousness of history, with the nation at war, could hardly be gainsaid. Most of the students enrolled in my courses came to class, although the existence of "Phi Bete" notes made this unnecessary. Long before I reached California some shrewd entrepreneur had thought up the idea of employing good students—prospective Phi Betes—to take careful notes in large lecture courses, which he then had typed and mimeographed for sale to hard-pressed students. While I advised my students to take their own notes, I was powerless to stamp out the racket, and on occasion gave my approval to competent note-takers. To get credit for my course, or any other large lecture course, students need only buy the Phi Bete notes, read them and the various assignments, write such papers as might be required, then pass the required examinations. There can be no doubt that some students bought or plagiarized required papers, and sometimes even hired other students to take their examinations for them. A campus story, no doubt apocryphal, has it that a fraternity once decided to put their dog through the university, registered him under an appropriate name, paid his fees each semester for four years, divided up his work among themselves and turned it in, took all his examinations for him, and won him his degree. My guess is that the pooch, if ever registered, failed to make it through the first semester. But it's a good story.

There were always a few students on campus who took pride in the fact that they never attended lectures. I think they cheated themselves; there is so much that can be conveyed by word of mouth, by emphasis and inflection, that the reader of a single-spaced typescript of notes taken by someone else is likely to miss. Nor were the note-takers always dependable, for the things they often made the poor "prof" say were a far cry from what he actually had said. Now and then a Phi Bete employee who was a true believer in some offbeat faith plugged his favorite ideas, especially if he happened to be impressed with the gospel according to Marx. Sometimes students who came to class regularly also bought Phi-Bete notes; some found them better than the notes they took for themselves. In my larger courses there were always a number of auditors or visitors who never expected to take an examination. Perhaps on this account, I occasionally got a good round of applause on an individual lecture, although such behavior was rare and highly selective. California students usually reserved their applause for the last day of a given semester. I confess to a certain amount of emotional reaction when my class of five or six hundred students, after my last lecture in class at the University of California, gave me what the reporters call a standing ovation.

All large lecture courses in history at California that were designed primarily for freshmen made the customary provision for small weekly sections. I did what I could to extend this practice to the survey course in American history, which was designed primarily for sophomores, and in this I succeeded after a few years. But I failed to get away with anything more than optional sections for upperclass students. During the war I was able to recruit as helpers in my survey course two capable married women, Irene Prescott and Edna Daniels, who gave far more out-of-class time and attention to students than was nominated in the bond. Their mature attitude toward youngsters of college age let them in for much unrecorded counseling. Mrs. Prescott had been a student of mine many years before at the University of Nebraska; Mrs. Daniels had had experience as a trained nurse. One wartime incident I shall never forget. During one of my lectures I saw a girl slip to the floor from an aisle seat, presumably in a faint. I immediately started from the rostrum to take charge, but I had not taken three steps before a half-dozen navy men in uniform were on their feet carrying out the fallen colleague the way they had been taught to do. With Edna at the rear door to take charge, I went on with my lecture, hardly losing a word.

Discussion sections, whether required or voluntary, were in my judgment extremely useful. They gave an opportunity for self-expression to students who craved it, and provided special assistance for those who needed extra help. They made possible individual contacts between students and teachers. In California beginning courses, the number of students per section was held down to twenty-five or less, and the number of sections per assistant to four or five. Thus each teaching assistant could easily get to know all the students assigned to him, and in practice he usually did. One of the obligations I laid on my assistants was to arrive at an estimate of each student's worth, based on personal contacts, both within and without the sections. We then used this estimate in making out the semester grades.

Most critics of the lecture system ignore the existence of these "clean-up" sections, or infer that the teaching assistants are incompetent or uninterested. At a university such as California, where there are so many graduate students of exceptional ability, some even with previous teaching experience, this criticism is quite unintelligent. Most of our teaching assistants had already had at least a year of graduate work, and many of them already held a Master's degree. They all expected to make careers of teaching, and as far as my experience went they seemed eager to teach well. Frequently these younger teachers did a better job with the undergraduates than the professor in charge could possibly have done. They were closer to the students in age and interests and could understand them better.

Another frequently repeated canard is that university teachers do nothing toward teaching their graduate students how to teach. While I was teaching the beginning course in American history, per contra, I always held a group meeting of the section leaders involved by way of preparation for their work. On these occasions we would consider together what subjects should be featured in the sections, how to avoid a mere rehash of the lectures and the text, and in what ways to encourage the free expression of different points of view. Although the teaching assistants were usually quite scornful of whatever courses in education they had been obliged to take, they were interested in methods of teaching and contributed many ingenious ideas during these sessions.

One of the primary purposes of the sections, I tried to emphasize, was to induce the students to talk. The proof of a good section leader could almost be measured by how much of the time he could keep his students talking and how little of the time he himself consumed. Students, for all they say about self-expression, prefer it the other way around, and will trick a section leader, if they can, into doing all the talking himself. My advice to the section leaders in dealing with such cases was to hew to the subject, turn all loaded questions back to the class, draw the students out despite their efforts to resist, reveal their ignorance when they were ignorant, and encourage them to display wisdom when they were wise.

I had many excellent teachers among my helpers, and I am sure that nearly all of them became better teachers for their experience as graduate assistants. Most of them were also at one time or another members of my graduate seminars. There I tried to get over the idea that the reports they gave were in part practice lectures, to be so constructed and so delivered as to hold the attention of the class.

Examinations are a necessity in classes of almost any size, and will remain so as long as grades and credits are required. The problem of giving these tests, however, and reading the resulting papers becomes increasingly perplexing as the size of the class grows larger. Some teachers dodge the difficulties involved by giving so-called objective tests. These tests depend on four main types of questions: true and false, with a single alternative; multiple choice, with several opportunities to go wrong; completion tests, which again give the students a variety of right and wrong alternatives; and association tests, which require the pairing up of related items listed in two columns, but out of their proper order, such combinations, for example, as events and dates. The trouble with these tests is that there is nothing objective about them except the grading. The instructor, or educational expert who makes them out, decides which is the right answer and how much weight to give each question in the totals. In practice, matters of the least consequence are often equated with matters of great significance; in such cases the unimportant blunders count as much against the student's grade as those of a fundamental nature. The value judgments involved in the test are all purely subjective, all dependent on what the maker of the test happens to think, for he and he alone decides both the correctness and the relative worth of the questions he poses.

Students who take these tests learn to become expert guessers. In most of them anyone who is good at cards or has a strong puzzle-solving instinct can achieve results far beyond his knowledge of the subject. The multiple-choice or completion question, for example, ordinarily lists one totally absurd alternative, one deemed correct by the test-maker, and two or three other partly true alternatives. The shrewd guesser, whether he has cracked a book or not, can usually throw out the absurd answer at sight, then deduce from the others which is the most likely risk. Per contra, the conscientious student, who has read a lot and who has really thought his way through the subject, is apt to be confused by the fact that there is truth in several of the alternatives given. He finds by sad experience that in preparation he can do best by concentrating on a single book (the one his test-maker uses), and by memorizing exactly what the book says. If he permits himself to be exposed to conflicting opinions, he is in deep trouble. Many times students have asked me at the beginning of a course whether I would give objective or essay-type examinations. When I asked why it made any difference to them, they invariably replied in substance: "Oh, we study differently for objective tests. With them we have to know exactly what is in the book and what the lecturer has said, and shut out everything else. But with essay-type examinations we must read for thought and formulate ideas of our own."

I've never been one to decry a little memory work; in a subject such as history, and in most subjects, there is no such thing as avoiding it. But the mere memorizing of assorted facts and opinions is not enough. The student should learn to analyze what he has read and heard, to think about it, and to understand its implications. If he disagrees with expressed opinions and can buttress his disagreement with sound argument, so much the better for him. Also, he needs to learn to write well, to express his thoughts clearly and forcefully, something the objective tests never require of him. In an essay-type examination, if the questions are well conceived, he gets good practice in the use of the English language. I have even encouraged students to ask themselves in advance the questions they think they might be asked on an examination, then to write out the best answers they can devise for their own questions. Those who were willing to try this method (I can recall using it myself as a student) rarely failed to profit from the exercise.

With hundreds of students in each class, who is to read the papers? In my courses, when there were teaching assistants who held quiz sections, they ordinarily read the bluebooks for the students they taught. In upper-division courses, where there were no assistants, we recruited readers from among other graduate students who could be trusted to do a competent and conscientious job. The great trouble was that some readers were stiffer graders than others. I solved this problem in two ways. If the class was small enough, each reader could read certain designated questions in all the papers; I have at times taken over part of the task myself. Or, when the numbers were great, as they usually were at California, each reader would read all of his fair share of the papers, and rate them according to some agreed-upon numerical scale (usually 10 points for a really excellent paper, and less for those not so good). Then the readers would bring all the papers to my office and I would "cut the curve," that is, I would decide where the A's left off and the B's began, and where the B's left off and the C's began, etc., in each pile of papers, doing the best I could to equalize matters between the "tough" and the "easy" graders. I tried also to inspect and put my personal O.K. on all papers marked F.

I doubt if we were guilty of many rank injustices. If anything, we probably erred on the side of generosity. I always instructed my readers to mark clearly anything they found wrong and to make appropriate—but never sarcastic—comments. Students, rightfully, I think, resent low grades when they find not a mark on the paper to tell them what was wrong. They will even accept without protest low grades on good papers, if only the papers are marked up enough. Grading is, of course, purely subjective, and never very accurate. But I'm sure we never failed people without good reason, and I doubt if any students got C's when they should have had A's, or vice versa. The number who might as well have had an A as a B, or a B as a C, is of course legion.

My examinations were never very popular and were never meant to be. The average student prefers as an examination question some paraphrase of the idea, Tell me back what I told you, or What does the textbook say? I tried to devise questions that would not only test the students' knowledge but would also encourage them in independent thinking. For students who chose so to interpret these questions, they offered an opportunity of self-expression and a chance to reveal how well they could think. I encouraged my readers to keep an eye out for originality and to read papers not so much for what they failed to say as for what they said. Mere repetition of the textbook and the lectures might rate a B if well done, but never an A. I argued that we were entitled to a little interest on our investment.

Student prowess in passing examinations with only a minimum of work was particularly phenomenal at California. For final examinations and sometimes for mid-terms also, many students depended on off-campus seminars, so called, which were mere cram sessions, in which the seminar leader, for a consideration, undertook to prepare a number of students for a given examination. These enterprising operators always managed to get hold of old examination questions, and did a pretty fair job of predicting what the instructor might ask. I kept a file of my own previous examinations and tried not to repeat myself too often. If, as occasionally happened, my questions were a bit un-expected and led to protests, it was probably because I was trying a little too hard to cross up the off-campus coaches whose business it was to help slothful students beat the game. Good students, even when, as occasionally happened, they were among the loudest protesters, rarely failed to write good papers. I had a stock answer for the argu-ment that the examination was unfair. "Well, what of that?" I would say. "The purpose of an education is to prepare you for life, and if you get the idea that what's going to happen to you after college will always be fair, you're in for a great surprise." I never refused to reread papers that students thought had been unfairly graded, but I took such cases only on appeal; the student had to consult the reader first, and me only afterward. Few came back after an interview with the reader; many failed even to go that far.

One of the big surprises after World War II was the discovery that the returning veterans were about the best students we had ever had. Our sociologists and psychologists had led us to believe that we would find the returners, or at least many of them, neurotic, maladjusted, and undependable. President Sproul even called an all-university con-ference to enable us to plan how to deal with these prospective problem students. But when the men who had spent from one to four years in military service, instead of in college classes, got back to the campus, we found them to be a very superior group. They were mature, punc-tilious in behavior (they almost saluted us), and determined to make up for the time they had lost. I doubt if the federal government ever made a better investment than the educational benefits it provided for veterans under the G.I. Bill of Rights. The numbers that descended upon us taxed our facilities to the limit; our classrooms were over-crowded, our office space was reduced to a minimum, and our in-structional staff was painfully inadequate. The shortage in faculty was due less to financial pressures on the university budget than to the fact that for four years most of our graduate students and potential Ph.D.'s were members of the armed services. But the eagerness and interest of the students made up for all these deficiencies. An amazing phe-nomenon, also, was the way in which the girls, especially the freshman

girls, on an average at least two or three years younger than the returning veterans, rose to the competition and kept right up with the men.
The postwar years thus provided additional evidence, if any were
needed, to indicate that, given the proper stimulus, our college students
can accomplish far more than we tend to regard as normal. Unfortunately, the change in the student climate lasted only as long as the
G.I.'s lasted; once they were gone, the undergraduates tended to
revert to their previous standards.

The graduate students, of course, both pre- and post-G.I., could be
counted on to show due diligence. An imported French instructor,
surprised at the contempt some college students showed for their superlatively zealous confreres, reacted in horror: "They call them e-gair
be-vairs!" The good graduate student is by definition an "e-gair
be-vair." Among the most eager, both graduate and undergraduate,
were those who were married. This was something new to the campus,
but by no means difficult to explain. Many of the returning servicemen
were old enough to be married, even if classified as freshmen, and many
of them found wives. This extra burden no doubt contributed to their
seriousness; they had need to make up for lost time. Graduate students,
who in my youth were of necessity unmarried, after the war were more
often married than not. Frequently the wives of students got jobs and
helped their husbands financially, but wives have a way of becoming
mothers, and the student with a family to support had himself a problem. The surprising thing was how often and how well such students
worked their problems out. I've seen student parents take turns pushing
the stroller on campus while one or the other attended classes. I've even
seen babies in libraries, strapped to a parent's back, Oriental fashion.

After the war my seminars were crowded, as they had not been while
the fighting continued, and I was soon turning out a steady stream of
Ph.D.'s. To have been consistent with my earlier record, which had
shown an interest first in Populism, then in Progressivism, I suppose I
should have moved on to the New Deal as the central focus of interest
for myself and my graduate students. Instead, I chose to direct my
attention mainly to the 1920's; the New Deal, I insisted, was still too
close in point of time for us to get a good perspective on it. Besides,
right after the war I had agreed to do a book for the "New American
Nation Series" on the post–World War I period, and I preferred to
direct my main attention toward those years.

Many of my students were content to work along with me on one aspect or another of the 1920's; for example, Gladys Waldron Gilmore, who wrote on "Antiforeign Movements in California, 1919–1929," Russell M. Posner, whose subject was "State Politics and the Bank of America," and Sister Gertrude Mary (Gray), who chose a thoroughly secular subject, "Oil in Anglo-American Diplomatic Relations, 1920–1928." But others preferred quite different themes, and I made no effort to discourage them. It was not my practice to assign thesis subjects; rather, I made it clear that this responsibility lay with the student himself; if he couldn't even come up with a satisfactory topic on which he wished to work, he had better not go any farther in history. There were at least four considerations, or so it seemed to me, in the choice of a subject: it must have some significance (a purely subjective matter, I suppose, on which my judgment had to be final); it should be something in which the student already was or could become deeply interested; it must not have been done to death already; and the essential sources must be available—"no documents, no history."

In providing us with material, our Bancroft Library was indispensable: most of my Ph.D. candidates at California drew mainly from its treasures. Fortunately, the antiquarian interest, which would have restricted the Bancroft collections to the early periods only, was on the wane after the war, and the library was on the alert for twentieth-century manuscripts, such, for example, as the papers of the governors. Nor was its spread of interest limited to the California boundaries; its collections included material on the whole Pacific Coast, on the Rocky Mountain area, and on the westward movement generally.

I had no objection to subjects of a local nature, provided they were sufficiently meaningful. Edward Everett France, for example, wrote on "The Migration of the Negro to the San Francisco Bay Area Since 1940," and I had a number of M.A. theses on other equally local themes. My interest in agricultural history frequently cropped out, as in Rolf W. Ordal's "History of the California Walnut Industry." Ordal, I recall, had on his examining committee two of our most distinguished agricultural economists, but he knew their language and acquitted himself well. I also remember well a similar study—an M.A. thesis—by Elizabeth Riley on "The California Almond Industry," the writer of which still presents me each Christmas with a valued gift of salted almonds.

Most Ph.D. theses are not ready for publication at the time they are accepted, a fact I emphasized whenever I thought it necessary. This did not mean that the thesis was itself unworthy, only that it required further polishing and sometimes further specified research. It has always seemed to me a mistake to withhold a degree from a candidate whose work amply proves his worth simply because his thesis is not yet ready for publication. Indeed, most subjects of sufficient importance to warrant a Ph.D. degree are likely to require more time and work than the student has immediately available. It is a pity, however, that so many students who receive their degrees on theses not yet ready for publication get mired down with other duties and let their theses gather dust. But who is to sit in judgment on them? Even the so-called "still-born" Ph.D., who never writes a line after he becomes a doctor, has learned much from his experience and may become an able teacher.

A number of the theses written under my direction at the University of California became books. Vincent Carosso's *The California Wine Industry, 1830–1895* (1951) aroused the irritation of some of my colleagues in the College of Agriculture, where there was a whole division devoted to this subject, but the book was delightfully done, and exploited a theme on which the author had the advantage of family experience to guide him. Clarke A. Chambers, in *California Farm Organizations, 1929–1941* (1952), adventured into the New Deal field, despite my misgivings, and taught me enough about the differences between California and middle western protest movements to make me reluctant thereafter to describe myself as either an agricultural or an agrarian historian. Robert E. Burke's *Olsen's New Deal for California* (1953) introduced me to the almost equally incredible complications of twentieth-century California politics. Gilman Ostrander, left an academic orphan by the death of his major professor, Dixon Wecter, wrote, with a minimum of help from me, *The Prohibition Movement in California, 1848–1933* (1957), including earlier manifestations of which I had known nothing until he brought the subject to life. Gerald D. Nash took a long romp through California administrative history and came up with a very original study, *State Government and Economic Development, 1849–1933* (1964), which emphasized the fact that the development of the California economy was hardly less the result of governmental activities than of private enterprise.

Within the department I fought a losing battle against the tendency to make drastic changes in the requirements for both the M.A. and the Ph.D. degrees. Part of our trouble came from our expansion to include so many new specializations. Modern European history, which in earlier years had been regarded as one, was now split both horizontally —before and after the French Revolution—and vertically—Western Europe, Central Europe, and Eastern Europe. English history likewise got itself divided chronologically, while the Renaissance and the Reformation cut into both late medieval and early modern Europe. The Far East, or Eastern Asia, and the Middle East also required recognition. Only ancient history clung to its early boundaries, and it did this primarily because of a lack of personnel, both teachers and students. In American history the colonial and the national periods began to come apart, and the sharp division between Latin American history and the rest of the Americas, long resisted at California by the Bolton school, became more and more apparent. Naturally, the new specialties and specialists demanded their fair share of graduate students, most of whom tended to concentrate on the United States, modern Europe, and Latin America.

Our new requirements virtually knocked out the Master's thesis by providing an easier alternative, three seminar papers to be written in three different seminars. This spread the students around, but destroyed their opportunity to get a good start on a Ph.D. thesis by writing an M.A. thesis with a developmental potential. Furthermore, the difference between one sustained research project, such as an M.A. thesis, and three term papers was very great. Course requirements for the Ph.D. were also multiplied and diversified. This gave more instructors a crack at the Ph.D. candidates, but lengthened greatly the period of preparation for examinations. Indeed, it was soon taking two or three years beyond the M.A. degree for students to get ready for the qualifying examinations, and only after that could they get down to business on their Ph.D. theses. By that time many of them had lost their original drive and wrote mediocre theses when, if only they could have begun their research sooner, they could have done very well. I could cite specific instances among my own students. It was my conviction, and still is, that for the well-prepared student the Ph.D. should require not more than three or four years beyond the Bachelor's degree. He can never hope to learn as a graduate student nearly all he needs to know; he will have to learn as he teaches. Why handicap him by requiring what is conventionally known as "well-rounded knowledge," but in practice means mainly taking courses in subjects far removed from his principal field of interest? If he has to teach those subjects later, he can work them up when the time comes.

Fortunately, the case against the long-drawn-out period of Ph.D. training won many converts when the population explosion of the war period began to affect college and university enrollments. If teachers were to be found in sufficient numbers to meet the new needs, university faculties would have to let their graduate students complete their work in more reasonable time. Fundamental changes along this line are now in progress at the University of California and elsewhere, one way in which the 1960's are a long lap ahead of the 1940's and 1950's.

XIII. Dutch Flat

BEGINNING IN 1945 the Hicks family spent at first weeks each summer, then later months, in the little mountain village of Dutch Flat, just off Highway 40 (Interstate 80) some 60 miles east of Sacramento and about 140 miles from Berkeley. I'll let my old friend Bill Adams, in his day a writer of note, tell you about this village.

AN OLD SUBSCRIBER CHANGES HIS ADDRESS

DUTCH FLAT, May 15, 1929

MY DEAR OUTLOOK AND INDEPENDENT:

Did you ever hear of Dutch Flat? I can find no flat ground and devil a Dutchman at all.

Dutch Flat's a grand place. There isn't a movie within twenty miles, nor a doctor. There are maybe 150 people. In the school are nine pupils. Cows with bells on their necks wander the streets, browse round old abandoned houses, doze beneath the pines. There is one store which is also postoffice and phone exchange. I was down there a while ago and found it closed. The keeper was gone home to dinner, I suppose. There is a quaint old hotel built in 1856. In the rooms are huge walnut bedsteads, that came over the plains by ox-team; old walnut bureaus too. The old emigrant trail wound close by where Dutch Flat now is.

In the days of gold, Dutch Flat was a jostling busy place. In the hotel are registers and ledgers dating back from that time. You may read how Jim Hughs brought in gold dust which he traded for schnapps and a new pick, also some dynamite. In those days there were saloons, livery stables, a lumber yard, clothing stores, grocery stores, all manner of stores in Dutch Flat. Today along Main Street stands a row of rotting buildings, long ago closed. Pheasant's eye narcissus and daffodils flourish all over Dutch Flat. English may is in bloom. It was brought here long long ago by Englishmen who yearned for their homeland. Peonies and tulips, flowering locust, and yellow laburnum grow in old gardens along Main Street. A mile away passes the main highway, but it doesn't trouble Dutch Flat. From beyond a high pine-clad mountain there flares at night an

235

air-mail beacon. Once in a while a plane roars high above Dutch Flat. No one looks up. Dutch Flat is sufficient. From the top of the ridge behind Main Street you look down upon great naked gullies where vast white boulders glisten in the sun. Banks of red earth, pinnacles of red earth, stand above the deep gullies. Here and there lie lengths of rusted iron pipe through which in bygone years the water poured, to wash away the soil and so expose the glittering gold. Today hydraulic mining is forbidden by law. It had to be forbidden, for thanks to it the valley river beds were filling in with silt, the rivers rising, so that the safety of towns along their banks was threatened.

Dutch Flat's a fine place. I've been here a week and no one has so much as asked me what my business is. The first day I was here I started down a winding hill road. A man driving a rusty old car passed, and stopped to ask me would I care to ride. He drove me down to Bear River, two miles away, and when he set me down said, "You'll have a steep climb back up. If you can't make it, just sit down. I'll come and get you if I don't see you round town when I get back." He returned to town by another road, and as I was walking up the sunny hill that afternoon I met him coming to look for me.

Yesterday I met a man dressed in city clothes, with a good pair of shoes and a fine hat. His eyes looked red. "A pretty place," said I. He said, "I've just come back this morning, the first time in thirty-five years. It breaks my heart to see the old place so. I was born and raised here."

There are robins and juncos and swallows, gold finches, stella jays, bandtailed pigeons, woodpeckers, sapsuckers, and many another bird in Dutch Flat. There are trout in the streams and deer on the hill slopes. Down the road a way are the old gold camps of "Red Dog" and "You Bet." Up the road a way is Donner Lake, where the people of the Donner Party froze and starved to death, caught by the winter snow in the Sierras.

I'll be strolling down to the post office to mail you this letter now. A letter to New York. Skyscrapers, elevated trains, electric lights by the million, tramp of ceaseless feet, roar, rush, greed, and "be damned to you," "every man for himself and the devil take the hindermost" . . . civilization! progress! . . .

There's peace in Dutch Flat! Look in when you come by.

BILL ADAMS

P.S. Would you tell the circulation man that my address is now Dutch Flat?[1]

By the time we reached Dutch Flat it had changed a little, but it was still "a fine place." We saw "devil" a cow in the streets and some of the

[1] *Outlook and Independent*, August 21, 1929.

old houses were beginning to take on a definitely spruced-up appearance, among them an ornate old one which Bill Adams had long
maintained and a neat little one in which, as an old man, he now lived
alone. Perhaps his keen appreciation of the village had won converts.
The number of unoccupied buildings had diminished to the extent that
no one could now properly call the place a ghost town. The one
general store was well kept and prospering, although still in the same
stone building built for the purpose in 1854; the major part of the old
hotel still stood, the property of appreciative owners who kept it up
for its historical interest, despite the fact that prohibitive insurance
rates made running it as a hotel impossible. The Masonic and Odd
Fellows buildings stood side by side, each showing unmistakable
symptoms of decay but also a firm determination on the part of the
two rival orders to keep them intact. Even the narrow road which
enclosed the central village "flat" (only plainsmen ever say "flats")
was now paved after a fashion.

Our introduction to Dutch Flat coincided with a prolonged series
of celebrations by means of which Californians reminded themselves
that their American beginnings had taken place a full hundred years or
so before—celebrations of events such as the Mexican War, the Bear
Flag Revolt, the discovery of gold, the formation of the state, its
admission to the Union, and all that. Renewed interest in the early days
meant a rash of historical markers, one of which, near the village store,
proclaimed that Dutch Flat was founded in the spring of 1851 by two
Germans, Joseph and Charles Dornbach. The Dornbachs, one learned
from other sources, had led a covered-wagon train all the way from
St. Louis, and had built the first house of the settlement—a log cabin
near the northeast corner of the flat, only a stone's throw from the
house we now live in each summer. Joseph soon returned to the East,
but Charles stayed on long enough to give a name to the region. First
it was known as "the Dutchman's Flat," or "Dutch Charlie's Flat,"
but in due time it became just plain "Dutch Flat." Charlie's daughter,
Louise, was the first white child born in the village.

Other markers reveal that the first story of the hotel was built in
1852; that the walls of the store were constructed of volcanic tufa
quarried nearby; that part of the J. H. Runckel house on Main Street
was built about 1854, making it the oldest original dwelling still standing; that the Masonic Lodge dates back to 1852 and the Odd Fellows
Hall to 1856; that the trim little Methodist church was begun in 1859

and completed in 1861; that the old abandoned adobe building at the southeast entrance to the flat was built by the Chinese in the 1870's. The two-story, four-room, frame schoolhouse, topped by an appropriate belfry, that stands opposite the Methodist church is too young to rate a marker, for it dates back only to the turn of the century, but it is an important village landmark. The principal town marker, after paying its respects to the Dornbachs, goes on to recite that Dutch Flat from 1854 to 1882 "was noted for its rich hydraulic mines. In 1860 it had the largest voting population in Placer County. Chinese inhabitants numbered about 2,000. Here Theodore Judah and Dr. D. W. Strong made the original subscription to build the first continental railroad."

Dr. Strong, one soon discovers, was a "noted" physician and pharmacist who ran a drugstore in Dutch Flat. He had long had the vision of a railroad to the Pacific and had even marked out the route through the mountains over which it could be—and eventually was—built. He it was who interested Judah in the project, and together they undertook to raise the capital needed to start construction. Dutch Flat subscribers contributed a total of $45,000, and were duly rewarded when the railhead reached their town in 1866. The railroad tracks were located about a mile up the hill from the flat, but the railroad station bore the name Dutch Flat as long as it existed. For years it was flanked by frame buildings of considerable size, one of which, the three-story Fowler Hotel, was destroyed in 1899 by a locomotive explosion. When we arrived, all that was left of the railroad complex was an unoccupied boxlike building, perhaps ten by twelve feet in size, completely devoid of furniture, but still proudly bearing the Dutch Flat label. For a while some passenger trains respected it as a flag stop, but ultimately even that service was discontinued and the building came down.

In its heyday Dutch Flat was a prosperous town of five or six thousand inhabitants. After the completion of the transcontinental railroad in 1869 it stayed alive to furnish fuel for wood-burning locomotives, to produce lumber, and to continue the quest for gold. The Chinese, brought in originally to help build the railroad, frugally worked the tailings that white miners discarded and clung to their quarters as long as they could. Fires took a heavy toll; for years Dutch Flat was derided as the "Tinder City." Two of the worst fires, one in 1873 and another in 1881, virtually destroyed the Chinese quarter, which extended along both sides of the road from the village proper to the railroad tracks, but by a miracle the houses on the flat escaped.

After the outlawing of hydraulic mining in the 1880's, the decline of the village was rapid. All the Chinese moved away and all but one or two hundred of the whites. Thereafter, individual houses that burned down or that the snow collapsed were rarely replaced; when Bill Adams discovered the village, the number of houses in the flat area had dwindled to about two score.

Oddly, however, the spirit of the village survived, this in spite of the fact that only for a few months in 1872 was it ever even incorporated. Unofficial town meetings dealt, usually successfully, with such community problems as arose. A case in point was the Dutch Flat Fire Department, a volunteer organization that has remained in continuous existence from about 1854 to the present. When we first became aware of it, the fire department was busily engaged in raising money to pay for some government-surplus fire-fighting equipment it had just acquired. Private subscriptions, supplemented by a benefit concert, footed the bill. Similarly financed, also, was a much needed firehouse, built on land contributed by the storekeeper, Kirby Quinn. The village water mains and fire hydrants are really not the property of anybody. They were installed sometime in the 1870's at the expense of local merchants, most of whom later went broke or moved away. But the fire department assumed control of the pipes and has maintained the water system, after a fashion, ever since. Efforts to create a tax district for this purpose met vigorous and successful resistance.

Community self-reliance has long exhibited itself in a number of other ways. A Ladies' Aid Society, unconnected with the church, raises money by such well-worn devices as bake sales and bazaars to support worthy projects. Once in the early days, according to legend, when a respected saloonkeeper was burned out, the Ladies' Aid helped him make a new start. (Nowadays, one can't buy liquor by the drink anywhere in the village.) The Society acquired by bequest a small building on Main Street, where it holds its meetings—a women's club, really, although the women who belong to it insist on doing something for others rather than merely for themselves.

A Dutch Flat Swimming Pool Corporation, composed of public-spirited local citizens, long ago constructed and has maintained ever since a delightful swimming pool for free use by residents of the community. Here both children and parents find relief from the heat on summer afternoons. For a long time an annual barbecue (of which more later), complete with the crowning of a queen (for selling the most tickets) and an aquacade, raised most of the required funds, and contributions did the rest.

The Methodist church, although technically denominational, also wins generous support. With the centenary of its founding in prospect, the community raised the money to straighten the church belfry, which had begun to lean backward a little, as if weary with age, and to effect other needed repairs, including a new paint job. Church attendance is ordinarily sparse, except for weddings and funerals, but everyone turned out to celebrate a one hundredth anniversary service, with Bishop Donald H. Tippett, our near neighbor in Berkeley, presiding.

The Dutch Flat School District long stood its ground against consolidation, even after the number of pupils declined to one-room, one-teacher proportions. When at last competent teachers for an ungraded school could no longer be found, the Gold Run, Dutch Flat, and Alta school districts combined, and buses took the children to Alta, where the accommodations were most up-to-date. Children of high school age are sent to Colfax, ten miles away. These changes left the Dutch Flat schoolhouse without a tenant, but it had long served as a kind of community center, and it is now owned by a self-styled Community Club, founded in 1951. This development meant more solicitations and more contributions, but there were few complaints. The Community Club holds regular well-attended dinner meetings, discusses in town-meeting style the village crises that constantly occur, and makes democracy work. Currently the chief issue is what to do about the franchise, long held by one Arthur Nicholls, to deliver water to the residents of the flat. "Old Art," when he died, willed his rights, whatever they were, to the users, some say just to get even with his critics. But since he did not own the water mains, and since they are all in a sad state of repair, most of us think that the water district, once voted down, must be created. Nevertheless, strong opposition exists. As one leading citizen said to me a few days ago, "If we had to vote on whether the sun should rise tomorrow, somebody would be against it." Bill Adams had it right. Dutch Flat is a grand place.

I would like to be able to record that all this civic righteousness was what brought us to Dutch Flat, but the truth is quite otherwise. These things we discovered only later. We came first as guests of our Berkeley neighbors, Luigi and Teresita Piccirillo, who had found the place long before and had told us of its wonderful summer climate. The whole Bay area, including Berkeley, is cold during most of the summer, with a thick morning fog that chills one to the bone; during most of July and August the thermometer hovers persistently between 50° and 65° Fahrenheit. In Dutch Flat, the Piccirillos claimed, the sun shone dependably all summer long; we could count on being comfortably warm by day and comfortably cool by night. Besides, there were interesting things for the children to do (the Piccirillos had two daughters) and a summer colony we would be sure to like. A trial trip and we were hooked. In 1945 and again in 1946 we found places to rent for a few weeks and began to look around for a place of our own. The summer of 1947, which we spent in Hawaii, served only to increase our interest in the climate of the Sierra foothills, and the next summer it happened.

When the academic year of 1947–1948 ended, Lucile and I and our two daughters, Carolyn and Marjorie (Jane Harriet was now married) drove back to the Middle West to visit friends and relatives in Nebraska, Minnesota, and Wisconsin. Dutch Flat lay along our route, so we stopped there to investigate a story, brought to us by our good friend Dr. George Hahn, a Berkeley orthodontist. George and his wife, Dorothy, had an attractive summer residence on Dutch Flat's Main Street, a half mile north of the village proper, next door to a cottage in which we had already spent a summer. He told us that Guy Gilchrist, another confirmed Dutch-Flatter, had just purchased an old house in the center of the village and would like to sell it. Guy had bought the place for back taxes, not because he wanted it, but primarily to keep the acre of land on which it stood from being turned into a trailer camp by someone who had no respect for the character of the town. We had hoped to find a location farther out, somewhere in the big trees, but we decided that Guy's real estate would at least be worth a look.

What we saw would certainly have discouraged saner people. The house was a wreck. Obviously it had not seen a coat of paint in the twentieth century. Decrepit porches that ran halfway around it were dropping off; one porch had dropped clear off. Across the rear was a shed-roofed kitchen, obviously an afterthought, and at one corner of the kitchen a tower-like addition with a sign on it: "Kline the Tailor; Suits Cleaned and Pressed." Kline was the last occupant of the house, but a fire had gutted his shop so that it stood up only by a miracle. Down the hill a piece were remnants of a cow shed and other tumble-down outbuildings. Tall native grass or, far worse, rampant black-berry vines covered what had once been a vegetable garden.

On the positive side, the original four-room house was an honest L-shaped structure that seemed redeemable. The front door needed only to be repainted to be made attractive, and above it was an eye-catching transom of red and blue glass. Next to the ground there was some evidence of dry rot, but none of termites, and overhead Guy had put on a new roof. Furthermore, the place was historic; the exact year in which it was built was in dispute, but all the old-timers agreed that it would soon be a hundred years old. Most entrancing of all was a weathered board, labeled "Gold Trees," that swayed on wires from two huge trees just within the front gate. According to Gilchrist, the name came from a tall tale told to tenderfeet by the miners. Some of the best gold, the sourdoughs claimed, was to be found in the tops of the trees, carried up there as the trees grew, the taller the trees the richer the deposits. A more plausible explanation was that the two ancient cherry trees from which the sign hung bore fruit that was golden colored before it ripened. Or maybe the name came from the imposing poplars out back whose leaves turned a bright yellow in the fall.

At any rate, we liked the sign, and the price was within our means. We drove on eastward without reaching a decision, but the farther away we got, the more interested we became. Finally I wrote Gilchrist that we would take the place and sent him a check to bind the bargain. We went on with our tour as scheduled, but we could hardly wait to get back to see "Gold Trees" again. When, at long last, we returned to it, all the romance seemed suddenly to have vanished—how could we ever make anything out of that miserable old house? Closer inves-tigation revealed indescribable filth within; instead of taking up a worn-out rug, for example, the occupants had only put down another on top of it, or maybe a layer of linoleum. Some floors, we discovered, had six layers of carpeting, with newspapers of World War I vintage at the bottom. There was furniture galore, both within the house and under it, but not a whole chair or a whole bed or a whole bureau in the lot. The kitchen, the porches, and Kline's burnt-out tower would all have to come down.

We considered trying to sell the place, but we knew that nobody else would be so foolish as to buy it. The only thing to do was to go through with the plans we had made. Fortunately, the Piccirillos were just then building a new house in the thick wooded area near the Hahns, so we got their contractor to help us make a start. Our house had only rotted wooden pilings as a foundation, and had listed about nine inches from one corner to its opposite, so the first thing to do was to jack the house up, level it off, and build a new foundation. Since our contractor found it impossible even to guess how much this improvement would cost, he consented to take the job only on a cost-plus basis —the cost of labor and materials plus a 17 per cent commission. By the time he had the house squared up on a decent underpinning, we had put into it more money than we had expected to spend on the entire job of reconditioning—for a while we called it "the Hicks Foundation," but it made no grants.

Although Gilchrist had had the house reroofed, the need for that job had been so long postponed that much of the plaster was ruined, while three out of the four rooms had to have new floors laid over the old. Instead of a new plaster job, however, our contractor used plaster-board where the disintegration had gone too far. We were amazed to see how lavish the original builders had been with lumber. Where carpenters of today would use only two-by-four studding, those mid-century mountaineers did not hesitate to use four-by-fours. The wood sills on which they began construction were invariably eight-by-eight, and the joints, according to some sidewalk supervisor, were the kind ship carpenters made. As for the laths, now standardized at four feet, the early Sierra sawmills turned them out the length of the log they happened to be sawing—often ten or twelve feet.

We had to return to Berkeley in time for the opening of the academic year, but we paid frequent visits to Dutch Flat that fall and spring to watch the progress of reconstruction. Costs mounted disastrously. All that tearing down cost money, and besides we had to have an entirely new kitchen and an adjacent "combination" room— sitting, eating, sleeping, etc. Of necessity we decided to do with our own hands everything that we could possibly do.

Our first few summers in the new (old) house were thus monumentally occupied. We took over ourselves all the painting, inside and out, the patching of such plaster as could be saved, the sanding of the floors, even the hanging of wallpaper. Lucile proved to be most competent with a tempersome sander we rented; I won a monopoly on the plaster-patching (sometimes on lath I had had to insert); the girls and

I did the wallpapering (with ten-and-one-half-foot ceilings this was no joke). We had had no experience with wallpapering, but we learned. Soon red roses ran riot on the walls of the living room and yellow roses dominated one bedroom; Currier and Ives sailing ships, racing locomotives, speeding horses, and snow scenes down on the farm brightened up the dining room; and by way of contrast a plain peach-colored paper with a dignified narrow border identified the master bedroom. We all painted like mad. The inside ceilings and the outside gables were the worst. To reach the ceilings I recall standing on a two-by-twelve-inch plank, six feet long, that rested on the tops of two stepladders. The outside gables were several feet too high for the twenty-foot extension ladder we had bought, so we mounted it on a wobbly old table to achieve the extra altitude. Nobody got hurt, everybody got excited about the job we were doing; we all rose early and worked late through the long, hot days.

Once I forgot all about an overdue index for the third edition of *The American Nation*, and when the publishers reminded me, I had to drive all the way to Berkeley to do it—a scandalous waste of time. An absolutely essential revision of the table of contents I overlooked entirely until it was much too late to get it in, but when I wrote in about my dereliction, I got back from a delightful editorial pen pal—Dora L. Peeples—this reassuring note: "Don't worry. I've done it for you. Get on back to the plastering."

Living in the house as we worked on it made us acutely furniture conscious. Whatever items seemed salvageable we stored in one bedroom, while we slept on mattresses or cots wherever we could. Piece by piece we began to rescue the articles we needed. Two of our Berkeley friends, Frank ("Rusty") and Mildred ("Billie") Russell, gave us infinite aid and comfort. They both knew old furniture and were completely entranced with the riches we had acquired. With the ssells' help, a beaten-up old kitchen table, complete with three ves found in assorted places, was promoted to the dining room, here it still serves us well. With enough elbow grease, dilapidated old icture frames turned out to be beautiful walnut or mahogany antiques. Billie knew enough about American folkways to look beneath the currently exhibited atrocities, and to find buried, sometimes several pictures deep, some delightful old prints. Two painted kitchen cupboards, after the use of much paint remover and more sanding, became attractive pine period pieces. An old walnut bedstead, with a headboard seven and one-half feet tall, with bureau and commode to match; eight cane-backed and cane-bottomed Victorian chairs; a solid walnut table; a carpenter-built pine cabinet—according to Billie the oldest piece in the house—all these and more we painfully rescued and re-assembled. One walnut picture frame, size two feet by one and one-half, enclosed a colorful, glass-covered certificate of membership in the Improved Order of Red Men, issued to one John Simon, a resident of Gold Trees, "on the 18 of the Travelling Moon, G.S.D. 391, A.D. 1882." Lucile irreverently mounted Simon's pride and joy on four spindles recovered from a fallen porch, and called it a tea table. And so on.

Rusty and Billie came often, and always left us richer as a result of their visit. When we found ourselves short of bedsteads to go with our oversupply of springs and mattresses, Rusty built the frames we needed. Billie inevitably snooped around and found something we had overlooked—a good mirror, for example, enclosed in a frame painted a violent red. She took the paint off and brought to the surface the original mahogany. She saw merit in the fragments of a tiny Franklin stove, and inspired Lucile to get it patched together.

When we began to invite in other visitors to see what we had done, they remembered Victorian pieces that they had long ago retired to their attics, and presented them to us. In this way we acquired an old mantle clock, a plaster statue of Venus and Adonis, an ancient foot-stool, an old stereopticon set, framed prints from *Godey's Ladies' Book*, and the like. Adeline Gilchrist lent us an old piano that had come around the Horn in 1851. It couldn't be tuned, so when her son re-claimed it a few years later we were consoled by her gift to us of an old parlor organ. Finally Lucile found an ornate old upright piano of 1880's vintage that was still in good condition, so now we have the parlor organ in the dining room and the piano in the parlor.

From time to time we bought a few articles that we thought would be appropriate—a roll of hitherto unused ingrain carpet that made a rug the right size for our living room, a tiny old desk that exactly fitted the space between our two front windows, a whatnot for the display of useless curios, a sturdy but ancient chesterfield with flowered uphol-stery, a huge wardrobe of the kind our ancestors used instead of closets, a tiny corner cupboard, and other items too numerous to mention.

Our move in Berkeley to the new and smaller house we had built there also netted Gold Trees some important acquisitions, among them a round walnut center table that had been a part of Lucile's grand-mother's wedding furniture; a half-dozen eighteenth-century chairs that we had bought in Boston in 1930; an old plush-covered family album that Lucile had inherited from her mother; an antique spool bedstead, made of butternut, that we had purchased for a fraction of its value during the depression; and books galore, brought up for summer reading and never taken back.

As a matter of fact, many interesting old books came into our pos-session along with the house. There was Agassiz's *A Journey to Brazil* (1869), for example, and Livingstone's *Perilous Adventures and Dis-coveries in the Interior of Africa* (1872), "sold only by subscription." Also, Lunette's *The American Gentleman's Guide to Politeness and Fashion* (1860), and Miss Leslie's *The Behavior Book; A Manual for Ladies* (1853). When we discovered this last-mentioned item, it won instant promotion to the living room center table, alongside the family album. Not only was *The Behavior Book* handsomely bound, but it contained some quite unusual literary gems. A chapter entitled "Sug-gestions to Visiters" warns the troubled guest to avoid letting her hostess know "that you have found or felt insects in your bed. . . . If you have positive proof that your bed is not free from these intolerable nuisances, confide this fact to the chambermaid only, and desire her to attend to it speedily." There is a section, too, on how to behave toward slaves, if you happen to visit in the South, and a somewhat ambiguous warning that "in her intercourse with gentlemen, a lady should take care to avoid all pecuniary obligations."

Sharing space on the center table with the family Album and *The Behavior Book* is a morocco-bound copy of *Collier's Cyclopedia of Com-mercial and Social Information* (1885). This impressive volume, accord-ing to the preface, presents "useful knowledge" in attractive form. A sequence of listings in its table of contents reads as follows: "Algebra, Gymnastics, Riding, Driving, Lessons in Bicycle Riding, Swimming, Drowning, Rowing," etc. There is a guide, too, for the pianoforte player, a disquisition on letter-writing, and a select list of prose quota-tions; everything, indeed, that a lady or gentleman of culture should know. Obviously, some of our predecessors at Gold Trees must have been quite elegant people.

Our fireplace was a kind of afterthought. We didn't really need a fireplace, for we had one little sheet-iron stove in the living room and another in the dining room that, taken together, could bring the whole house, even in the coldest weather, close to the boiling point. But the fact that we had a living room wall appropriate for a fireplace did not go unnoticed. So when Lucile and the girls couldn't stand it any longer without one, they got it. Built of rock gathered nearby—thirteen tons of same that cost me a dollar a ton ungathered—the chimney rises majestically above the house outside, and inside presents a handsome, nearly white, crystalline face that visitors are never permitted to ignore. The narrow mantle is faced with some walnut trimming taken from the headboard of an old bed, the rest of which was missing. So we retired the living room stove, and in due time the dining room stove gave way to an anachronistic electric heater. To have kept the house in character, perhaps we should have had a hard-coal base-burner, but hard coal was hard to come by in the Far West, and such luxuries fell only to those who had struck it rich. For years on years firewood was the principal fuel in our mountains, even for locomotives.

Like previous owners, we soon found that our house was not big enough and began to add to it. Our eldest daughter, Jane Harriet, came home after an unhappy marriage that lasted four years, and joined the annual trek to Dutch Flat. Young men began to drive up to call on the girls, and we needed a place to put them up overnight. Then, in quick succession, all three daughters were married, and for a time made their homes in Berkeley. Next the grandchildren, of whom there are now ten, began to come. We tried hard to keep up with the demand for space. Our first expansion was a basement excavation that netted us another bedroom and bath, plus space for an electric washer, a prime necessity after the appearance of the first grandchild. Next we built a wide screened-in sleeping porch along one whole side of the house, and another bathroom. We now had sleeping space for fourteen bodies within the house, and sometimes there were that many of us. Too many, we concluded, so next we built a guest house, complete with kitchen, bedroom, bathroom, and sleeping porch. Our oldest and youngest daughters no longer live in Berkeley, and so spend little time at Dutch Flat, but our second daughter, Carolyn, her husband, and their three children occupy the guest house a month or more each summer. When Marjorie, our youngest, with her family of six, visited us recently, we abandoned the "big house" to them and retreated to the "little house." If we had to, however, we could accommodate the whole tribe at once, all eighteen of us, but that hasn't happened yet. The period of expansion, we think, is over.

During our first frantic efforts to make our house habitable, we paid little attention to the yard outside. But gradually a transformation took place there also. The two great cherry trees in front were nearly dead and had to come down. This required outside help, but the competent workmen who took them down anchored a line in the process to a third cherry tree at the side of the house and brought it down, too. After some unseemly shrubs and a locust tree were removed, the house presented an extraordinarily bare face to the road, although one large cedar tree stood its ground at one side of the house and an elderly pear tree at the other. We observed numerous brave little cedars here and there, and some struggling walnuts; for no good reason we let them grow, even adding a couple of knee-high pines. Out back there were more pear trees, more walnuts, and some seedling cherries. Time did wonderful things to all the trees. Now our house is so surrounded by them that it can hardly be seen from the street. In fact, we cut down trees enough each year to furnish fuel for our fireplace.

To begin with, part of our lot was reasonably clear of everything but cover grass, but part of it was infected with blackberries, on which as soon as we could we made determined war. Only those who know what mountain blackberries can do will understand what an obnoxious adversary we had to fight. We tried several varieties of poison, but after a short period of wilted leaves, up they came again, bright and vigorous. We tried burning them off late in the fall after the rains had begun, but next spring there they were again. Finally we took to digging them up, painfully, root by root. After about ten years we won, although we still have to be on guard against guerrilla attacks.

To remove those two unsightly cherry tree stumps in the front yard required more power with an ax than my muscles afforded. One of them yielded to a young man who came up in a navy hellcat to visit Carolyn, first buzzing the village, then landing at the nearby Blue Canyon emergency air field. These deeds of derring-do, impressive as they were, rated far behind his destruction of one of the stumps, but Carolyn was unimpressed and turned him down. The other stump continued to glare at us until our youngest son-in-law accepted the challenge and won.

Then there was the matter of the fence. The wire one that existed was designed, obviously, just to keep the cows in, but there were half-rotted pickets here and there which suggested that we ought to have a white picket fence, at least across the front. We found a refugee from an old soldiers' home (he turned out to be my age to the day) who agreed to build us such a fence for a consideration, if we'd let him do it his way. Since no pickets existed anywhere the exact shape of the originals, we induced a neighbor with a machine saw to cut them out for us at ten cents a picket. Even when it was new this fence looked old, but now that it has survived many winters and much punching around by growing trees, it looks as if it might be as old as the house itself.

The front yard soon became quite presentable. We built a cement patio to fill out the ell of the house, next to the fireplace chimney, mowed the native grass so that with the stumps removed it made a quite respectable imitation of a lawn, and put up a temporary fence to mark the boundary between the tamed and the untamed areas. Two dark red peonies competed in season with the old-fashioned roses that bordered the walk; a trumpet vine, a holly tree, a smoke bush, and sundry native shrubs screened from view the dilapidated old garage at the corner of the lot; an untamable grape vine ran riot in the young trees and shrubs farther down the hill. (The grapes, which are delectable, unfortunately do not ripen until too late in the fall for us to harvest them.) For a while Marjorie's horse (her second one, a palomino mare, Milady) had the run of the back half of the lot and, whenever we had guests on the patio, stretched her neck across the fence to join us.

In time progress took its toll, even in the back yard. The unsightly cow sheds and other outbuildings came down, and apple trees grew where the sheds had stood. After Marjorie's marriage the presence of the horse was removed. The sons-in-law took the matter of landscaping into their hands, leveled and hard-surfaced a spot large enough for a badminton court, turned the red-dirt areas next to the house into lawns, marked out an appropriate section for a croquet court, and even created an elaborate back-yard lighting system for the use of after-dark players. As the second generation grew older the courts were used correspondingly less, but now that the grandchildren are growing up, interest in outdoor games is reviving. Since the back lawns are now heavily shaded, we often take our party guests out there. On the edges we display a small vegetable garden, a patch of raspberries, and spots where in season the native flowers—California poppies, larkspur, columbine, and primroses—still hold sway. If we come up early enough in the spring, violets and daffodils are everywhere, even in the grass.

From the beginning we participated actively in various aspects of village life. One of the big events of the summer season turned out to be a Fourth of July parade. This event is quite unlike anything I have ever seen anywhere else. An adult committee makes the plans, interested mothers produce the costumes, but children do the marching. There are prizes for enough different types of entrants to make sure that every child will get some reward, so the kids show up in droves. Naturally, the Hicks grandchildren appear regularly; last year, the youngest granddaughter became a "Liberty Belle" (fourth prize among the Patriotic entries), while an eleven-year-old joined with a visiting friend the same age to take first prize in the Animal class. Their exhibit, according to a picketer's-type placard they carried, was "Three Pairs of Twins"—themselves in red, white, and blue; two black kittens they held in their arms; and the two Hicks silver-gray poodles on leashes. A few American Legionnaires, with guns, set the pace, and the children marched valiantly past the hotel, where the judges sat, then more haltingly the long way around the town to the schoolhouse. There, after "The Star-Spangled Banner" and a short patriotic speech (three and one-half minutes by yours truly), the prizes were awarded, and everyone was invited to patronize the cafeteria-style luncheon arranged by the Community Club, the proceeds from which covered the cost of the prizes. For this occasion the whole town turned out, and was joined by a surprisingly large number of outsiders.

The platform from which I spoke was that of an old narrow-gauge railroad caboose, which now sits on an appropriate length of rails in the schoolhouse yard. The caboose once belonged to the Towle Brothers Lumber Company, and for years followed through the mountains a train that brought in lumber from the sawmills to Towle, a railroad point, now extinct, on the main line near Dutch Flat. Local history buffs, motivated by Adeline Gilchrist, I think, persuaded the Towle estate, which still exists, to restore the caboose (it had long leaned against a shed near the village store) and to present it to the village. Katherine Towle, dean of students at the University of California and a former WAC colonel, made the presentation speech from the caboose platform, and with a bottle of champagne dedicated the trophy. Mindful of the danger to bare feet from broken glass, however, she refused to break the bottle and instead merely released the cork. The resounding whoosh with which the cork and most of the champagne left the bottle won enthusiastic applause from the crowd. Miss Towle told us that she had played in the caboose as a child.

Dutch Flat has another relic from the past, an ornate, horse-drawn, glass-sided hearse, with silver trimmings and plumes. There is a "Hearse House" at one end of Main Street in which the vehicle has gathered dust for years, except on the rare occasions when it was taken out for public inspection. Once, with one of these public appearances imminent, Byron Emerick, a long-time resident of Dutch Flat, came to Gold Trees to get Lucile's help in polishing the silver, because, he said truthfully, "she's not afraid of work." Recently Schatzi Rettenmayer, of whom more later, had the Hearse House renovated at her own expense and a window cut in so that the public could view the relic at will.

When I first came to Dutch Flat I was told a story about the hearse that is probably mythical, but why all this obsession with destroying myths anyway? In the earliest days Dutch-Flatters hauled their dead to the cemetery in wagons, but a few public-spirited citizens felt the need for a more dignified conveyance. So they took up a collection to buy a hearse, not neglecting to highjack the local madams, who, at any rate, in the normal course of events would provide a disproportionate amount of business for it. With the money in hand, a delegation left for San Francisco to buy the coveted vehicle. To their great distress they found that they had not enough money to buy a hearse with plumes, so they returned to Dutch Flat determined to collect the extra sum needed. Again they asked the madams for help, but the old gals said they'd be damned if they'd kick in another cent. Finally, however, they accepted a compromise proposal. They would announce a dollar day the length and breadth of the diggings, and if they took in enough extra cash that way, they'd help buy the plumes. Apparently the cut rate must have turned the trick, for the hearse certainly has plumes. Shatzi says it wasn't that way at all, but why spoil a good story?

The cemetery, high on the hillside above the church, is worth a visit. It is far better populated than the village itself; the tombstones have a lot to tell. Once when Bill Hesseltine was visiting us, he and I undertook to find out how much of the history of Dutch Flat we could glean if we had only the inscriptions to go on. Onlookers, of whom fortunately there were none, might have been surprised to observe two elderly gentlemen on their knees before tombstone after tombstone, pulling out the grass at the base of each, brushing away the dirt with a whisk broom, and taking notes on what they found. By the dates we could easily measure the growth and decline of the village.

We could spot years in which epidemics carried whole families away. We could tell where the residents of Dutch Flat had come from ("Native of England," etc.); we often learned what their occupations had been. We were left in no doubt as to their fraternal connections; indeed, the Masons had a whole section to themselves. We could guess a little about their conduct; for example, on the headstone of one relatively young woman we read "The Path of Glory Leads but to the Grave." So they knew their poets, too. And we could learn a lot about their religious views:

> Death unto me no warning gave,
> But quickly took me to my grave.
> Oh, flee to Christ without delay
> For no man knows his dying day.

As for the Chinese burial ground, there was only a remnant of masonry left, and it later disappeared—some ghoulish builder no doubt coveted the old brick. The Orientals, we were told, operated a primitive crematory, but sent the bones of their dead back to China for burial. Maybe; certainly we found no Chang or Wong inscriptions. For the Chinese chapter of Dutch Flat's history the cemetery helped very little.

I have already mentioned the Dutch Flat annual barbecue. This event is as much a social occasion as a money-making venture, and the whole community takes part in the project. The day before the feast some of the younger and stronger men build a roaring log fire in a deep rectangular pit near the swimming pool. This pit, once merely a hole in the ground, has acquired quite recently sturdy brick walls that prevent cave-ins. For years Leo Quinn, who heads a highway maintenance crew, has stayed up all night with the fire to make sure that the wood is properly consumed and that by morning it has turned into a glowing bed of coals. The village men gather to prepare hundreds of pounds of beef, done up in thirty-or forty-pound rolls, for the roasting.

Henry Ford could hardly have planned a more effective assembly line than now takes over. Operating on long tables built for the purpose, one or two individuals begin the process by cutting six-foot lengths of cheese cloth, wrapping paper, and burlap. Another detail thoroughly saturates each roll of beef with barbecue sauce (prepared in advance by Jean Quinn, the woman with the most know-how), while at the same time wrapping it with cheese cloth to hold the flavor in; another group rewraps it with the butcher paper; still another encases it in burlap, coating it as they go with a heavy layer of fire clay. Then a few skilled workmen fasten wires around both ends of each sticky bundle and attach to them long lengths of wire with loops at the end through which a rod can be passed. Next two of the strongest and tallest men present shoulder the burden and, with one of them walking on each side of the pit, lower it into place, carefully securing the wire ends so that they can be used again when the time comes to recover the roast. As each "pig" settles into the bed of coals, men at the side with shovels cover it over with sand. Long experience or careful indoctrination ensures that each person does his task with skill. It's hard work but a lot of fun.

When the job is over, a number of the participants often retire to the home of some one of them for an eye-opener or two. For years Dr. Gerald Stoodley, owner of the old hotel, served on these occasions highly sophisticated gin fizzes, each containing enough fruit and cream (as well as gin) to drown all thought of a proper breakfast.

Meanwhile the women have made tubs of potato salad, baked bushels of beans, cut and buttered loaf after loaf of French bread, readied watermelon for dessert and coffee or punch for drink. A committee sends out notices to every female resident, telling her in advance where to go, at what time, and for what duties. For years, by common consent, a summer resident, Mabel Ferrier, who lacked the sense of smell, chopped the onions for the potato salad; since her departure others less well adapted to the task have had to cry it through. The women do most of the serving, too, from the same tables used earlier to prepare the meat, and provide clean-up squads whose duties extend over into the next day. The men, however, lift the meat from the pit and do the carving. The number of people served each year (at two dollars per person) exceeds many times over the number of Dutch Flat residents —well over a thousand is not uncommon, and below seven hundred is regarded with some dismay.

Until recently profits from the barbecue, supplemented by individual contributions, have sufficed to keep the pool in operation. The Swimming Pool Corporation has handled all funds, hired the necessary life guards, planned and supervised improvements. Mounting costs, however, particularly those incurred to comply with more exacting health requirements, led at length to the formation of a tax district through which to acquire additional funds for pool maintenance. To some members of the community this development amounts to disturbing evidence that our greatly cherished individual initiative is on the way out.

On his last visit to Dutch Flat, Bill Hesseltine, as he sat puffing away at his pipe on our patio, ruminated as follows: "Yes, Hicks has come full circle. Born and brought up in a small town, he went away to college, won fame and fortune [a gross exaggeration], saw the world, then wound up right where he started from."

Maybe he was right. The Dutch Flat setting is different from the settings of the small towns in which I lived as a boy; the agricultural hinterland that was so important to them is lacking; the summer colony is unique. But in many respects our town is like every other American small town. Everyone knows and takes an interest in every-one else. Most of us call each other by our first names. We meet con-stantly at the store, or the post office, or the swimming pool, and when we meet we take the time to talk a little. We visit back and forth, eat and drink at each other's expense, attend community gatherings, wrestle (sometimes heatedly) with local problems.

Dutch Flat, as Bill Adams pointed out, is a haven of refuge from the modern city, a place of escape from the tumult of industry, the chaos of transportation, the pollution of the atmosphere, the clash of races, the disease of unemployment, and all the other ills that make our urban society so intolerable. Part of its residents live there the year around, others only summers, but all because they enjoy the immunity it gives them from city life. Let me introduce a few of my neighbors.

I must begin with Luigi and Teresita Piccirillo, for it was they who introduced us to the village. Luigi (in the phone book, Louis) is a successful San Francisco attorney by profession, but by avocation a devotee of music and a playwright. Occasionally he writes and directs the annual extravaganza put on by the Berkeley Hillside Club. His most outstanding success, in my opinion, was his "Land o' Gold," which featured such historic characters as Sam Brannon, Lola Montez, and Lotta Crabtree (played by Lucile). For our twenty-fifth wedding anniversary he wrote a skit entitled "The Wedding of John and Lucile," which he staged in his Berkeley house, with two of our neighbors, Francis and Kay Hutchens, standing in for us. Luigi was born in San Francisco and remembers well the earthquake and fire, but Teresita was Italian-born, and lived for a time in South America, where her name acquired the Spanish diminutive. Almost single-handed she created the Department of Italian in the University of California, Berkeley, and during World War II came back to it to teach Italian to servicemen presumably bound for duty in Italy. One of the two Piccirillo daughters, Laura, was the age of our Carolyn and attended the same school. The spacious Piccirillo summer home in Dutch Flat took form while Gold Trees was being reconstructed, with the same contractor dividing his time between the two projects. Hospitable almost to a fault, the Piccirillos are always entertaining interesting guests, whom they unfailingly share with us.

Across the street from us when we first came to Dutch Flat lived Dr. George Runckel and his wife. The Doctor had come full circle, too, for he was born in Dutch Flat, went away for his medical education, practiced for years in northern California, then came back home to retire. But how can a doctor retire? The whole village took its complaints to him and he took care of us. He was one of the no-nonsense kind. I recall going to see him once about a sick daughter. After listening to my description of her symptoms, he put on over his head the already tied four-in-hand necktie that he always wore when he made house calls, took down from a shelf the medicine he expected to prescribe, and came back with me to examine the patient. Sure enough, he had diagnosed the trouble correctly and could leave the pills he had brought. Next day he came again, noted marked improvement, took back with him the unused pills—"It's not always easy to get to a drugstore up here," he explained, "so why waste them?" He cured most of our ills when he recommended that we carry our drinking water from his springhouse, where it was protected against the pine pollen so plentiful in these parts. He was not even above mending our dogs when they got hurt, and he never sent bills. His charge for a season (I always insisted on paying him) was about four dollars.

Our appreciation of the Doctor grew with the years. We left our keys with him when we were away; once, when he was sure that too much rain was going down our chimney, he brought his ladder over, climbed up on the roof, and put a bucket upside down over the opening. He knew a lot about early Dutch Flat and entertained us with his reminiscences. When spading in his garden one day he dug up a ball of metal which he took to be lead. He left it on the workbench in his garage until one time he accidentally knocked it off. To his surprise, it broke in two, so he had it assayed and found that it was some old-timer's cache of gold held together with mercury. It brought him over three hundred dollars and reminded him of an unexplained murder in Chinatown, about that gold, he surmised. He showed us the place up the hill behind his house where in his youth the Indians used to camp. They were acorn eaters, and the holes their pestles had bored, during the grinding process, in a big flat table stone were still quite visible.

Then a short block from us clockwise around the town there were the Gilchrists, Guy and Adeline (everyone called her "Adaween"), well-to-do San Franciscans who lived about half of each year in Dutch Flat and made it their voting place. They called their property "China Hill," because it had once been in the Chinese section. They were extremely hospitable; on their patio and around their swimming pool we met most of the people in Dutch Flat that we came to know well. Adaween was a devoted student of local history and helped locate the nearby markers which the Centennial Commission built and which she and I helped dedicate.

Next door to the Gilchrists lived Anna Young, a former San Francisco Opera singer, who had named her acreage appropriately "Harmony Farm" (the notes were written on her sign so that all who could read them could whistle the tune). Frequently the breezes wafted the sound of music our way, so naturally she and Lucile became good friends. Indeed, during the winter months Lucile went from Berkeley to San Francisco each week for years to take singing lessons from Anna. In her patio, too, Dutch-Flatters often forgathered.

Farther down the hill lived Rob and "Biddie" Waybur, Piedmont residents who had moved to Dutch Flat permanently after Rob's retirement. Rob was well read and loved to talk, and he and I fought happily over the issues of the day, political, social, and economic. The Wayburs knew the mountains well, and with them we took many expeditions up and down and around the ranges. They, too, had bought an old house, although one not as far advanced toward disintegration as ours, and they had made it over into an attractive residence. They, too, had daughters—one of them was married in the Dutch Flat church. So we had much in common. Eventually Bob's health declined and they moved to an easier winter climate.

Their successors were Phil and Julia Hindley. Phil had been on the editorial staff of the San Francisco *Examiner* and had retired to Dutch Flat, only to take a commuting job with an Auburn paper. Julia had a passion for cookbooks and owned a remarkable collection of them. Before long the Dutch Flat Ladies' Aid was selling a Dutch Flat cookbook, with recipes furnished by the local ladies and assembled by Julia.

On a side street near the Wayburs, Harrison and Jeanne McClung took over another old house and made a showpiece of it. Harrison had put on exhibits for the United States at trade fairs all over the world until he got into trouble during the Eisenhower administration. A stickler for efficiency, he refused, although himself a Republican, to appoint an incompetent Republican office seeker to his staff. So he was forced out. He was ready to retire anyway, and enjoyed himself hugely at Dutch Flat for the few years of life he had left. Now Jeanne lives on alone, but with frequent visits from children and grandchildren.

Next door to the McClungs live Matt and Betty Bailey. Matt is a graduate in engineering, but he abhors city life and took a job with the Pacific Gas and Electric Company that enables him to live up here in the mountains the year around. Betty is a well-educated eastern girl who endears herself to all and sundry by writing a chatty column of personals for the Colfax *Record*. We can hardly wait—winter no less than summer—for the weekly issue that will tell us all about the local doings. The Baileys have three lovely daughters who remind us of our own children at comparable ages. For them Matt built the most wonderful playhouse I have ever seen. Whether for his daughters or for himself, I am not sure, but he also long harbored three big donkeys —Ramona, Lucinda, and Clarence. They were lovable creatures, but noisy, and Matt got sensitive about their heehaws, so now only Lucinda is left. I always enjoyed their salutes to the dawn; they were inconsequential in comparison with the sonic booms that have begun increasingly to blast our ears.

Down the hill from the Hindleys is the home of Kirby Quinn, the former storekeeper, who is still the commanding officer at the annual barbecue. Approximately my age, Kirby could turn out more work in a day than most men could manage in a week. He had the welfare of the whole community on his mind; he needed no school of business administration to instil in him the idea of service. When we needed help we knew we could turn to Kirby for it. Before we got an electric refrigerator, he personally delivered the ice for our icebox. When we required items he didn't have in stock, he ordered them. He took equally good care of the "snipers," lowly successors to the miners, who eked out a living by panning gold down on Bear River. He accepted their gold dust in payment for groceries—many times I've seen him weighing out their hoards. Since their product was far from pure, he valued it at only twenty-nine dollars an ounce, but that was probably more than it brought him.

I doubt if Kirby ever took an inventory of his stock or ever disposed of anything merely because it was no longer in demand. Some articles that took up space in his overhead storeroom certainly dated back to a very different age. Once, for example, he dug out a keg of nose rings for swine, the kind that in my youth Missouri farmers put in the pigs' noses to keep them from rooting their way out under the fence. Another time he found and displayed some of the old pans used by the miners in "O, Susannah" days—we bought one for a patio ash tray. It was Kirby's wife, Jean, who always made the sauce for the annual barbecue, and his nephew, Leo, who sat up all night with the fire. For years Kirby did more work on that occasion than any other three men. He took great pride in the celebration. "This thing must go on," I've heard him say, meaning that someone else must carry on the tradition after he no longer could do it. I think Leo got the message.

Reversing ourselves and going back toward Depot Hill, we find many more interesting people. Across the street from the Gilchrists, Marsh and Harriet Evans have rescued another of Dutch Flat's old houses. Marsh is a United Airlines pilot who, by a miracle, chanced to be in charge of the plane when Lucile and I flew with two of our grandchildren from San Francisco to Los Angeles, bound for Disneyland. When we left the plane, Marsh in his pilot's uniform took the children by hand and led them to the Disneyland helicopter, a more important event by far than any they were about to encounter. "Hat" grows an incredibly prolific flower garden, harbors a big turtle named Napoleon, and gives parties under an apple tree that bears the biggest apples I ever saw. All the village wept—quite literally—when Tat, the younger of the two Evans boys and a universal favorite, died of cancer.

Farther up the hill on the Gilchrist side we find Anna Lindberg in a big house once owned by her father, a somewhat eccentric gentleman who is remembered for having had all the trees cut down that blocked his view of the passing trains. Beyond Anna is Anita Crellin, a very intelligent former librarian, who has long made Dutch Flat her permanent home. She has acres of fruit trees, mostly pears, which she markets in years when the yield is good. She is chock full of good deeds. When a neighbor's house burned down, she gave him one that stood unused on her property, and he moved it down the hill and around the corner to a lot he owned a half block from our house. That house-moving project monopolized the attention of the village for as long as it took. Still farther up the hill are John and Kathryn McGinis, an Oakland couple who advertised for the kind of summer place they wanted for themselves and their two boys, and thus found Dutch Flat. Beyond them, David and Jean McKibben; David is a member of the University of California accounting staff whom we also know in Berkeley, and whose parents lived in Dutch Flat when we first came up here.

Again retracing our steps and making the turn into Main Street, we pass the Hearse House and the old Runckel place and come to where Hans and Zenobia Haldorsen live. Hans is a retired railroad carpenter with a continuing yen for work. He built our sleeping porch and guest house, and keeps us in repairs generally. His wife, Zenobia, has a hobby shop in front of their residence, where one can buy notions; for good measure she also presides over a regional lending library that is renewed at regular intervals. George Parkhill, the current store-keeper, has finished a house that one of his predecessors had begun, back of the store, so attractively as to make it quite the talk of the town. Next door to the store our superlatively efficient postmaster (not post-mistress), Marguerite Wilson, now raises and lowers the Stars and Stripes each day before a separate building; time was when she had to compete for space with groceries inside the store. Maggie, as most people call her, now lives with her husband, Perry, in what was once Bill Adams' big house. She has completely redone it and throws a fabulous party each year for the whole community.

Farther up the street are many other good friends, including Margaret Flournoy, a former schoolteacher who until recently was the harassed president of the Community Club; Gene Smart, by common consent the titular mayor of Dutch Flat; Judge Richard Sims and his wife, Dale, whose house, "Wild Honey," is another of the older places and is now undergoing reconstruction; and until recently, Warren and Mabel Ferrier. Warren was a professor of law in the University of California, but summers he roared around the town in an army jeep, fished the rivers dry, and gathered prickly wild gooseberries to give to his friends. Still farther out, along the winding Drum Power House Road, are two old-timers, but new acquaintances to us, Bill and Louise Melton. Bill is a former miner who has discovered a knack for cooking and proudly exhibits his products each year at the county fair. Louise is a former architect for the Auburn Lumber Company, whose imaginative draftsmanship is exhibited in our new guest house.

George and Dorothy Hahn have, high up in the pines near the Piccirillos, a big house with a wide front porch facing the road and on the opposite side an equally spacious patio facing the trees. Although George is one of the world's most distinguished orthodontists, he is really a farmer at heart, and grows Dutch Flat's largest and best vegetable garden—a great boon to all his friends. Dorothy lived in Wyoming as a young girl, so we share many interesting memories. Each year she has us over for a breakfast of sourdough pancakes, baked on an old-fashioned wood-burning range—the only way to do it right, she says.

The year we lived next door to the Hahns they were unexpected hosts to a most unusual party. The way to George's heart was fertilizer —more precisely, manure—for his garden. He ranged far and wide in his pickup to find it. One evening Marj's horse left a large deposit in our yard, so I shoveled it up and started over to George's with it, followed by family and friends. After disposing of our trophy appropriately, we decided to stay a while and put on a show. Roe and Horty Stebbins from the University of Wisconsin had shown up in their *wagon-lit*, and being natural-born vaudevillians, they started it off. George played and Lucile sang. With each act the crowd grew larger, as univited guests, attracted by the tumult, appeared at windows and doors. Dorothy danced. Gertrude Moir and her daughter, Babs, visitors from Hawaii, put on some very sophisticated hulas. By that time Roe and Horty had thought up something else, so the cycle began all over. Dutch Flat theater.

One of our most unforgettable characters is Schatzi Rettenmayer. Schatzi's given name was Philippine, because she was supposed to have been a boy named Philip, but no one ever calls her or thinks of her except as Schatzi. Shortly before we came to Dutch Flat she made over an old miner's cabin into a delightful summer cottage, but that was only the beginning. Soon she built a barn, so called, but in reality a garage that looks like a barn and has living space inside for guests and helpers. Next came a big, beautiful, modern house, up a few steps from the cottage—"Top Side," she calls it. Her shaded patio, enclosed by the two houses and a swimming pool, provides space for some of Dutch Flat's most original entertaining. Schatzi is a born artist. Her houses are in every detail works of art. She has a loom and weaves, even teaches some of our grandchildren to weave. She is an expert at needlework. She makes unique art objects for the Ladies' Aid bazaars. She excels in exotic cooking. I'm sure there is only one like her, and the pattern got lost.

From a totally different mold was Bill Adams, one of my first and most cherished Dutch Flat friends. A tall, spare figure in his seventies, he sometimes appeared at the village swimming pool with every muscle of his shoulders and arms and legs as clearly outlined as the spars on the sailing ships he loved to talk about. He called on us regularly while we were working on our house, arriving at any time of day. We knew who was coming when the gate clicked to the accompaniment of his tuneless whistle, and I, for one, always knocked off whatever I was doing to keep him talking as long as I could. He was a native of England, born in the Wye River country, had a good public school education, and handled the English language with rare felicity. True, he told the same stories over and over, but he told them in such a fascinating way that they were well worth rehearing. He had gone to sea as a young man, and although illness cut this experience short, it left a deep imprint on him. After two or three trips around the Horn he stayed in California to recover from tuberculosis; it was the health-giving air of the red-dirt country, I think, that brought him to Dutch Flat. He soon discovered his talent for writing and wrote tall tales of the sea. To some of the literal minded, who failed to see that he was a fictionist, he was an "old fraud," but to me he was as honest a man as I ever knew. He wrote a book, *Ships and Women* (1937), in which he uncovered many similarities between the two; but whereas he claimed to know something about ships, he admitted that understanding women was quite beyond him.

Bill's first marriage (he told me this himself) was of the common-law variety because he and his wife were too closely related, in an odd sort of way—not as close as cousins—for the English statutes of the time. When later the law was changed and they could have married legally, they refused the indignity of it. The death of his wife hurt him deeply, but two later marriages, each strictly according to law, failed miserably. He would never talk of them. His last wife, a Mills College English teacher, took his big house from him, and after that he lived in the little cottage back of the old hotel. Bill's literary capital lay in his sea stories, but in his later years interest in the old windjammers he loved to write about had run out; only now and then could he sell one. His last story, however, "Man Overboard," appeared after his death. Obviously, he was thinking of himself as he wrote it—he knew his end was near.

Bill had great tales to tell of early Dutch Flat, but he was reluctant to put them in writing, for he wanted to live in peace with his neighbors. One that he could have elaborated upon more fully was of a meeting, held by the local volunteer fire department the day after a disastrous fire. The trouble was that the fire fighters had no sooner ostentatiously unrolled their hose than it split open from one end to the other. So all they could do was to watch while the building burned to the ground. Bill attended the meeting called the next day to consider the situation. According to his report, the chairman, not much of a talker himself, finally prodded out the motion he needed: "I move, by God," said one volunteer, "that we get a new roll of hose."

After a long pause came the second: "Well, by Jesus Christ, I second the motion."

Without further ado the chairman put the motion: "It's moved by God and seconded by Jesus Christ that we get a new roll of hose." The motion carried.

I have not named nearly all the people we know in Dutch Flat, or nearly all that I ought to name, but this sample will have to suffice. Somehow Dutch Flat attracts the kind of people we like. Many others besides Bill Adams that we used to know are now gone, among them Warren Ferrier, Adaween Gilchrist, Julia Hindley, and the elder McKibbens. But they all live in our memories, and we know most of the newcomers who have taken their places.

Pardon me, gentle reader (if any) for including all this personal material in what started out to be a strictly academic autobiography. You may skip it if you choose. But maybe, as a bit of social history, it is quite as important as any of the rest.

XIV. California (Part 2)

ALTHOUGH I HAVE BEEN four times the chairman of a history department and twice a university dean, I have never aspired to an administrative career. On the other hand, I have always maintained that every
faculty member should accept his share of administrative responsibilities. Only by shouldering ourselves as much of this kind of work
as possible can we hope to escape the development within universities
of a separate—and often quite unpalatable—administrative caste.
Admittedly, it is not easy for any individual to engage in teaching,
research, and administration all at the same time, but the fact that some
persons do succeed in this endeavor proves that it can be done. Moreover, there is no reason why the same individual should remain
indefinitely in any particular administrative office. Departmental
chairmanships can be, often are, and usually should be rotated frequently; the same thing could be true of deanships, directorships, and
the like. One obstacle to the latter course is that an administrator's
salary is usually greater than a professor's, and few faculty members
can ever bring themselves to take a cut in salary voluntarily. Unfortunately, also, many professors, once they accept administrative duties,
find excuses for neglecting, then eventually giving up entirely, both
their teaching and their research. As a matter of fact, after a too prolonged vacation, they are not likely to be much good for either. Some
even develop an appetite for power and keep grasping for more.
Despite the old adage, a little learning is probably better than none,
but a little power in the wrong hands is certainly a dangerous thing.

World War II was not yet over when I found myself, almost in-
explicably, saddled with the deanship of the Graduate Division at
Berkeley. My predecessor, Charles Lipman, a plant physiologist, had
died in office, and because of the preeminence of the sciences in
graduate work at Berkeley it was generally assumed that some distinguished scientist would take his place. However, the California

committee system, with which I was beginning to be familiar, produces some interesting upsets. In choosing a new dean the president, according to custom, asks our committee on committees to appoint an *ad hoc* faculty committee, the duty of which is to nominate suitable candidates for the position. Someone on that committee (presumably my colleague, Raymond J. Sontag) succeeded in putting my name on a list that I am positive was otherwise composed exclusively of scientists. Perhaps President Sproul was unwilling to choose any one of the eminent scientists suggested for fear of offending the others, or perhaps he thought that the time had come to recognize the importance of the non-science fields. At any rate his choice fell on me.

I was reluctant to take the job and before doing so consulted a number of my friends. Most of them urged me to accept, not only on the theory that it would be a step up for me personally, but also because my appointment would constitute a much needed recognition of the growing importance of the social studies and humanities at California. Paxson's advice was tongue-in-cheek: "Go ahead and take it," he said. "Join the Bohemian Club and become a big shot." This was only his way of saying that I would have to go one way or the other. (The Bohemian Club never asked me.)

I suppose flattery had something to do with my becoming a dean again; I had felt a bit rejected by my new colleagues, and here was a chance to show that I was somebody after all. In my heart I knew that Paxson was right, that a deanship would be a handicap to one whose interest lay primarily in the writing and teaching of history, but once more I attempted to compromise. In accepting, I made it clear to the President that I would not give up my teaching—not even a single class—and that in case I could not discharge adequately my double responsibilities as dean and as professor, I would resign the deanship. Also, I asked permission to retain my office ("study," we sometimes called it) in the library as headquarters for my activities as a history professor. By this time the number of graduate students who looked to me for guidance had begun to multiply, and I was unwilling to subject them to the ordeal of having to break through the barriers that the graduate office, more or less of necessity, had to set up to protect the dean's time in his "holy of holies."

One interesting by-product of my being made graduate dean was my election to an honorary membership in Phi Beta Kappa, an attainment I had failed to achieve as an undergraduate at Northwestern

University. Dean Lipman, it chanced, had been a Phi Beta Kappa senator, an honor that some loyal Californians believed should not be lost to the university. They therefore suggested my name as a replacement, assuming that I was of course a member of the society. When to their chagrin they found that I was not, they could think of no better solution than to plug for Clarence A. Dykstra, newly chosen provost at UCLA. So Dykstra got the honor instead of a Berkeleyan. But the men who had promoted my abortive candidacy did what they could to overcome their embarrassment by inducing the Alpha chapter of California to make me an honorary member. In this fashion I achieved the status that I had failed to make on my own nearly a third of a century earlier. I was selected also to give the annual Phi Beta Kappa address that year at Berkeley, and spoke on "The American Tradition of Democracy," a theme to which I frequently recurred on later occasions.[1]

Lipman left me a well-staffed office that in many ways could carry on about as well without a dean as with one. Carefully defined rules covered nearly every possible situation. The interpretation of these rules, however, without a dean's active intervention from time to time, tended to grow too formal and rigid. I found myself inevitably drawn into the business of applying the graduate regulations to individual cases in such a way as to avoid unintentional injustices. Because I was more accessible in my library office than in the dean's office, students who had occasion to see me as dean began to compete with my history clientele in seeking me out in my library refuge.

I have no doubt that some of my colleagues thought I was neglecting my work as dean, but I could point to the budget in justification of my giving most of my time to my work as a professor of history. About seven-eighths of my salary was charged to the history department and only about one-eighth to the Graduate Division; if arithmetic meant anything, the deanship was entitled to one-eighth of my working time. But of course it was not meant to mean anything. This well-worn statistical device for pretending that the costs of administration were less than they really were had always irked me; I resented the siphoning off of money technically allotted to teaching for use in paying administrative salaries.

To cut down as much as possible on my administrative chores I dispensed with some of the duties with which Dean Lipman had

[1] John D. Hicks, *The American Tradition* (1955).

encumbered himself. He had, for example, taken a personal interest in the appointment of examining committees for each Ph.D. candidate, whatever his field, a prerogative that in my opinion might better be surrendered to the departments directly concerned. He had also insisted on personal interviews with every Ph.D. candidate, a nice gesture, perhaps, but there were just too many Ph.D.'s being born for a one-eighth-time dean to interview them all.

Partly because of the pressures on the dean's time and partly because I felt uneasy in my contacts with the sciences, I persuaded President Sproul to appoint as assistant dean Morris A. Stewart, a parasitologist who knew his way about in most scientific fields. Morris was interested in administrative detail to a degree that I never could be, and as the numbers of post–World War II graduate students began to pour in, his help became indispensable. After my resignation as graduate dean, he carried on for a year as acting dean, then for several years as associate dean under Will Dennis, then finally as graduate dean in his own right. His genuine appreciation of the importance of administration made a far deeper imprint on the Graduate Division than anything I had done.

A Graduate Council of twenty-one members, representing as nearly as possible every scholarly interest of the university, existed to advise the graduate dean. Since the committee on committees, rather than the dean, determined the membership of the Council, it was anything but a rubber stamp. For many important decisions I leaned on it heavily, or upon a smaller executive committee selected from it. One of the Council's most exacting duties was the awarding of graduate fellowships and scholarships. At Wisconsin this task fell primarily to the various departments, with the Graduate Office (whenever options existed) merely making specific allotments to fields. I would have preferred to follow a similar procedure at California, but the long-established practice was otherwise. So once each spring the Council remained in session for an entire week end to make the final awards for the entire campus. Fortunately, the organization of applications and departmental recommendations was in the hands of a superbly qualified member of the graduate staff, Miss Florence Mullins (later Mrs. Scott Pyle), whose painstaking labor furnished us with indispensable guidance. In cases where differences in opinion developed, the Council made the decision by majority vote, the dean's vote counting no more than that of any other member.

The seriousness with which members of the Council prepared for this ordeal can hardly be overstated. For days and nights before the concluding sessions they pored over the records, listing the various candidates in order of preference. I doubt if we made many serious mistakes, although it was not easy to balance the merits of candidates in such divergent fields, for example, as chemistry and political science. How does one compare such diverse qualifications? We learned not to depend completely on grades. In the social studies and the humanities, where the grading is less exact, a B-plus average could be as hard to win as an A average in mathematics or a laboratory science. Grading standards varied. An A plus in a second-rate college might be worth less than a B minus in a first-rate university. Recommendations from men we could trust might mean far more than grades. Some letters that came in, however, could be accepted only at a heavy discount. Too many professors are inclined to think that all their good students are potential scholars. Also, if I had not known it before, I would have learned then the wisdom of writing discriminating rather than effusive recommendations. Sometimes a few words are better than many. I recall with a degree of pride the occasional handwritten notation I used to find on a blank sent me by Henry Moe of the Guggenheim Foundation: "Is this man worth it? Yes, or No." If I said "Yes," the candidate was usually in.

Within less than a year after I had accepted the graduate deanship I knew I had made a mistake. The distractions of the office began to eat into my thinking time; instead of pondering problems relating to history when I lay awake of a night, I would more likely be dreaming up solutions for some perplexing administrative snarl. Nor was I sure that I was accomplishing anything worth while as dean. The office carried with it little real power. Lipman had already written the ground rules necessary to protect the university against unworthy programs leading to higher degrees; there was little left for me to do along that line other than to apply existing rules. In the making of university policy the graduate dean had influence, but very little else. He had no important prerogatives. He was in fact little more than a glorified registrar. He did, indeed, sit in on the Administrative Council, an unwieldy group of high-ranking officers from whom the president occasionally asked advice, but his was only one voice among many, and in my case one seldom raised.

However inconsequential his powers might be, the graduate dean marched third in academic procession, right after the president and the provost. On one such occasion I exchanged a few words with President Truman, the year he came to Berkeley as our commencement speaker. As happens during most processions, this one was unaccountably stalled for a few seconds, and by chance President Truman, President Sproul, and I confronted each other in a gateway to the stadium. "Give-'Em-Hell" Harry was speaking his mind freely about the Republican opposition, as was his wont, so I sounded a warning: "Be careful, Mr. President: you're in the presence of the enemy," indicating Sproul, a lifelong Republican. "How do you know you can trust this man?"

"Haw! Haw! Haw!" Sproul roared. "*You* have to trust me." Then the parade marched on. I have written about all our national Presidents and have seen and heard several of them from a distance, but this was the only direct personal contact I ever had with any one of them.

My relationship with President Sproul was much closer, although not especially more intimate, during my term as graduate dean than before or after. I got to know him best, perhaps, during a tour of northern California, arranged by Bob Sibley, our alumni secretary, to warm the hearts of the university's alumni. Dr. Stafford Warren, dean of the new UCLA Medical School, and I went along to help Sproul and Sibley with the speech-making. Also, as a kind of social garnish, the wives of the four principals were members of the party. We hit it off together admirably, and certainly the loyal alumni who turned out to listen to us were no less loyal for our coming. As for our speeches, we got a little tired of listening to each other, and threatened occasionally to give the other fellow's speech instead of our own, as each of us easily could have done before the tour ended. The wives criticized our jokes and insisted that we come up with some new ones, which with their help we did. Wherever he was and whatever he did, Sproul always remained in character. I never found anything devious about him—a rare quality in a university president. If he rejected your advice, he was honest enough to say so, but you had the feeling that he had weighed it for what it was worth. Some of his critics complained that he tried to do too much and should have delegated more authority to subordinates. Probably they were right, but he had an incredible memory for persons and details, met new people and new situations with easy aplomb, and muffed few decisions. As Dixon Wecter once put it: "Doubtless God could have made a better university president than Robert Gordon Sproul, but doubtless God never did."

Although I knew that I would not retain the dean's office very long, I began to reflect on what powers it should have to make it worth a good man's time. My conclusion was that, if this particular deanship was to mean anything, its holder should become a kind of director of university research, not in the sense that he should tell the scholars of the university what their research should be, but in the sense that he should be able to help find the support they needed for the work they wanted to do. With this thought in mind I took seriously my duties as an ex officio member of the committee on research, over which Professor Raymond T. Birge, chairman of the physics department, presided with exceptional skill. Really, it seemed to me, the head of that committee should be ex officio dean, instead of the other way around, for he had in his hands most of the loaves and fishes. I would gladly have turned over my office to Birge, but that was not mine to do. Nor could I take over his duties in the face of the long-established practice of powerful Senate-chosen committees.

I discovered, however, that the graduate dean was chairman of a somewhat moribund Institute of Social Sciences, created years before to implement a research grant to the university from some outside agency. The Institute had used up all its original funds, and now existed only by virtue of a small annual subsidy from the president's budget. Logically this fund should have been transferred to Birge's budget and the Institute liquidated, but I resisted this solution and persuaded the President instead to funnel more money in our direction. The net result was that the Institute continued to provide support for some non-science projects that Birge's committee might have overlooked. The Institute, I believe, still exists.

Another problem about which I began to have deep concern was the multiplication of research grants for specific projects, with some branch of the national government, or of the armed services, or even a private corporation providing the largess. To what extent would the possibility of obtaining these huge grants seduce our men—particularly our scientists—into doing research that someone else wanted them to do instead of determining themselves independently the direction of their activities? In particular, I feared that pure research might give way too frequently to applied research. I finally persuaded the President to route through my office all university research projects for which outside funds were provided. But by the time these proposals came to my desk they were practically always beyond recall; the only thing I could do was to sign my name in the space provided. As a matter of fact, neither Morris Stewart nor I knew enough about most of these projects to warrant any interference, and I had a feeling that the same thing was true about the President and his advisers. Could the university under these circumstances, I queried, remain in control of its research activities, or would it become a mere vehicle through which governmental and private agencies sought to promote their own ends? I never came up with an answer to this question. The best hope for the university, I suspect, lies in the judgment and integrity of the individual faculty members concerned. After all, the university is only as good as the professors who compose it, a situation that mere administration cannot control.

My touchiness about outside influence on our research program did not set well with some representatives of the various foundations, all of whom seemed to think that they knew better what we should be doing than we ourselves could possibly know. Most of these gentry visited my office during their visits to the campus, and I can remember several amiable conversations on the subject, and one that became quite heated. My theory was that the foundations would serve their purpose best if they would support whatever worthy projects our faculty members, as groups or as individuals, were ready to propose. The foundation point of view, however, seemed to be that they were in a better position to judge what subjects we should emphasize than we were. I suppose their idea was to divide fields of research among the various universities in such a way as to avoid overlapping. But it seemed to me that the University of California was large enough and important enough to make its own decisions. It is possible that my stand may have lost the university some grants, but I think I was right.

The foundations also had a penchant for encouraging the creation of separate interdepartmental organizations, usually called institutes, thus multiplying administrative officers and activities, when existing facilities could have handled the work equally well. Every time a person got to be a director of such an institute he inevitably concluded that he must have more office space, additional secretarial assistance, and freedom from some of his teaching responsibilities. The university thus often stood to lose as much from one of these grants as it gained. As a general rule, however, if the foundations were willing to put up the money, they got whatever concessions they demanded.

When after due deliberation I finally told President Sproul of my intention to resign as graduate dean, he asked me to stay on another year in order to give him time to select my successor. This I agreed to do, but when the year rolled around there was still no successor in sight. Perhaps he had thought that I would change my mind. To make sure that I would be out, I took my name off the graduate office budget, leaving my fate in the hands of the history department. Thereupon the President made Morris Stewart acting dean, and for some time after I stepped out Morris had to carry on the work alone. At long length the customary faculty committee was chosen to make nominations, but it had a hard time making up its mind. As a member of it, I first recommended that Morris Stewart should have the place, but the committee thought he was too young and not yet far enough advanced as a scholar. I then proposed my good friend Theodore C. Blegen, dean of the Graduate School at the University of Minnesota, whose experience in a comparable office would give him a great advantage over most of our own men. President Sproul knew Blegen and liked the idea, but the committee held that it would be an insult to our own faculty to assume that we did not have anyone on the campus good enough for the position.

Actually the committee wanted to select Alva R. Davis for the graduate deanship, and would have done so, I think, had I not argued them out of it. I was also on the committee to nominate a new dean for the College of Letters and Science, and I wanted (and eventually succeeded in getting) Davis for this post. "Sailor" Davis, as everyone called him, had administrative talent of the highest order. I knew him well. He never jumped to conclusions; he thought out each problem step by step in painstaking deliberation; he arrived at decisions that almost invariably turned out to be correct. It would be a pity to waste his talents on as impotent a post as the graduate deanship. In the end, William R. Dennes, a distinguished member of our Department of Philosophy, headed the committee's list and, as already noted, was named graduate dean by the President. But Dennes, too, soon became weary of the job and returned to his department. After that Morris Stewart had proved his worth so completely that his succession to the post was almost automatic.

Sailor Davis was chairman of the powerful Budget Committee while I was one of its members, and it was through our association there that I came to appreciate his truly extraordinary talents. He knew every aspect of the university's activities, loved the institution with all his heart, had the complete confidence of both the President and the faculty. It was the function of the Budget Committee, among other things, to make final recommendations to the president on all new appointments and all promotions; in general, its recommendations on such matters were decisive, although the president had the authority to overrule it, if he chose. My thought was that Davis should have the deanship of Letters and Science with the full budgetary authority that was common to that office in nearly every other American university, but not in California; at least, not yet.

I can recall writing a long memorandum to the President on this subject. There was a glaring defect, I argued, in the pattern of organization that had grown up at Berkeley. Deans, as such, possessed no budgetary power whatever; in Letters and Science departmental chairmen made their recommendations directly to the president, completely bypassing the dean, who existed only to enforce the rules of the college respecting students. The inevitable result was overcentralization; the president's office had more to handle than was humanly possible. To be sure, there was a vice president and provost (one and the same man), Monroe E. Deutsch, but his functions were not clearly differentiated from those of the president; he was, in effect, only the president's alter ego, exercising presidential power on sufferance. There should be someone with *real* power, including budgetary power, between the departmental chairmen and the president's office.

The professional colleges (or schools) had all recognized this problem long ago and had solved it in an awkward but, for their purposes, a satisfactory way. Each such college was also a department, and its dean got his budgetary authority, not by virtue of his being its dean, but because he was its departmental chairman. As dean he was little more than a titular head, but as chairman he had all the power he needed. For subordinate units that in Letters and Science would have been designated "departments" the professional colleges used the term "divisions." Each division had a chairman, but he had to clear his budget through the departmental chairman, who was of course also the dean. It was an anomaly that Letters and Science, the largest and most important of all the colleges, had no single head with the same kind of authority that the professional college deans (as chairmen) regularly exercised. Why should the professional colleges always have a powerful representative at court, while Letters and Science was dependent for its leadership on a score or more of competing departmental chairmen?

The President accepted my memorandum without resentment and told me that, in case I could carry my proposition in the Academic Senate (i.e., the faculty governing body), he would be glad to give the dean of Letters and Science the kind of budgetary authority I had suggested. He was the more willing to make this concession, I am sure, because Davis would be the person to exercise the power involved, for Sproul too often thought of the delegation of power as something given to an individual rather than to an office. The same was probably true of the faculty—it would consent to placing power in Davis's hands, whereas it might have reservations when it came to deans in general. Quoting a Scandinavian friend on this subject, Dean Blegen used to say: "Deans? Some people look up to them, and some people look down on them. But me, I yoost look at them!"

Whatever their misgivings, a majority of the Senate went along with me, and the President was as good as his word. For many years Dean Davis served our academic community well. Letters and Science chairmen could now get from him in far less time the answers to budgetary questions that formerly they could clear only through the president's office. It was obvious, however, that the tremendous growth of the university, involving as it did the addition of many new campuses, called for a complete reorganization of the whole system of administration. When the time came to work out the new plans, Dean Davis's advice, on both means and ends, proved to be of fundamental importance.

While I was still graduate dean I was asked to deliver the keynote speech for an All-University Faculty Conference, to be held in Davis in the spring of 1947. This was the second of a series of such conferences, designed in part to get the faculties of our various campuses better acquainted with each other, and in part to promote discussion of whatever current problems seemed most significant. A large faculty committee, with equal numbers drawn from the Berkeley and the Los Angeles campuses and smaller numbers from the others, made all the preliminary arrangements, including the creation of subcommittees to bring in special reports. Considerable rivalry existed between the Berkeley and the Los Angeles faculties, and in the committee sessions evidence of ill feeling was often close to the surface. Gordon Watkins, who was chairman of the second conference, was singularly successful in holding friction to a minimum, and when it was my turn to be chairman the following year I profited greatly by his example. Only a small fraction of the total faculty personnel could be invited to a given conference, but care was taken to pass the honor around and to represent all ranks and as nearly as possible all fields. The university footed the bill for sessions lasting about three days.

In my 1947 keynote speech I undertook to emphasize the necessity of good teaching at the University level, whether for undergraduates or for graduates. While faculty members in a great university must indeed do creditable research, there is no good reason, I argued, why the same individuals should not show competence as teachers. Research and teaching should complement each other; anyone on the alert could discover in his teaching new openings for research, and in his research new ideas to plow back into his teaching. But good teaching required a conscientious effort; just because a man was a good scholar it did not follow automatically that he was a good teacher. I went on to identify some good and some bad teaching practices, and to advocate a more conscientious effort to employ the former.[2]

By and large my keynote speech fell flat. Nearly every faculty member cherishes the illusion that he is a good teacher, however contrary to fact that assumption may be. And everyone knows that the road to promotion in most of our great universities lies primarily in research and publication. Moreover, the problem of evaluating good teaching is also perplexing. Student approval can be, and often is, derided as evidence of "playing to the galleries," mere exhibitionism. Indeed, it is a dangerous thing for a young teacher to have students flock to his classes; if he has not yet achieved tenure, he stands a good chance of losing his job. According to some stodgy critics, popularity in itself is evidence of "superficiality," a badly overworked word in academic circles. Reasons for the dismissal of a promising young teacher are rarely stated with candor, sometimes, of course, to his advantage. It is always possible to say that he does not "show enough research promise," or that he somehow "does not fit in," when the real trouble, far more frequently than it should be, is more closely akin to jealousy. For the most part my opening remarks at the Conference were merely

    [2] "The Place of the State University in a Democratic Society," *Proceedings* of the University of California Second All-University Conference, February 8, 9, and 10, 1947 (Berkeley: University of California, 1947), pp. 13–17; reprinted in *Journal of Dental Education*, XII (December 1947), 68–78.

ignored, but one dean said candidly, although regretfully, that he regularly advised young scholars not to let their teaching stand in the way of their research. The Conference went on to discuss many other important matters, and on the whole it was a success. But it revealed no burning desire to improve classroom performance.

Shortly before I left the graduate office, President Sproul paid me a call to ask me if I would accept the chairmanship of the Department of History. This offer was not entirely unanticipated, for I knew that the time for Paxson's retirement had arrived. But it was not quite accurate to say, as my successor in the dean's office frequently did, that I had resigned the deanship in order to accept the chairmanship. The two decisions were quite unrelated. In agreeing to accept the chairmanship, however, I made one condition, and I made it very clearly. It was that President Sproul himself should inform my colleague Robert J. Kerner, in advance of any public announcement, that it would be I and not Kerner who would succeed Paxson. I knew that Kerner was almost pathologically eager for the job; indeed, he had already called on me to solicit my help in getting the place for him. He even made it clear that he would pay a price for my assistance; if he became chairman, I would have a free hand in all matters pertaining to American history. At one time I had thought that making Kerner chairman would be the best way to deal with a somewhat cantankerous colleague; responsibility often tempers the behavior of such persons. But I had had to change my mind. Kerner was a distinguished scholar and, when he could forget himself sufficiently, an excellent teacher. But in all matters, administrative or otherwise, in which his own personal interests were involved, his judgment deserted him. Most members of the department believed him to be temperamentally unfitted for the chairmanship, and in this opinion President Sproul concurred. Sproul agreed to inform Kerner in advance of my appointment, but failed to do so. When I protested later, he said that he had asked Provost Deutsch to do the honors, but that Deutsch had probably forgotten it. I'm not sure that anybody forgot. Certainly I shall never forget my first interview with Kerner after my appointment was announced. But when the initial fireworks were over, we learned to live together amicably. Kerner used to argue that it was impossible to disagree without being disagreeable, and for him that was the truth. But as soon as his anger had spent itself he could act as if nothing had happened. We were on friendly terms— most of the time—until his death.

Between the deanship and the chairmanship, I enjoyed a pleasant interlude as a 1947 summer-session instructor at the University of Hawaii. At this time our oldest daughter, Jane Harriet, was married, so she could not accompany us, but we took the other two with us, and rounded out the family number by adding Barbara ("Bobby") Walrond, one of Marjorie's friends, to our group. Bobby lived a block up the street from our house on Southampton Avenue, and we knew both her and her parents well. For the outgoing trip we wangled a lanai suite on the *Matsonia* and invited all our friends and neighbors down to the ship to see us off. It was a lively party. The ocean trip then lasted about four days, and still does, but now one may go more cheaply by air in as many hours. This was our first, but not our last, trip on the calm Pacific.

By good luck we were able to exchange our house in Berkeley for a house in Honolulu; we made the trade with a physician who had spent the war years in the Islands and was eager to visit the mainland. So we lived in considerable elegance "out about three showers," as some of the local residents expressed it, up Nuuwanu toward the Pali. The doctor took over our two cars in Berkeley, leaving us by way of compensation one car (which was enough) and the use of his beach house out across the Pali in Kailua. So we spent each week on a beach as marvelous as Waikiki, but less thickly populated. My teaching duties were not arduous and the students, especially those of Oriental ancestry, were bright and eager. My one real problem was the absence of graduate students to help me in grading the several hundred blue-books turned in when examination time came. I pressed the whole family into service, and we did the best we could. But I was not very convinced of the correctness of the marks I turned in that summer.

Naturally, we tried to do all the things that tourists do in Hawaii. We drove all over and around Oahu, and after the summer session ended spent several days each in Maui and the "Big Island," Hawaii. We were particularly entranced with Kona, and saw there a system of loading cattle now no longer in use. Since the water along the pier was too shallow for large ships to dock, the cattle had to be floated out to sea for loading. First, cowhands on specially trained horses herded the cattle into the water, then lassoed them one by one and tied them by their necks to lighters, four animals on each side. Then the boats towed them slowly out to sea, where each animal was hoisted on a bellyband, feet sprawling, into the ship. They were then taken to Honolulu for slaughter. Although the island of Hawaii boasted the largest cattle ranch in the world, the beef supply for the Islands had to be supplemented by shipments from the mainland.

On Maui, Jack Moir, manager of a sugar cane plantation, and his wife, Gertrude, took us to their splendid home and put us up in regal fashion. Their daughter, Babs, had attended Mills College while Carolyn was there, and the two girls had become good friends. Jack took us to the Haliakala crater, showed us sugar cane and pineapple plantations, guided us through a sugar mill, introduced us to local VIPs at the Hana Ranch, and told us more about Hawaii than we had ever read in books. He was still in a state of shock over the ruthless way in which Harry Bridges had organized farm labor in the Islands. Fortunately, we could reach the other islands from Oahu by air; in earlier years, when such travel was possible only by sea, the crossings might have given us more grief. As it was, we could get from island to island in about half an hour. The airline hostesses on these flights all were part Hawaiian, and quite the most beautiful girls I have ever seen. The Hawaiian-Oriental-Caucasian intermarriages have produced offspring that in many instances far surpass in looks any one of the original races. The peoples mingle freely, whatever their racial origins, and if left alone would produce a new race. But the white influx since World War II, and particularly since statehood, may in the long run bleach the natives out.

We had intended to see Kauai, but when the girls learned that the battleship *Iowa*, with a thousand midshipmen aboard, was coming into port just at the time we had planned this trip, they refused to budge from Honolulu. They knew that they had friends and acquaintances aboard, and soon we did too, for numbers of the visitors arrived at our house almost by instinct, and always very hungry. We should have sent the navy a bill for board. After the *Iowa* went to sea, it was time for us to return to California, but on this trip we rated far less sumptuous quarters than from San Francisco out, and there was no going-away party. The impression that Hawaii left on us was one of lasting delight. We have returned repeatedly.

The chairmanship of a department at California is a position of some importance. I can remember Sproul remarking on one occasion that he could understand anyone wanting to be a chairman, but could not see why anyone should ever want to be a dean. When I was chosen my appointment came directly from the President, and in those days the chairman was directly responsible to the President. After the delegation of budgetary authority to Dean Davis, however, the Dean nominated chairmen for Letters and Science, following a formal or informal consultation with members of the department concerned. I do not know to what extent, if any, my colleagues in history had anything to do with my being made chairman; I suspect that the President acted primarily upon the recommendation of Professor Paxson, the retiring chairman. But if anyone other than Kerner had any serious objection to my appointment, I never knew about it. Since I had made so strong a plea for the increase of the dean's powers, after that happened I was always scrupulously correct about clearing with Dean Davis all matters that were beyond my jurisdiction. I think that other chairmen, also, did far less running to the President about everything than they had previously deemed necessary. All budget recommendations, in any event, now went first to Dean Davis's office, not directly to the president's, as formerly.

The California committee system is a fearful and wonderful thing, especially as viewed from the angle of a departmental chairman. This form of faculty participation in university government grew out of a well-remembered "revolt" that occurred in 1919–1920, during the presidency of Benjamin Ide Wheeler. At that time, with the full consent of the regents, the Academic Senate won the right to choose its own presiding officer, or chairman, and to select by secret ballot a committee on committees with authority to appoint all other Senate committees. Most important of those other committees was one on budget and interdepartmental affairs, which had the right to scrutinize all budgetary recommendations. Thus the Budget Committee had to be consulted with reference to all promotions from a lower to a higher rank and all appointments of outsiders to positions above the grade of instructor on the California faculty.

Over the years a hard and fast procedure developed for the processing of such recommendations. First, the chairman would send them to the president (later, to the dean or chancellor), who in turn would pass them along to the Budget Committee for its advice. Then the Budget Committee, before ruling on any given case, would appoint an *ad hoc* subcommittee, drawn entirely from outside its ranks, to study the recommendation and report back its findings. The subcommittee, consisting usually of three members for assistant professors and five for higher ranks, might not include the recommending officer, but must include one or more members from outside the department concerned. Printed instructions warned all members of subcommittees to keep their assignments secret; hence the harassed chairman had to document each case in the fullest detail. The preparing of an annual budget under these circumstances became a kind of nightmare. By experience I found that unless I supplied two or three single-spaced pages of typescript for each personnel recommendation, I could count on being asked for additional information.

As for the Budget Committee, it was in what seemed like almost continuous session—the year I was a member of it, I estimated that it consumed on an average about fifteen hours of my time each week. Fortunately, as chairman of a department I was exempt from service on the Budget Committee, although merely holding a deanship had not let me out. Most members of the Budget Committee teach one less course than usual and most deans teach only one course. But I always taught my normal load of two lecture courses and a seminar, whatever my other responsibilities. Imagine my surprise when Kerner reported to me, shortly after I became dean, that the talk around the Faculty Club was that I was lazy.

Official policy directed that the chairmen of departments should seek committee advice in making their budget recommendations. Strictly interpreted, this could mean the appointment within the department of a separate committee to study each case for promotion. During my years as chairman the normal schedule of advancement left an instructor in his lowly rank for not more than two years; at the end of that period he either became an assistant professor or he was out. If he won promotion, he might serve for six years longer as assistant professor, with stipulated salary advancements (provided he was deemed worthy of them) at the end of each two-year period. Since promotion to associate professor involved permanent tenure, I followed the common practice of appointing an assessment committee to study each assistant professor's record two years before his term in that rank must end. For advice on all other promotions I consulted standing committees chosen on the basis of rank. Associate professors, like assistant professors, went through three periods of grace before becoming full professors, and for these advancements I obtained recommendations from a committee consisting of the full professors. Similarly, the full professors and the associate professors, sitting together, ruled on the fate of assistant professors. The chairman might accept or reject all such advice, but if he rejected it he was supposed so to state in his own recommendations, and to supply the arguments on both sides. In practice I found it fairly easy to obtain a consensus of opinion, but the process of constant consultation consumed a lot of time. Promotions in salary for full professors I recommended on my own, but the Budget Committee did not always support the figures I urged. With reference to my own salary, I consistently refused to make any recommendation.

The most important duty of a chairman is the recruiting of new members of his department as needed. When I took over in 1947, the membership of the history department was about twenty-five and a period of expansion was at hand. The war had served to emphasize the inadequacy of our offerings in fields that lay beyond the borders of the Americas and Western Europe. To remedy these deficiencies, we made a number of appointments, the original recommendation in each case coming from the members of the department most familiar with the fields concerned. We had shortages, also, in the more traditional fields, and here, too, we made some headway. In American history we lacked specialists both in foreign relations and in social and intellectual history; as already noted, I had felt obliged to teach courses in both these subjects in spite of the fact that I could not regard myself as a specialist in either. As a result of Bolton's emphasis on all the Americas, Latin American history was about the only field in which we believed ourselves to be adequately staffed.

Left over from Paxson's administration was the appointment of his successor. Paxson had held one of the named professorships, and the selection of one of our own number to fill his chair was deemed inappropriate. In fact, when I mentioned the name of one of our men as a possible candidate for the place, Sproul replied: "If that is the best you can do, we'll just leave the chair vacant for all time."

So the appointment had to go to an outsider. Foreseeing some of the difficulties, I had urged Paxson, while he was still chairman, to start the ponderous machinery working. Hoping possibly to expedite matters, Paxson asked the Budget Committee to appoint a subcommittee to conduct the search; if it came up with a satisfactory nomination, there would be no need for the name to be submitted to another subcommittee. The Budget Committee complied, making our own Raymond J. Sontag chairman of the subcommittee. In due time Sontag's group recommended three preferred names, along with several other possibilities. The preferred nominees were Dixon Wecter of UCLA,

Merle Curti of the University of Wisconsin, and Thomas A. Bailey of Stanford. The report ran us immediately into roadblocks. Intra-university policy strongly condemned the idea of one campus robbing another, and UCLA was particularly sensitive about Berkeley's poaching on its preserves. That seemed to rule out Wecter. There was also a tacit agreement between the presidents of California and Stanford binding them not to raid each other's faculties. That ruled out Bailey. Then, when we made an offer to Curti, he declined. Eventually we persuaded the President that his agreement with Stanford was no longer binding, but a tentative approach to Bailey made it clear that Bailey had no intention of moving. To teach American diplomacy, however, we presently brought in one of his ablest students, Armin Rappaport.

Luckily for us, by the time I became chairman, Wecter was more closely identified with the Huntington Library than with UCLA, although he still taught a class on the Los Angeles campus. Moreover, it was rumored that he might be ready to make a change. When I asked the President to find out how the land lay, he not only found out, but reported to me happily: "I've landed Wecter."

To achieve this end, however, he had had to agree to a salary figure substantially higher than any other member of our department, including myself, then received. This pleased me, for it gave me a weapon to use in obtaining higher salaries for others on our staff, but it did not please all of them. Wecter, moreover, had moved over into social and intellectual history from American literature, and a few of our men held his background against him. Once he was on campus, he quickly won his way with all of us. His premature death in June, 1950, just as I was about to take off for a year in Europe, left our problem of a successor to Paxson still unresolved.

Our solution, reached hastily that summer, was to bring in Carl Bridenbaugh from Williamsburg. Although he eventually took over Wecter's course in social and intellectual history, Bridenbaugh was essentially a colonialist. His location on the Pacific Coast proved to be so unsatisfactory to him that he finally accepted an offer from Brown University, and returned to the Atlantic seaboard. Meantime, however, he had won the presidency of the American Historical Association, an honor which three other members of the Berkeley department— Henry Morse Stephens, Herbert E. Bolton, and Frederic L. Paxson— had also held. After Bridenbaugh resigned, named professorships in history at Berkeley regularly went to men who had already rendered distinguished service on our campus.

When I first became chairman of the department at Berkeley, we managed adequately with only one full-time secretary and some student help. By the time I left for Europe three years later, we had an office staff of two full-time employees. Perhaps we needed more help than we had, but I was never one to multiply paper work, and we got along. Members of the staff took care of many administrative chores. I persuaded John J. Van Nostrand, our senior active member, to serve as vice-chairman, and he relieved me of all details in the selection of teaching assistants and the nomination of candidates for fellowships and scholarships. George H. Guttridge handled most of the annoying problems connected with the scheduling of courses. Larry Harper fought our battles for more space. Paul Schaeffer made the important decisions on departmental recommendation of manuscripts for publication in the University history series. And so on. Practically always someone other than myself served as acting chairman during the summer sessions, for, delightful as the Hawaiian experience had been, I had resolved never again to teach in summer school.

On one matter I think I may have done the department a disservice. Before my time and to some extent after it, although over my opposition, we had become more inbred than I thought desirable. Bolton had filled all vacancies in his field with his own students; Palm and Kerner competed in pushing their students for such openings as developed in European history; Paxson brought in only his own men (myself included) when he needed an Americanist. I resolved to set a good example by never permitting the appointment of one of my own Ph.D.'s to our staff while I was chairman. As a result I passed over opportunities to bring in several of my ablest former students, among them George E. Mowry, Vincent P. Carosso, and Clarke E. Chambers, all of whom now hold important positions elsewhere. I am not sure that I did right, either by them or by the department.

My final year as chairman was marred by the distressing oath controversy, our local contribution to the McCarthy era. Hoping to complete my book on the 1920's, I had taken a year's leave in residence. This status freed me from two of my three courses and from all committee assignments, including the committee on committees, to which I had been elected the preceding year. Instead of taking the year off on part time, I might better have chosen the other alternative, a full semester off without any university responsibilities, but I knew that unless I got clear out of town I would still have my candidates for degrees to advise, so I chose to keep my seminar and, for good measure, the chairmanship. The result was that I got exactly nowhere with my research and writing; instead, the oath controversy occupied almost my entire time.

With charges rife that we were harboring Communists on our faculty, President Sproul, on the advice of James Corley, his chief agent in dealing with the legislature, sought to dispel this false allegation by including a new clause in the oath of allegiance to which the faculty was required to subscribe. Each person must swear that he was "not a member of the Communist Party or under any oath, or a party to any agreement, or under any commitment that [was] in conflict with [his] obligation under oath." For good measure the same requirement was extended to every other individual of the university's payroll.

Neither the President who suggested the revised oath nor the board of regents who voted to impose it foresaw clearly the results of their surrender to expediency. The regents themselves were already on record as opposed to the employment of Communists by the university, and most of them assumed that recognition of this fact by the facu..y would serve only to implement an existing, generally accepted policy. The purpose that the board had in mind was not at all to bait the professors, but rather to clear them of untrue charges, and incidentally to promote legislative appropriations of the generous sums for which the university was asking. At a later session of the regents doubts arose. Regent John Francis Neylan, who had not been present at the earlier session, asserted firmly: "We will make a mistake if we are at loggerheads with the faculty," and Regent Farnham Griffiths inquired what the board would do if some eminent professor, under no suspicion of Communist taint, refused to sign the oath. But the President and the others who favored it talked them down.

Most of the faculty, myself included, while irritated and annoyed by the new oath, were willing to accept it as a necessary evil. Nearly all of us resented the implication that professors were *ipso facto* unreliable characters whose loyalty to their government needed to be nailed down with particular emphasis. But we assumed, probably correctly, that the current mood of intolerance would soon pass, and with it such nonsensical pledges as we were being asked to give. At least the requirement did not involve us in swearing to something that was not true.

A relatively small minority, however, saw in the new wording of the oath a challenge to academic freedom. As Ernst Kantorowicz, one of my colleagues in history, put it: "The harmlessness of the proposed oath is not a protection when a principle is involved." If this initial restriction were accepted, what new ones would be added? If membership in one political party was to be proscribed, why not membership in another? Where would it all end? To some former Europeans on the faculty, men like Kantorowicz who had a vivid recollection of the cumulative nature of totalitarian restrictions on liberty, this risk seemed particularly grave.

Thus, to the considerable surprise of the President and most of the regents, the problem of what to do about non-signers arose, a problem that led to long negotiations between the board and a series of faculty committees. Efforts to revise the oath so as to avoid the implication of "guilt by association" failed to satisfy either the extremists among the regents or the dedicated non-signers. Hardening of the arteries set in, and emotion began to triumph over reason.

When it became apparent that a majority of the board were determined to fire all non-signers, some of whom were as bitterly anti-Communist as the most conservative regent, the proposed violation of tenure rights brought the faculty as a whole into the fight. It was at this point that I became involved. Quite against my wishes I was made chairman of a Committee of Seven, the purpose of which was to implement in every way we could the strong position taken by another faculty committee, headed by Malcolm Davisson, that tenure members should not be dismissed merely because they refused to sign the revised oath.

The Committee of Seven did everything in its power to bring public opinion around to our side of the issue. In this process, with my consent, my name was used repeatedly in statements put out for newspaper publication, statements that I would never have dreamed up myself and that I often read for the first time when I saw them in print. Although I found this personal publicity particularly galling, I endured the embarrassment as part of my contribution to the cause. I was repeatedly accused of being a Communist and asked why, if I weren't, wouldn't I sign that oath. The fact that I had signed it already and that my committee was in the fight primarily on the tenure issue simply never got over. I doubt if the general public would have seen much point to faculty tenure, anyway, even if they had understood what it was all about.

Our committee also did its bit toward working out an acceptable compromise. We even went so far as to obtain by mail ballot a faculty vote condemning by an overwhelming majority the employment by the University of Communist party members. Unofficially, Regent Neylan (who had at first opposed the oath only to become its most vigorous protagonist) had given the committee to understand that if this action were taken the obnoxious section of the oath would be dropped. But when the showdown came the board voted, ten to ten, not to go through with their part of the bargain, Regent Neylan voting to retain the anti-Communist clause and President Sproul, who had introduced it, voting now to strike it out. To many disillusioned faculty members, this was the "great double cross."

I was present and spoke at the Santa Barbara meeting of the board of regents when it refused by a tie vote to expunge from the oath the offensive anti-Communist statement—with the change of a single vote, we would have won. From this time on, the division within the board was never healed, but the extremists, who had almost lost, soon got the upper hand again and carried on with great determination. A strong minority, however, including President Sproul and Governor Earl Warren, stood firmly, if helplessly, with us.

Finally an alumni committee undertook to negotiate an agreement between the faculty and the board. The resulting bargain permitted each person to sign without amendment the customary oath of allegiance, but required him also to accept his appointment in a separate document containing the words "I am not a member of the Communist Party." This change seemed to me and to many of my colleagues a distinction without a difference, a defeat for the non-signers rather than a compromise. Fortunately, perhaps, I was out of town when the Committee of Seven agreed to it.

We thought, however, that a way had been left open for the non-signers. The agreement stipulated that, in case anyone refused to sign the proposed contract, he should be given a hearing by the appropriate Senate Committee on Privilege and Tenure (Berkeley or Los Angeles, as the case might be). It was our understanding that non-signers who were cleared after such a hearing would not be dismissed. Inevitably many who had refused to sign the oath also refused to sign the contract, so a prolonged series of hearings resulted. In the end, the two Committees on Privilege and Tenure cleared all the Senate (i.e., tenure) non-signers except six individuals who refused utterly to cooperate in the hearings. But the majority of the board of regents were dissatisfied with only six scalps, and promptly dismissed all non-signers, whether they had been cleared of Communist affiliations or not. To an outraged faculty, this was simply another double cross. As for non-tenure academic employees, such as teaching assistants, they had already been liquidated, although only to take effect at the end of the academic year, so that their dismissal amounted to little more than a denial of reappointment. The fact that there were only thirty-one dismissals of tenure members was due in part to personal economic pressure—many who would have preferred not to sign had families to support. Also, faculty signers put much pressure on the dissidents, for almost everyone was tired of the long turmoil and wanted an end to the strife.

After the advent of the alumni compromise, my part in the oath controversy diminished rapidly. The Committee of Seven had lost whatever excuse for existence it had had, and was liquidated. In the late summer of 1950 I left with my wife and youngest daughter for the University of Cambridge, where I had accepted a temporary one-year appointment. I was thus spared the dismal post-mortem period that followed our defeat.

As for the non-signers, their only recourse now was the courts of law. Armed with generous faculty contributions, they sought a legal decision on the correctness of the action taken by the board. In the district court of Appeal they won a unanimous decision, but the California State Supreme Court took jurisdiction of the case and turned what looked like a clear-cut victory into something else. For meantime the state legislature, at Governor Warren's suggestion, had passed the Levering Act, requiring of all state employees an oath not essentially different from the one the board of regents had prescribed for the faculty. The verdict of the Supreme Court was that the legislature had long ago preoccupied the field of oath legislation, so that the regents' oath was illegal, whereas the Levering Act was legitimate. As for the non-signing members of the faculty, they had only to take the Levering Oath to be reinstated.

By this time (October 17, 1952) only twenty-four of the non-signers were left—the others had already severed whatever ties they might have had with the university. Of these twenty-four, to whom the board now issued letters of employment, "seven resigned immediately, two accepted appointment for the spring semester, 1953, remained on leave without pay during that semester, and then resigned on July 1, 1953; two, having reached retirement age on June 30, 1952, were appointed to emeritus status; seven accepted appointment but remained on leave without pay or on sabbatical for varying periods of time; and six accepted appointments and returned to the University for the spring term 1953." [3]

To me and many other participants the whole oath controversy seemed to be an exercise in futility. There was little gained by all the turmoil—certainly no vindication of high principle; it was just a firecracker that fizzled out. There was much lost. For many of us it was impossible during the year of the oath to keep our teaching and research up to par. My leave of absence was completely vitiated. The university lost many good men to other institutions and failed to recruit many others who, but for the controversy, would have accepted California offers.

The conflict engendered much lasting bitterness. Regents were set against regents, faculty members against each other, regents against faculty, friends against friends. I personally, as a would-be peacemaker, was caught in the middle and much reviled by extremists on both sides. The President survived the ordeal—by a miracle—but he had had to reverse himself, and his stature in many minds was considerably reduced. In one sense the controversy had been a power struggle between him and Regent Neylan, who quite obviously had hoped to oust the President. In another sense it was a battle between the regents and the faculty over who had the right to choose and promote faculty personnel, and over the right of faculty members to tenure. It was all a grand mix-up in which no one came off the winner and nearly everyone the loser.

Eventually the university pulled out of the slump, as so great an institution was sure to do, and resumed its normal position of eminence. But the ordeal left lasting scars on those who were caught up in it. For me it was the most traumatic experience of my life.

[3] David P. Gardner, *The California Oath Controversy* (1967), p. 253. This book provides the first scholarly and dispassionate study of the imbroglio. I have depended on it for most statements of fact. See also John Caughey, "A Battlefield Revisited," *Law in Transition Quarterly*, IV (September 1967), 172–178.

XV. Cambridge, England

THE YEAR after the oath I spent as visiting professor of American history and institutions at the University of Cambridge, England. This stroke of luck came my way, I am sure, because of a recommendation from Henry Steele Commager, with whom I had long been on friendly terms. He thought that it might be desirable for Cambridge to experience an honest-to-goodness middle westerner, and he knew that the year abroad would be good for me. Strange as it may seem, I had up to that time had no foreign experience whatever, except for occasional forays north of the forty-ninth parallel into Canada and south of the border into Lower California. I had visited nearly every state in the Union, and also the Territory of Hawaii, but I had not yet set foot in Europe, Asia, Africa, or even South America. At my age such provincialism was almost a disgrace.

The news that I would be asked to spend an "academical" year at Cambridge came in a letter from the tutor of Trinity Hall, C. W. Crawley, who explained that I would also be made a fellow of his college, one of the oldest, but not one of the largest of the Cambridge group. I accepted with alacrity. My letter of acceptance, however, was somewhat delayed in reaching its English destination, for I had addressed it mistakenly to Cambridge, Massachusetts. The net result, I consoled myself, would be that the Cambridge authorities would think that I had given the matter long and serious consideration.

Financially speaking, I really would have had good reason to ponder the offer well, for I was certain to lose money on the deal. This circumstance aroused the compassion of my good friend Dean Morris Stewart of the Graduate Division, who made every effort to obtain for me some kind of supplementary grant, either from the university or from some educational foundation. The best he could do was a Fulbright offer to pay my travel expenses, but since this item was included in the Cambridge offer, the Dean's intervention netted me exactly nothing. Later on, members of the University of California faculty who have held analogous posts have usually received some kind of compensatory grant, but I received nothing of the sort and in the end took quite a beating. The treasurer of the University of Cambridge assured me that a convention between the United States and the United Kingdom exempted my English salary (about half what I would have received in California) from taxation in either country, but he was wrong. The convention that he had misinterpreted was meant merely to ensure against the taxation of the same salary by both countries. Some time after my return to the United States I was obliged to pay about half of my English salary to the United States Internal Revenue Service. But if I lost financially on the venture, I gained in every other way.

One problem involved in our leaving the United States for a year was what to do with our daughters. We decided finally to permit the two older girls to keep house at home, and to take Marjorie with us. Jane Harriet and Carolyn would visit us after we were settled. We also invited our next-door neighbor, Mrs. H. O. Fisher (Zoe), whose husband had died recently, to join us in New York and make the trip to England with us. From New York we would take the *Parthia*, an eight-day ship, to Liverpool, then go by train first to London, where we would spend several days, then on to Cambridge. Following that, while I was getting acquainted with my new duties, the three women would tour the Continent.

During the long sea voyage I began a diary that I kept with reasonable regularity until our return to the United States. At one time I thought the document might be worthy of publication, but rejections from two commercial publishers discouraged me, so I put it aside. On rereading it seventeen years later I am not sure that this decision was right. Many of my entries were strictly personal, and to hardened travelers they may have seemed naïve. As one of my friends consoled me after the first rejection, "No one should ever visit England for the first time." But some of my observations, especially in the realm of international opinion, make interesting reading today. I was not always accurate in my predictions, but I reflected pretty closely the thinking of the time, now often forgotten.

With London, it was for us love at first sight. We took double-decker buses to the end of the line, saw many bombed-out areas, visited St. Paul's and Westminster Abbey, watched the changing of the guard at Buckingham Palace, rode in the London tubes and compared them favorably with our New York subways, listened to the speech-making in Hyde Park, visited the Waxworks, and all that. Somehow everything seemed so familiar. For the English who insist that Americans have no history, we had found a ready answer. We have all of theirs, and our own besides.

In Cambridge we received a friendly welcome and were shown our way to Southacre, a huge manorial type of building that the university had acquired and had turned into flats for university personnel. We were assigned an L-shaped apartment of six rooms, entirely adequate for our purposes, and with two electrically heated rooms, a real luxury at that time. The flat had furniture, but few furnishings, so we stayed in a little hotel on the Cam while Lucile and Zoe shopped for the essential kitchen utensils, dishes, blankets, *et al.* Prices were lower than in the United States, but austerity was in full swing, and the range of choices was not great. Everything that could be shipped abroad to improve the balance of payments was hard to get.

Before leaving America we had contracted for an Austin car, a little station wagon, or shootingbrake, as the English called it. A condition of the purchase was that we should take it back with us to the United States; to serve this purpose it was even left-drive. When we reached Cambridge, there it was, waiting for us. It made the business of getting about much easier for us, both for local and for more distant trips. Before we left we had seen a lot of England, a little of Scotland, and had driven through four countries on the Continent. It took some doing to learn to drive on the left side of the road, but eventually we were so proficient at it that we had to watch ourselves closely, when we came home, to keep consistently to the right.

The origin of the Cambridge professorship I held goes back to World War II, which served to make the English aware of the fact that they should know more about the United States, even including its history. Since the number of English scholars who had specialized in this subject was very small, the Cambridge idea (following an Oxford precedent) was to establish a chair to which a different American scholar should be called each year. The position I held, often called inaccurately the Pitt Professorship, was more or less the Cambridge equivalent of the Harmsworth Professorship at Oxford.

As it seemed to me, the choices of Americans for the Cambridge chair were somewhat whimsical. Probably J. Frank Dobie of Texas, for example, had never fancied himself a historian until he received the appointment. But he was a marvelous success. His wide-brimmed western hat, from which he was almost inseparable, his deep and abiding interest in Cambridge pubs, and his Texas wisecracks made him the pride of the town. He even influenced the architecture of his college, Emmanuel, the same that had once housed John Harvard. Dobie, as a thin-blooded Texan, found the damp chill of the English climate hard to take and complained bitterly of the open archways, through which for many centuries Cambridge undergraduates had mounted the staircases to their rooms. Why should these staircases and halls be open to the cold all the time? asked Dobie. "Any Indian," he said, "would know enough to hang a bull-hide over a hole." So they hung doors on at least one Emmanuel College archway, a memorable victory for the American influence. Dobie was a folklorist primarily; my immediate predecessor was trained in English history rather than American; and the man selected while I was there to serve the second year after my tenure was an economist. But as Americans they all knew a lot more about American history than the Cambridge undergraduates.

Warned in advance, I soon found out for myself that the formalities of English university life were much more rigid than I had been accustomed to. I knew that I would be expected to lecture in gown, but, quite correctly, I left my American academic regalia at home, since such inferior insignia would not be recognized in Cambridge. To make up for this slight discourtesy, however, I was awarded a Cambridge M.A. shortly after my arrival. Thereafter, not only when I lectured, but also when I went to chapel (not often), or when I dined at high table, or when I attended any of the numerous college or university functions, I always wore my English gown. It amused me slightly thus to be demoted from a Ph.D. to an M.A., but the M.A. gown was just as warm; and owing to the abnormally low room temperatures I encountered, I learned to take great comfort in wrapping it about me. I found it somewhat confusing that my name on the Trinity Hall staircase was preceded by the title "Dr.," a label that in America I have always sought to avoid. Wasn't this a bit inconsistent? Or was it a delicate English gibe? They really don't think much of our Ph.D.'s over there.

As a fellow of Trinity Hall, I was assigned to a well-appointed sitting room, complete with fireplace, where I could receive guests and hold conferences with students—or undergraduates, as they are more correctly called, unless they chance to be graduates, in which case one avoids calling them anything at all. In England the word "student," whether applied to graduates or undergraduates, is frowned upon as too pretentious, perhaps for somewhat the same reason that Americans object to calling school children "scholars." If a fellow of a college is unmarried, or if his wife is out of town, he may live in, as I did while Lucile was on the Continent. During that period I rated also a bedroom adjacent to my sitting room, but the minute my wife returned I had to give up my sleeping quarters. One of the constantly recurring problems of the college was to have enough unattached fellows living in; the presence of a few mature men was thought to have a salutary effect upon the undergraduates. Until the 1870's, indeed, fellows at Cambridge were forbidden to have wives, with results that in an American university might have seemed quite extraordinary.

A college servant, known as a "gyp" (a "scout" at Oxford), exercised great authority over my life, particularly for the month I lived in. He it was who decided that seven-thirty in the morning was plenty late for me to sleep. If, through no fault of his own, I failed to hear him heavy-handedly lighting the fire in my sitting room, he stomped into my bedroom with a solemn "It's seven-thirty, sir," and even when I had only just begun to dent the frigidity of my monkish bed, I crawled obediently out. He drew water for my bath when, and only when, he thought I merited one. Sometimes, when I seemed inclined to argue the point, he explained patiently "I'm sorry, sir, someone else (it was usually the chaplain) got your bath this morning"— meaning that the hot water had given out. I was easily consoled, for the trip to the bathroom—out through the hall, down a staircase, past an open archway, and around a corner—was in itself discouraging.

Each day I rated more service than I had ever known before. At eight o'clock my gyp brought breakfast to my sitting room, and if I failed to eat what was set before me, he brought the same thing again the next time it was available. Usually I gave in and ate what I got, but one English morning delicacy, cold baked beans on cold toast, I resisted with great obstinacy, in spite of the hurt looks he gave me each time he hauled the untouched portion away. A woman of discreet age, in this case the gyp's wife, served as bedmaker, or "bedder," sent my laundry out, and kept my rooms tidied up. The two of them conspired to keep my windows open. English windows, regardless of the weather, are to be kept open, not closed. If you don't like it that way, I soon learned, you can go back to America. Over there no one is ever allowed to die of suffocation or overheating. They may have something, at that. The first cold I had in Europe came only after I had abandoned the rigors of the English climate for the genial sunshine of Nice.

My professorial duties were light by American standards, with only two or three lectures a week and an additional class for special students during the second term. I was relieved to find that the English students, as I still insisted on calling them, were quite comparable to their American counterparts; they even understood my wisecracks. As for my middle western accent, it troubled them not at all. From one hundred to two hundred students came to my lectures during the first two terms, but only a handful during the third. The reason for this, I discovered, was that the "tripos," or examination, set in American history for Cambridge degrees included nothing beyond the Civil War, and my third-term subject was the United States after 1900. This was an attitude that I could well understand; to American students it would have been like taking a course without credit. Most of the men had spent two years in military service before entering the university, and showed the same kind of maturity that I had noted in our own returning G.I.s. Unfortunately, my contacts with the great majority of the students to whom I lectured were even less than with classes of comparable size in the United States. I invited them to call on me at Trinity Hall, but the response was no better than after similar invitations to my American classes. Furthermore, since the examining function and the teaching function are separated at Cambridge (and Oxford), I had no responsibility for examinations, gave none, graded none, and had no complainers about grades to deal with. In American universities, this situation is reversed, and provides a very dependable incentive for student-teacher contacts. Attendance at lectures at Cambridge was, of course, entirely optional.

During the second term I joined forces with Denis Brogan of Peterhouse and Frank Thistlethwaite of St. John's to conduct a class for about thirty-five students. We held our meetings each Tuesday from five o'clock to seven o'clock—after tea and before dinner. Our general theme was the American frontier, and to begin with we drew up a list of topics long enough to meet the needs of the unexpectedly long list of enrollees. Each student, under the supervision of some one of us, was expected to prepare a twenty-minute paper which, when his turn came, he would read to the class. Since the numbers were so large, we had to listen to three papers each session. After the papers, whichever one of us presided opened the subject for general discussion.

This class gave me an excellent opportunity to get better acquainted with some of the Cambridge undergraduates. The men I met were uniformly superior to the run-of-mine students in any ordinary American university. They were, of course, a very select group even for Great Britain. Cambridge and Oxford together then accounted for less than fifteen thousand students—as I figured it, only three out of every ten thousand inhabitants of Great Britain—whereas the University of California, by way of comparison, had forty students for every ten thousand Californians. I met the young men whose topics I supervised as many times as they chose to call on me, and usually talked with them about many subjects other than the one they were writing on. The papers they produced were by no means knockouts, although the composition was usually excellent. The trouble was that these young Englishmen, like their elders, lacked an adequate background in American history, and often in addition had absorbed much from our movie westerns that simply was not true. Discussions following the reading of the papers in class were always lively; participation was far more general than I would have expected from American undergraduates.

It took me a little time to figure out the relationship between the university and the colleges at Cambridge. Like most Americans, I suspect, I had the notion that in all matters, including instruction, the colleges were quite separate and independent. Actually it is quite otherwise. What exists bears a certain analogy to the federal system of government in the United States. The university is roughly comparable to the nation and the colleges to the states. The university supplies classrooms, laboratories, libraries, and lecturers, while the colleges supply, as far as possible, living quarters, food and drink (Cambridge undergraduates may buy beer and wine from the college supplies), supervision, and discipline. Salaries of professors and others who give general instruction are paid by the university. But the professor, or lecturer, or reader who holds an appointment from the university is ordinarily attached to a college, where he has dining privileges and a place to receive students and dispense hospitality. His salary comes from the university, but the college credits him with a sum that ordinarily covers the cost of all the meals he takes in college and such essential room requirements as beer, wine, and coal.

The college is primarily a place where the students live, chaperoned after a fashion by what Americans would call members of the faculty. The word "dormitory" has a totally different connotation in England, but in the American sense of the term that is really what a college is. A few unmarried or unattached fellows live in, as I did during my first month, and as many of the students who are affiliated with the college as its buildings will house. Students who do not live in are permitted to rent quarters, usually called "digs," in private homes. Every effort is made to ensure that each undergraduate lives in college during a part of his three years' residence, but very few have that privilege all the time. In fact, some of the young men, after a brief term in college, prefer the greater freedom that comes with living outside the college walls. For walls they are, quite literally, and those who stay out longer than the prescribed hours must rouse the porter to get in. For this, or for any other unseemly conduct, such, for example, as failing to wear a gown, there are penalties, usually in the shape of fines. And there are proctors who walk the streets at night in search of sinners. Each proctor is accompanied by two "bulldogs," college servants whose business it is to run offenders down on command of the proctor. On occasion, however, a friendly "bulldog" has been known to whisper, when hard on the heels of a culprit, "Can't you run a little faster, sir?"

At the head of each college is a master, next to whom in rank, at least at Trinity Hall, comes the tutor. I found, to my surprise, that the tutor does very little tutoring, if any, but is primarily an administrative officer. He assigns rooms to the undergraduates, gives special dispensations and permissions as needed, and functions *in loco parentis*, more or less in the manner of an American dean of men. And finally we come to the supervisor, lowliest of all, who does whatever actual tutoring is done. He sets papers to be written, suggests books to be read, and each week talks directly with the undergraduates entrusted to his care. Professors are ineligible for any of these minor chores; except for lectures and an occasional class, they are free to confine their efforts to writing and research. And there are no minor grades of professor, such as assistant professors and associate professors. Either a person is a professor or he isn't. Supposing, as I always had before I came to Cambridge, that the English university operated very differently from an American university, with direct tutoring the essence of the system, I was appalled on one occasion to hear a young supervisor remark that all the undergraduates needed to do to pass their examinations was to attend lectures, take full notes, and study their notes faithfully. If they did that, he said, they needn't ever crack a book. This all seemed so painfully familiar.

My month living in at Trinity Hall was soon over, but my contacts with the college remained close throughout the year. Together with some of my colleagues, I had lunch there each day in the "combination room," a large, cold, well-appointed all-purpose room, fully equipped with newspapers and periodicals, where the fellows were free to tarry at will, but in view of the lack of a fire in the fireplace—or any other heating—seldom willed to tarry very long. Luncheon was self-service, but always adequate. Each Tuesday night the master and fellows dined together at high table in the Great Hall, with the undergraduates partaking of somewhat simpler fare down below. After dinner we adjourned to a semicircular table in the combination room for fruit and biscuits (crackers to Americans), coffee, and port. My admiration for the Master of Trinity Hall, Professor H. R. Dean, who set the tone for these occasions, was unrestrained; he was one of the gentlest gentlemen I ever knew. From time to time he accorded to each of us the privilege of sitting beside him, and so kept in close touch with the personnel of the college. When he arose to go, we all arose to go. The evening was over. There were many other college contacts that meant much to a visitor—up and down the staircases, in each other's sitting rooms, out together for a walk or a beer, in each other's homes for dinner. By the end of the year I had the comfortable feeling of belonging.

As a visiting professor I was shown many courtesies by colleges other than my own. There were very few of them in which I did not dine in hall as the guest of some one of their fellows. On such occasions I was often, but not always, seated next to the master of the college, invariably a man of distinction whom I found it a pleasure to meet. I was invited also to many college feasts, audit feasts they were frequently called, because originally they were held in celebration of the fact that the year's accounts had been settled up; here in America we no doubt would have called them, more prosaically, annual banquets. Some of these invitations called for white tie, some for black tie, but they always involved formal clothes; and whatever the tie, the Cambridge gown was an essential part of the uniform. White-tie affairs license doctors of the university to wear their scarlet robes, so that, without the presence of women, these occasions had a dressed-up, colorful appearance. Quite in contrast to similar events in the United States, there was a great absence of speech-making during or after the meal, and little serious talk at any time. But there was a great plenty of wine drinking and an endless flow of conversational banter. Lucile was greatly annoyed at the exclusion of women from all these festivities. She said she had never spent so many lonely evenings at home in her life. England, she decided, was primarily a masculine civilization, with women cast in a strictly secondary role.

Before leaving America I had made up my mind that, rather than to settle down on some research project, I would use my spare time to get better acquainted with England and the English people. I therefore accepted such invitations to speak as came my way, even when they involved a good deal of travel. One excursion, for example, took us all the way to Edinburgh, another to the British Museum, yet another to Oxford, others to such "red-brick" universities as Birmingham and Reading, and still others to towns and cities within easier reach of Cambridge. One of the most interesting of these trips was to Boston, where I made a Thanksgiving speech in the American tradition. Boston, Lincolnshire, I learned, and Boston, Massachusetts, have developed a close relationship and take every opportunity to cultivate it. Often my invitations came from a chapter of the United Nations Association or the English-Speaking Union and called for speeches on the American attitude toward the UN or on Anglo-American relations. Locally I spoke to history clubs in the various colleges, to the Rotary Club (without benefit of horseplay), to women's clubs, to church and school groups, even to a Fabian Society (which gave me a bad time).

The British are a very ritualistic people, and the speech-making ritual varies little from time to time or place to place. I was pleasantly introduced by the chairman, spoke a given length of time, and was then subjected to questioning by the audience. Regardless of what I talked about, invariably one of the first questions was: What about the Negro problem? How I would enjoy now to reply to that one, "Do you mean yours or ours?" But at that time I had no alibi and could only try to explain how long it takes to live down historical prejudices. When occasionally I was harried more than I thought justifiable, I pointed out that many white Americans had "died to make men free," and asked how many Englishmen had done the same. Occasionally, after the question period, the audience was invited to talk back to the speaker.

In both the question period and the talking-back period there was little pulling of punches. The English people are very reticent about expressing controversial opinions at dinner parties or other social occasions, but let anyone make a speech and he is considered fair game. Many were the times that I stood literally with my back to the wall, shivering with cold in a room that any American audience would have deserted in five minutes, fighting warmly for my country with every forensic weapon at my disposal. There is nothing better calculated to make a person at least one hundred and one per cent American than to be put on the defensive by a foreign audience.

American foreign policy, a subject I was frequently asked to discuss, rarely escaped a thorough panning, especially when it diverged from British policy. I was never able to satisfy a British audience that the United States had a case for not recognizing Red China, or for not consenting to its representation in the United Nations, or for not facilitating the Chinese conquest of Formosa, or for not keeping MacArthur south of the thirty-eighth parallel in Korea. I could not defend Senator McCarthy, but I was rarely believed when I asserted that he in no way spoke for the American government. Sometimes I had to deal with tormentors whose pronunciation of MacArthur and McCarthy was so similar that I could not be sure which they intended to denounce. All I could hope was that on each occasion I had given the best defense I could make of my country and had not always come off second best in the argument. At the close of each meeting the English ritual required someone from the audience, selected for the purpose in advance, to thank the speaker, and usually the official thanker discharged his duty most pleasantly. Only once did I get a panning from this last speaker, whom I couldn't answer back, and he turned out to be a South African, not an Englishman at all. British sportsmanship disapproves such tactics. Certainly I learned a good deal about what the English were thinking, and I'm sure that many who listened to me heard, probably for the first time, a defense of the American point of view.

Despite these differences of opinions, which it took a speech to bring out, the friendliness of the British people to us as Americans was really extraordinary. Everywhere we went we met this all-pervasive be-kind-to-Americans attitude. We were thanked personally for the help that Americans had given the British during the dark days of World War II. In particular, people we met spoke appreciatively of the "Bundles for

Britain," the Care packages, and the food parcels sent them by individual Americans. They were by no means unaware of the importance of our Lend-Lease outlay, our postwar loans, the Marshall aid they received, and American assistance in British rearmament. But all this they could discount as governmental policy, from which the United States hoped in some way to obtain value received. Individual gifts were different. They were from the heart, with no thought for return favors, and they made a tremendous impression.

American troops in Britain also left a helpful legacy. When invited into British homes they sometimes failed to appear, which made for irritation, but when they did come they usually behaved themselves well. Undoubtedly there were exceptions. There was for example, the duchess—there is always a duchess for example—who, according to a well-worn legend, invited into her house a number of soldiers, mostly colored. "What did you think of the Americans?" she was asked after they left.

"Oh, I liked the Americans all right," she replied, "but I didn't think much of those white fellows they brought along with them." Usually, even the "white fellows" made a good impression.

Also, such British troops as were for one reason or another stationed for a while in the United States found in American hospitality an unforgettable experience. Both over here and over there the ease with which Americans of high and low degree met strangers, their total unconsciousness of class barriers, their amiability and generosity all promoted friendly relations. American visitors during the years I was in Great Britain were cashing in on this treasury of good will. If, as often happened, Lucile and I should be standing on a London street corner baffled as to which way to turn, some Englishman would at once appear with a courteous "Pardon me, is there anything I can do to help you?" And help us he would, even to the extent of missing his bus or going blocks out of his way to straighten us out.

How Britishers can spot an American so surely, even before he utters a word, remained to me a mystery to the end. They said it was my hat, so I got a French beret. But did they mistake me for a Frenchman? They did not. They said it was my necktie, so I got a Swiss necktie. But did they mistake me for a Switzer? They did not. They said it was my overcoat, so I got an Austrian overcoat. But did they mistake me for an Austrian? They did not. Wearing a French beret, a Swiss necktie, and an Austrian overcoat, and driving an English Austin with a large "G.B " for "Great Britain" on the license plate, I was spotted as an American everywhere, just as far as I could be seen. "Oh, it's just the way you look and walk," said a cockney waitress in Harrod's. But she had spotted me as an American when I was sitting down, looking the other way.

By the time the Christmas holidays rolled around, our family situation had altered considerably. Zoe Fisher and Marjorie had gone back to Berkeley, and our second daughter, Carolyn had joined us. Thoroughly fed up with the dreary English weather, we had decided to spend our vacation in southern France and Italy. Fortunately, while Lucile and her companions were on their European tour, I had spent a few days with them in Paris; and since I had taken a profound dislike to Parisians, we felt free to concentrate this time on Rome. First we flew to Nice, where we basked in the sun for a few days, then we took a bus along the coast to Genoa to join forces with Bob Reynolds and his family. Bob, a former colleague of mine both at Lincoln and at Madison, was in Genoa on leave of absence to work in the archives there. Bob's family consisted of Sarah, his wife; Sam and Sally, two of his three children; and Sarah's mother, Mrs. Chickering, who proved to be a delightful partner in our adventures. Following a big Christmas dinner in the Reynolds' Genoa apartment, we all set out for Rome, where after a few days, Jane Harriet, our oldest daughter, joined us.

The trip by train to Rome was quite an experience. Marshall aid had served to spruce up the trains, which were electrified throughout, ran smoothly, and were usually on time. The coaches were similar to those we had become accustomed to in England, but with three classes of accommodations instead of only two (called confusingly in England first and third). The number of passengers traveling first class from Genoa to Rome was negligible, second class was comfortably filled, but third class was intolerably overcrowded. This circumstance told us a lot about Italy, for wherever we went the poor were always with us in catastrophic numbers, good-natured, uncomplaining, but obviously poor. In Italy we encountered for the first time begging on a really serious scale—from both children and grown-ups, including monks. To our surprise, the beggars were rarely turned down, perhaps because a ten-lira note was so valueless that it was easier to give than to refuse.

Since Bob and Sarah both knew Rome well and spoke Italian, we were in luck. They had made reservations for us at a small but excellent hotel just across the street from a second-century Roman wall and gateway, both practically intact. Each day we set forth in two taxis to see the sights. First, of course, we went to the old forum, the Colosseum, and the surrounding ruins. Rome took very little bombing during World War II, so what we saw were mostly ancient ruins. On the train from Genoa, however, when I called Bob's attention to some damaged masonry and asked him about its antiquity, his reply was direct and to the point. "No," he said, "them's American ruins." Our second day we drove out to Tivoli, saw the sixteenth-century palace of the D'Este family, with its fountain-filled garden, and inspected the second-century ruins of Emperor Hadrian's villa. Thereafter we shopped around for more ruins, visited the great Roman baths, drove out the Appian Way, examined the tomb of the Scipios, and saw some of the huge aqueducts that once brought water across the Campagna from the Alban Hills. The *Viri Romae* of my high school days seemed at last to come alive.

After we had done all the ruins we had time for, we turned from pagan to Christian Rome, beginning quite properly with St. Peter's, which was quite as huge and beautiful as we had been led to expect. We were amused to note that not Americans alone, but even Romans, are capable of a little high-class bragging. As we walked toward the center of the church we observed marks on the floor, each indicating how far back some other great cathedral would come if measured from St. Peter's altar. They all fell far short. The dome, of course, was also the biggest. An unexpected diversion was the baptism of an infant Roman, who resented with all his lung power being made a Christian, a throwback, maybe, to pagan times.

One whole day we devoted to the Vatican Museum, starting with the Sistine Chapel, which so entranced us that we could hardly tear ourselves away. There before our eyes—or above them—were the Michelangelo originals of all the Sunday school cards we had ever seen. We went through acres of rooms adorned with frescoes, statues, and paintings, and emerged at length with picture post cards of the items that had impressed us most; some of the cards we mailed, complete with Vatican stamps, to our Catholic friends back home.

During the following days we saw all the principal Roman churches, visited the catacombs at St. Sebastian's, found our way to the top layer of the castle of St. Angelo, and drove out to Ostia and inspected the ruins there. On Epiphany, the twelfth day after Christmas and reputedly the day on which the Wise Men brought their gifts to the infant Jesus, we took a turn around the city to see what was going on. This is an important holiday in Italy, the day on which Italian children get the gifts we ordinarily give to our children on Christmas. The crowds were out in the streets, in the churches, and in the markets. Everywhere the children were proudly displaying their gifts. One little girl had a puppy, another a doll as large as herself, and the number of cowboy suits we saw on little Romans proved beyond a doubt the power of the American influence—probably conveyed through the movies—on postwar Italy.

After nearly two weeks in Rome, Lucile and I and our two daughters parted company with the Reynolds family and took the train for Naples. There we had reservations at the Hotel Vesuvio, a new structure built with American aid money to replace one bombed out during the war. When we reached our rooms, they turned out to be so sumptuous that I questioned my ability to pay for them, but I found out eventually that they were no more expensive than more ordinary quarters in New York. The next day, under American Express Company guidance, we drove by way of Salerno and Amalfi to Sorrento. On the way we saw Mount Vesuvius and the ruins of Pompeii. Our rooms at Sorrento were even larger than those we had enjoyed in Naples, but the worn-out elegance of the furniture was quite a contrast. The view we had that night from our windows of the Bay of Naples was the finest we had seen since our last glimpse of San Francisco Bay, of which it reminded us. Our days in Italy had been sunny and warm during our entire visit, but the nights were cool, and the Sorrento hotel in particular lacked nothing so much as heat.

This hotel, for all its grandeur, was mostly unoccupied, since early January was not exactly the tourist season. Perhaps that was the reason we had our dinner in a small room that ordinarily, we guessed, was used as a bar. As we came in, the radio was blaring away full blast with news from Korea, but since none of us could understand what was being said I asked the waiter to interpret. Unfortunately, his English was adequate only for gastronomic necessities and hardly equal to the occasion. He made it clear, however, that the UN forces were in full retreat. Continuing, more with poses and gestures than with words, he managed to get over a pretty important message to us. "You Americans," he communicated, "you are used to winning. We Italians, we are used to losing; we get beaten all the time. But don't worry," he consoled us, with a sympathetic shrug of his shoulders, "we have come out all right, and you will too." Somehow we were comforted.

We got up early the next day to visit Capri, saw the famous blue grotto, and took a guided tour of the island. At the far end of our journey we were thrilled to see from a high eminence the Faraglione, two huge pillars of stone that rise dramatically out of the sea just off-shore. An etching of this very scene had long hung in our Berkeley living room without our knowing what it was. "There's our picture," we said in unison as it came into view. Our trip ended with a boat trip back to Naples, where we boarded the train for Rome. The next morning I left by plane for England, while Lucile and the two girls stayed on to visit Florence, several cities in Switzerland, and Paris, and after ten days to rejoin me in Cambridge.

Between the second and third terms at Cambridge there was another long vacation, long enough to permit me to accept an invitation to teach for a month at the Salzburg Seminar in American Studies. We decided that, for the sake of greater mobility, we would take our Austin shootingbrake with us, which meant a drive to Dover via London, a ferry across the channel to Dunkirk (service to Calais was not available at that season), then a drive across northern France and western Germany to Austria. Our daughters were by this time back in Berkeley, so Lucile and I had room enough to invite a St. John's undergraduate, Alec Campbell, who had been accepted as a student by the Seminar, to accompany us. His ability to speak French with fair fluency turned out to be a great help.

Unraveling the red tape necessary to enable us to get our car out of England was a real experience. On inquiry, I discovered that since our Austin was bought for ultimate shipment to the United States, we would have to give bond for its full value as assurance that we would bring it back to England and not dispose of it on the Continent. It never occurred to me that giving bond would mean anything more than paying a small fee to a bonding company, so I let the matter slide until a few days before the time set for our departure. To my consternation I then discovered that the English concept of giving bond differed markedly from our own. I found out, to my dismay, that what I had to do was to put up £500 ($1,400), the estimated value of the car, in cash. Since my account at Barclay's contained substantially less than that sum, and since there was a Bank of England rule against lending to aliens (I had found that out before), I was in a predicament.

What to do? I had an account in Berkeley with enough money in it to meet the required sum, and offered to draw a check on it for the full amount. A polite official explained to me that this wouldn't do, for my check would have to be cleared, meaning, in effect, that it would have to go to America and the money would have to come back before the Austin could leave England. This would take about two weeks, more time than I had at my disposal. So I had to think again. Salary payments at Cambridge came quarterly, and my second payment would soon be due. Suppose I sign over my right to my next check to meet the required bond. That one took a lot of consultation and much hand-wringing (on the officer's part, not mine), but it, too, was turned down. Fortunately my third idea worked. In desperation I went to the treasurer of Cambridge University and asked him to advance me enough money on my next check (which I had already earned) to permit me to take off. He agreed without hesitation, so all was well.

The trip to Salzburg was exciting. We saw for the first time the white cliffs of Dover, landed at Dunkirk amid the most indescribable ruins, and drove on through tree-lined roads to Arras, where we spent our first night on the Continent. There was a vast difference, we discovered, between Parisians and provincials; we received the most cordial treatment everywhere, including smiles and Churchillian V-signs from children, and no attempts whatever at exploitation. The next day we drove through Rheims, where we saw the cathedral, badly damaged but with its great rose window still intact, then across a section of World War I entrenchments, then on through many peasant villages with big manure piles in front of each house, and finally to Strasbourg, where we spent the night. Here we learned the hard way that a room with bath in Europe did not always include other and even more important items than a bathtub. Our route in Germany took us through the Black Forest, somewhat denuded by ruthless cutting during World War II, but still impressive. The strangest thing about it to us was its clean floor; unlike all the American forests we had ever seen, there was not a branch or a twig left to go to waste, to say nothing of fallen trees. Finally we reached the Autobahn, which reminded us of home, except for such signs as "Ausfahrt" and "Infahrt," the meanings of which, however, seemed perfectly clear. We spent a night in Munich with a former Berkeley student of mine, and in due time reached Salzburg.

This city, with its central Festung on a mountain high above the surrounding houses, with its abundance of church spires and its quaint winding streets, seemed to take us back in time hundreds of years. But the headquarters of the Seminar, Schloss Leopoldskron, was right out of the eighteenth century, as completely baroque as its builders could make it. Before the war, we were told, it had belonged to Max Reinhardt, and the Seminar rented it from his widow. It was a huge affair, only half of which had central heat and was being used by the Seminar.

Our Salzburg experience was very unusual. The Seminar was almost continuously in session, with a different set of students every month or six weeks. It was organized after World War II by a group of Harvard students, and, following a period of administrative chaos, won from foundations and individual donors the support it needed to carry on with good efficiency. The idea was to bring in for short periods of a month or six weeks many different groups of students from the nations of Western Europe. At Salzburg they were directed in their studies by such American professors as chanced to be available at the time in Europe and willing to undertake the assignment. Beyond room, board, and travel expense, the faculty, if one could so designate it, received no remuneration; indeed, since we so much appreciated the privilege, I put in no bill for travel. The subject of the Seminar changed with each session, but it was always on an American theme. The month I participated was devoted to American history, with Charles S. Sydnor of Duke, then Harmsworth Professor at Oxford, and George E. Mowry of UCLA, a Fulbrighter teaching in France, also participating as leaders.

The Salzburg students were carefully screened for entrance, and were usually accepted only after a personal interview with the director. They were housed and fed without cost to themselves, and there was no tuition, so their only expense was for travel. The month we were there some forty-five students were present, several each from Great Britain, Ireland, France, Norway, Sweden, Denmark, Finland, Holland, Belgium, Switzerland, Germany, Austria, and Italy. All spoke, read, and wrote English with fair facility, and classes were conducted in English. Before many days national lines broke down, and the Seminar became, as its founders intended, just people living together, people who no doubt learned more from one another than from their professors. Undoubtedly one purpose of the Seminar was to promote good will toward the United States, and to some extent we may have succeeded in softening the Old World antagonism toward the New. However that may have been, we later met a number of the participants as students or travelers on our side of the Atlantic.

Once toward the close of the Seminar we had a meeting for general discussion, partly to find out what the students thought of the United States. The subject they chose to discuss, however, turned out to be in reality an accusation: Should the United States use Marshall aid to force its policies on Western Europe? I got the impression that the students present believed, almost to the last person, that the United States, openly or secretly, was using European aid to subvert the liberties of the poor Europeans. Some, however, especially representatives of the defeated nations, thought that the United States ought to use its power still further to force their own governments, which they completely distrusted, to do whatever each speaker thought should be done. One Italian argued that the United States should compel Brazil to take in Italian immigrants, since Italy had too many people. To which one of the staff replied: "So you think the United States should take responsibility for Italian unwillingness to practice birth control?" The attitude of the British was least irrational, but nearly everyone took occasion to blame the United States for some European misfortune. I tried, in vain, I fear, to point out that the United States had no ax to grind other than the desire to produce peace and prosperity in Western Europe and to restrain the spread of Communism. But they simply would not believe that any government would be so foolish as to hand out money without expecting some more direct and tangible advantage for itself in return. "The United States," said one Italian lad, "will always be remembered as the nation with the worst foreign policy."

I revealed a little of the hurt I felt for myself and for my country to some of the English students after the session was over. "How would you like it," I lamented, "if your nation had done all this for other nations and had received only scorn and contempt in return?" To which one of them, with great perspicacity, replied: "Oh, I don't think we would much mind."

That reply taught me a lesson. The English, when they were top dog, had never minded in the least what other nations thought of them. Now that we had succeeded them in the leadership of the Western world, we would have to cultivate that attitude. The leader could never be loved; jealousy would take care of that. Virtue would have to be its own reward. On my return to the United States I tried repeatedly to make this clear to American audiences, but it never got over. Unlike our British predecessors, we are still too thin-skinned for our own good.

We returned to Cambridge, after the Seminar ended, by a somewhat different route. This time, besides Alec Campbell, we had with us Rodney Green, another Seminar student, whose cheerful wit and Irish brogue enlivened our conversation all the way to London, where he left us. From Salzburg we drove to Karlsruhe for our first night out. Emma Paxson, Fred Paxson's second daughter, whom I had known since she was four years old, was in Karlsruhe with some American agency, so we looked her up and spent the evening with her. The next morning we found our way to the right bank of the Rhine and drove slowly along it from Mainz to near Cologne. We passed dozens of castles, saw the spot where the Lorelei was supposed to have exerted her charms, viewed the remains of the Remagen bridge, ate lunch in a tiny restaurant overlooking the river, and watched with fascination the passing procession of barges. We explored through Coblenz in search of an American Express Company office which we didn't find, but we saw the ghastly ruins made by Allied bombing, a scene repeated at Cologne, where we spent a night and also visited the cathedral, still structurally intact but badly damaged. We then drove westward through Liège, Brussels, Louvain, and Ostend to Dunkirk, with war damage about us all the way. And yet, with every meal among the ruins we were reminded of the fact that the people on the Continent were eating better than the British. Even the poor people looked well fed; some were very fat. In one Rhine-bank restaurant at which we ate, the well-upholstered waiter took time out between our main course and our dessert to devour a huge meal right before our eyes.

The third term at Cambridge was soon over, and in June, 1951, we took ship from Southampton to New York on the *Queen Elizabeth*. Our daughter Marjorie was to be married at the end of the month, and we had to "make it to the church on time." Aboard ship we had a chance to reflect on what we had seen and heard. The friendliness that was so apparent toward us as Americans, we realized, did not extend to our government and business structure. Europeans were seriously alarmed for fear American leadership would be unable to avoid another economic crash, such as had come in 1929, a crash that would leave Europe, no less than the United States, in unbelievable chaos. Many of them also feared our lack of experience in world affairs and our brashness. Could the United States be trusted with world leadership? The English, in particular, would have felt so much more secure if they could only have taken over our State Department and run it for us. The French were seriously worried about their remnants of empire in

Indo-China and North Africa. Would American aid be used to influence their policy in those areas? Every nation involved in the American demand for rearmament was disturbed. Would these expenditures result in more inflation? Why shouldn't the United States, with all its riches, carry this burden alone?

I suppose it was the specter of World War III more than anything else that determined the attitude of Europeans toward the United States. Some of the continentals were not very sure that we were trying hard to avoid war; even if peace was our goal, would not some miscalculation on our part destroy it? They were frightened by the Korean War, which they blamed on the United States. At best this conflict would drain off American military might from the defense of Europe to the defense of South Korea; at worst it could become the prelude to another world war. Even the British were frightened, as nearly as a Britisher can be brought to show fright, by the presence of American bomber bases in Britain, which, in the event of atomic attack, would furnish the targets for the destruction of British civilization. Continental nations that had been fought over and liberated had no desire to be fought over and liberated again, and some of their people were not sure that the United States, in the last analysis, had anything better to offer. They looked with some askance at our establishment of closer relations with Spain. Could that mean that the United States expected to see all the rest of Europe conquered by the Russians, with the task of reconquest to begin at the Pyrenees? We had countered all these arguments, one by one, as they were presented to us, but we knew that we had made few, if any, converts.

Back in California, and soon to be confronted by my classes, what had I gained from my year overseas? As far as my teaching potential was concerned, quite a bit. A teacher of American history could not help profiting from a glimpse of how other peoples regarded his nation and his subject. But when I reflected on what the English university system had to offer for the reform of our own, I came up with very little. Americans quite generally fail to understand the nature of Cambridge and Oxford. Thinking of our own distinction between small colleges and large universities, they frequently conjure up visions of a flock of little New England colleges, each responsible for the whole educational process, all located together on the same oversized campus but with interrelationships held to a minimum. Such a system might have its merits—I doubt it—but this is not the Cambridge-Oxford system, and attempts to reproduce something in America that never existed in England are not likely to get very far. The Harvard and Yale experiments, with "houses" and "residential colleges," respectively, were, of course, based on a real understanding of the British system, but I wonder if they have scored any very notable results. Returning Rhodes scholars, deeply impressed by the tutorial system, have also got that phase of Oxford life quite out of focus; only lately have we begun to hear from the returning American teachers.

As it seemed to me, the differences between British and American universities, even Oxford and Cambridge, to say nothing of the newer "red-brick" universities, are quite overplayed, and have more to do with form than with substance. Both systems involve lectures and classes, large and small, and much attention to individuals, in both countries usually assigned to lower-ranking personnel—teaching assistants, we call them. The British do a rather better job with undergraduates than we do, largely because the young men and women who come to their universities are farther along with their studies than ours, and are much more carefully screened. But we do an infinitely better job with graduate students, whom the British universities, at least when I was there, had not yet learned how to handle. There can be no doubt that both the British and the American systems can be bettered, but I came back with the conclusion that each nation could learn more from its own experience than from anything it could borrow from the other.

XVI. The Later Years

WHEN WE RETURNED from England in the summer of 1951 I had only six years left for active duty. It seemed reasonable that during this period I should ease off from general university responsibilities and devote my time primarily to teaching and writing. One great advantage of my prolonged leave of absence was the complete wiping out of all my committee assignments, and for the future I hoped to keep this kind of time-consuming activity to a minimum. I was barely back on campus, however, when I was asked to serve again on the Budget Committee. I begged off, and when I was asked to suggest someone else from the history department for this duty I wished the job off on George Guttridge. Perhaps he enjoyed the experience. There certainly could be no better way to learn the pattern of university behavior than to serve on that committee.

I was not long unencumbered by extra duties. To succeed me as chairman, I had nominated, after due consultation within the department, John J. Van Nostrand, who had served us well as vice-chairman. Probably Sontag, whom I personally would have preferred, would have been a better choice, but Sontag recently (1946–1949) had been absent in Washington in government service, and, as it transpired, was soon to go there again. Members of the department thought that Van Nostrand was the logical choice, although some of them expressed the hope that when I came home he would turn the office back to me. That, in point of fact, was about what happened, for only one semester after I returned to Berkeley, Van took leave and went to Japan. With Sontag away, there seemed no alternative to my assuming Van's duties, although only as acting chairman and presumably for one semester only. But since Van liked his work in Japan so well—or disliked his work as chairman so much—that he stayed on for a year and a half, it was a full year before I could get rid of his job.

I regretted the necessity of having to resume administrative duties, and for once claimed the right to teach only two courses instead of the customary three. But the two courses I taught were practically a full load. My seminar ran to a dozen or more students, many of whom were working for the Ph.D., and my lecture course regularly numbered at least four or five hundred. The maintenance of adequate departmental personnel also provided me with some difficult problems. It was not easy to find temporary replacements for the absentees, and there were other openings to fill. Moreover, some of the younger and newer members of the department, quite naturally, were beginning to be restive under the rule of the elders. While I did my best to consult my colleagues about all matters of importance, I did not hesitate to make what I regarded as minor decisions on my own. If the answers were fairly obvious, I reasoned, why waste all that time in consultation? When I detected an undercurrent of unrest with my "autocratic" rule, I refused to stay on as acting chairman for a third semester, and recommended to Dean Davis as my successor the youngest full professor in the department, James F. King. King took over as acting chairman until the end of the year and then became chairman. So I was over that hurdle.

Among the problems that I left to King was the promotion to tenure rank of two assistant professors whose original appointments had occurred when Paxson was chairman. The time had come when they must either be elevated to full tenure as associate professors or dismissed. In each case the real test came over the quality and quantity of their publications, and in both cases the quantity, at least, was meager, although both men had worked hard on their research. One of them had undertaken a new and difficult field, in which he had published a short monograph, but was this enough? The other had invested considerable time on a biographical study only to discover that a descendant, who had control of the documents, would not permit the unflattering interpretations of his ancestor that the conscientious biographer felt obliged to make. Both assistant professors, in my opinion, had a case for tenure, and I fought hard for them. So, also, did King, the new chairman. The problem of replacement was also a factor; I knew by experience how difficult it would be to get better men than those we already had. Furthermore, while both men had signed the offensive 1950 oath, they had been more conspicuous in their opposition to it than any other members of the department except Kantorowicz, who was one of the non-signers. Some observers were sure to say that this was the reason they got the ax. In the end, by a bare majority, the department voted for dismissal. I felt outraged, but there was nothing I could do about it except to help both men get better jobs, which they did. It was apparent that within the department a new generation had arisen "which knew not Joseph." From then on I kept clear of departmental politics and concentrated on my teaching and writing.

That is, as much as I could, for I had not retreated completely to that ivory tower about which I have heard so much and known so little. I have always thought of myself as a liberal, and on political matters that is no doubt true. But my support in academic circles has come mainly from educational conservatives, men who are unwilling to promote change just for the sake of change and who see virtue in St. Paul's admonition to "hold fast that which is good." My adherence to such views led to some of my friends putting me up for election to a newly created Representative Assembly, to which for a time our Academic Senate delegated many of its prerogatives. The Representative Assembly was a much smaller body than the Senate, and in my opinion it gave a good account of itself. It got lost in the general reorganization that took place a few years later, but there is talk of its revival. The Academic Senate, as a legislative body of more than a thousand members, is too unwieldy to be effective. Moreover, its requirement of a minimum quorum of only seventy-five means that its decisions are at the mercy of the few who choose to attend, or who stay on after impatient members have gone home to dinner. Paradoxically, Senate committees are very effective. One reason for the difference is that they are chosen by the committee on committees, which in turn is elected by a mail ballot of the whole Senate; furthermore, they have well-defined and important duties.

I served also for a period as a member of the Senate committee on privilege and tenure. One case that came before us in my time involved the dismissal of an acting assistant professor. After giving the individual concerned a tedious hearing, we agreed that whatever the administration had done to him was amply justified. Following this case, which attracted considerable attention, faculty legalists insisted on the appointment of an all-university committee to lay down elaborate rules for such proceedings. As a member of that committee, I did what I could to keep the rules simple, but it was not enough. As I saw it, we had no need to model our procedures on those of law courts; for our purposes our own academic precedents were adequate. Members of the committee on privilege and tenure had a hard time at best, and to introduce further complications was both unneccessary and unwise. Nevertheless, the *ad hoc* committee proposed new rules that probably made matters worse rather than better.

More or less because of geographical necessity, I had cut down somewhat after coming to California on my commitments to historical organizations. I occasionally attended meetings of the Mississippi Valley Historical Association, particularly those held west of the Mississippi River, for they came in the spring when air flights were pretty dependable. The American Historical Association, however, persisted in holding its annual meetings between Christmas and New Year's, the worst flying season of the year, and also a poor time for a holiday-loving father and grandfather to be away from home. For a while I carried on a one-man war against this winter meeting date, but I got exactly nowhere with my agitation, and my absence from the annual meetings was accepted with remarkable equanimity.

Members of the American Historical Association who lived in the far western states had long held a consolation meeting each year for what they called the Pacific Coast Branch. This organization within an organization dated back to the time when travel by train—four days each way—was the only mode of transportation to the eastern seaboard states, unless one went by sea, which took longer. Since not many westerners could afford either the time or the cost of the trip, the parent organization gave its blessing and several hundred dollars each year to the Pacific Coast Branch, which held its meeting in the West while the national association was holding its meeting in the East. Oddly enough, when I was chairman of the A.H.A. committee on reorganization during the depression years, my committee had voted to cut off the subsidy to the western branch, for the Association was desperately hard up. But an eloquent plea by Edgar E. Robinson of Stanford University led us to reverse ourselves and permit the Branch to live. Branch members generally subscribed to the *Pacific Historical Review*, which specialized to some extent in articles having to do with the "rim of the Pacific," a quite extensive area.

After coming to California I attended nearly every meeting of the Pacific Coast Branch, and had something to do, perhaps, with persuading its governing body to change the date of meeting from December to late August or early September. This made better sense because air flights to the East were now short and safe at any season, so that members who had the cash and wished to do so could attend both the western and the eastern meetings. Nor did the parent group withdraw its support, logical as such a course might have been. Branch meetings continued to be well attended, and many members found them more enjoyable than the national meetings, where the rapidly increasing numbers had made easy fraternization almost impossible.

In the course of time I was made president of the Pacific Coast Branch, an honor passed along to a different person each year. At the 1955 meeting held in Berkeley (still in December), I took as the subject of my address "What's Right with the History Profession." Actually, this theme was in a sense a reversal of what I had originally intended to say, for my first thought had been to use the occasion to dress down some of my colleagues who needed it. But on second thought it occurred to me that I could get my message across better by emphasizing the positive; if anyone fell short of the generally respectable behavior of the profession, he could make his own deductions. Curiously, my address was frequently referred to as "Hicks' Reply to Beale," something it was not intended to be at all. In fact, when I wrote it, I had not even read Howard Beale's article, "The Professional Historian; His Theory and His Practice," although it had appeared in the August, 1953, number of the *Pacific Historical Review*. Beale's strictures, while probably true enough, item by item, with respect to particular individuals in specific cases, made it appear that the historical profession as a whole was incompetent and dishonest. His argument was shot through with generalizations based on insufficient evidence. But I was happily ignorant of these charges when I wrote my "reply." American teachers and writers of history are a pretty decent lot, I think, and this is what I tried to say. Exceptions, of course, there are, and not anyone is perfect. But it's unfair to damn everyone for the sins of a few, or even for a few unintended sins of his own.

Some of my graduate students undertook to celebrate my attainment of the P.C.B. presidency by inducing Houghton Mifflin Company to publish eight of my occasional addresses as a little book, *The American Tradition* (1955). Undoubtedly the publishers knew in advance that, financially speaking, this book would be a total loss, but they nevertheless dressed it up handsomely and had it available for distribution at the time I gave my "What's Right" address. To speed matters up, I had agreed to leave the proofreading, both galley and page proof, to the publishers, a sad mistake, for a number of glaring typos got through. But I was greatly touched by the spirit behind the move, and if the book did not sell the fault lay with me, and not with my students or the publishers. It contains in the appendix a list of the names of the men and women who up to that time had taken their Ph.D.'s under my direction, but omits the names of those who arrived at that goal after 1955. Among those omitted were Gerald D. Nash, Richard B. Rice, Galen R. Fisher, and Edward Everett France. The number of graduate students who received their doctor's degrees with me as their major professor reached forty-five.

One interesting assignment that came my way during the postwar years was service on a War (later Army) Department committee set up to give advice on the writing of an elaborate history of World War II. My membership on this committee involved annual trips to Washington from 1947 to 1953, and gave me an interesting behind-the-scenes glimpse into the making of the multivolume series. My selection as a member of the committee, I have always assumed, was due to the influence of my good friend Henry Steele Commager, who was also a a member of the committee; but Kent Roberts Greenfield, the chief army historian, was another long-time acquaintance, and he may have been responsible. The decision to produce this official history grew out of the discovery during World War II that the record of much of the army's experience in World War I was virtually unavailable for use— still hidden in mountains of undigested documents. Accordingly a Historical Division (later, Office of Military History) was charged with the duty of ensuring that such a mistake should not be made again. The original plan called for about one hundred volumes, but the number was later scaled down to eighty-five. The first dozen or so of these handsomely illustrated and sumptuously printed volumes appeared while I was a member of the committee.

On one of my visits to Washington, General Eisenhower, then Chief of Staff, met with the Historical Division and in an extemporaneous address showed clearly that he knew about what was going on and thoroughly approved of the project. As President, however, he, or more likely someone acting for him, suggested that appointments to the advisory committee be rotated, and I as an undeserving Democrat was promptly rotated off. By way of consolation I received a Department of the Army "Certificate of Achievement" at the San Francisco Presidio, August 2, 1954, from the hands of Major General

William F. Dean, then Deputy Commander of the Sixth Army. My family all attended the ceremony, and it was quite a show. According to the citation, my "participation in the activities and counsels of the Committee contributed materially to the development of the Army Historical Program," while my "long service in the national interest" had been "of great benefit to the entire military establishment"—a gross exaggeration.

In an earlier chapter I have alluded to the constantly recurring task of revision that every writer of a successful textbook must face. While I was on the way to Europe in 1950, my publishers induced me to pay a visit to their office in Boston. Leaving Lucile in New York with Zoe Fisher, I took Marjorie with me, a great experience for her, for my Houghton Mifflin Company friends gave us the full red-carpet treatment. The reason for all this, I was soon to discover, was that William C. Cobb, the individual chiefly responsible for what happened to my books, wanted to bring them out in a totally new format, with two columns to the page and on slick paper in order to permit profuse illustrations. It took all of his salesmanship to bring me around to this departure, for I liked the books as they were and thought that the new treatment would cheapen them. But at length I capitulated, on the understanding that I could postpone work on the revisions until after my return from England.

Many people who should know better assume that the revision and republication of textbooks is a perfunctory undertaking, designed mainly to dress up the same old copy in a new format that will help restrain second-hand sales. They are so wrong. For one thing, two of my textbooks, *The American Nation* and the *Short History*, required constant "updating," to use the publishers' inelegant term. Since these books first appeared, the world has experienced more than a quarter century of probably the most tumultuous and complicated happenings it has ever known. My course in recent American history helped me keep abreast of current events, but the task of organizing and writing always turned out to be far harder than I had foreseen. Furthermore, a textbook cannot be permitted to grow indefinitely in size; in general, an equivalent condensation of what he has already written is the price a writer must pay for each new page he adds. He finds invariably that he has given too much space not only to the last presidential election, but to many other items, also; all of which get cut down to size in the revising process. (Currently, I have my knife out for those two whole pages I wasted in defeating Goldwater in 1964.) In the first edition of *The American Nation*, the election of 1940 was the last subject treated. In the fourth edition of the same book the shortened version of that election appears nearly two hundred pages before the end of the book.

Important as the tasks of updating and condensation are, they cause the conscientious textbook writer less trouble than some of his other obligations. History, whatever the layman may think, is not set in a permanent, inelastic mold. Fashions in history change, although the proponents of new concepts don't like to have it put that way. During the past two decades, for example, historians have tended to place much more emphasis on social and intellectual history and to downgrade political and economic history correspondingly. New interpretations, based sometimes (but not always) on new research, appear constantly, and ambitious young writers make a cult of "revisionism." Keeping up with new bibliography is a never ending task. Once when I congratulated an ancient history expert on having fewer changes to deal with than the modernists, he replied testily: "You don't know what you are talking about. They even change the dates on us!"

Since the first editions of the "Hicks histories" came out, historians have changed their minds, one might almost say, about every important development in American history. What they once accepted as gospel, they now denounce as myth; what they once regarded as reasonable generalizations, they now discard altogether or replace with modified versions. Perspective also makes a difference. With the passing of time, events that once seemed of major significance prove to be relatively unimportant, while others that contemporary writers regarded as of little consequence now loom large. The easiest changes to make are corrections of a merely factual, rather than interpretative, nature. Recently someone demonstrated, for example, that Alexander Hamilton, while still reckoned the youngest Secretary of the Treasury, was actually two years older than stated by all his earlier biographers; also that the ringing declaration "Fifty-four forty or fight," long accepted as an expansionist battle cry in the election of 1844, was apparently of post-election origin. In making these corrections, however, it is wise to point out that they are being made, and why. Otherwise, letters soon begin to pour in saying "You've got Hamilton's birth date wrong," or the equivalent, and quoting Lodge or Bassett to prove it.

Before our trip to Europe, *The American Nation* had experienced a second edition, so the first pictorial edition of the two-volume text came in 1952 for *The Federal Union* and in 1955 for *The American Nation*. A third edition of *The Federal Union*, with a new chapter on Reconstruction but otherwise nearly identical with the second, appeared in 1957. All this work I did myself, except for some valuable assistance in my office from Helen B. Gray (later Mrs. Robert E. Burke), who was especially helpful with proofreading and running down new bibliography. The virtually simultaneous demand for a new pictorial edition of the *Short History*, however, was simply more than I could handle, so I induced George E. Mowry of UCLA to do the job for me, a task he finished in 1956. Fortunately, a Houghton Mifflin art editor ran down the illustrations for these editions, but we often had to decide which of several to take, and we wrote the captions for all of them.

For the fourth editions of *The Federal Union* and *The American Nation*, Mowry rewrote all the chapters that dealt primarily with social and intellectual history; Robert E. Burke of the University of Washington, a really phenomenal bibliographer, brought the book lists up to date; and I reworked the rest. We all collaborated, however, in the task of bringing the books into harmony with the findings of recent scholarship. In this undertaking we received much help from criticisms of the earlier editions, obtained for us by the publishers from about a dozen competent historians. Experience seemed to show that, for the task of revision, three heads were better than one. Both Mowry and Burke could see defects to which I was quite blind, and could initiate changes that never would have occurred to me if I had been working alone. In our last and closest collaboration, the third edition of the *Short History*, which appeared in 1966, we not only shortened the text, but we also dropped the word "Short" from the title, so that the book became merely *A History of American Democracy*, symbolic, perhaps, of the fact that it was no longer really the same book. It is possible, nevertheless, that these books all profited from being written by one author originally; it is difficult otherwise to maintain an even consistency of composition, pace, and emphasis. The more common method —that of dividing the field chronologically among two or three authors—leads inevitably to as many different shifts in style and point of view.

A new feature of *The Federal Union* and *The American Nation*, fourth editions, was the inclusion in each volume of sixteen colored plates, through which, together with the accompanying captions, we sought to present a glimpse into the history of American art. Unfortunately, the new one-volume *History of American Democracy* omitted the colored plates, a great mistake, in the opinion of the authors.

Another burden on the textbook writer, and one not generally known, is the necessity of participating in the production of manuals for students and teachers. As far as those for students were concerned, Professor Harry D. Berg of Michigan State University, an expert in the teaching of history, did most of the work, while I provided only short introductions for each of the various periods into which we divided the textbook material. For the teachers' manuals, however, I wrote quite elaborate commentaries on every chapter of every book, commentaries designed primarily to help the teacher whose familiarity with the subject was slight. I provided also essay-type questions for examinations, lists of topics for term-paper assignments, and short bibliographical notes. To Berg fell the task of inventing the objective tests, so generally in demand these days, together with an indication of what he regarded as the correct answer to each question. To save my sanity, I never even read proof on those questions, but teachers who have used them say they are very satisfactory. The student's manual (one each for all the later editions) was made available for purchase and carried small royalties; the instructor's manual, also revised with each revision, was a giveaway job (for carefully screened teachers of the text only) that carried no royalties, but cost both the publishers and the authors good money. I contributed my part of the work gratis, while the rather considerable fees paid to Berg for his help came out of textbook royalties. Over the years I had a part in the making of about ten such manuals, not heady intellectual work, maybe, but time-consuming.

The textbook revisions of the 1950's drew me away from my principal postwar research undertaking, a history of the 1920's for the "New American Nation Series," edited by Henry Steele Commager and Richard B. Morris, and published by Harper and Row. As far back as 1946 I had signed a contract to write this volume, but time to work on the project had never seemed to materialize. The leave of absence "in residence" that I took in 1949–1950 was designed mainly to enable me to finish the manuscript, but turned out instead to be the dismal "year of the oath." I might have used my year in England for this purpose, but I chose, rightly, I think, to spend my spare time there in seeing the country and exchanging views with English audiences. By 1956 I had another leave coming—only the third in my entire career—so I took the spring semester off and Lucile and I went to Washington, where I could work in the Library of Congress. By this time, with our daughters all married and away from home, we had decided that wherever we went we would go together. Like the oxen at the end of the Oregon Trail, we needed to lean together to keep from falling down. We got a housekeeping room at the Coronet Hotel, not far from the Library, and both of us went to work, Lucile in the newspaper room and I in the manuscript division. Lucile really helped me a lot, but working with microfilm seriously damaged her eyes, and from that time on she had to wear glasses. Later she was to type most of the manuscript, a task she had also assumed with some of the textbooks.

We had been in Washington many times before, but we took advantage of this visit to see some of the things we had missed and to make a memorable pilgrimage to Colonial Williamsburg. There we renewed our acquaintance with Ed and Alice Alexander, whom we had known in Madison while Ed was director of the State Historical Society of Wisconsin. We were greatly impressed with the faithfulness of the reproductions we saw, although I was reminded of Paxson's comment on Drakes' Plate, a cherished possession of the Bancroft Library at Berkeley. "The only thing against it," I once heard Paxson remark, "is that it is just too perfect."

Washington is the place to go if you want to meet your friends in the historical profession. They all flock to the Library of Congress whenever they can, and ever since the years of the New Deal many of them have accepted temporary or even permanent jobs with the federal government. Some, too, have retired to live in Washington. In earlier days those of us who knew each other used to have lunch together somewhere on "ptomaine row," the block of third-rate restaurants that used to deface one whole side of the Capitol Plaza. But by 1956 we could choose between such reputable eating places as those provided by the Library of Congress itself, or the Supreme Court, or the Methodists.

I was unable to finish my book on the 1920's until after my retirement in 1957. Then I had the free time I needed and saw the manuscript through to publication in 1960. The title of the book, *Republican Ascendancy, 1921–1933*, was not my first choice; I would have preferred *Normalcy and Reaction*, the title of a chapter in the Morison and Commager textbook *The Growth of the American Republic* that I had meant to plagiarize. But the editors were determined to have the word "Republican" in the title, and I contributed "Ascendancy." One unfortunate result of the title was the inference often drawn that I blamed all the calamities of the "boom and bust" cycle on the Republican party. Reviews in Republican newspapers seemed particularly on the defensive in this regard, especially since the book appeared on the eve of a presidential election. In general, the reviews in scholarly publications were favorable, although by no means as flattering as those I had received three decades earlier on *The Populist Revolt*.

A by-product of this book was another but smaller volume on the years 1918 to 1921. My original assignment for the "New American Nation Series," at least as I interpreted it, included the whole period from the end of World War I to the beginning of the New Deal. To avoid any misunderstandings, however, I wrote to Arthur S. Link, who had the assignment of World War I, and to William E. Leuchtenburg, who was to do the New Deal, asking the former to set his ending date and the latter his beginning date. Link wrote back that his book would be quite incomplete without the election of 1920, while Leuchtenburg wanted to begin his volume with the election of 1932. All this was fine with me, for I had already begun to worry about how to keep within the 80,000-word limit the editors had set. So I cut out my first three chapters and left unwritten most of what was to have been my last chapter. Even so my manuscript ran to about 100,000 words, despite painful abridgements. A request from the University of Florida that I give three lectures on that campus enabled me to revise and adapt for public presentation the omitted initial chapters. Since they dealt mainly with the business boom and collapse of 1919–1920, I could not resist giving them the title *Rehearsal For Disaster* (1961), although the parallel with the big boom of the middle twenties and the panic of 1929 was far from exact, as I well knew. Beautifully published by the University of Florida Press, this book, like *The American Tradition*, was noted chiefly for the small number of sales it attracted.

One interesting legacy from my work on the 1920's was the addition to my library of several hundred volumes relating to that period. I soon discovered that there was no percentage in taking full notes from books that were on my shelves; a note on where to find what I wanted when writing was sufficient. It was easy enough to progress from that stage to collecting as many as possible of the books I needed. Since I am not especially adept at spotting such books in miscellaneous second-hand bookstore collections, I turned over the task to Robert E. Burke, who was then a member of the Bancroft Library staff. Burke can look at shelves loaded with books and almost instantly pick out the one he wants. He in turn enlisted the interest of Rudy Lapp, who was similarly gifted and was working at Berkeley for a Ph.D. in American history. Together they found most of the books I wanted and many more of which I had had no previous knowledge. Ephemera of the 1920's were then not very expensive, so that for a surprisingly small sum I obtained an excellent collection. Most of the secondary titles listed in the bibliography of *Republican Ascendancy* are, or once were, on my shelves. Some of them, however, I have given away to covetous friends or to the "gifts and exchange" division of the university library. Since I have space on my office shelves for not to exceed two thousand volumes, I have made it a rule to eliminate as many books as I add. Those I have turned over to "gifts and exchange" have been given with the understanding that homes will be found for them in one or another of the several new libraries that the University of California is attempting to create on its various new campuses.

Fortunately, retirement from teaching had meant no serious change in my office routine. Unlike many other universities, California is willing to give space to its emeriti as long as they continue to be productive, so I remained undisturbed among my books in my fourth-floor library haunt.

I had had some secret concern about how I would react to the absence of classroom contacts, but I found to my relief that I was quite content with things as they were. Out of deference to my supposed retirement, I did go home at four o'clock each afternoon, instead of at five or five-thirty as formerly, but mornings I arrived on campus as usual at nine o'clock or soon after. I continued my habit of having lunch with familiar friends at the Faculty Club, and thus kept up on university gossip. In my office for a while I had frequent and pleasant interruptions from graduate students, while on campus hundreds of the undergraduates I had taught still recognized me. Because my classes had been large, I had always asked my students to greet me when they saw me—they would know me even if I didn't know them—and as long as they lasted they continued the practice. College generations are short, but by the time no one I met knew who I was I didn't much mind.

I could have taught every year for the next ten after I retired, had I chosen to do so. President Paul Giddens of Hamline University, where I had begun my teaching career, was the first to ask me, an offer that touched me deeply, but I declined, telling myself that I remembered those Minnesota winters too well. When the chairman of the Department of History at the University of Redlands duplicated the offer, I again refused, although the winter involved would have been one of California's mildest. The fact was that I really didn't care to undertake a new teaching assignment. After that I declined all offers, including wisely one that would have taken me to New Delhi. One year, when the University of California asked me back, I was tempted, but I suggested a possible alternate, who accepted. It was well that he did, for the week I was to have begun teaching I went to the hospital instead. For several years during the early 1960's I battled a series of illnesses, as most old men must do, but I survived and got to my office regularly enough to hold it. The past academic year, 1966–1967, I could have taught at the American University in Beirut, and had that offer come nine or ten years earlier I might have accepted it. Only last fall, although I was then in my seventy-eighth year, I was asked to teach a class at San Francisco State College. Our current practice of granting frequent sabbaticals, plus the difficulty of filling new positions in a hurry, account in large part for the numerous temporary appointments available to emeriti.

While I so regularly refused to accept a teaching assignment, I did agree to undertake a tour of duty in 1958–1959 as visiting scholar for Phi Beta Kappa. This assignment came my way on the recommendation of Peter Odegard, our distinguished political scientist, who knew me pretty well and had heard me speak. The program was financed jointly by the central and the local Phi Beta Kappa organizations, the former paying the bulk of the bill, but the latter providing for the entertainment of the speaker and the scheduling of his activities. I accepted the mission only on condition that Lucile should accompany me, and this she did. In Los Angeles, our first assignment, we divided a week between the University of Southern California and UCLA. Since I had taught summer school in both places, we found ourselves on familiar ground and among friends. My lectures were open not only to all the students but also to the general public, and were well attended.

My principal address on these and similar subsequent occasions was a comparison of the 1920's and the 1950's, a subject that permitted me to speak my mind on a number of things.[1] The postwar lapse into conservatism was pronounced in both decades, and I questioned the adequacy of the current American commitment to liberal policies, both at home and abroad. Other subjects upon which I spoke included my 1957 observations on Europe, a lecture on Theodore Roosevelt that I had given a short time before at the University of Omaha to commemorate the one hundredth anniversary of T.R.'s birth, the role of third parties in American politics, and the background of Populism. I tried to suit my subjects to the interests of the groups before which I spoke. Often I took over a class in American history, fitting my remarks to the theme then under discussion. On one occasion, at least, I participated in a Phi Beta Kappa initiation. At each place I made myself available for private interviews with graduate students or potential graduate students, especially those planning to continue their work in history or related subjects. The number of such interviews varied, but I rarely had less than a dozen or so consultations at each place.

After the Los Angeles visit, we made three more trips, one to the Northeast, one to the Southeast, and one to the Northwest. The trip to the northeast was a long one which we undertook in the dead of winter. We visited New York University, the University of Delaware, Bucknell University, Hobart College, and William Smith College, all on the first lap; then Kenyon College, Gambier, Ohio, the Universities of Indiana and Wisconsin, Lawrence College, and Beloit on the second lap. We made two campuses a week and managed not to miss a single engagement, although we encountered a miserable blizzard in central New York and two more in Wisconsin. Most of our trips were by air, but the planes were grounded in Wisconsin, and the train that took us to Chicago was stalled by the snow several times. The adventure into the Southeast took us to Wofford College in Spartanburg, South Carolina, the University of South Carolina, and the University of Oklahoma. On our return trip we attended the Denver meeting of the Mississippi Valley Historical Association and saw many old friends. The trip to the Northwest involved only two stops, Reed College in Portland, and Washington State at Pullman.

I got as much as I gave on these trips. Among other things I learned for a fact that the small colleges quite outdid the large universities in the intimacy of student-faculty relationships, while the drive for distinction in graduate work eclipsed almost every other consideration in the universities. The alertness and responsiveness of the students every-

[1] "Two Postwar Decades," *Nebraska History*, XL (December 1959), 243–264.

where was heartening. At every opportunity I gave them the chance to ask questions and express their own points of view. They seemed to be trying earnestly to think their way through the problems of the present, and I did what I could to assure them, as any historian would, that an adequate knowledge of the past was a prime essential to an understanding of the present. Between the two South Carolina engagements we got in a visit to Charleston, which we had never seen before, and inspected also the remarkable semitropical gardens in the vicinity.

After my year as visiting scholar, the Phi Beta Kappa central office kept me on its list of speakers available for alumni organizations. This resulted in several additional speaking engagements, but for the most part my invitations came from former students and professional acquaintances. Probably I accepted many more such obligations than I should have, but I always enjoyed the new contacts and the challenge of a new audience. Of late years, as on the Phi Beta Kappa tours, I have always taken Lucile with me, even when the honorarium was too small to pay the way for both of us. Some of the most interesting of our recent trips have taken us to Lincoln, Nebraska, where I helped Union College celebrate its seventy-fifth anniversary;[2] to Lewis and Clark College, Portland, Oregon, where I gave the annual Throckmorton lecture;[3] to the University of Wyoming, Laramie, where I chose to tell the students what their state was like sixty years ago; to the United States Air Force Academy, Denver University, and Colorado State University at Fort Collins, all in one well-filled week; and to the University of New Mexico in Albuquerque.

At Fort Collins I spoke two evenings to unusually receptive student audiences of six or seven hundred, the first time on our rural heritage and the next on the urban civilization that had succeeded it.[4] My contention was that in our old town-and-country America we had produced a viable society, one that we could live with and that could live with itself, a state of grace that our fast-growing city economy has by no means reached. At a luncheon session of the Western History Association in San Francisco, October 14, 1967, I exploited the same

2 "Then (1891) and Now (1966); Some Comparisons and Contrasts," *Nebraska History*, XLVII (June 1966), 139–155.
3 "The Urban Revolution," *Pacific Northwest Quarterly*, LVII (October 1966), 181–188.
4 *The Transformation of America* (Norman F. Furniss Lectures in History; Colorado State University, 1967).

theme in an address entitled (with a bow to Turner) "The Significance of the Small Town in American History."

Like most university professors, I have always been an easy touch for local organizations in need of a speaker. From my first teaching years at Hamline on down to the present, I have found it harder to refuse than to accept such invitations. As a result I have spoken to innumerable men's clubs, women's clubs, breakfast clubs, luncheon clubs, dinner clubs, church societies, graduating classes, even political rallies. For these appearances I assume, usually correctly, that there will be no fee; many organizations seem to think that they are doing a mere professor a favor by asking him to speak to them. I have always excused my willingness to accept these invitations on the ground that I was promoting good public relations for my university, but I suspect that the real reason was that I enjoyed each occasion, probably more than my audience enjoyed it. In addition to the outside speeches, I must have made scores—more likely hundreds—of speeches to local campus organizations. Those who think that a university professor's position is a sinecure ought to try following him around.

American audiences, whether they agree with the speaker or not, are invariably courteous and attentive—or so I have found them. I can remember only two occasions when I was completely undone—once in a small Nebraska town where five lusty infants cried in unison and their parents made no move to take them out, and once in a university student union where the room in which I spoke was separated by only a thin fabric curtain from a blues singer, supported by a noisy orchestra. Since on such occasions it was not my habit to use either notes or manuscript, my train of thought was quite completely wrecked.

Nowadays when one confesses that he is from the Berkeley campus, he usually gets the fishy eye. For Berkeley, ever since the Free Speech Movement of 1964, has been associated in the public mind with student rioting and mob violence, a reputation we had won even before the outbreak in the Watts district of Los Angeles. As an emeritus professor I ran no risk of becoming involved directly in these proceedings—an immunity which, unhappily, I had not enjoyed during the year of the oath. But I was on campus throughout the turmoil and as frequently as possible crossed the picket lines that the strikers set up. The trouble started almost accidentally, when some old rules, recast to fit new conditions, seemed to restrain unduly the rights of students to promote political ends on campus. There was nothing in the new wording that was not negotiable; indeed, the administration showed an almost craven eagerness to revise its position to meet the demands of the protesters. The real objective of the agitators, I believed then, and I believe now, was not the redress of grievances, but trouble for trouble's sake. What they wanted to do, although this was not fully understood by most of their followers, was to strike a body blow at the "Establishment," whatever it was and whatever it stood for.

The most astonishing thing in the whole unsavory mess was the behavior of the faculty. As one of my colleagues, Raymond Sontag, once remarked, there are always a number of people who begin to salivate when the words "free speech" are uttered; this attitude, I suspect, is disproportionately high in faculty circles. Some quiet behind-the-scenes maneuvering by our principal droolers eventually placed the University Senate on record, by an overwhelming majority, in favor of the student agitators and against the administration. Bad as this was, the administration itself, unfortunately, was not of one mind, with the Berkeley chancellor and the university president somewhat at odds. Had the trouble come on a campus other than Berkeley, it is unlikely that the president would have interfered, but the over-all administration of the university and the president's residence were both in Berkeley. In army terms, the local commandant was hampered by the fact that the "old man" lived on the post. President Kerr's proximity to the conflict and his belief in his abilities as a conciliator (he had had much experience in settling labor disputes) inevitably drew him in. At the present time, I believe, the president would refuse to play a leading role in any such disturbance and would leave the chancellor free to operate as he thought best. But the separation of functions was not then as clearly drawn as at present. Certainly the differences between the president and the chancellor, which led eventually to the chancellor's resignation, added to the unsavory nature of the conflict.

In the end the F.S.M. got nearly everything its leaders asked for, but meanwhile several hundred students and nonstudents had staged a sit-down strike in Sproul Hall, and by order of the governor of the state had been arrested. Their appeal to civil disobedience had in a sense paid off, although those arrested had to stand trial and many of them took stiff sentences. When, two years later, another flare-up occurred, the Senate reversed its attitude and stood by the administration, with many of the former recalcitrants now supporting the loyalists against the rebels. Perhaps the faculty had by this time realized that the chief promoters of unrest were less interested in furthering a cause than in producing a conflict. In both the first and the second disturbances the attitude of the overwhelming majority of the students varied from indifference to downright hostility toward the troublemakers.

It was ironic that Clark Kerr, who had somehow got the train back on the track again, was at this late date dismissed by the regents. But there was, of course, a political factor involved. Ronald Reagan, as candidate for governor, had taken full advantage of public resentment against disorder in the university, and had virtually declared war against Kerr for his handling of the situation. At the first meeting of the board of regents after Reagan's election, the new Governor discovered that he had the votes he needed to fire Kerr, and joined happily in the execution. The political nature of this removal was quite as obvious as in the removal of Glenn Frank by the LaFollette forces in Wisconsin more than two decades before.

The spirit of protest on the part of modern youth, both inside and outside our universities, is not something we can ignore. We may take comfort from the fact that the extremists are only a noisy minority, but they are numerous enough that we need to find out, if we can, the causes of their dissidence. There is good reason to believe that their rebellious attitude is in some way related to our current affluence. The historic lot of mankind is to struggle; even in America, as long as rural conditions predominated, the struggle for existence was very real. Now, in our mainly urban environment, machines do most of the work and mankind no longer has to struggle very hard. And yet the urge to struggle, whether instinct or tradition, remains. Is it so surprising that youngsters who find themselves bereft of the necessity of struggling *for* something turn in desperation to struggling *against* what they have?

Nor can we blame everything on the younger generation. Ours is an age of violent antagonisms. As John Gardner, until recently Secretary of Health, Education and Welfare, once said: "More and more, hostility and venom are the hallmarks of any conversation on the affairs of the nation. Today, all seem caught up in mutual recriminations—Negro and white, rich and poor, conservative and liberal, hawk and dove, labor and management, North and South, young and old." Perhaps he should have added "students and teachers." Currently our Berkeley activists are busy protesting the war in Vietnam and picketing the Oakland draft center. But if the war were to end today and the draft tomorrow, the dawn of the following day would see a new protest movement take form, led by the same discontented intransigents.

Within our campuses I give little credence to the inconsequential but chronic student gripes that professional protesters try to build up into causes. For example, the notion that students grieve deeply because they can't see more of their professors is totally phony. In general, they want to see less rather than more of their teachers. Trying to get students to come in for personal conferences, as all of us who are honest know, is like pulling teeth. Young people have so many more interesting things to do than chewing the fat with untrustworthy characters over thirty. Even so, the agitators would still be unappeased if we could provide two young (but bearded) professors to shoot the bull continuously with each hairy student, taking time out only for free love as needed and an occasional psychedelic trip. Most of the hell-raisers really don't know what they want, but they are not about to give up until they get it.

Sometimes I look back with a degree of respect to the Communist-inspired rebels of the 1930's. They at least had a vision of something they thought worth while, a plan toward which to work. They dreamed of an ideal society which would take from each according to his abilities and give to each according to his needs. But the social dropouts of today want only to live as parasites, taking everything they can get and giving nothing in return. If they believe in anything, it is that whatever is, is wrong, and that there is no remedy in sight but total destruction. To be consistent, they should welcome, not protest against, an atomic war, for that would get the world over its sickness in a hurry.

Occasionally I am asked, "Are you an optimist or a pessimist?" My answer to that question is double-barreled. In the short run, considering only the immediate future, I find it hard not to be a pessimist. There are so many problems for which we can think of no quick and easy answers. But in the long run I think I am an optimist. As far as our great universities are concerned, they will not be destroyed, even if perchance for a few days they may come close to a "grinding halt." Such an institution as the University of California, for example, has picked up far too much momentum to be held back. It will continue. From it and from other centers of learning will come the new knowledge that will enable society to grapple more successfully with the problems that confront it. If the scientists of our time can put a man on the moon, as they seem about to do, surely scientists of the future can find cures for our limping civilization, ways to clean up the air we breathe and the water we drink, to restrain the population explosion, and to conserve our dwindling resources. Surely, too, we can count on our experts in the social studies and the humanities to provide adequate underpinnings for that "great society" we all long to achieve. From their efforts we may expect an abatement of the curse of war, improved systems of city government, better race relations, greater efficiency in both business and government, closer cooperation between labor and management, decent housing and job security for all. As a nation, as a civilization, we have come a long way. Why should we now falter and fail?

There is an element of hope in the recognition of an existing evil, and I think we recognize clearly most of the evils that now beset us. And we are working, however haltingly, to restrain them. We know that the millennium is not just around the corner, that equal justice for all is a distant, not an immediate, goal, that peace is not likely to come in our time; but as long as our will to strive for worthy ends endures, we have a right to cling to our faith in man and in man's ability to cope with the problems he has created.

As a footnote to my long-range optimism, I can cite a series of heartening interviews I had recently with high school seniors who had applied for university scholarships. Since, presumably, I had nothing better to do (and that certainly turned out to be the truth), I was asked to meet seventeen of these youngsters, each for a half hour, to rate them on personality traits. Grade screening had already established their superior scholarship; each candidate had a practically straight-A average. Also, they all came from low-income families; perhaps that, too, was a condition of eligibility. The experience was unexpectedly exciting; no one could possibly doubt the high potential of these boys and girls for constructive leadership. Several of them had grown up without a father in the home and had helped with the support of the family. Indeed, for some of the boys, the necessity of assuming responsibility that should have belonged to a father had quite clearly firmed up their characters. Many of the applicants had held class offices; some from the humblest of homes were senior class presidents. Not one of them was yet eighteen years of age. They were all so beautiful, so full of vitality, so competent beyond their years. Sometimes, between interviews, I had to take time out to wipe the tears from my eyes. If our country can produce children like these, all is not yet lost.

XVII. Other Lands and Seas

My STORY would not be complete without some account of the foreign travel Lucile and I have been able to work in during the years of my retirement. I am not a compulsive traveler—quite the reverse—but Lucile enjoys going places and seeing things, and with no teaching responsibilities to bar the way I had trouble in thinking up excuses for thwarting her wishes. We had long agreed that we would celebrate the year of my retirement with another trip to Europe. I had attempted to find an excuse for this extravagance by offering my services gratis to the Salzburg Seminar for any month, or even a longer period, during the summer or fall of 1957. The local director of the Seminar, George W. Adams (the same who had been one of my Harvard readers) so recommended, but the American managers apparently had other plans, for when their invitation came it was for January, 1958. Since we had no more interest in a European winter than in one of our own choice mid-western winters, I turned the offer down and the two of us set out on an unconducted tour, leaving early in the fall for a two-and-one-half-month venture. We had had our fill of crossing the Atlantic by ship, so this time we planned to make the long jumps by air. We flew first by way of New York to Scotland and took in the famous Edinburgh Music Festival, a fascinating experience. Most thrilling of all was the final military tattoo, with the massed bands and marchers assembled in the courtyard of Edinburgh Castle.

Leaving Edinburgh, we took a bus through the lake country of northern England, which we had somehow missed before, then on down through western England to London. A group of noisy and smelly German students detracted somewhat from the pleasure of this experience, but we met an Englishwoman whose intelligent conversation balanced them out. We saw Windsor Castle with an expensive guide, then went by train to Cambridge, where we revisited the familiar scenes of seven years before. Most of the people we had known were away on vacation, but the Christopher Morrises of King's College insisted on our being their house guests, and gave us another fine example of English hospitality.

Our continental tour included Berlin, Vienna, Milan, and Venice, cities we had missed before; also portions of Switzerland, Greece, Sicily, Spain, and Portugal. We were impressed both with the increase in the amount of tourism and the facilities available for handling it. We found Europe much more prosperous than it had been seven years before, with an incredible amount of building going on. The scars of war were less in evidence, and the success of American aid under the Marshall Plan was obvious. The remarkable comeback of Germany, together with the hardness of the mark, were constant subjects of conversation. Much of the change, we thought, was due to the affinity of the German people for hard work, a characteristic less in evidence among the English.

While some of the recent building was primarily to replace wartime destruction, some of it seemed also to suggest the beginning of a new era. West Berlin was in the process of being made over into a different, more beautiful, and quite un-German-looking city, in striking contrast to the Stalinist efforts in East Berlin, which we also saw. The Vienna Opera House lived again, partly a restoration, but partly newly conceived. We worked in two operas while we were there. In Salzburg we were surprised by a new highrise hotel, in design not unlike the United Nations building in New York. Even more amazing was a new Catholic church we visited. I had always supposed that in Europe people *had* their churches, much as in Boston the dowagers *have* their hats, but here was as modern a building as we had ever seen, with utterly unchurchlike lines and an impressionistic Christ sketched on its façade. Inside, the altar was in the center of the church and consisted merely of a great stone slab surmounted by an unadorned cross. The stations of the cross were mere marks on the wall, and outside the door by which we left were crude, almost childlike drawings, done in the cement while it was still wet. There was something about the building that made it seem peculiarly appropriate to our age, as if Christianity were a little ahead of the rest of the world in liquidating the past and starting over.

Asked repeatedly after we got home what country or what people we liked best, we were completely at a loss for a reply. We loved the English; among them we felt more as if we were visiting relatives whom we liked than as if we were travelers in a foreign land. But the English climate is dreadful and sometimes the food isn't much better. We liked the friendliness of the Germans and Austrians, at least as individuals. In groups they sometimes bothered us, as, for example, when we changed planes in Frankfort, and were jostled by the strictly German passengers, who ran all over us and each other in their efforts to be first to board the plane. After the politeness of the English queues, this was hard to take. We liked the miraculous cleanliness of the Swiss and the beauty of the Alps, but the people of Switzerland seemed a bit calculating, and a little above it all. Here, incidentally, we saw more evidence of military might than anywhere else in Europe. The Swiss are proud of their army and their defenses, and by design, I suppose, leave much of the latter out in the open for all the world to ponder. We admired the palaces of Austria, the churches of Rome, the broad avenues of Madrid, the ruins of Greece and Sicily, the quaintness of Portuguese Nazaré; but we could hardly say which we liked most. We liked least the glimpses we got of abject poverty; these are not to be seen on the usual tourist routes, and we saw them only occasionally and fleetingly. But they were there and they were terrifying. We shall never forget a visit we made, without benefit of tourist agents, to some Palermo slums.

There was much about Spain that intrigued us. The pinkish hue of the landscape, as viewed from the air, was not altogether dispelled by more intimate contact, and the high plains and mountains reminded us of our own American West. We also liked the Spanish people we met. They served us well without being obsequious. They were models of dignity and restraint, unlike the Greeks and Italians, who were all over us like a cloud all the time. The Spanish were understandably proud of their ancient monuments, and enjoyed talking about their former imperial greatness. But they showed no regret that those times had passed. Indeed, they seemed a little sorry for people who were going through that experience. Their interest lay in bettering their conditions at home, without thought of expanding Spanish culture or civilization abroad. They were glad to have tourists and treated them well, but were unwilling to do any groveling for anyone. Once I tried to give our Spanish driver a tip when we were halfway through a trip of several days, but he rejected it in embarrassment. "I'm not through yet," he said simply. That was the first money I'd offered anyone in Europe that hadn't been reached for before I got my pocketbook open.

Politically, the Spanish accepted Franco as better than chaos, but they showed no enthusiasm for him.

We were interested, of course, in the attitude of our European allies toward the United States. I got the distinct impression that they would be with us and for us only as long as we were top dog. Great Britian would, of course, resist invasion; she had not known that humiliation since 1066, or at least since 1216. But the rest of them would fight only as long as they thought we could win for them. There is a limit to the number of times a people can be conquered and retain its will to resist. Take Italy, for example, and Sicily in particular. Everybody has romped over Sicily from the beginning of time. The Phoenicians got there thirty centuries ago, the Greeks in the eighth century B.C., and after that in turn came the Carthaginians, the Romans, the Vandals, the Goths, the Byzantines, the Saracens, the Normans, the French, the Spanish, the mainland Italians, the Americans, and no doubt a few others I've forgotten. Each wave of invaders left its train of ruins, not among the least the Americans, whose landing beach we saw. Is it any wonder that the Sicilians of our time have come to the conclusion that their best course is to yield to any conqueror who comes in force? They suffer less that way; besides, for the great majority, what is there to lose anyway? Sicily, of course, was an extreme example, but we got the impression that other parts of Europe also had had about all the beatings they could take.

Possibly we profited most from our visit to Greece. We found conditions there less comfortable for us than in Western Europe, for the Greeks were only just beginning to cultivate tourism. But, as one of our party remarked, "They try so hard." Admittedly they have little but their ruins to offer, for Eastern Europe had no Renaissance to produce the magnificent cathedrals and palaces we saw in the West. We visited a little Byzantine church in Athens and a nineteenth-century church; apparently there were no churches worth seeing in between. Nor was there any Reformation, either Protestant or Catholic, in Eastern Europe; as nearly as we could tell, the Greek Orthodox Church stood about where it had stood a thousand years before, uninfluenced by a Martin Luther, a John Calvin, or an Ignatius Loyola. The great poverty of the country was also depressing; in so many places deforestation and erosion had destroyed the very foundations of agriculture. Some of the lesser Greek islands we visited had lost nearly every handful of soil into the sea. It was hard to believe that once they had sustained great centers of civilization.

But the ruins were everywhere, impressive reminders that our own civilization, like that of the ancient Greeks, might sometime consist mainly of ruins. Over the entrance to a Swiss cemetery we had read recently in German: "What you are, we were; what we are, you will be." That might go for civilizations as well as for individuals; the ruins of the Old World would seem to prove it. Worst of all, so many of the ruins were man-made. After allowing as much as possible for the damage done by earthquakes and time, the evidence was still conclusive that city after city had met its end at the hands of some ruthless invaders. At Corinth, where the Roman soldiers had done their worst to destroy what they found, I managed to come up with a happy thought. In the end, I reflected, the superior aspects of Greek culture triumphed even over the Romans. And after Rome went down before the barbarians, the barbarians in turn recognized that what they had conquered was better than what they had, so they likewise absorbed the superior culture. Applying all this to our own age, in which only a "balance of terror" keeps the peace, I wondered if our culture wouldn't in the end survive even if we did go down before our current adversaries and our cities became mere rubble. Maybe, in the end, even if we lost, like the Greeks, we'd win.

In the fall of 1958 we were off again, this time for a three-week tour of Mexico, accompanied by our close friends Frank and Mildred ("Billie") Russell. The four of us drove together to Tijuana, then took a plane to Guadalajara, where our guide, Tulio del Pino, met us with an ancient DeSoto. Tulio worked for a Mexico City tourist agency and was to serve as our driver and constant companion during the rest of our trip. He was a young man thirty-one years of age, of excellent intelligence, one-fourth Italian and three-fourths Chamula Indian, amiable and eager to please. He was born, he told us, far to the south, near the Guatemala border, one of a family of nine, all living in a one-room shack with no windows and a dirt floor. For clothes he wore only a breachcloth and a serape with a hole in it to enable him to pull it on over his head. Until he was twelve years old he never had a pair of shoes. He went to the village school, and because he was the brightest boy in his class, the government gave him a scholarship to continue his education in Mexico City. His mother was all for his accepting this opportunity, but his father opposed it, for he needed Tulio's help on the land. Tulio's father was a peon, hardly freer from the patron who owned the land than a slave. Women, Tulio insisted, had no rights in a Mexican family, where the husband and father made all decisions, but somehow, despite his father's objections, Tulio made it to the capital, where he acquired a good knowledge of Spanish and English, and enough history and economics to pass the examinations in those subjects required to become a guide. He hoped eventually to get into the diplomatic service and to obtain an assignment with the United Nations in New York, but that, he said, would require a knowledge of six different languages. He was full of misconceptions about the United States, but he was ahead of his time in arguing that the Washington government should parallel its Marshall Plan with equivalent aid to Latin America—this long before the Alliance for Progress took form. Tulio's wife, whom we met in Mexico City, was pure Aztec, but the Del Pino family lived respectably with their children in a little apartment and had definitely middle-class standards. From meeting them and a few others like them, we took heart that the beginning of a middle class in Mexico might be in sight.

Our itinerary took us through the larger cities of central Mexico, nearly but not quite as far east as Veracruz, and south to Oaxaca. With one exception we stayed everywhere at modern hotels, but what is known variously as the "tourista," "the Aztec curse," and "Montezuma's revenge" followed us relentlessly wherever we went. Only Billie, about whose health we had had the most concern, remained fairly normal throughout the trip. I understood and later repeated the remark of one of my friends, who had preceded us on a similar junket, that he had seen Mexico "from all the best bathrooms." My first glimpse of Popocatepetl, I recall, was from exactly this position. We took every possible precaution, but within twenty-four hours after entering Mexico I was miserable, despite the sulfasuxidine I had brought with me and the *vio formo interno* pills that Tulio had recommended. Frequently the only way I could ensure myself against trouble going from one city to another was by taking an overdose of paregoric. Sanitation is just not one of Mexico's outstanding accomplishments. Even the natives suffer from diarrhea frequently, according to Tulio, who once had a bout with it himself during our tour. An early entry in Lucile's diary tells a lot about Mexico. "Guadalajara," she wrote, "has narrow streets, open-door shops, flies, and a beautiful cathedral."

Perhaps my internal disorder warped my judgment, but I found Mexico far more foreign than any nation I had visited in Europe.

Oddly, the next most foreign area I recalled seeing was French Canada, also in the Western Hemisphere. Of course, the Mexican people, with a few exceptions, are not European at all, but Indian, and dark-skinned at that. Nor were the clothes they wore very suggestive of Europe— wide-brimmed straw hats and sandals for the men, long black skirts and *robozas*, or shawls, for the women. The presence of donkeys in large numbers was not unlike southern Europe, but the donkey is every- where only a badge of poverty, and the Mexicans were certainly poor. The population explosion had something to do with that situation; nearly half the women carried babies wound up somewhere in their *robozas*—no baby buggies. If not encumbered by babies, they often had big baskets of clothes or other burdens on their heads. Passenger buses infested the roads, with people standing in the aisles, spilling out on the steps, or even riding on the roofs. On second-class buses they took along pigs, chickens, turkeys, and bundles of every size and shape. The villages through which we drove were appallingly filthy, squalid, and ugly. Farmhouses at the side of the road followed the same pattern, but the larger cities were much better. Mexico City was a modern metropolis by any standards. There we lived in a fine modern hotel, but the insecurity of what should have been terra firma made it list slightly to one side. The whole city seems to be sinking.

Our tourist bureau tried to show us a little of everything in Mexico and succeeded pretty well. We stayed one night in Uruapan, a city of less than twenty thousand, but not visited often enough by tourists to have anything better than a Mexican-type hotel. The hotel floors were bare, the beds were hard, the toilet (which I used constantly) was primitive, and the bath tub needed scouring. We were the only guests at table and the menu was the same noon and night—not bad, although the beef was freshly killed. There was one bellhop, a thirteen-year-old boy, whom we sent all over town in search of an electric light bulb strong enough to enable us to read by it—in vain. There was a hand- loom factory in town, which Lucile and Billie visited, acquiring in the process quantities of beautiful colored fabrics. To most women, I've learned both by experience and by observation, shopping is the better part of travel. We soon added two huge hampers to our luggage, one for the Russells and one for ourselves, into which the loot went for transportation home. We had to carry it back home ourselves; Tulio and others who seemed to know admitted that the risk of its being stolen if mailed back was too great to take. Poverty and light-fingeredness go together. The wages of the Uruapan loom workers were $1.20 per day.

The roads over which Tulio drove us were sometimes good, but more often terrible. The mountain curves were a little breath-taking, particularly the way Tulio took them. The hillsides were brilliantly green, with occasional cornfields on the steepest slopes, oxen drawing crude implements; only once did we spot a tractor. The government was doing something, Tulio said, toward dividing up the great estates, but what the country needed most was an agricultural revolution to bring it into the twentieth century. East of Mexico City we got into the tropical areas where bananas, coffee, citrus fruits, and sugar cane were the chief products, often intermingled in what appeared to be impenetrable jungles.

Tourism was by no means new to Mexico, so there were plenty of luxury resorts. We stayed at several of them, including San Jose de Purua, where mineral baths were the special attraction; a sumptuous hotel in Taxco, the silversmiths' center where our women lost their heads and their money; the Hacienda Vista Hermosa, a former sugar refinery now converted into a hotel; and a place in Fortin where exotic flowers bloomed in the patios and baskets of gardenias floated in the swimming pool. We kept away from Acapulco, which seemed to be too completely a tourist trap for our purposes and not worth the cost, but we were twice in Mexico City and altogether spent about a week there. Here we had less trouble with the "tourista," and in addition had many interesting sights to see. We visited churches, museums, government buildings, and especially the university, where elaborate mosaics on the exterior walls of the buildings provided a unique touch —"cartoons," my friend Bill Hesseltine called them. We went to a bull fight, but after the death of the first bull we retired, slightly shaken. On our trip south we visited the ruins at Mitla and the pyramids of Monte Alban.

Mainly we got the feel of a different and distinctive nationality. The extremes of wealth and poverty, with too little in between, were painfully apparent, but we left with the impression that there was hope ahead—that education was making slow headway, and that at least a small fraction of the lower class were on the way up. Politically, the appearance of democracy was deceptive. Despite pretenses to the contrary, the governing party had no notion of permitting the opposition to grow strong. One got the impression, however, that the nation's leaders had the welfare of the people at heart and were doing what they could to overcome the heavy load of inertia they had inherited.

Our next trip outside the United States was delayed until 1964, mainly because of illnesses that overtook me in the early 1960's. We had long promised our oldest granddaughter, Kathleen Pierce, a trip around the world after her tenth birthday, but my doctor vetoed the Indian and African sectors of that junket, so she had to settle for a visit to Japan and East Asia. With her teacher's consent we took her out of school early in May and flew first to Hawaii, which she loved so much we could hardly tear her away. There we met a small tour group— only eight all told—with which we traveled for the next five weeks. We were fortunate in our companions, whose presence made the trip much more interesting than if the three of us had gone on our own. We had an escort who saw us from country to country and, in addition, a local guide in each. Kathleen, the only child in the party, soon became a universal favorite; also, she proved to be as helpful to the guide in keeping us rounded up as a sheep dog to a herder. We were not wrong on our theory that the age of ten years would be ideal for taking a child on a trip. Kathleen had eyes for everything and remembered more about what she saw then either of her grandparents. Moreover, she was as capable of taking care of herself as an adult and was immune alike to children's diseases and adolescent emotions.

We landed at Tokyo and put up for several days at the Imperial hotel—the new section, not the old Frank Lloyd Wright creation. On walking through the latter we decided that our travel agent had done well to place us where he did. The old section, we thought, was cut up into too many small rooms, and showed little feeling for light and space. We were impressed, as no doubt all visitors to Japan are, with the hordes of people everywhere; the dense crowds, almost any time any place, resembled the masses of people we were accustomed to see only as we were leaving a football stadium. School children in attractive uniforms were much in evidence at the appropriate times of day, not just in hundreds but in thousands. The whole city was torn up in preparation for the coming Olympics, but we saw no evidence of impatience or bad manners. The Japanese have to be well disciplined, I suppose, just to be able to live together in such prodigious numbers.

We submitted willingly to the tyranny of our guide, Mr. Sugita, a miracle of efficiency. Why people think they can do so much better fumbling around by themselves, I'll never know. The experts in tourism know better than the tourists what is worth seeing and the guides know how to get you there. One of our most interesting trips was by train to Nikko, where we visited the Toshuga shrine, a marvel of complicated architecture, with decorations so intricate as to make European baroque seem like simplicity itself. Busloads of children were everywhere, always well behaved and completely obedient to their sponsors. How do they do it? we wondered. When we asked Mr. Sugita, he said: "Oh, that's just our way of life." A dinner at the Mikado, a Tokyo night club, gave us an opportunity to see some remarkably original acts, one of which was a dance of the fountains, with colored lights playing on patterns of water that took up one whole side of the room. Another night we saw a girlie show (three hundred of them) that quite eclipsed the Rockettes, except that all Japanese girls have crooked legs, the result, I suppose, of sitting the way they do. To most places we visited we went by bus, with a little "beep-beep" girl, smaller than Kathleen, always on hand to help the driver with the inevitable parking problem. She would hop outside when occasion demanded, and by beeps from her whistle guide our unwieldy vehicle into spaces that looked to be about half the size of the bus.

One noon we had as our guests at lunch a Japanese teacher, T. Gamo, Jr., with whom I had corresponded for years, and his tiny wife. After lunch they took us by subway to their home, a typically fragile Japanese house, with sliding doors between the rooms, mats on the floors, and for furniture only low tables and pillows. We met Mr. Gamo's father, a distinguished scholar who, like his son, spoke English acceptably, Mrs. Gamo, Sr., the two little Gamo children, and an aunt who put us through the tea ceremony (we flunked miserably). We came off second best, too, in the exchange of gifts, although I consoled myself with the thought that I had previously sent Mr. Gamo several books. Kathleen emerged with one of those elaborately over-dressed Japanese dolls.

Just how my correspondence with the junior Gamo began, I cannot now recall, but it started soon after World War II with an exchange of opinions on international affairs. Both father and son were intensely anti-Communist and appreciated deeply the postwar aid the United States had given Japan. They have been sent separately on educational missions to the United States, and both of them have been in our Berkeley home. The senior Gamo, incidentally, translated with ease the ornate old Japanese calligraphy of a *kakemono* that hangs on our

OTHER LANDS AND SEAS   341

dining-room wall. I had assured Lucile, when I first saw it, that it was a come-on sign for a brothel, but it turned out to be a very formal note of congratulation to the master of the house on reaching the age of seventy.

From Tokyo we flew to Osaka and got a good view of Fujiyama on the way, a good thing, for when we approached it later by land the fog closed it in. We then took a ship through the Inland Sea to Beppu, where we experienced the elaborate hospitality of a Japanese inn, then by rail to Hiroshima, the restoration of which seemed to be quite complete. On the train, just before we reached Hiroshima, a messenger from the mayor delivered to me, as the oldest member of the party, a huge bouquet by way of welcome. It was, of course, a mere tourist ploy, but I was deeply touched and made a little speech of acceptance. Somehow I can't quite imagine a greeter from Pearl Harbor carrying gifts to a visiting Japanese professor, although the Honolulu Chamber of Commerce thinks of nearly everything.

Our admiration for the Japanese people, their intelligence, their industry, their politeness, their ability to get things done increased with each new contact. They have even made the grade in sanitation. When Mr. Sugita told us that we could safely drink tap water anywhere in Japan and eat whatever food our hotels offered, we were skeptical. But he was right; no "tourista." What a contrast to Mexico! Another, quite different contrast—the Japanese don't mind being photographed; indeed, when they have finished posing for you, they often produce a camera and ask you to pose for them. Kathleen, who to them was a pronounced blond, they found particularly entrancing, and they repeatedly captured her on film.

We saw all we could of Japan in the time allotted, then flew on to Taipei, the capital of Taiwan, the Formosa of our old geographies. By some stroke of luck we were routed first class for this trip instead of tourist, as our tickets called for, and as a result were served the most elaborate dinner we had ever eaten—drinks before and after, and more courses with a different wine for each than we could remember. Our hotel in Taipei was very elaborate, too, a show place built, no doubt, with American money. But the few days we spent on the island revealed pretty clearly that by Oriental standards Taiwan was prosperous. Chiang Kai-shek's government might not be popular with the natives, although no one there told us that, but it had at least done a competent economic job. While American aid had no doubt played a great part in bringing this about, the day of dependence on outside help was about over. We looked in vain for evidence of the long pre–World War II Japanese occupation; perhaps its chief legacy was to condition the residents of the island to alien rule. To our eyes, everything we saw was Chinese, not Japanese. There was a sharp contrast, for example, between the spic-and-span condition of the Japanese temples and the unkempt Chinese temples of Taipei. Before leaving Taiwan we spent a few days in the luxurious surroundings of Sun-Moon Lake, a tourist's paradise.

Our next flight took us to Manila, where Ron and Janet Baird, old friends from Berkeley temporarily stationed in the Philippines, helped make our stay interesting. I was pleased to note that my mental picture of Manila Bay, which played quite a role in American history, was reasonably accurate. We felt quite at home, with English signs to guide us and "jeepneys" coursing through the streets. The combination of American and Spanish influence reminded us of what we had seen along the Mexican border. And felt, too, for Lucile promptly came down with the "tourista." Despite that handicap she acquired some interesting examples of Philippine wood carving and other art treasures toward which Janet had guided her.

The trouble with these tours, of course, is that one sees too many countries too fast. After a few days we flew from Manila to Saigon, where we touched down only to change planes and were not permitted even to leave the airport. We talked to some uniformed American flyers in the airport, but they were completely discreet and told us not a thing about local conditions. A small local plane with French pilots took us on to Pnompenh, where we were to change planes again for Angkor Wat. As we entered the Pnompenh airport, I heard a familiar booming voice and said to Lucile: "There's only one person in the world who talks like that." We turned around to greet our next-door neighbor, Edward Kent, who with his wife and two other neighbors were on their way to Thailand and India. "It's a small world," we recited in unison. As a matter of fact, only a few days before in Kyoto we had had a similar meeting with Professor and Mrs. George Stewart, also of Berkeley. We Americans do get around.

The ruins of Angkor Wat were vast and awesome, but the damp days we drew there brought out the smell of all the urine that had accumulated through the ages, and hastened us on our way. Not, however, until we had nearly lost our minds trying to keep an eye on Kathleen, who climbed to the steepest temple eminences like a mountain goat. Our hotel in nearby Siemreap was French in character, like everything else European in the area, and not very good. We also got the feeling that our presence there was merely tolerated and by no means desired. The food was bad, service nonexistent, and all signs of welcome totally missing. We were glad when our brandied-up pilots got us out, with another stop at Pnompenh, for Bangkok.

Bangkok had a lot to show. Probably there are more richly decorated temples and golden Buddhas to be seen here than anywhere else in the world, and we must have seen most of them. By this time, however, the "tourista" had caught up with both Kathleen and me, and we sometimes preferred to stay in our air-conditioned room at the Hotel Rama. We all managed to inspect the King's Palace, where, despite the stifling heat, protocol required the men to wear their coats and ties. The plentiful use of gold in the elaborate decorations contrasted markedly with the poverty so in evidence elsewhere in the city, particularly along the *klongs*. We worked our way in a little open launch through the city's intricate network of canals, and saw sights on the banks alongside that did little to settle our stomachs. The *klongs* are little better than open sewers, but the people use the water for every known purpose. At one point we landed for lunch, but no one seemed to have much of an appetite. The women of our party, unable to escape the spray raised by our boat and others, could hardly wait to get back to their rooms to rid themselves of every stitch they had on and to take prolonged baths.

Street scenes—for there are also streets—showed school children in uniform, each with a big brief case in hand, a kind of status symbol, we assumed; workers weaving through the crowds, carrying great baskets of produce, one basket at each end of a pole slung across their shoulders; tiny tots playing on the sidewalks outside dark and dirty shops. Then, of course, there are sections with European-style buildings, where only the people look strange.

We flew via Kuala Lumpur to Singapore and from our plane windows could see the curious landforms that constitute the Malay Peninsula. A day or two in the hot and sticky former outpost of British imperialism was all that we could stand. Our guide told us that the temperatures were at all seasons just about as we found them—hot to hotter, morning, noon, and night. He took us to see where the Japanese had invaded from Johore; how, we wondered, could the British have expected anything else? Our guide was Jewish, and I had the temerity to ask him how his people got along with the Chinese, whose dominance in business seemed so obvious. "Oh, we can't compete with them," he replied. "Our people are leaving. There were once about eight hundred of us, now only three or four hundred."

Our tour took us from Singapore to Brunei in British Borneo, a mistake in planning, we thought, but we were wrong. The Brunei hotel accommodations were primitive, with no hot water except that heated by the sun on the outside pipes, but we found it a relief to be in a clean little town, free from great hordes of people, especially tourists. Only during the preceding two years had Brunei been on any tourist route, and it was still generally bypassed, but we thought it well worth the trip. The river city, where about fifteen thousand natives live in houses on stilts, particularly impressed us. Unlike the dwellings along the Bangkok *klongs*, the Brunei river cottages were attractive, sometimes painted in bright colors, and with a fresh, clean look about them. The secret of the cleanliness was in large part the river current, which was swift enough to carry all debris away. Children, many of them naked, rushed to the railings everywhere to greet us. Our guide (Chinese, inevitably) pointed out two small hospitals, a midwife's residence, a schoolhouse wide open to the breezes, and small grocery stores, all on the river. People get around in boats, one of which is tied in front of each cottage. The government is trying to induce the river dwellers to accept gifts of land and move ashore, but they like the way they live and refuse to leave.

Another high point of our trip to Brunei was the mosque, said to be the largest and most beautiful building of its kind in Southeast Asia. The territory around Brunei and the city itself consitute a British protectorate, but ostensibly it is ruled by a Sultan, who, needless to say, gets along well with his advisers. He collects oil revenues, so he is not without means, but we noted that his palace is quite unostentatious. When it came to the mosque, however, he had spared no expense. Its main feature is an immense gold dome, balanced by a strikingly tall minaret off to one side. We took an elevator part way up the minaret, but to reach the windows at the top we had also several flights of stairs to climb. The inner halls of the mosque are spacious and light, with handsome, well-kept tile floors. During our tour of inspection someone out of sight was chanting, perhaps a muezzin calling the faithful to prayer. Near one entrance to the mosque was a large pool of clear water, meant probably for the ablutions of the people coming in to pray, but being used at the moment by children happily dumping buckets of water over each other.

Our next and final stop was at Hong Kong, left until the last, no doubt, so that the women could spend all their remaining traveler's checks on bargains. Between purchases we did the customary sightseeing, and what we saw was certainly worth the effort. But the squalor of life that enveloped the great majority of the residents, including the water people, was oppressive. Adding to the population pressure was the constant flow of refugees from Red China. We visited the New Territory, saw where the British colony left off and the domain of Mao Tse-tung began, reflected on how hopeless Hong Kong would be against a determined attack from the mainland. Local residents, including our guide, refused to worry about that. Hong Kong, they said, was too important to Red China as an exchange center to the West; on this account it would not be molested. We were carefully warned however, against buying from any of the Communist-owned stores, since goods from Red China would not be passed by the American customs. As a matter of fact, some of the things Lucile bought from recommended dealers failed to get through. We took the hydrofoil from Hong Kong to Macao, saw what little was worth seeing there, and realized that the Portuguese colony, like Hong Kong, existed only by sufferance.

From Hong Kong to Tokyo, from Tokyo to Honolulu, and from Honolulu to San Francisco. Back to our own sufficiently crowded streets, we could understand the inquiry of a visitor from Japan: "Where are all the people?"

Two years later we were off again, this time in late October, with a party of thirty-three on a luxury cruise to the South Pacific. Life on shipboard, as I had previously experienced it, made me pretty skeptical about spending five or six weeks at sea, but I took a chance that I was now old enough and tired enough to welcome the endless hours of inactivity. Our ship, the *Mariposa*, was a triumph of aquatic splendor. It could care for over three hundred passengers and a considerable burden of freight—much of the latter, we learned, consisted of frozen foods for residents of the tropical islands we were to visit. Our party, most of whom we had never met before, had a common interest in the Children's Hospital of the East Bay, to which the Matson Line had agreed to contribute a percentage of our passage money. So, for whatever comfort it might give us, we could reflect that we were serving a good cause and our own pleasure at the same time.

Life aboard ship was like a continuous house party. Our group held down a half-dozen tables in one corner of the dining room and we soon got to know each other well. There was the usual high proportion of widows among us, but this fact provoked an attitude of gallantry among the outnumbered men that was good for all concerned. The *Mariposa* was a happy ship, with friendliness between officers, crew, and passengers in constant evidence. There were ship parties of one kind or another nearly every night; my black tie was almost worn out by the time we got back home. Whenever the ship failed to serve free drinks before dinner, we took turns serving them to each other in our staterooms or in the cocktail lounge; no one was allowed to remain thirsty for long. There were the usual bingo bouts and horse races, fancy-hat and costume parties, and a variety of musical events, deck sports, shuffleboard, calesthenics, and the like, but one could ignore such activities at will and I often so willed. We had a commodious stateroom, with two comfortable chairs, two beds, and a table on which we could write. We brought a box of books along and I got caught up with my reading. Also I did some writing—several chapters of this book took form on the ship.

We docked first at Los Angeles, then for a full week plowed straight ahead into the tropics. By day it was hot on deck, and many of the passengers sprawled about near the swimming pool, cultivating a sun tan and sometimes achieving instead some painful blisters. Others were content to plant themselves in deck chairs and watch the endless motion of the sea. The motion of the ship was insignificant; at the first sign of turbulence the stabilizers took over, but they were rarely needed. Inside, the ship was air-conditioned throughout. This distressed me, for I have always noted that colds and air conditioning go together. There was nothing we could do about it, for the portholes of our stateroom were not made to be opened. The results were predictable. With cool air circulating rapidly throughout the ship, everybody's germs got a free ride to everybody else, and a severe respiratory infection spread through the passengers and crew. Lucile and I waited apprehensively until our turn came, but we hadn't long to wait. The ship doctor took good care of us, but for ten days or so we were well below par. I think a study should be made of the relationship between air conditioning and colds with a view to preventing the former from promoting the latter.

Our first landfall was Bora Bora. Everyone got up early that morning to watch the island's most striking feature, a high mountain shaped like a plug hat, rise above the horizon. This view should be familiar to all Americans who turn the advertising pages of our slick magazines, for during the past year the Matson Line has run a picture of it in most of them. Time after time we watched while a high-powered team of professionals arranged and photographed a dinner scene on deck (where no one ever ate), with the Bora Bora mountain in the background. Lucile and many other passengers took advantage of the opportunity to get the same picture with their cameras. Included in the group of diners was a young French couple, only recently wed, both of whom had just completed a pharmacy course in Paris, and who were on their way to Nouméa, in New Caledonia. There they were to take over a pharmacy owned and operated by the bride's parents, who were scheduled to leave at once for a long stay in Paris. Speculation ran riot among the women in our party as to how well the groom would adjust to the tedium of life in the South Seas. The youngsters were a handsome pair and should have rated pay as models for all their posing, but they told us that they didn't.

Since Bora Bora afforded no dock facilities to accommodate our ship, we anchored out in the harbor and went ashore by launch. Except for the lush green foliage and the people, who were quite like the native Hawaiians, there was not much to see. The Bora Bora Hotel, which consisted of eight or ten thatch-roofed cottages, served us an excellent lunch, after which we took "le truck," an open-air bus with no springs, to the village. There the native women had set up tables with souvenirs and shell beads for sale to the tourists. They did a brisk business, not overlooking the opportunity to take advantage of American unfamiliarity with their French currency.

We visited two more islands in the Society group, as they are called, Mooréa and Tahiti. Coconut palms grow everywhere along the beaches and copra is the principal product, but ground flowers and trees with bright blossoms abound. These islands are still relatively unspoiled, perhaps because in the tropics the scars made by civilization heal easily, but tourism is having its effect. There is a big hotel on Mooréa, with thatched cottages, landscaped grounds, and many native dancers to entertain visitors, both after lunch and after dinner. These Polynesians have the same look as their Hawaiian kinsmen, but the dances they stage are more vigorous and earthy. On Tahiti, the largest of the three islands we visited, we took a bus clear around it, some eighty-two miles, in the course of which we inspected the Gauguin memorial and ate an elaborate lunch from beach tables covered with ti leaves and flowers. To our surprise, most of the food available in these parts, except for fruits and vegetables, comes from the United States. We took a quick look at Papeete, a bustling little city, very French, very dirty, and very full of motor scooters—more per capita, I venture, than anywhere else in the world.

We did not leave the *Mariposa* again until we reached Auckland (pronounced locally "Oakland," to our considerable confusion), although some natives came aboard at Rarotonga with wares to sell. Our tour called for us to stay five days in New Zealand while our ship went on to Sydney, so we packed the minimum necessities in suitcases, preparatory to travel by bus and plane. We got a quick look at Auckland from the top of Mount Eden, but were soon off by bus, bound for Rotorua. The New Zealand countryside revealed endless numbers of bright green pastures, surrounded by darker green hedges, and each pasture with its quota of sheep. The agricultural patterns, unlike the rectangular fields of America, are totally irregular; in this, as in so many other ways, the New Zealanders followed British precedents. At intervals there were one-story farmhouses, usually painted in pastel colors, and all very neat in appearance. In this latitude, well to the south of the equator, it was springtime, and flowers bloomed profusely.

By the end of the day we were at Lake Rotorua, the thermal region, in a hotel that faced a huge geyser, which at frequent intervals played sixty feet in the air. There were also many smaller geysers, and some bubbling mud puddles such as one sees in our Yellowstone National Park. En route to Rotorua we had seen another strange natural phenomenon—some dark caves, the ceilings of which were covered with millions of glowworms, each, like the stars in the heavens, giving forth its little glimmer of light. The most interesting part of the Rotorua trip, however, was the glimpse we got of the old Maori civilization. The Maoris are light-skinned, and by far the most advanced of the Polynesian peoples. They quickly absorbed Western ways, but were proud of their past and made every effort to preserve its memory. That evening a group of high school youngsters gave us a sample of the old songs and dances, and the next day we visited a reconstructed Maori village. The Maoris, unlike the American Indians, made quick terms with their conquerors and learned to live with them in peace. As nearly as we could tell, their descendants have no feeling of inferiority whatever and associate with the whites on equal terms.

From Rotorua we went by plane to Wellington, a modern city built around a fine harbor, then on to Christchurch in the southern island, where we spent a night. The high point of our trip came the next day as we flew through the snow-covered, jagged peaks of the Southern Alps, so close to them at times that it seemed as if the wings of our plane would surely touch them. By great good luck, we drew brilliant sunshine instead of the often encountered fog, so we didn't miss a thrill. Mount Cook, more than twelve thousand feet high, lay straight ahead of us, and our pilot let us take turns riding with him so that we could see and photograph it face to face. We spent the night at Wanaka, then went the next day to Milford Sound, a deep fiord that winds in and out among the mountains. A launch took us through it to the sea, ten miles away, and back again, with each succeeding view seemingly outdoing every other. We were two nights in a hotel on the sound, then went by bus to Invercargill, the farthest south we ever expect to be, then back by plane to Christchurch, from which we flew to Sydney to overtake the *Mariposa*.

Our inspection of New Zealand was too casual to warrant us in drawing many conclusions. But we could not fail to note the over-dependence of the economy on sheep. A glance in store windows indicated, too, that the economic ties of the islands with England were painfully close. Rivalry with Australia, rather than partnership, seemed also in evidence, and the virtual absence of American products betrayed the existence of tariffs high enough to keep them out. The people seemed devoted to their welfare-state economy, and prided themselves on having escaped the customary extremes of the very rich and the very poor.

A tale told me about the method of agricultural expansion then in progress on the South Island interested me greatly. There the bush is gradually being cleared to make way for productive agriculture, but the state takes the initiative, not individuals. First a state authority clears the land of its worthless growth; then, because the land is not very rich, builds it up with fertilizer; then, since native grasses are not nutritious, sows the proper seed to produce good pasture; then puts a tenant in charge for a long enough period to prove that the new fields are really ready to use; then, and only then, offers the land for sale. To an American this sounded like the frontier process in reverse.

Sydney is a beautiful but widely divided city. It surrounds a bay, with long tongues of water extending into the land, and equally long peninsulas extending into the water. A huge steel-arch bridge, shaped like a gigantic coat hanger, spans the bay from north to south, but one must still drive great distances to get from one arm of the city to another. We went to the zoo to see such strange creatures as koala bears and kangaroos, but they looked no different there than in our own zoos. We also took a launch trip around the bay and viewed with considerable wonderment the extraordinary opera house, now under construction. It rises from the shores of the bay in great sail-like concrete structures, so intricately interwoven as to suggest a fleet of sloops blown together by a high wind. Residents of the city are not pleased with the slow growth and enormous cost of this edifice, and would like to forget it. But they just can't. A friend of one of our shipmates took us for lunch to the ritzy American Club; from its high eminence we looked down on the opera house, the harbor, and much of the surrounding city.

We were sorry not to have had time to see more of Australia, but after two or three days in Sydney, the *Mariposa* was off to Nouméa in New Caledonia. Here we lost our young French couple. We had only a few hours ashore, and most of that during siesta time, so our dedicated shoppers were somewhat aggrieved. But we saw some interesting sights nevertheless. Most unusual to our eyes were the umbrella-like flamboyant trees, the bright red blossoms of which lit up spectacularly the whole city square. We also visited an aquarium that exhibited many strange types of South Pacific fish, sometimes with live coral growing in the tank. The live coral tentacles, instead of being rigid the way we ordinarily see them, moved and squirmed like the boughs of a tree in a heavy wind. The natives here are Melanesians rather than Polynesians, have darker skins, Negroid features, and frizzly hair. Like the Hawaiians, they did not thrive on white supremacy and declined greatly in numbers after the French invasion.

After Nouméa we had only three stops left. The first was at Suva, in the Fiji Islands, where a big market was open and the women had a field day buying native wares. Native singers and dancers, and an excellent band, trained by the police department, celebrated our coming and going. Here, too, the natives are Melanesian, although their larger size indicates some admixture of Polynesian blood. Our next stop was Pago Pago (pronounced "Pango Pango") on American Samoa (Polynesians here). Bad luck again for the shoppers; it was a Sunday, and the missionaries had done their work so well that most of the stores were closed. The Pago Pago harbor, however, was the most spectacular we had ever seen. It was formed by the crater of a volcano that sank into the sea, completely on one side, but on the other leaving a high semi-circular rim of mountains. Across the harbor, from rim to rim, there is a cable tram, which of course we could hardly wait to ride. This event turned out to be quite exciting, not only because of the spectacular view, but also because our car couldn't quite make the last two feet to the landing platform. So two or three of us—I was one elected—clambered up with the waters of the harbor a whole mountain's height below. Thus relieved, the tram docked successfully. Our last stop was Honolulu, where we spent two delightful days. But the Fiftieth State was not new to us; it was our sixth visit to Hawaii, we figured, when we filled out a Chamber of Commerce card asking us how many times we had been there and why.

In a sense our last trip, made in June, 1967, was anticlimactic, for it took us only as far as Carcross in Canada, on the old route marked out in the late 1890's by the Klondike gold seekers. The reasons for this trip were somewhat mixed. I had a yen to see the Inside Passage to Alaska and to set foot upon the soil of the Forty-ninth State. Lucile's interest in travel of any kind was perpetual. And we had another grand-daughter, Louise West, who was now eleven years of age and would not much longer be eligible for half fare. In taking Kathleen Pierce, our oldest grandchild, across the Pacific in 1964, we had set an expensive precedent, for when her brother, Donald, reached the appropriate age, he, too, expected a trip. His sister had been so entranced with Hawaii that he would have been disappointed with any other choice, so in 1966 we spent two weeks with him there, visiting again the four major islands. We could hardly do Hawaii again so soon, so Louise had to settle for Alaska.

Our route took us by air to Vancouver, where we spent a day, then by water up the Inside Passage to Skagway. Our ship, the Canadian National *Prince George*, was a pygmy in comparison with the *Mariposa*, and decidedly less luxurious, but she was able to accommodate almost as many passengers. We were aboard her for four days going north and for four days coming back. The weather, all our knowing friends told us, would be intolerably bad and we would not see a thing. Actually, we had rain only one day, and we saw everything our eyes could take in. Our routes north and south were different, but headed one way or the other we went ashore at Prince Rupert, Ketchikan,

Wrangell, and Juneau. These towns were all small and primitive, still swallowed up in their wilderness surroundings, and strongly suggestive of frontier conditions. We saw the tallest totem pole in the world, others not so tall, and numerous museum relics of earlier days. Most of all, we saw a lot of nature in the raw—high, snow-capped mountains; dense, spreading forests; rugged promontories; unpeopled islands; even glaciers dropping their ice blocks into the sea.

At Skagway we rode on the narrow-gauge railway that follows the old trail toward the Klondike. Frequently we could make out the path that men and beasts had worn into the mountainsides, and could try to visualize the incredible hardships they had suffered in their usually ill-fated quest for gold. The most spectacular sight of all came where the land trail turned to a waterway, and the gold-seekers had had to use their wits to fashion whatever wood they could find into boats. Here the still waters of Lake Bennett reflected every detail of the surrounding mountains with such uncanny accuracy that, in the pictures we took, we could hardly tell the difference between up and down.

After our return to Vancouver we took the ferry to Victoria, where Helen Burke and her daughter, Libby, had come from Seattle to meet us. We spent a night at the Empress Hotel and the day following in inspecting probably the most British city in the world—except, perhaps, Christchurch, New Zealand—then took the ferry across Puget Sound to Seattle, and went, the next day, by air, home.

All the familiar clichés about the value of foreign travel are true. It widens the traveler's horizons and gives him a better understanding of other nationalities and a better perspective on his own. It gets him out of whatever rut he has got himself into and forces him to make new acquaintances, new judgments. It deepens his longing for peace; people everywhere are just people; why should they be trying to harm or destroy each other? An American can hardly fail to realize how fortunate he is, how well fed, well clothed, and well housed, in comparison with so many others and how free from hampering laws and customs. It is hard, too, for him to escape a feeling of responsibility for the less-favored peoples of the earth; why should we have so much and they so little? How can we help those who need help?

Unfortunately, too many travelers are too old to get the maximum benefit from their foreign experiences; they should have gone abroad before, not after, their minds had set. But changes in this situation are coming fast. Young Americans are traveling now in far greater numbers than formerly. The costs are less prohibitive, there are scholarships and student exchanges to help, and the educational value of living among other peoples is more clearly recognized. The Peace Corps struck a responsive chord because the young people of the nation were so ready for it. If peace is to come in our time, or in any time, it will have to be preceded by a better understanding and a greater tolerance among the peoples of the world. And one way to promote these ends lies through their intermingling in foreign travel.

XVIII. A Summing Up

LIFE HAS BEEN kind to me. The psychologists tell us that a feeling of security is of primary importance to a child, and I was born into a secure home. My father was as kindly and considerate a person as I have ever known; he loved his children and they all loved him. My mother could show affection when things went right and temper when they went wrong; above all, she was practical and foresighted. If my father always paid his bills, it was because my mother knew how to keep them down and how, when necessary, to earn a little extra cash. Family discipline and indoctrination fell mostly to her. It was she, not my preacher father, who quoted endlessly to me II Timothy, 2:15, "Study to show thyself approved unto God, a workman that needeth not to be ashamed, rightly dividing the word of truth." It was she who watched over my progress in school and laid out a program for my college education. It was she who pulled me up sharp when I needed correction. Children need to know what they can do and what they can't do; this, indeed, is the essence of child security. I was never left in doubt.

The small-town environment in which I grew up added to this sense of security. By the end of the nineteenth century small-town America had developed a viable pattern of life. The people who lived in these towns had jobs, not very well-paying jobs, but jobs that made them a living. The word "unemployment" did not enter my vocabulary until I found out about its existence in cities. People in the towns were aware of each other. If calamity struck, they were never left to bear their sorrows alone; if good fortune, that, too, was recognized, even if not without a trace of envy. Town-dwellers understood where the food they needed came from; they saw it growing on the surrounding farms, and some of it they grew themselves in their own gardens or in nearby pastures. They had problems, but almost never the problem of where the next meal was coming from. They were to a remarkable degree self-sufficient, with churches to meet their religious needs, schools to educate their children, and jobs enough to go around. Their lives were not very exciting, and many of the young people left the towns for the cities, sometimes replacing security with insecurity. But not always insecurity, for, before the age of automation, even the city provided jobs for the multitides.

Furthermore, the world of the late nineteenth and early twentieth centuries was a secure world. Wars of great dimensions, such as the American Civil War and the Bismarckian wars, were thought to be outmoded. At home the Indians were rounded up with finality on reservations; the Wounded Knee massacre, which marked their last resistance, took place in the year of my birth. The Atlantic and Pacific Oceans, with the diplomatic assistance of the Monroe Doctrine, protected the Western Hemisphere from all foreign wars, or so we thought. We might have to do a little missionary work with bullets, as in the Spanish-American War and the Philippine Insurrection, but the world had outgrown the kind of general wars associated with the French Revolution and Napoleon. Before World War I young Americans were unworried about the imminence of the draft, or the prospect of long military service overseas, or the disrupting effects of war itself. Ours was a secure age.

These factors explain in part the differences between the young people of the age into which I was born and the young people of today. Young men and women nowadays are often frantic from insecurity. Broken homes are about as common as homes presided over by an enduring father-mother alliance. Cities promote no such sense of security as existed in the old town-and-country communities, still the dominant American way of life at the turn of the century. Peace and prosperity are no longer the normal expectations. The United States has been involved in four hot wars during the last half century, a Great Depression, and a continuing cold war that depends only on a balance of terror to stave off atomic destruction. The feeling of security that young people had in my youth helped them not to lose faith during the low blows they were to suffer in middle age. But young people born since World War I have had all too little reason to hope for a secure future. Small wonder that so many of our juveniles today become dropouts from society and live only for the moment.

In addition to being born into a secure world, I had the advantage of "domestic tranquility," although I doubt if my use of that term is exactly what the Founding Fathers had in mind when they wrote it into the Preamble to the Constitution. Marriage is a hazardous undertaking at best. When I was contemplating it, one of my friends, who, I had supposed, was happily married, observed: "Well, whichever you do, you'll regret it." Another obliged with the cheering thought: "If you come to after six months and find you haven't made a fool of yourself, you're lucky." I was lucky, although maybe foresight had a little to do with it. Once Chancellor Avery of the University of Nebraska laid down in my hearing a policy on divorce: "If members of our faculty get divorces," he said, "we will of course retain them, but when it comes to recruiting, I'm against hiring anyone who has been divorced. Why take a chance on a person who has proved his bad judgment by making a mistake in the most important decision of life?" Whether by accident or by good judgment, my marriage was not a mistake; I have had the advantage of a peaceful and happy home.

Not that Lucile's interests and mine have always been the same, for they have not. She, for example, has always had a far deeper devotion to music than I ever could. But I encouraged her in it; with our first savings we bought a piano. Likewise, she has made terms with my interests, whatever they have happened to be. There have been very few harsh words between us in all these nearly fifty years. We have had our deep disappointments and our sorrows—the death of our infant son, of our first infant grandson, and of many loved friends and relatives. But these misfortunes have served only to bring us closer together. We have comforted each other and faced the world as one.

Never once have I regretted my choice of a profession. I used to hear, no doubt both from my parents and from my teachers, a constant refrain (based obviously on the Protestant ethic): "If you don't find happiness in your *work*, you'll *never* find it." I did find happiness in my work, from my first college teaching day to my last. And I believed in it. Nor did the "publish or perish" requirement, so often the despair of university teachers, hold any terrors for me. I picked subjects for research that I enjoyed living with, and I found writing almost as much fun as teaching. A writer takes great satisfaction in turning out a sentence that says what he wants it to say and sounds right when he reads it aloud; he delights in composing a paragraph that clings tightly to its topic sentence, in producing an article or a chapter in which the paragraphs really hang together and tell what he means them to tell.

An artist can get no more satisfaction out of a well-executed painting than a writer out of a carefully wrought book.

The variety of institutions in which I had the privilege of teaching was another stroke of luck. Somewhat to my disappointment, my first job was in a small denominational college, where I had to teach many subjects outside my speciality. But this was one of the best things that could have happened to me; the teacher to be sorry for is the one who gets his first job where he took his Ph.D. and thereafter never confronts another campus. I taught also in a southern women's college, in a small university, in a large university, and in a "multiversity." I taught summer school in nine universities other than those to which I belonged and held temporary positions at Harvard, at the University of Cambridge, England, and at the Salzburg Seminar in American Studies. I learned a lot, and maybe grew a little, with each new move. I taught nearly every subject in American history that appears in a university curriculum. Once Paxson said to me: "Anyone who can teach any course in American history should be able to teach them all." Probably he was right, but I doubt if I taught them all equally well.

My greatest good luck, I think, was in not being seduced permanently into administrative work. To have a taste of it, as I did, as a departmental chairman and dean, was not amiss; I learned a lot about universities that way. But a too prolonged experience in such positions is a hazard. For all of them, rotation in office is a good thing, both for the jobs themselves and for the men who hold them. The same goes for committee work, of which I also had my fill. Service of this kind should be generously passed around.

On retirement my interest in writing and research stood me in good stead. I still had work to do that I enjoyed and that I thought to be useful. So many of my friends, particularly high-ranking business executives, are lost on retirement. One day they are indispensable, the next they are forgotten and left to fade away. This sometimes happens even to university administrators. If they have concentrated too long on their duties as deans or directors or what-not and have lost contact with their subjects, what are they to do when they have nothing to administer? Of course, there's always travel, golf, and bowling on the green. But who wants to make a career of things like that? Since retirement, I have also accepted invitations to speak on historical subjects, both locally and at a distance. I suspect that these later speeches were better prepared than those I gave when my campus duties required so much of my time, and they have led to many interesting new contacts.

Inevitably the question arises: If you had it all to do over again, what would you do differently? The answer, I suppose, is: Not very much. A few bad blunders I would be glad to correct, but on the whole, considering my limitations, I did about the best I could. An old man's opinion on his life is, of course, purely subjective, distorted by his ability to remember what he wants to remember and to forget what he wants to forget; but for whatever it is worth, I think I have had a good life.

Index

DATE DUE

F			
Γ			